Understanding Film Theory

Understanding Film Theory

Christine Etherington-Wright

and

Ruth Doughty

First published 2011 by
PALGRAVE MACMILLAN

Palgrave Macmillan in the UK is an imprint of Macmillan Publishers Limited, registered in England, company number 785998, of Houndmills, Basingstoke, Hampshire RG21 6XS.

Palgrave Macmillan in the US is a division of St Martin's Press LLC, 175 Fifth Avenue, New York, NY 10010.

Palgrave Macmillan is the global academic imprint of the above companies and has companies and representatives throughout the world.

Palgrave® and Macmillan® are registered trademarks in the United States, the United Kingdom, Europe and other countries

ISBN 978–0–230–21710–2 hardback
ISBN 978–0–230–21711–9 paperback

This book is printed on paper suitable for recycling and made from fully managed and sustained forest sources. Logging, pulping and manufacturing processes are expected to conform to the environmental regulations of the country of origin.

A catalogue record for this book is available from the British Library.

Library of Congress Cataloging-in-Publication Data
Etherington-Wright, Christine, 1950-
Understanding film theory : theoretical and critical perspectives / Christine Etherington-Wright, Ruth Doughty.
      p. cm.
Includes index.
ISBN 978-0-230-21711-9 (pbk.)
1. Motion pictures--Philosophy. 2. Film criticism.
I. Doughty, Ruth. II. Title.
PN1995.E84 2011
791.4301--dc22
2011008000

10   9   8   7   6   5   4   3   2   1
20 19 18 17 16 15 14 13 12 11

Printed in China

Contents

Illustrations

Acknowledgments

We would like to thank the following people for their advice and time taken to read material: Rhona Doughty, Emma Dyson, Stephen Harper, Sue Harper, Paul McDonald, Alison Raimes, Deborah Shaw, Sally Shaw, Justin Smith and Paul Spicer.

We would like to thank Portsmouth Film Studies students past, present and future. This book developed out of lively seminar discussions and the frustration at not being able to find any student-friendly books on film theory.

We would like to thank Belinda Latchford for her patience and keen eye for detail. Similarly, we are indebted to Paul Sng at Palgrave, who went way above and beyond the call of duty. His guidance, support, humour and willingness to 'muck in' really helped us across the 'finish line'.

Finally, we would like to thank our 'other halves' Andrew Barnicoat and Barrie Etherington-Wright for putting up with us throughout this long process. Our progress was not as smooth as it might have been due to the arrival of Briony Barnicoat. However, her understanding of Freud and Baudrillard is exemplary for a baby.

Introduction

Theory has a bad reputation. It often sends a shudder of despair down the spine of students and academics alike. The reasons for this are because it is challenging, it is difficult, it can take time to grasp and can often leave the reader feeling inadequate and frustrated. Theory can often seem old-fashioned and stuffy and therefore it can be hard to see its modern-day relevance. The aim of this book is to try to disassociate theory from these negative connotations. It is for this reason that the book has been written. In short, our intention is to take the 'fear' out of theory.

What is theory?

Theory is a system of trying to understand and explain things from a specific point of view. Theories develop and evolve through debate and the interchange of ideas. For example, someone comes up with an idea which they commit to paper. This forms the basis for discussion and often vehement criticism. Over time ideas are questioned and more people contribute to the field of debate. As a result, theories should be thought of as chains of ideas and responses.

Interestingly, not all approaches to reading a film text are recognized as traditional theoretical modes. This can be attributed to hierarchical bias. For example, theories that developed out of philosophy and literary criticism have a long-established history and, for that reason, they are often granted the status of theory (Formalism, Structuralism, Marxism and Psychoanalysis). Alternatively, in the 1970s a number of new approaches emerged that were concerned with looking at groups that had previously been marginalized (Feminism, Queer Theory, Race and Ethnicity). As with all new ways of thinking, modern approaches are often met with controversy. However, this can fuel intellectual discussion and in turn can lead to new ideas. For example our chapter on Masculinity can be read as a response to Feminist readings. Additionally a further widening occurred when film scholars began to use empirical research to inform their findings (Stars, Audience Research and Reception).

This division between which theories are traditionally classed as such and which may more appropriately be classed as critical perspectives is both reductive and redundant. All approaches are methodologies that enhance our understanding and appreciation of the film text. Which approaches earn the status of 'theory' remains a contested notion and is to a large extent subjective. Nevertheless, Film Studies is a more recent academic pursuit, and as films are a modern cultural format, innovative theoretical ideas offer new and exciting lines of study.

Why study theory?

Theory can be interesting and exciting as it enriches our understanding of filmic texts. It can provide new ways of looking at some of our favourite films. More importantly, it can help us gain a new level of appreciation for texts that we feel we know inside out. Theory encourages debate as it enables different readings of texts; it provides another degree of interpretation. It can also offer a way of making sense of a film that may at first seem inaccessible such as avant-garde, surrealist filmmaking.

Theory can be difficult to comprehend and therefore it is important to invest a little time. Complex ideas cannot be understood and appreciated in a few minutes. Some theorists have spent their entire career debating and writing about one specific area; as a result it can be an arduous task trying to extract the intention of their theses. The process of finding that hidden nugget can be overwhelming. However, when the ideas finally fall into place, the 'light bulb' moment is exciting, generating a huge sense of achievement and satisfaction.

The problems with theoretical writing

One of the main problems with theoretical texts is that they were often written a long time ago. Accordingly, the style of writing is typically archaic and dense, rendering it inaccessible to a modern reader. This is compounded by the fact that many texts were originally written in a different language and have since been translated into English. Unfortunately, this has set a precedent and even modern-day theorists tend to adopt a formal tone when bringing their ideas to life. This impenetrable and complex tone often works to alienate the reader. As a result, we are often left feeling intimidated and giving up seems the only option.

Our approach

In this book, we provide a definition of each theory as a starting point, all of which have been taken from the Oxford English Dictionary online, and set out to summarize the main concepts proposed by key thinkers. Our intention has been to summarize, yet not necessarily oversimplify, seminal texts. Throughout each chapter you will find 'Reflect and Respond' sections. These have been designed in order for you to explore and attempt to apply ideas to see if you have grasped the main points. These questions also ask you to find contemporary examples so that you are aware of the theory's relevance to a modern-day viewer.

It is important to note that, even though we have separated theories into distinct chapters, there is a lot of overlap in ideas and individual theorists can be linked to more than one theory. Therefore, theories should not be thought of in isolation (neatly defined 'boxes'). It is from this movement and cross-fertilization between areas that new theories can emerge as theory is constantly evolving.

Two final important points: this book is not intended to be read from cover to cover, although you may wish to do that. It has been organized so that you can easily dip in and out to find specific information. The second thing is that it would be impossible to cover all ideas and academics associated with each theoretical perspective. Consequently, this book should be thought of as a starting point for further research. It is important to expand on our summaries and seek out original writing for yourself.

Hopefully, this book will act as a 'springboard' and encourage you to confidently explore and enjoy film theory.

Auteur Theory

Auteur

1. A film director whose personal influence and artistic control over his or her films are so great that he or she may be regarded as their author, and whose films may be regarded collectively as a body of work sharing common themes or techniques and expressing an individual style or vision.

Setting the scene

Historically the notion of authorship conjured up the image of an isolated individual passionately working to create bodies of art. Characters such as those in Baz Luhrmann's *Moulin Rouge!* (2001) help perpetuate this romantic stereotype of the tortured Bohemian artist. When applying ideas of authorship to the field of Film Studies it is typically the director that is acknowledged as the creative force. The term auteur is French for author and the word derives from the prefix 'auto', meaning one.

The idea of a single controlling figure was acknowledged as early as the 1910s in the British fan magazine *Bioscope* where certain directors were identified as special. Similarly, in Germany the term *Autoren* film was used, which also promoted the idea of the director as author. However, screenwriters campaigned for their right to be recognized as the creative force. This debate from the 1910s continues to resonate a century later and is one of the founding ideas of film theory.

The idea that film is the sole work of a single contributor is problematic. Film is a collaborative process and therefore to attribute control to the director above all others is contentious. The number of people involved in producing a film is extensive: actors, writers, set designers, camera operators, musicians, financial backers, technical advisors, costume and make-up artists, editors, marketing and distribution staff, etc. To understand this debate fully, it is necessary to trace the emergence and development of Auteur Theory and explore its complexity. These debates about the auteur were initiated by an influential text from filmmaker and novelist Alexandre Astruc.

Astruc coined the term *caméra-stylo*, which literally translates as 'camera pen'. He wanted to bring film into line with other forms of art, namely raising its status from a working-class form of entertainment to match that of opera, ballet, poetry, literature and fine art. His article, 'The Birth of a New Avant-Garde: *La Caméra-Stylo*' (1948), called for a new language in filmmaking. He posited that the camera should be used in the same way that a writer would use a pen. He rallied filmmakers to move beyond institutionalized forms of cinema in favour of more personal ways of storytelling. The emphasis that Astruc placed on the 'personal' has fuelled debate. The most vigorous participants in this debate came from France.

The *Cahiers* group

The *Cinémathèque Française* in Paris was much more than a typical cinema, as it was home to a group of enthusiasts who collectively sought to revolutionize cinema. Led by Henri Langlois, the group showed films throughout the day and night, attracting the attention of likeminded individuals. Their fascination in cinema instigated a forum for debate and experimentation. For example, they would watch films without any sound so that they could focus solely on the importance of the image. This fanaticism and attempt to comprehend the very essence of cinema resulted in two major developments in film history: the journal *Cahiers du cinéma* and the *Nouvelle Vague*/French New Wave school of filmmaking.

These 'filmoholics' were often referred to as *cinéphiles* as they were obsessed with filmmaking. Among the key members of the group were:

- André Bazin (theorist)
- Claude Chabrol (New Wave director and writer)
- Jean-Luc Godard (New Wave director, writer and theorist)
- Henri Langlois (archivist)
- Alain Resnais (New Wave director)
- Jacques Rivette (New Wave director and writer)
- François Truffaut (New Wave director, writer and theorist)
- Roger Vadim (New Wave director and writer).

From within this influential group of filmmakers and thinkers, François Truffaut energized the debate with his article, 'Une Certaine Tendance du Cinéma Français'.

François Truffaut

'Une Certaine Tendance du Cinéma Français' (1954)

Truffaut's seminal text 'Une Certaine Tendance du Cinéma Français', signalled a radical shift in the auteur debate. He and his fellow *cinéphiles* found traditional French filmmaking conservative and unexciting. '*Tradition de la qualité*' was the term used to describe films that were typically based on adaptations of literary classics. The *Cahiers* group mocked this mode of production, calling it '*Cinéma du Papa*' (Dad's cinema) as they felt it was stuffy and outdated. More importantly this form of filmmaking privileged the role of the writer rather than acknowledging the director. In contrast to '*tradition de la qualité*' they aspired to create films that spoke to their generation. Their intention was to attack the ideology of bourgeois culture.

During World War II foreign imported films were limited due to the Nazi occupation of France. Post-war the influx of films, particularly from Hollywood, strongly inspired the *Cahiers* group. In spite of studio stipulations, they recognized that certain directors' films exhibited identifiable stylistic traits. As a result of these observations Truffaut developed '*la politique des auteurs*' (auteur policy). It is important to establish that Truffaut never intended for his work to form the basis of a theory; it represented a policy, an attitude and a critical approach to reading film. The two over-riding principles he put forward were:

1   *Mise-en-scène* is crucial to the reading of cinema and is essential in film analysis and criticism.
2   The director's personal expression is key in distinguishing whether they should be afforded the title of auteur.

Truffaut was concerned with the focus on film style (*mise-en-scène* and thematics) rather than film plot (content).

Reflect and respond

1   How did the *Cahiers* group change the previous sense of the auteur?
2   Why do you think Truffaut favours *mise-en-scène* over other aspects of filmmaking?
3   Can you identify any directors who are instantly recognizable due to the consistency in *mise-en-scène* throughout their films?

Mise-en-scène

The term *mise-en-scène* literally translates as 'put into the scene'. Originating from the theatre, it describes everything that appears in the frame. This can be divided into four specific components:

1   set design (props and décor)
2   lighting (and shadow)
3   acting (movement and gesture, not dialogue)
4   costume and make-up.

In order to understand the importance of *mise-en-scène* in relation to Auteur Theory, it is necessary to identify consistent stylistic traits across films to decide whether or not a director can be classed as an auteur.

Tim Burton provides an interesting study as his films have a distinctive aesthetic style. Consider the films *Sleepy Hollow* (1999) and *Big Fish* (2003). The narratives in both films are located in the woods, a typical trope found across Burton's oeuvre, with the gnarled, eerie trees serving to create a foreboding atmosphere. The viewer is drawn into an uncomfortable world, as generically Burton falls between the two camps of Horror and Fantasy. This is enhanced by the artistic use of light and shadow to anticipate the arrival of nightfall and unspoken horrors.

Burton owes a great debt to German Expressionism; this can be seen through the use of curves, the angular objects within the frame and the surreal nature of his storytelling. The lead protagonist, though central to the composition, is intimidated by the pervading forest. These elements of

Figure 1.1 *Sleepy Hollow* (Tim Burton, 1999)

the *mise-en-scène* combine to induce a sense of menace where man is pitted against nature, a recurring dynamic in Burton's work.

In addition to the importance of set design and lighting, the aesthetic consistency can also be applied to Burton's use of costume and make-up. A typical feature of an auteur is a director who uses the same actors time and time again. Throughout Burton's career Johnny Depp has been cast in numerous leading roles. Despite the disparate characters Depp has played, Burton recycles and develops roles rather than abandoning characters. Sweeney Todd can be seen as an extension, and in many respects an inversion, of Edward Scissorhands. The naïve, fearful and introverted character from the 90s is transformed into the cynical, murderous and predatory demon barber of Fleet Street; a ghost of his former self.

To examine this in more detail it is appropriate to focus on costume and make-up. In both films Depp sports a dishevelled look with unkempt hair. Similarly his black and white clothing

Figure 1.2 *The Nightmare Before Christmas* (Tim Burton, 1993)

is reminiscent of a Gothic, Romantic artist, a familiar motif woven throughout Burton's repertoire. The costume is flamboyantly adorned with frills typical of swashbuckling heroes of old. Yet unlike with the conventional heroes, the garments are crumpled and suggestive of neglect. The razor-sharp fingers that were imposed on the earlier character of Scissorhands become a fundamental part of Todd's character and once more integral to the narrative.

The consistency in design across Burton's work is exemplified by the highly stylized look explicit in the *mise-en-scène* of his films. Figures 1.1 and 1.2 exemplify tropes discussed above; extreme use of light and shadow, curves and angles, influence of both German Expressionism and the Gothic. Furthermore the compositions of the images are incredibly similar. The images above reflect Burton's consistent preoccupation with the macabre. His use of dark tones, spooky landscapes and scary objects provide an appropriate backdrop for his Gothic tales. These have become synonymous with his oeuvre.

Personal filmmaking

Another facet of the auteur argument is the notion of directors pursuing projects that hold personal significance. These personal aspects can manifest in many forms, such as political, social and cultural. For example Spike Lee is typically drawn to narratives about race and Martin Scorsese is interested in Catholicism.

To continue with Burton as an illustration, it can be seen that the theme of childhood isolation is pertinent within his films. As a child Burton was estranged from his parents, living with his grandmother from the ages of twelve to sixteen. During this period he sought solace by escaping into his imagination, which was fuelled by fairytales and classic monster movies. Burton identified with the monster rather than the hero as he was himself a loner. He states:

> Every kid responds to some image, some fairy-tale image, and I felt most monsters were basically misperceived, they usually had much more heartfelt souls than the human characters around them. My fairy-tales were probably those monster movies, to me they're fairly similar. (Salisbury, 2006, p.3)

The film *Edward Scissorhands* (1990) is probably his most autobiographical to date. The unlikely hero of the narrative can be seen as Burton's *alter ego*. The resemblance to these main characters is also evident in Burton's physical appearance. He is often photographed looking awkward in crumpled suits and with long, tousled hair. The link between personal experience and filmic storytelling in *Edward Scissorhands* and many of his other films exemplifies the recurring sentiment in Burton's work.

In addition to thematic consistency, directors can also include personal signatures within their oeuvre. This can consist of a visual motif that is repeated across a body of texts. Earlier we discussed Burton's Gothic *mise-en-scène* as an illustration of a personal signature. Another example can be found in the films of Spike Lee where he places an actor on a dolly with the camera. The effect is that the character appears to float rather than walk and this technique is instantly recognizable as Lee's signature.

The importance of *mise-en-scène* and a director's personal signature are fundamental to the auteur debate. The ideas of the *Cahiers* group and Truffaut in the 50s were taken up and complicated by Andrew Sarris, an American critic writing in the 60s.

Andrew Sarris

'Notes on the *Auteur* Theory' (1962)

Sarris is most famous for mistranslating Truffaut's '*La Politique des Auteurs*' as Auteur Theory. Although it is predominantly referred to as a theory, it should be considered as a device for reading film. Sarris starts his essay by pointing out the flaws in Truffaut's thesis. He questions whether a director can be the author of a film and therefore solely responsible for its distinctive quality. He continues by stating that Auteur Theory: 'makes it difficult to think of a bad director making a good film and almost impossible to think of a good director making a bad one' (Sarris, 1962, p.561).

Sarris discussed his interpretation of Auteur Theory in terms of concentric circles (see diagram below): 'The outer circle as technique; the middle circle, personal style; and the inner circle, interior meaning' (p.563). He believed that for a director to reach the status of auteur, they would have to be accomplished in all areas. Most important, for Sarris, is the inner circle. Many directors are able to achieve the outer circles but if a filmmaker's work consistently attains 'interior meaning', this would suggest it is the work of an auteur. Here Sarris raises the important debate concerning the *metteur-en-scène* (see below).

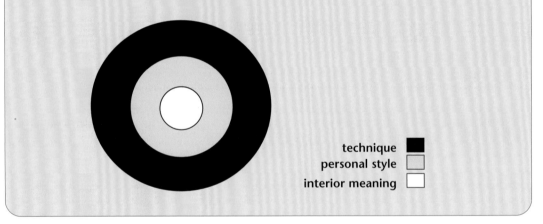

technique ■
personal style □
interior meaning □

Metteur-en-scène

The term *metteur-en-scène* was first coined by André Bazin, another *Cahiers* writer. A *metteur* is different from an auteur in that the former is a competent, and often very good, technician. Whereas an auteur can make a good movie out of a poor script, a *metteur-en-scène* would struggle; they merely adapt material given to them rather than making it their own. In other words, they may exhibit some of the attributes associated with an auteur but lack the extra depth involved.

Production

Another area for consideration is the budget that a director is able to secure. It does not necessarily follow that a large budget is an indication of auteur status; in fact the reverse can often be true. A director could be successful working in a specific genre and therefore accrue monetary backing as future projects are likely to be commercially successful. In contrast, many auteurs work outside the mainstream studio system and accordingly struggle to attract financial support. Often in the case of the latter, big-name actors appear in films at a reduced fee as they are more interested in the critical acclaim that can be gained from working with such a director. For example Tom Cruise worked with Paul Thomas Anderson on the film *Magnolia* (1999) and more recently Duncan Jones, son of David Bowie, managed to acquire the vocal talent of Kevin Spacey for his film *Moon* (2009) as the voice of the robot companion, GERTY.

Interestingly, this leads to another aspect of the auteur debate. *Moon* was Duncan Jones's debut film. Although it has been critically praised, we cannot deduce whether Jones qualifies as an auteur because he has only made one film to date. It begs the question: Does a director have to produce a certain number of films before he can be ascribed the status of auteur? Or should artistic ability be measured by quality rather than quantity? This is one of many obstacles that problematize the issue of authorship.

Problematizing the auteur

One of the main criticisms of the director as author is that film is a collaborative process involving an eclectic team of artisans, whose input is ignored when applying the theory. Peter Wollen refers to the additional layers of film production as 'noise' (Caughie, 1981, p.143). He stated that viewers have to separate the 'voice' of the director from superfluous 'noise'. Wollen was referring to other forms of interference such as input from actors, producers, camera operators. Once more this emphasizes the personal, distinctive vision of the director and asks the audience to be active in locating and hearing a continued narrative. Conversely, what he dismisses as superfluous 'noise' can be privileged as an alternative to the vision of the director. Here we will consider four possible candidates for the role of auteur in order to further the debate on authorship:

1 Actor

The actor has a unique presence within a film, not only on screen but also as a marketing tool to attract an audience. Films are more frequently advertised using the name of the star rather than that of the director. Certain stars have the kudos to ensure a film is realized. For example Alejandro Amenábar's *Abre los Ojos/Open Your Eyes* (1997) was remade as *Vanilla Sky* (Cameron Crowe, 2001) due to Tom Cruise's enthusiasm for the Spanish film. Similarly Tom Hanks was highly influential in bringing the film *My Big Fat Greek Wedding* (Joel Zwick, 2002) to the screen. Additionally, some actors have made the transition into directing, for example, Clint Eastwood, Mel Gibson and Kevin Costner.

2 Cinematographer

One of the main preoccupations in discussions of the director as auteur is the focus on visual style. The responsibility for style often lies behind the camera. The selection of specific angles and depth of field influences the spectator's understanding of an entire scene. Therefore the cinematographer is key in the overall look of the film and could be considered an auteur. Interestingly in America they are known as the 'director of photography' (DP). There are certain directors who have also undertaken this role, for example David Lean and Lars von Trier; however, these are exceptions.

3 Writer

This is possibly the most problematic category. If we consider *The Lord of the Rings*: J. R. R. Tolkien penned the original books; Peter Jackson directed the franchise (2001–3); yet it was Fran Walsh and Philippa Boyens, with Peter Jackson, who wrote the screenplay. This clearly calls the idea of authorship into question. The British director Richard Curtis believes that it is paramount that a writer is part of the filmmaking process because:

> A film is made at least four times. Once in the writing. Then in the shooting, which is the second film. Then in the editing, which is the third film. Then there might be a fourth film … losing bits that you love … . The screenplay is only the beginning. (Owen, 2003, p.96)

4 Composer

Many directors work repeatedly with the same composers: Steven Spielberg with John Williams, Sergio Leone with Ennio Morricone, Tim Burton with Danny Elfman. Therefore much of the distinctive style associated with these directors is reliant on this collaborative process. The score and soundtrack are once again integral to audience interpretation.

These four ways of discussing authorship signal a move away from Truffaut's *Politique*; this idea was further complicated by the work of Roland Barthes.

Roland Barthes

'Death of the Author' (1968)

Roland Barthes was a theorist, critic and writer on cultural and social meaning. His seminal text 'Death of the Author' was written for literary criticism. However, a look at his ideas will show how they are easily applied to questions of authorship in film. According to Barthes, Western culture places too much emphasis on the creative force; assigning meaning of the text to the author. He challenged this tradition by giving preference to the reader. He maintained that it was the reader who gave a text meaning. The reader is the interpreter and there can never be one definitive reading of a text, be it film or literature. We all interpret information in different ways.

In order to fully appreciate messages contained in a work, it would be necessary to have knowledge of an author's intended purpose. But this author-centred approach closes down the full range of possible meanings. The traditional notion of the author needs to be reviewed. The onus instead is placed firmly on the reader/viewer, as they need to engage with the material and become an active reader. Whereas the passive reader allows information to be absorbed without any conscious effort, the active reader will question and challenge the text. This allows an endless play of meaning; the text is no longer closed but instead remains open. The 'death of the author' leads to the 'birth' of the reader.

Reflect and respond

1   To what extent do you agree or disagree with the ideas of Barthes?
2   It is now common to speak of a Scorsese or a Tarantino film. What characteristics would you expect to see in a film by either of these two directors?
3   Can a film's meanings be attributed to a single creative source?
4   Why do we place so much emphasis on 'authorship'? Why do audiences and critics continue to want a cinematic author?
5   Can you name any famous cinematographers, composers, editors or other technical crew members?
6   Is Auteur Theory now an outdated mode of analysis for Film Studies? If yes, what are the alternatives?

Making a case for an auteur

The diagram on p.12 should help you focus your thoughts when trying to make an argument for a director as auteur or not.

It is important to note that there are arrows leading to and from the 'Biographical details' box. This is to indicate that a director's life can, and typically does, influence aesthetic and thematic choices.

Using this template as a starting point, the following case studies may help you ascertain whether a director deserves the title of auteur.

Case study: Alfred Hitchcock

Alfred Hitchcock was involved with every aspect of filmmaking both before and during a shoot and exercised a great deal of control over his work. On most projects he developed the screenplay; was active in casting; and influenced the choice of soundtrack and visual style. In exercising such control to produce a highly personal artistic vision he was able to override the constraints of the studio system; this entailed him having authority over the final cut (a privilege afforded most auteurs). It was Hitchcock's complete control over all elements that led to Truffaut citing the director as an example in early auteur debates (see Hitchcock interview, 1967, in Truffaut, 1986).

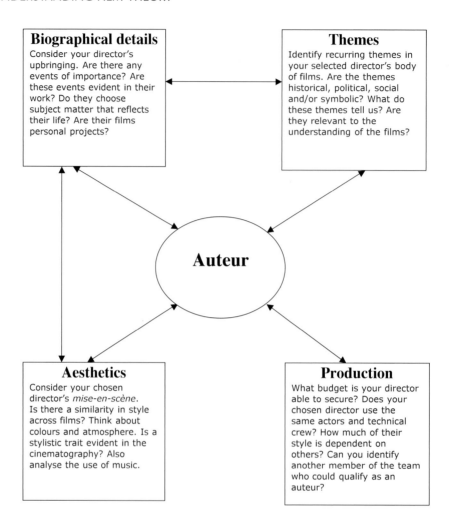

Biographical details
Consider your director's upbringing. Are there any events of importance? Are these events evident in their work? Do they choose subject matter that reflects their life? Are their films personal projects?

Themes
Identify recurring themes in your selected director's body of films. Are the themes historical, political, social and/or symbolic? What do these themes tell us? Are they relevant to the understanding of the films?

Auteur

Aesthetics
Consider your chosen director's *mise-en-scène*. Is there a similarity in style across films? Think about colours and atmosphere. Is a stylistic trait evident in the cinematography? Also analyse the use of music.

Production
What budget is your director able to secure? Does your chosen director use the same actors and technical crew? How much of their style is dependent on others? Can you identify another member of the team who could qualify as an auteur?

The most commonly examined areas attest to his title as 'master of suspense'. He is recognized as revolutionizing the thriller genre, playing with an audience's nerves and fears and often tackling subjects of a taboo nature. For example, *Strangers on a Train* (1951) touches on issues of homosexuality; *Psycho* (1960) deals with the Oedipus Complex; and *Marnie* (1964) looks at repressed memory.

Devices such as recurring themes, camera technique, editing, particular use of sound and silences, chiaroscuro lighting, the MacGuffin (an object that serves as the impetus for the plot) and cameo appearances all combine to present Hitchcock's personal vision of the world in his thrillers. Due to the array of innovative stylistic features that were employed by Hitchcock only a few examples can be selected here. This study will look first at those characteristics that are concerned with filmmaking (aesthetics and production) and second at those characteristics rooted in Hitchcock and his personal vision (biographical details and themes), which together combine to suggest his auteur status.

Aesthetics

Hitchcock is considered an expert of cinematic technique. His dialogue, sound, plot and character were always secondary to the image.

However, he used all these components in imaginative ways. In *Blackmail* (1929), his first sound film, he utilized silence and dialogue to dramatic effect. Repetition of the word 'knife' is amplified within a conversation; this device aurally represents the violent stabbing action of the knife and psychologically gnaws away at the guilty character. Similarly, Bernard Herrmann's score for *Psycho* was composed with the distinct intention of emphasizing the violence of the famous shower sequence after many images had to be cut due to censors. Here the staccato strings accentuate the physical assault.

It is probably for his innovative camera techniques and editing that Hitchcock is considered a master. The placement and movement of the camera was carefully controlled. Dolly zooms, which became known as the 'Hitchcock Zoom', are seen in *Vertigo* (1958). They were combined with strange camera angles to heighten dramatic meaning in many films, especially when psychological elements were involved. Returning to the shower scene, Hitchcock builds suspense by using cuts that get progressively shorter until the victim lies dead, with her blood trickling down the plug hole.

Themes

The act of murder in his films points to another of Hitchcock's motifs; a fascination with eyes. Hitchcock understood how the eyes, as windows to the soul, revealed what a character thinks or needs. Extreme close-up shots and point-of-view editing force spectators to experience the perspective of both the victim and the killer. In a voyeuristic way the audience enters the violent, frightening scene. The film *Frenzy* (1972) engages shot/reverse-shot to mirror the eyes of both the murderer and his prey.

Hitchcock's preoccupation with eyes continues throughout his oeuvre. In *Rear Window* (1954), Jimmy Stewart's character repeatedly watches his neighbours through a pair of binoculars. Norman Bates (Anthony Perkins) spies on Janet Leigh through a peephole cleverly hidden behind a painting. The director takes his obsession with eyes to an extreme level. Consider the images below (Figures 1.3 and 1.4). Here horrific blindness is enforced on elderly victims. The vivid desecration of the skull shocks the audience and highlights the fragility of the human body.

Figure 1.3 *Psycho* (Alfred Hitchcock, 1960)   **Figure 1.4** *The Birds* (Alfred Hitchcock, 1963)

Production

A typical trait of an auteur is to employ the same actors and technical crew time and time again. A look across fifty years of Hitchcock films shows that he tended to choose the same screen-writers, art directors, composers and actors, usually working with them over a short period of time. Bernard Herrmann, the composer, was the exception to this, working on eight films over a period of nine years from 1955. Herrmann was responsible for some of the most successful scores in Hitchcock's films; notably *Vertigo, Psycho* and *North by Northwest* (1959). Additionally, Jimmy Stewart and Cary Grant each appeared in four Hitchcock films while Ingrid Bergman and Grace Kelly each starred in three films.

Biographical details

Command of the *mise-en-scène* and familiar cast and crew are only part of the vision of an auteur. Integral to the auteurist position are aspects of the director's own life which are deemed to have influenced his work. Critical writing on Hitchcock often focuses on his childhood, Catholic upbringing and fascination with aspects of guilt, punishment, fear and morality. Critics and jour-nalists soon began to recognize these familiar tropes and discuss them at length, speculating on their origins. Hitchcock fostered this speculation, by alluding to childhood experiences when interviewed.

In particular he spoke of an incident when he was punished by his father (Spoto, 1983, p. 4). This is often read as the motivation for Hitchcock's fears and distrust of authority and also for his recur-ring theme of the innocent man wrongly accused. In this anecdotal tale, Hitchcock was sent to a police station by his father as punishment for a minor offence. There he was locked, terrified, in a cell for a short time. The experience engendered a fascination with the plight of the ordinary man when the victim of mistaken identity, wrongfully accused or imprisoned. His early film *The Lodger* (1926), and many later films, among them, *The Thirty-nine Steps* (1935), *The Wrong Man* (1957), *Vertigo* and *North by Northwest*, all share and develop this theme and all include a character trying to prove his innocence.

The recurring themes in his films of loneliness and depressive illness can be traced back to his childhood. He felt that he was an outsider, 'I don't ever recall having a playmate [...] I looked and observed a great deal' (Spoto, 1983, p.20). Outsiders who feature in his films include an amnesiac accused of murder in *Spellbound* (1945), a woman with a fear of sexual contact in *Marnie* and a serial killer made psychotic due to his sexual impotence in *Frenzy*. However, it is not only villains who are outsiders; alienated heroes appear in *Rear Window* and *Vertigo*.

Alongside this alienation there is evidence of Hitchcock's misogyny and episodes of sadism are to be found in biographical accounts. These similarly became dominant themes in many of his films. Tormented blonde heroines are foregrounded as vehicles for male voyeurism and as objects of sadis-tic male fantasies. It appears that Hitchcock saw female sexual vulnerability as a powerful dramatic device to be exploited, as can be witnessed in *Psycho, Marnie* and *Frenzy*. Furthermore, these hero-ines suffered violent deaths, further demonstrating the director's fascination with sadism. Violent death and murder, in particular strangulation, made an appearance from his earliest films.

Hitchcock was an accomplished self-publicist and carefully manufactured his public image. Unusually for the time, Hitchcock's name featured prominently in the marketing and promotion of his films. His cameo roles formed part of this promotion, while his narration of prologues and epilogues in his TV shows increased his visibility to another audience. His striking way of signing his name was made up of a series of eight strokes of his pen to create a silhouette likeness of himself. This, alongside his highly visible, rotund figure, combined to market his image as a director. Another aspect of this self-promotion was his decision to restrict his work to the narrow focus of a single genre, thus establishing his brand-name as the master of suspense.

Conclusion

However, whether Hitchcock can be considered an auteur remains a contentious issue. While Hitchcock's worldview and stylistic tone are very apparent across some fifty years of filmmaking, of his forty-four films from *Blackmail* to *Family Plot* (1976), thirty-seven were literary adaptations. Unfortunately, in Hollywood the screenwriter is often seen as a technician rather than as a creative person. That is, to make a novel into a screenplay is a mechanical process that can be learned by hacks. David O. Selznick, a 'hands-on' producer who worked with Hitchcock until *Notorious* (1946) was keen that film adaptations should be faithful to the original book. This did not suit Hitchcock. Therefore to establish and maintain his status as auteur, Hitchcock needed to move authorship away from the original author. Rather than be recognized for literary adaptations which would dissipate his auteur status, Hitchcock chose to make films from relatively unknown books and authors. This enabled him to buy, for example, *Psycho* (novel by Robert Bloch) and *Strangers on a Train* (novel by Patricia Highsmith) cheaply. After banning the novelists from any further intervention, Hitchcock remodelled the plots to allow for his personal interpretation. In his interview with Truffaut, Hitchcock noted that, 'What I do is to read a story once, and if I like the basic idea, I just forget all about the book and start to create cinema' (Truffaut, 1986, p.71). Hitchcock's strategies worked, as very few of the novelists are connected with their adapted texts even if they later gained fame. For instance, Patricia Highsmith is known for the Ripley character but not as the writer of *Strangers on a Train*. Despite the involvement of screenwriters, novelists, playwrights, composers, art directors and cinematographers, Hitchcock's personal worldview shines through and coheres fifty years of filmmaking.

Case study: Guillermo del Toro

At what point a director can be accepted as an auteur is a question that has been asked since debates concerning directorial authority first began. The contemporary Mexican director Guillermo del Toro is being discussed in both academic and popular publications as a potential auteur. He is an interesting candidate as he has directed only seven films to date:

- *Cronos* (1993)
- *Mimic* (1997)
- *El Espinazo del Diablo/The Devil's Backbone* (2001)
- *Blade II* (2002)
- *Hellboy* (2004)
- *El Laberinto del Fauno/Pan's Labyrinth* (2006)
- *Hellboy II: The Golden Army* (2008).

Biographical details

Del Toro is one of three Mexican directors who have received critical attention over the last ten years. Affectionately referred to as the Three Amigos, del Toro along with Alejandro Gonzalez Iñárritu and Alfonso Cuarón all share the same ideology and strive to promote Mexican filmmaking on a global scale. A similar political agenda is woven throughout their films and a case could be made for any one of the group to be labelled as an auteur, but here we will turn our attention specifically to del Toro.

Following the success of his debut vampire picture *Cronos*, del Toro was invited to direct his first Hollywood film. The experience was less than ideal, as he felt his authority was constantly being undermined by the studio. Once *Mimic* was completed he fled back to his native Mexico where he made *The Devil's Backbone*. He was motivated to return to the US in 1998 when his father was kidnapped. Although del Toro has made films in Mexico, America and Spain and is able to attract funding for blockbusters and independent art-house productions, a stylistic and thematic consistency still runs throughout the body of his work.

Themes

Del Toro can be considered a generic filmmaker. As early as 2002, Kimberley Chun referred to del Toro as 'one of the most original and ambitious horror auteurs since David Cronenberg' (2002, p.28). His films are primarily a hybrid of the Horror and Fantasy genres. He is more specifically influenced by the world of fairytales and fables as his films continue to explore boundaries between reality and the world of imagination and the supernatural. Accordingly, del Toro often manages to go against the grain of generic conventions, for example, the character of *Hellboy* is not your usual comic-book adaptation. Rather than a moral, altruistic superhero, Hellboy is a jealous, jaded and flawed character.

At the heart of the majority of the director's work is the theme of childhood. Del Toro is akin to Ingmar Bergman in his innate ability to capture childhood innocence and depth on screen. His two art-house successes *The Devil's Backbone* and *Pan's Labyrinth* both enquire into the workings of the child's mind. Del Toro often relates the importance of his own childhood and convincingly describes encounters with monsters and ghosts, which he claims fuelled his filmmaking in later life. Yet his films do not cater for a younger audience as children in his movies often experience extreme violence, which once more is not typical of traditional filmmaking.

Another key theme inherent in his works is a political agenda. Occasionally films will take place at a specific moment in history, making the political subtext apparent (the Spanish Civil War is integral to both *The Devil's Backbone* and *Pan's Labyrinth*); even when not explicitly expressed an anti-authoritarian message underlies most of his films.

Aesthetics

In numerous interviews del Toro cites the Spanish artist Francisco de Goya as an influence. Stylistic similarities can be seen between the colour palette adopted by Goya and the tones and atmosphere captured in a del Toro production. In particular he often discusses the impact that *Saturno devorando a su hijo/Saturn Devouring His Children* had on him as a child (Figure 1.5). This painting is part of a collection known as the 'Black Paintings'; also in this group is *The Great He Goat/The Witches' Sabbath*. Here the silhouetted horned figure, which appears in many of Goya's paintings, bears a striking resemblance to the iconic Faun featured in *Pan's Labyrinth*. Del Toro's love of chiaroscuro lighting can similarly be recognized in the dark shadows that are eerily cast in Goya's brush strokes.

The imaginary, surreal worlds typically inhabited by the lead protagonists in the films of del Toro are frequently located underground. This adventure into a world of darkness and the unknown is also evident in the literary writings of Lewis Carroll. Ofelia's journey into the labyrinthine world of Pan draws parallels with that of Alice's into Wonderland. In the press notes that accompany the film, del Toro talks of the symbolism apparent in the journey:

Figure 1.5   Francisco de Goya, *Saturn Devouring His Children* (1819–23)

> I tried to reconnect with the perversity and very sexual content of his work. In fairy tales, all stories are either about the return to the womb (heaven, home) or wandering out into the world and facing your own dragon. We are all children wandering through our own fable. (2006)

The symbolism throughout del Toro's oeuvre demands closer attention. The iconography is often reflective of his fascination with insects and clockwork mechanisms but many images hold greater spiritual and religious connotations.

Production

Del Toro's films manage to traverse big-budget commercial Hollywood filmmaking and low-budget art cinema. The director is fortunate to be in a position to secure large budgets. Conversely he funds his art-house ventures from his own production company, 'Tequila Gang'. Del Toro founded his company following his experience of being produced by El Deseo (a production company established by the Spanish director Pedro Almodóvar). Both the Tequila Gang and El Deseo were set up to nurture up-and-coming filmmakers from Mexico, Spain and Latin America. Whereas many directors see working for Hollywood studios as a betrayal of artistic integrity, del Toro does not distinguish between his films in this way, naming *Pan's Labyrinth* and *Hellboy* as the films he takes greatest pride in.

Del Toro typically works with the same cast and crew. After casting Ron Perlman in his 1993 film *Cronos* and *Blade II* in 2002, he petitioned for Perlman to take the lead in the comic-book adaptation *Hellboy*. Perlman was predominantly known for his television role in *Beauty and the Beast* (1987–90) but producers felt they needed a star to sell the film and had Vin Diesel in mind. Del Toro refused to compromise and as a result Perlman was hired. Another actor who has

Figure 1.6 *Hellboy* (Guillermo del Toro, 2004)

Figure 1.7 *Pan's Labyrinth* (Guillermo del Toro, 2006)

featured in a number of his films is Doug Jones. Jones first appeared in the director's American debut *Mimic* as an extra. He was then cast as one of the lead characters in the *Hellboy* franchise. His role as the psychic amphibian 'Abe Sapien' (Figure 1.6), and more importantly his physicality, must have inspired del Toro as the director went on to cast Jones as the two most memorable characters in *Pan's Labyrinth* – that of the Pale Man (Figure 1.7) and the Faun.

Del Toro also tends to use the same Mexican cinematographer, Guillermo Navarro. Navarro has been instrumental in shooting his films with the exceptions of *Mimic* and *Blade II*. More recently the director has returned to the same editor. Bernat Vilaplana first worked with him on *Pan's Labyrinth*. He has since worked on *Hellboy II: The Golden Army*, which suggests that the collaborative relationship may continue.

Conclusion

Del Toro is a director, producer and writer. There is a distinct magical darkness to his films. Thematically he is concerned with childhood, memory, death and the politics of oppression. He can be classed as a generic filmmaker as his films adhere to the Fantasy/Horror blueprint, yet they are not contrived. Instead they provoke the audience to question wider political and social questions. Del Toro is becoming a household name and therefore attracting audiences on the strength of his previous work. The best illustration of this can be seen in the marketing of the Spanish film *El Orfanato/The Orphanage* (2007). *The Orphanage* was directed by Juan Antonio Bayona but was sold as a del Toro production. He produced the film and Bayona owes his mentor a great debt not just financially. *The Orphanage* covers the same ground as del Toro's *The Devil's Backbone*, with both films set in orphanages that are haunted by the ghosts of children and featuring a historical Spanish political subtext. Here del Toro proves himself an inspiration to younger directors. However, this influence goes far beyond style and content because he is also helping to support new talent. His name is increasingly recognized as an endorsement of quality, but whether he should be granted the status of auteur is yet to be seen.

Reflect and respond

1   Can you think of any reason why Hitchcock should not be considered an auteur?
2   To what extent do you think that Hitchcock's aesthetic is influenced by the composer Bernard Herrmann?
3   Make a case for whether you think del Toro is or is not an auteur.
4   What are your thoughts concerning the auteur status of Alejandro Gonzalez Iñárritu and Alfonso Cuarón?
5   Can you think of any other potential auteurs typically famous for making movies in one particular genre?
6   Comment on the tensions between art and industry in debates on auteurism.
7   Identify up-and-coming directors whom you believe may be accepted into the canon of great auteurs.
8   How have DVDs and Blu-ray changed the construction of the media personality of the director as author?

Conclusion

The question remains, why has Auteur Theory survived as a critical approach when filmmaking is clearly collaborative? Here are some possible answers:

- The director as auteur allows cinema to claim artistic and academic legitimacy; you have film artists just as you have literary or visual artists. Film should be scrutinized in a similar manner to traditional art forms.
- Academics and critics tend to champion the director as it is easier when writing to attribute responsibility to a sole individual. This practice of using the director as 'shorthand' has become accepted as the norm and in turn promotes Auteur Theory.
- Auteur Theory is key to the cultural capital of fan communities, cinema buffs, journalists and academics, all of whom publish using a variety of formats. The internet has given fans a platform to voice their opinions. Similarly newspapers, magazines, journals, radio and television all produce items promoting directors to their respective audiences.
- DVD and Blu-ray marketing include extra features to promote the role of the director: commentaries, 'making-of' documentaries, interviews and 'special edition' directors' cuts.
- Similarly a vast amount of journalism in print and on television features interviews with directors, not just stars, in order to promote the latest film offerings. Therefore Roland Barthes's idea that the author is theoretically dead appears, now more than ever, to be out of step with our contemporary media.

More recently academics have introduced the term 'post-auteur'. This can be seen as an extension of earlier criticisms where authorial intent has been questioned due to the dedicated involvement of actors, producers, screenwriters, etc.

Despite such recent trends, the director is still very much 'of the moment'. With the film industry struggling to come to terms with the drop in DVD sales and the emergence of peer-to-peer file-sharing (illegal downloads), actors and directors have become a stable commodity. Directors continue to garner respect, which can in turn draw people back into the auditorium. This is the case with a number of contemporary American indie auteurs such as Paul Thomas Anderson, Wes Anderson, Spike Jonze and Richard Linklater. Furthermore, viewers who are keen to see the work of these, and similar, directors could be enticed into the cinema to see a good copy of the film. Only once the DVD becomes available can a decent version of the film be illegally posted on the net (ripped from the DVD). Prior to this, unlawful recordings of the film taken from the cinema screen might be available to those who are impatient. However, these would be substitutes of poor quality. Accordingly, in this modern climate of illegal downloads, the auteur still manages to draw viewers back into the cinema. For that reason, academic enquiries into the role of the director will continue to be pertinent.

Bibliography

Astruc, A. (1948) 'The Birth of a New Avant-Garde: *La Caméra-Stylo*', in P. Graham (ed.) *The New Wave*, London: Secker & Warburg, pp.17–23.

Barthes, R. (1977) 'Death of the Author', in *Image, Music, Text,* London: Fontana (first published 1968).

Caughie, J. (ed.) (1981) *Theories of Authorship: A Reader,* London & New York: Routledge.

Chun, K. (2002) What Is a Ghost?: An Interview with Guillermo del Toro, *Cineaste* vol. 27 no. 2, pp.28–31.

Del Toro, G. (2006) 'Press Notes for *Pan's Labyrinth*', Tequila Gang.

Owen, A. (ed.) (2003) *Story and Character: Interviews with British Screenwriters,* London: Bloomsbury.

Rohmer, E. and Chabrol, C. (1979) *Hitchcock: The First Forty-four Films,* Oxford: Roundhouse.

Salisbury, M. (ed.) (2006) *Burton on Burton: Revised Edition,* London: Faber and Faber Ltd.

Sarris, A. (1962) 'Notes on the *Auteur* Theory', in L. Braudy and M. Cohen (eds) (2004) *Film Theory and Criticism: Introductory Readings,* 6th edn, Oxford: Oxford University Press.

Spoto, Donald (1983) *Dark Side of Genius: The Life of Alfred Hitchcock,* London: Collins.

Truffaut, F. (1954) 'Une Certaine Tendance du Cinéma Français', in J. Hollows, P. Hutchings and M. Jancovich (eds) (2000) *The Film Studies Reader,* London: Arnold.

Truffaut, T. (1986) *Hitchcock: The Definitive Study of Alfred Hitchcock,* New York: Simon & Schuster Inc. (first published 1967).

Genre Theory

```
Genre
1.a.Kind; sort; style
  b.A particular style or category of works of art; esp. a type of
    literary work characterized by a particular form, style, or
    purpose.
```

Setting the scene

Since the time of Greek and Roman literature, written texts have been classified as belonging to certain types or groups. The word *genre*, first used in literary studies, derives from the French word *genus*, meaning type. Over the years it has been used to distinguish between different forms of literature (prose, poetry, drama). Shakespearean drama, for example, can be classified as comedy, tragedy or history. Literary texts can be classified into these genres. Similarly in media texts the different categories of classification include Westerns, Musicals, Thrillers, Melodrama, Science Fiction, etc. Robert Stam notes that:

> While some genres are based on story content (the war film), others are borrowed from literature (comedy, melodrama) or from other media (the musical). Some are performer-based (Astaire–Rogers films) or budget-based (blockbusters), while others are based on artistic status (the art film), racial identity (Black cinema), locate [sic] (the Western) or sexual orientation (Queer cinema). (2000, p.14)

As early as the 50s, André Bazin was beginning to talk about genre. By the 60s and 70s genre criticism was seen as a systematic move away from the auteur concept. Genre Studies was seen to be a more inclusive discipline, which would encompass collaborative and commercial filmmaking practices.

In Film Studies, genre is more than just a means of grouping films into categories. The dictionary definition above appears to be straightforward, but many critics will often proffer contradictory definitions, which can be confusing for students and scholars alike.

Identifying genre: 'chicken-and-egg' dilemma

In order to begin our enquiry into the field of genre, the age-old saying of 'Which came first? The chicken or the egg?' is a good starting point. As Andrew Tudor notes:

To take a genre such as a Western, analyse it, and list its principal characteristics is to beg the question that we must first isolate the body of films that are Westerns. But they can only be isolated on the basis of the 'principal characteristics,' which can only be discovered from the films themselves after they have been isolated. (1974, p.5)

Or more simply: 'If we want to know what a western is, we must look at certain kinds of films. But how do we know which films to look at until we know what a western is?' (Buscombe, 1970, p.35). From these two quotes it is evident that there is no ideal place to start but for the purpose of this chapter we will turn to the writing of Andrew Tudor.

Andrew Tudor

Genre (1974)

Andrew Tudor takes the Western as a model for discussion. Tudor finds the term genre problematic and questions its usefulness due to the 'chicken-and-egg' dilemma outlined above.

To apply genre as a theory Tudor suggests that commonly recognized formal elements and common features of a specific genre need to be identified. He believes that these can be most clearly seen in filmic parodies. For example *Blazing Saddles* (Mel Brooks, 1974) mocks ideas of the traditional Western in a similar way to that in which *Scary Movie* (Keenen Ivory Wayans, 2000) plays with the conventions of Horror. In order for the humour to work, an understanding of generic traits is needed.

Tudor questions what the relationship between *auteur* and *genre* might be. How can a director use generic rules to his own ends? Both John Ford and Sam Peckinpah are cited here as rewriting the Western and changing the boundaries of the public understanding of the genre.

Most spectators are familiar with the established concept of a Western. Its characteristics cannot be manipulated by critics; they are what audiences collectively believe them to be. Furthermore, different cultures may not share the same preconception. Whereas East Asia has the ancient Wuxia genre, European culture has the tradition of Swashbuckling movies; the key components in both being swordplay and honour. In summary we can take from Tudor's discussion that he finds notions of genre ineffective and unreliable, with too many 'free-floating' variables.

Reflect and respond

1 Make a list of directors who are associated with specific genres. Are any of the directors you have listed considered to be auteurs?
2 How far are your cinemagoing decisions influenced by preference for a particular genre?
3 Tudor claims that the notion of 'genre' is ineffective. Discuss whether you agree or disagree with this statement.

Building on Tudor's ideas, we have below outlined two categories, 'Formal Elements' and 'Narrative', to help you start to understand Genre Theory.

Formal elements

Iconography (costume, setting, staging and stars)

This type of analysis is open to anyone from an early age. It can represent our initial steps into the world of genre, before knowing what genre actually means. So what is meant by 'iconography'? It is the symbolic meaning we attach to images. For example the Western is evoked by the following iconography: cowboy hat (costume), nineteenth-century American West (setting), saloon and rolling plains (staging) and John Wayne (star). This kind of identification holds true for all genres.

Tone (lighting, music and cinematography)

Tone requires a deeper level of analysis and a greater ability to read additional layers of film production. The way the frame is lit can be an indicator of genre, for example, chiaroscuro lighting is synonymous with German Expressionism and Film Noir. Similarly, musical instruments can become associated with specific genres, with the banjo, harmonica and Jew's harp often used in the Western. The Horror movie often includes point-of-view shots to keep an audience on the edge of its seat.

   Many theoreticians use different terminology to discuss these formal elements. Altman calls them 'semantics' (see boxes on pp.24–5). Formal elements are integral to the narrative as they dictate and restrict action. For example, you would not expect to see a UFO in the Wild West or tap dancing in a Thriller.

Narrative

Another way to identify genres is by considering narrative. Genres typically adhere to a formulaic way of telling a story. Narrative (and myth) will be covered in far more detail in other chapters because of the multifarious ways of reading narrative. However when looking at genre, narratives can be seen as blueprints that are frequently repeated across a number of films. For example, a traditional Musical could typically feature the girl falling in love with the boy nextdoor. Whereas in contemporary Horror movies if you are sexually active you are more likely to die because only the virginal heroine will survive.

   A number of theorists have written extensively on narrative structure in genre. Jim Kitses is probably the most renowned. Kitses approaches the narrative of the Western by focusing on the oppositions of wilderness/civilization, individual/community, savagery/humanity and many more. These broad themes identified by Kitses are synonymous with what Altman terms 'syntax' (see boxes on pp.24–5).

Rick Altman

'A Semantic/Syntactic Approach to Film Genre' (1984)

Altman begins his exploration by problematizing the way genre analysis is practised by critics. He points out that critics lack terminology and often contradict each other (p.27). He specifically identified three contradictions:

1   Genre analysis is both *inclusive* and *exclusive*. It is *inclusive* in that it is easy to construct a long list of films that fall into a specific genre (Musical, Western, Gangster). Yet there are certain texts that are considered to be *exclusive* (do not confuse this with exclusion); these films are canonized and are discussed as exemplary classic texts (p.7).
2   Genre Theory has become too preoccupied with semiotics (signs, iconography and meaning) rather than considering the historical emergence of genre movies. Theory ignores the fact that generic definitions were first introduced by the industry. In ignoring historical context there is no accounting for how genres develop, mutate and rise and fall in popularity, and the audience is forgotten (pp.7–8).
3   Genre is a lie that masquerades as truth. The audience is unknowingly manipulated by generic conventions; it feeds on desires for entertainment (ritual) yet at the same time transmits messages of mass conformity (ideology) (p.9).

Altman poses two approaches to analysing genre: semantic and syntactic. In literature semantics refers to words and meanings, whereas syntax refers to grammar and how sentences are constructed. When applied to film, semantics should be thought of as the building blocks of genre: costume, acting, cinematography, set, iconography, etc. (materials). Syntax on the other hand is the overlying structure, deeper meaning (arrangement) (p.11).

When analysing genre Altman believes that if you take both aspects into account you gain greater understanding. He adopts the semantic/syntactic approach in explaining how to deal with the three aforementioned contradictions:

1   Some films may have the semantic components yet omit the syntactic structure or *vice versa*. This allows the viewer to narrow the field rather than dealing with the broader nature of inclusiveness and exclusiveness (pp.12–13).
2   Historically and theoretically the correlation between the semantic and syntactic changes over time.
3   The shifting relationship between Hollywood and its audience (ritual) is under constant renegotiation. Ideas of mass conformity change depending on political, economic and social climate (ideology) (pp.13–14). This point can be illustrated through the development of both Linda Hamilton's and Arnold Schwarzenegger's characters in *The Terminator* franchise (James Cameron and Jonathan Mostow, 1984–91, 2003).

The genres that have proven the most durable (Western and Musical) have established the most 'coherent syntax' whereas those that quickly disappear are reliant on 'recurring semantic elements, never developing a stable syntax (Catastrophes and Newsroom films to name a few)' (p.16).

In 1999, Altman adds another component to his semantic/syntactic approach. He calls this additional level of analysis 'pragmatics'. Pragmatics refers to the context between the information on the screen and how it is interpreted. Meaning in film is never fixed; it is dependent on how the viewer reads the information. Altman identifies two areas of geography and chronology in order to understand this further. For example, depending on your nationality, race, age and the era in which you are viewing the material, the way you interpret information will differ.

Below are examples of how Altman's ideas of semantics and syntax can be applied to specific genres. Applying his ideas to Gangster films, it is clear that certain characteristics persist as the genre evolves and is taken up by different cultures.

Traditional American Gangster

Semantics	Prohibition era, speakeasies, bootlegging, jazz, guns, suits, flappers, police oppression, violence, class and individualism.
Syntax	Alcohol and criminality will lead to the downfall of American society. Exploration of the underclass. Critique of the 'American Dream'.
Examples	*The Public Enemy* (William A. Wellman, 1931), *Little Caesar* (Mervyn LeRoy, 1931) and *Scarface* (Howard Hawks, 1932).

Italian American Gangster

Semantics	Immigrant life, Little Italy, xenophobia, family, opera, guns, drugs, mafia/mob, violence, class, police, pasta, corruption and Catholicism.
Syntax	Celebration of the anti-hero. Questioning of capitalistic materialism. Exploration of the underclass. Critique of the 'American Dream'.
Examples	The *Godfather* trilogy (Francis Ford Coppola, 1972–90), *Goodfellas* (Martin Scorsese, 1990) and *Donnie Brasco* (Mike Newell, 1997).

African American Gangsta

Semantics	Inner-city ghettos, gang culture, rap, drugs, guns, 'bling', violence, class, brotherhood, drive-by shootings, racism, nihilism.
Syntax	Exposing the failings of American race relations. Results of disenfranchisement. Exploration of the underclass. Critique of the 'American Dream'.
Examples	*New Jack City* (Mario Van Peebles, 1991), *Boyz 'n the Hood* (John Singleton, 1991) and *Menace II Society* (Albert and Allen Hughes, 1993).

Reflect and respond

Using Altman's model founded on the ideas of semantics and syntax, apply your understanding of generic conventions to the genres below.

Science Fiction
Semantics
Syntax
Examples

Romantic Comedy
Semantics
Syntax
Examples

Horror
Semantics
Syntax
Examples

1   Are there any similarities across the three genres explored?
2   Was it more difficult to identify key characteristics in any of these genres? Why do you think this is so?
3   Which, if any, of the films you noted could be considered classic canonical texts?
4   From your findings here, which do you find more important – semantics or syntax?

It is important to note that many academics refer to the same idea using different terminology. For instance Edward Buscombe also explores what Altman calls 'semantics and syntax' but he calls them 'inner and outer meaning'.

Edward Buscombe

'The Idea of Genre in the American Cinema' (1970)

Edward Buscombe provokes debate concerning genre by asking (p.33):

- Do genres in the cinema really exist?
- What functions do they fulfil?
- How do specific genres originate or what gives rise to them?

These questions are pertinent to the heart of genre and its interpretation.

Borrowing from the literary work of Welleck and Warren, Buscombe uses the terms 'inner' and 'outer' forms for the crux of his argument. They define these as follows: '[o]uter form (specific metre or structure) … inner form (attitude, tone, purpose – more crudely, subject and audience)' (p.36). Buscombe believed both aspects to be of equal note, stating:

> [The] idea of both inner and outer forms seems essential, for if we require only the former, in terms of subject matter, then our concept will be too loose to be of much value; and if only the latter, then the genre will be ultimately meaningless, since devoid of any content. (p.36)

However, as film is a visual medium he places more emphasis on the range of 'outer forms', which he lists as setting, clothes, tools of the trade and miscellaneous physical objects. He suggests that these work as 'formal elements'. These four interlinking elements impact on the narrative framework and dictate to a certain extent how stories are told. He uses the case of the Western to illustrate the fact that violence is traditionally a core element. Accordingly, very few films treat the genre as nonviolent. Buscombe claims that genre enables good directors to excel. Yet at the same time it imposes limitations on a director.

Audiences

The audience is key when exploring ideas of genre. Rather than thinking of the audience as a coherent body, the industry often targets niche groups. These can be based on gender, sexuality, race, nationality or class. Certain film genres are associated with women (Musicals, Chick Flicks and Love Stories) and others with men (Science Fiction, Gangster and War movies). Tudor notes that 'art-house' films are often seen as elitist and therefore linked to educated intellectuals rather than the masses. He correctly points out that the term 'art movies' is used generically. It would be difficult to classify such films as the term incorporates many different genres, but overall they are more than often foreign, subtitled texts (1974, p.9).

Genre is dependent on audience expectation. For example, when we pay to see a Romantic Comedy we anticipate lighthearted entertainment with a 'feelgood' factor. The industry is aware of its audience and aims to deliver films that fit our expectations. Accordingly, the marketing of films is very important because it plays on our knowledge of genre. Bearing this in mind, consider the use of images on movie posters. Often the title alone does not immediately evoke the intended genre. It is the image that evokes the iconography associated with the specific genre.

Marketing relies on a level of audience cultural competency. The term cultural competency refers to knowledge that is acquired subconsciously over a period of time. Our recognition of iconography is dependent on our exposure to generic texts. However, it should be noted that genre restrictions are also dictated by economic factors. Studios are interested in profits and adhering to generic conventions is a tried and tested way of securing investment in projects.

Reflect and respond

1   Thinking about narrative structure, can you name any particular genre where recurring story-lines are frequently used?
2   Bearing in mind the film industry catering for specific groups, can you identify any films which could be marketed in relation to race, sexuality and nationality?
3   Make a list of film titles that are seemingly neutral. Can you think of how these films could be generically misread (e.g. *Saturday Night Fever* (John Badham, 1977) as a medical drama)?
4   What kind of images do you think the industry would use to promote the following genres: Science Fiction, Adventure and Sports movies?
5   Discuss how film posters use generic iconography in reference to posters of your choice.

The canon

The term canon is taken from English Literary Studies. Over the centuries, various intellectual groups have acted as an authority on literary texts to decide which were suitable for academic study. This elitist process created a hierarchy based on their selections. They included those texts they deemed to be artistically worthy rather than those that were popular with the masses.

Similarly in the field of Film Studies there is also a canon. Once again it is based on the writings of academics and critics without recognition of the filmgoing public. When applied to genre, some texts are considered canonical; all other films belonging to the same genre are compared to such classic examples. John Ford's films *Stagecoach* (1939) and *The Searchers* (1956) are seen to be exemplars of the Western. *Singin' in the Rain* (Stanley Donen and Gene Kelly, 1952) and *The Wizard of Oz* (Victor Fleming, 1939) are classic Musicals while *Metropolis* (Fritz Lang, 1927) and the original *Invasion of the Body Snatchers* (Don Siegel, 1956) are Science Fiction films also considered worthy of canonical status. However, the canon is constantly changing and expanding to include films that flaunt and challenge the traditional concepts of genre. But quality continues to be an overriding factor in the elitist, hierarchical process.

Steve Neale writes extensively on genre. Below you will find discussions on 'verisimilitude' and the way genre is viewed differently by the public and critics/academics.

Steve Neale

'Questions of Genre' (1990)

For Neale two things are central to the understanding of genre; verisimilitude and the 'question of social and cultural functions that genres perform' (p.160). Here, Neale is using verisimilitude to mean 'probable' or 'likely' rather than the traditional understanding connected to ideas of truth. He illustrates his definition with that of the Musical in which it is acceptable for characters to spontaneously burst into song, whereas in a Film Noir, singing would alienate an audience due to their prior knowledge of generic conventions. Neale highlights how some film genres hold verisimilitude as highly important (Gangster, War and Police dramas) whereas other types of generic films flout any adherence to this (Sci-fi, Horror and Comedy). Yet he also points out that breaking such generic traditions can often yield unexpected pleasure for audiences (p.162).

Neale identifies that there is a difference in the way genre is perceived by the film industry, whose prime focus is in attracting an audience, and the way theoreticians and critics talk about genre. The latter are instrumental in recognizing new genres, for example, Film Noir was a term first introduced by the *Cahiers du cinéma* group; '[N]o producer in the 1940s set out to make a film noir' (Stam, 2000, p.128). Rather than simply grouping these films into the already existent crime genre, they believed that the formal elements necessitated a new classification.

In addition, Neale highlights the fact that film genres borrow from other forms of media and entertainment. Here he cites how Melodrama originated on the stage, Comedy derived from vaudeville, circus and burlesque, and Musicals were often developed from Broadway shows (p.176). Neale states that more research into 'cross-media generic formations' is needed.

He concludes by pointing the way forward – the future of genre studies must consider the following:

1   prehistory (the development from other forms of media)
2   all films regardless of quality (not just canonical texts)
3   factors other than content (advertising, studio policy, stars, etc.).

However, Neale remains at the forefront of genre debates and continues to rework and challenge his own theories and those of others.

Reflect and respond

1   Why are some generic films considered classics?
2   Discuss whether you prefer genres that are based on verisimilitude or those that reject it.
3   Make a list of new genres that have occurred within your lifetime. How new are they? Do they rework old genres?

Genre revisionism

Revisionism began in the 50s but really came to the fore in the 60s and 70s. America was experiencing social upheaval both at home and abroad due to the fight for racial equality and the Vietnam War. The sensitivity surrounding these subjects caused directors to steer clear of dealing with them directly, instead addressing them allegorically.

The dominant ideology (formal elements and narrative) in traditional genres was no longer considered applicable to the time period. So in order to be relevant, genres developed in a manner that was pertinent to contemporary audiences. As a result of these developments, when genres re-emerged, many of the established features had evolved, mutated, become subverted or, in some cases, been omitted.

New generations of directors consciously played with the original characteristics in order to comment on contemporary concerns. Consider *Shrek* (Andrew Adamson and Vicky Jenson, 2001), a children's animated feature with a subtext that mocks the traditional Disney format. The table below illustrates how the Western has been revised over the last century.

1900s–1930s

- *The Great Train Robbery* (Edwin S. Porter, 1903) is identified as the first film Western. Prior to this the Western had existed in literature, pulp fiction, popular song and travelling Wild West Shows.
- Director John Ford teams with actor John Wayne in their first Western, *Stagecoach*.

1940s

- The 40s were dominated by John Ford, creating classics such as *My Darling Clementine* (1946), *Fort Apache* (1948) and *She Wore a Yellow Ribbon* (1949).
- *Duel in the Sun* (King Vidor, 1946) was unusual for a Western as it focused primarily on the passionate interracial relationship between the two main protagonists. It was fondly referred to at the time as 'Lust in the Dust'.

1950s

- *Rio Grande* (John Ford, 1950) and *Shane* (George Stevens, 1953) continued the classic tradition of the Western.
- The 50s saw the emergence of the Western Musical hybrid. The most famous examples, all made in this era, include: *Annie Get Your Gun* (George Sidney, 1950), *Calamity Jane* (David Butler, 1953) and *Oklahoma* (Fred Zinnemann, 1954).
- Traditional ideas of the Western were first challenged at this point in what have become known as 'revisionist Westerns'. Both *Broken Arrow* (Delmer Daves, 1950) and *The Searchers* attempted to address how the genre had been racist in its depiction of Native Americans, whereas *High Noon* (Fred Zinnemann, 1952) and *Johnny Guitar* (Nicholas Ray, 1954) can be read as allegory for the McCarthy witch hunt of suspected Communists. These revisionist texts looked to incorporate contemporary political and social issues.

1960s

- 1960 saw John Sturges borrow from the Japanese director Akira Kurosawa's *Seven Samurai* (1954), with *The Magnificent Seven* still considered a canonical text.
- Sergio Leone, in partnership with Ennio Morricone and Clint Eastwood, injected the Western with Italian flavour. *A Fistful of Dollars* (1964), *For a Few Dollars More* (1965) and *The Good, the Bad and the Ugly* (1966) initiated the emergence of 'Spaghetti Westerns', which were modern and redefined generic conventions. *Once Upon a Time in the West* (1968) explored the death of the genre; the frontier had become populated and weary old cowboys had lost their place in the modern world.
- 1969 witnessed a turning point with Sam Peckinpah's *The Wild Bunch*. This film used extreme violence to critique the social unrest afflicting America, with the war in Vietnam and the fight for civil rights at home.

1970s

- Many of the Westerns in the 70s continued to address the worries of the American people, with films such as *Soldier Blue* (Ralph Nelson, 1970) and *Little Big Man* (Arthur Penn, 1970) using the treatment of Native Americans as a metaphor for Vietnam and race relations.
- Interestingly, both *Buck and the Preacher* (1972), directed by the famous African American actor Sidney Poitier, and *Blazing Saddles* (Mel Brooks, 1974) introduced black cowboys as heroes of the narrative.
- Clint Eastwood directed his first Western *High Plains Drifter* (1973).

1980s

- The 80s saw a huge reversal in the popularity of the genre. This is epitomized by the colossal failure of the film *Heaven's Gate* (Michael Cimino, 1980). This disastrous production nearly bankrupted Universal Studios and resulted in the industry largely avoiding the genre for a decade.

1990s

- The blockbuster was pivotal in reviving the Western. *Back to the Future III* (Robert Zemeckis, 1990) and *Wild Wild West* (Barry Sonnenfeld, 1999) saw big-name stars like Michael J. Fox and Will Smith attract a new audience.
- The films that were at the forefront in attracting attention from the public, academics and critics were the intelligent Westerns, *Dances with Wolves* (Kevin Costner, 1990), *Unforgiven* (Clint Eastwood, 1992) and *Ride with the Devil* (Ang Lee, 1999).
- Jim Jarmusch took the genre in an entirely new direction with his experimental film *Dead Man* (1995).

2000s

- The intelligent, art-house approach to the Western continued into the next millennium, with the Oscar-winning films *Brokeback Mountain* (Ang Lee, 2005), which introduced the first gay-cowboy storyline and the Coen brothers' *No Country for Old Men* (2007).
- Joss Whedon developed his television series *Firefly* into the film *Serenity* (2005), which attracted a large cult following in part due to its hybridity, which expanded possibilities for the future of the Western.

Academics often divide the Western into two separate periods: 'Fordian' and 'post-Fordian' (Staiger, 2003, p.186). The former is considered to represent the genre in its purest form, whereas the latter is indicative of revisionist texts.

Hybridity

The idea of purity in genre is problematic. For example, most films, no matter what genre, typically include a romantic storyline. This does not, however, lead to the categorization of such

Figure 2.1 *Serenity* (Joss Whedon, 2005)

films as love stories. Hybridity refers to the merging of two or more objects to form a new entity; in this case film genres and subgenres. The boxes above reveal a number of examples where this occurs. In the 50s the Western was put to music, meaning that it could no longer be considered as belonging to one genre alone. The tradition of Musicals borrowing from other genres continues. For example, *Sweeney Todd: The Demon Barber of Fleet Street* (Tim Burton, 2007) is a Slasher/Musical and Andrew Lloyd Webber's Musical *Evita* (Alan Parker, 1996) marries politics, biography and music.

Reflect and respond

1 Look at Figure 2.1, the image for the film *Serenity*. Which genres have been merged? Justify your answer by reference to specific iconography.
2 Which of the genres appears to be more prominent?
3 Can you identify other films that combine more than one genre?
4 Why do you think the film industry makes such films?
5 Can you identify any genres that have merged to create a new genre in its own right (or hybrid genre)?

Robert Stam complicates the issue of revisionism and hybridity by introducing the term 'submerged' (2000, p.129). He adopts this to refer to instances when a genre may appear to fit one category, due to its archetypal iconography, but have an underlying theme associated with a different genre. The film *Easy Rider* (Dennis Hopper, 1969) can be read as the archetypal Road Movie, yet below the surface it shares numerous ideological traits with the Western – although it is knowingly playing with and subverting them. A key example is the scene when Wyatt (Peter Fonda) changes a tyre on his bike; this is juxtaposed with the shoeing of a horse.

Reflect and respond

1 Can you think of any films that consciously break with generic conventions – how did you react when viewing them?
2 Can you identify any other genres of film that you believe to have evolved from theoretical and critical writing?
3 What, if any, is the difference between a film movement, genre and school of filmmaking?

Case study: The Swashbuckler

Swashbuckling films fit into a hybrid genre of Action/Adventure movies. The name Swashbuckler originally derived from the small shield a swordsman carried, called a buckler, and the tradition that he was a poor fighter who covered his lack of skill with noise and bragging. Therefore the term came to function as a 'put-down'. Over the years Hollywood developed the Swashbuckling character into that of a loud, bragging, devil-may-care hero. This is an image not far from the dictionary definition of a 'swaggering adventurer, blustering, ostentatiously daring' (OED, 1996).

Subgenres and hybridity

This style of Adventure film has been in existence since the early 1900s. For the purpose of this case study we have identified two subgenres of Swashbuckling movies:

1   pirates and buccaneers
2   aristocrats and knights.

The first recorded Swashbucklers tended to be stories about pirates with tales of valiant knights and courtly honour emerging later. It is important to recognize that within the genre are a number of recurring characters and tales taken from legends, mythology and classic literature. The table below illustrates traditional characters found within each subgenre.

Pirates and buccaneers	Aristocrats and knights
Peter Pan	King Arthur and the Knights of the Round Table
Sinbad the Sailor	The Three Musketeers and D'Artagnan
	Robin Hood and his Merry Men
	The Scarlet Pimpernel
	Zorro
	Samurai/Wuxia – East Asian culture

What these tales have in common are heroic characters, villains, romance, codes of honour, exotic locations, swordfights, period costume, often a leading lady for romantic interest and a triumphant invigorating score. Furthermore these films encode ideas of brave deeds, justice and fair play, where the good vanquish the bad, usually through a swordfight that is choreographed for exciting dramatic effect rather than to show realistic swordplay.

Although typically recognized as Swashbuckling films, many of these character-based stories lend themselves to other genres. The list below gives a few examples of hybrid versions:

1   **Animation and puppetry**
   • *Peter Pan* (Clyde Geronimi, Wilfred Jackson and Hamilton Luske, 1953)
   • *Muppet Treasure Island* (Brian Henson, 1996)
   • *Mickey, Donald, Goofy: The Three Musketeers* (Donovan Cook, 2004)

2 **Musicals**
   • *Camelot* (Joshua Logan, 1967)
   • *Pirates of Penzance* (Wilford Leach, 1983)
3 **Comedy**
   • *A Connecticut Yankee in King Arthur's Court* (Tay Garnett, 1949)
   • *Don't Lose Your Head* (Gerald Thomas, 1966)
   • *Monty Python and the Holy Grail* (Terry Gilliam and Terry Jones, 1975)
4 **Science Fiction**
   • *The Spaceman and King Arthur* (Russ Mayberry, 1979).

Iconography

As we have discussed in this chapter, one of the ways in which to approach genre studies is to consider iconography and its greater meaning. While the iconography, tone and narrative are not always identical in the pirates/buccaneers and knights/aristocrats subgenres, many aspects are similar. The table below shows the similarities, development and the differences exhibited. It also clearly identifies the semantics and syntax explored by Altman.

	Pirates and buccaneers
Semantics	Characters: buccaneers and cutthroats, sailors and deckhands, captains, admirals and governors. Explorers, stowaways and missionaries. Daughters of rich officials.
	Rituals: walking the plank and keelhauling. Rum drinking (yo-ho-ho), hoisting the rigging. Sea battles and heroic, choreographed swordfights.
	Location: Caribbean, Southern Seas or the Spanish Main.
	Costume: scruffy shirts, ragged trousers or shirtless deckhands. Heroes dressed in pantaloons, long leather boots, white billowing–sleeved shirts with crossed leather straps for scabbards. Villain often wears seventeenth-century Cavalier jacket and three-cornered hat.
	Props: galleons flying the 'Jolly Roger' (skull and crossbones), parrot (pieces of eight), gold and the black spot (imminent doom).
	Narrative traits: search for buried treasure, shipwrecks and kidnapping.
Syntax	Code of brotherhood. Outlaws undermining the establishment. Strong anti-heroes – celebration of the underclass rather than the corrupt elite.
Examples	*The Black Pirate* (Albert Parker, 1926), *Captain Blood* (Michael Curtiz, 1935), *The Sea Hawk* (Michael Curtiz, 1940).
	Aristocrats and knights
Semantics	Characters: kings, queens, princes and princesses. Ladies-in-waiting, squires, sorcerers and magicians. Trained swordsmen, jesters. Mentors, wealthy landowners and oppressed commoners.
	Rituals: duels, jousting, archery tournaments. Crusades, coronations, weddings and medieval pageantry. Preparing for battle.

Locations: castles, dungeons, towns, villages and hamlets. Hidden lairs and rural nostalgia.

Costume: armour/chainmail, gauntlets, helmets, capes, robes and masks. Crowns, wimples, corsets, tights and codpieces, jewellery.

Props: quarterstaffs, bows, arrows, lances, swords and shields. Portcullis, coats of arms, pitchers and flagons.

Narrative traits: secrecy, ransom, exile, treachery, revenge, loyalty and code of honour. Romance and humour. Heroes in disguise rescuing damsels in distress.

Syntax	Collectivity rather than individualism. State vs religion. Redressing class divisions, stealing from the rich to give to the poor. Fight against the corrupt establishment and the oppression of the poor. Uniting the masses in order to overthrow the exploitative elite.
Examples	*The Three Musketeers* (Roland V. Lee, 1935) *The Three Musketeers* (George Sidney, 1948), *The Three Musketeers* (Richard Lester, 1973), *The Count of Monte Cristo* (Kevin Reynolds, 2002).

These popular narratives have an underlying moral message. All Swashbuckling stories expose the dangers of an all-powerful elite class, which, given free rein, tyrannizes and exploits the less fortunate for materialistic gain.

Stars

A different way of approaching the genre is to consider key actors who have become synonymous with the role of the sword-wielding hero. In brief, a study of the main lead characters shows that in the 20s Douglas Fairbanks became a famous matinee idol, followed by Errol Flynn in the 30s. Throughout the 40s numerous stars, such as Tyrone Power and Stewart Granger, played Swashbuckling heroes but no actor was predominantly associated with the genre. Whereas, in the 50s and early 60s a revisionist approach saw the emergence of female Swashbucklers alongside male leads. However, after the 60s Swashbuckling films lost their popularity until a small revival in the 80s and 90s.

More recently, Swashbuckling has undergone a huge resurgence with the success of the light-hearted *Pirates of the Caribbean* franchise (Gore Verbinski, 2003–7). The films can be seen as homage to Fairbanks and Flynn with Johnny Depp playing Captain Jack Sparrow. Similar to the heroines in the 60s films, Keira Knightley is adept at brandishing a cutlass and is often seen outsmarting her male counterparts.

Similarly, the knights and aristocrats subgenre has spawned a number of stars. Michael York is famously associated with the Musketeer films and has also played various kings and lords. Due to the iconic status of the famous heroes who inspire Swashbuckling narratives, these films can often attract well-known stars. King Arthur has been played by John Gielgud, Richard Gere and Clive Owen while Robin Hood has been undertaken by Sean Connery, Kevin Costner and Russell Crowe. Another Swashbuckling favourite is Antonio Banderas, who played the masked avenger Zorro in *The Mask of Zorro* and *The Legend of Zorro* (Martin Campbell, 1998 and 2005). He was ironically cast as the voice of Puss in Boots in the animated film *Shrek 2* (Andrew Adamson, Kelly Ashby and Conrad Vernon, 2004).

Political content

The political and social context is also significant when looking at Swashbuckling and other genres. The years 1934–41 saw the rise of fascism in Europe. To avoid censorship, filmmakers did not condemn regimes outright. However, they promoted chivalric honour to act as a vehicle for coded attacks. Rather than commenting on contemporary concerns, they used the historical setting of the Middle Ages to create distance and in order not to appear to be issuing a direct critique. This is apparent in *The Adventures of Robin Hood* (Michael Curtiz, 1938) which can be read as a metaphor for America's isolationist stance in the runup to World War II.

The introduction of the female Swashbuckler in the post-war period was 'in tune' with the emergence of the independent women who had contributed to the war effort. *The Wife of Monte Cristo* (Edgar G. Ulmer, 1946) provides a good example here. Equally at this time, men were returning from the war and faced difficult times demanding resourcefulness and strength of character. Flynn was an ideal star to represent this necessary masculinity.

The 50s saw the Cold War and McCarthyism at the forefront of concerns. Anti-Communist paranoia is alluded to in *The Flame and the Arrow* (Jacques Tourneur, 1950) and *The Crimson Pirate* (Robert Siodmak, 1952) starring Burt Lancaster. Covert messages were introduced by Communist writers and sympathizers. As Jeffrey Richards has noted, the Swashbuckling genre has not been dominated by auteurs; it is the scriptwriters who have instigated the political messages (Chapman *et al.*, 2007, p.120).

Conclusion

Swashbuckling is an interesting example for the 'chicken-and-egg dilemma'. The genre grew out of disparate myths and tales from around the world. These narratives provide a fertile ground for moral and political concerns although such messages are often veiled beneath a seemingly conservative plot. The longevity of the genre is due to the way such stories lend themselves to the big screen; they mix rumbustious behaviour and excitement with 'ripping good yarns'.

Case study: The Musical

The Musical is one of the film industry's most renowned and well-established genres. The first talking movie, *The Jazz Singer* (Alan Crosland, 1927), included a number of song-and-dance routines. Therefore, from the onset of sound on screen Musicals have been a staple form of entertainment.

Escapism

Musicals often attract audiences in times of social and political upheaval. Richard Dyer's seminal article 'Entertainment and Utopia' explores the escapist nature of the genre:

> Entertainment offers the image of 'something better' to escape into, or something we want deeply that our day-to-day lives don't provide. Alternatives, hopes, wishes – these are stuff of

utopia, the sense that things could be better, that something other than what is can be imagined and maybe realized. (1992, p.18)

For example, during the Great Depression, Americans sought refuge in the on-screen partnership
of Fred Astaire and Ginger Rogers. Musicals were at the height of their popularity during the war
years due to their escapist ideology. Their popularity waned in the 50s and 60s when the US was
struggling with the fight for civil rights and the Vietnam conflict. Cinema's escapist offerings
failed to overcome the violent images projected into homes via television. Throughout the rest of
the century, Musicals never regained significant popularity although some breakthrough films are
now revered as classics. These include *The Sound of Music* (Robert Wise, 1965), *Grease* (Randal
Kleiser, 1978) and *Annie* (John Huston, 1982).

More recently, Musicals have come back into favour. This may again be due to the escape they
represent from the political and social struggles of the new millennium such as the War on Terror
and the global recession. New Musicals that have reinvigorated the genre include *Moulin Rouge!*,
Chicago (Rob Marshall, 2002) and the *High School Musical* franchise (Kenny Ortega, 2006–8).

Setting

When sound was first introduced to cinema the industry struggled to supply enough films to cater
for public demand. Hollywood's solution was to use theatrical shows already being performed on
Broadway. Stage Musicals needed little adaptation for the screen as they were an already tried-and-
tested formula. Many early film Musicals were labelled as 'Revues' as they lacked a coherent storyline, instead comprising of various unconnected song-and-dance routines harking back to the
traditional music-hall and vaudeville shows. Revues typically took advantage of a backstage
setting, where the story of putting on a show could help weave together the disconnected musical numbers, yet these were not the only locations used to set a story to music.

Rick Altman has written extensively on Musicals as a genre. He categorizes the films into three
specific subgenres based on where the narratives are set (1987, p.127):

1 **Show**: Here we encounter a theatrical troupe putting on a production. The narrative is set
   backstage and the rehearsal format affords a naturalistic setting for song and dance. These
   films typically conclude with a show within a show. Examples include: *42nd Street* (Lloyd
   Bacon, 1933), *Singin' in the Rain, The Blues Brothers* (John Landis, 1980) and *Moulin Rouge!*.
2 **Fairytale**: This story is set in a magical kingdom where make-believe kings, queens, princes,
   princesses and magical creatures reside. Famous examples include *The Wizard of Oz, Chitty
   Chitty Bang Bang* (Ken Hughes, 1968), *Willy Wonka & the Chocolate Factory* (Mel Stuart, 1971)
   and *Beauty and the Beast* (Gary Trousdale and Kirk Wise, 1991).
3 **Folktale**: This is a nostalgic look at the past, typically involving families and communities
   pulling together. Rituals and cultural heritage are foregrounded. *Seven Brides for Seven Brothers*
   (Stanley Donen, 1954), *West Side Story* (Jerome Robbins and Robert Wise, 1961), *Fiddler on the
   Roof* (Norman Jewison, 1971) and *Bugsy Malone* (Alan Parker, 1976) are classic examples of this
   kind of musical.

Not all Musicals fit neatly into one specific category. Consider the 1978 Randal Kleiser Musical,
Grease. The narrative sits most comfortably in the folk category as the film fondly looks back at

50s American culture. The rituals include drive-in movies, drag racing (cars), sleepovers and hand jiving. However, there are elements of putting on a production when the television show, National Bandstand, broadcasts from Rydell High School. Similarly there is a nod to the fairytale formula in the final shot where Sandy and Danny's car takes to the sky and magically flies into the sunset. Therefore the three categories Altman suggests are not necessarily exclusive but do provide a useful starting point for any analysis.

Narrative structure

Altman also identifies that in most Musicals the plot is constructed on the idea of binary oppositions, which he calls the 'dual-focus narrative' (1987, pp.16–27). This is similar to the work that Jim Kitses did on the Western (Kitses and Rickman, 1998). Altman suggests that, rather than following the traditional cause-and-effect approach, the Musical is typically based on the relationship between the hero and heroine, their differences and similarities. He develops this further by stating that the *mise-en-scène* and characterization in Musicals are also dependent on opposing forces. The table below illustrates how Altman's 'dual-focus' can be applied to *Grease*.

Male	Female
Danny	Sandy
Kenickie	Rizzo
T-Birds	Pink Ladies
American	Australian
Sexually charged	Virginal
Black	Pink
Dark	Blonde
Rebel	Straight-laced
Popular	Geeks
Leather and denim	Cotton and lace

It is evident that much of the narrative conforms to Altman's theory. Interestingly, at the conclusion of the film Danny appears at the school fair dressed as a jock (athlete), willing to turn his back on his rock 'n' roll, bad-boy roots in order to gain the girl. Similarly Sandy sheds her innocent persona and makes an unforgettable entrance wearing skintight black trousers and a revealing top, with a cigarette hanging from her seductive red lips. This finale exemplifies the idea of binary oppositions as a framework for the Musical narrative.

Stars

As with all genres, the Musical has been responsible for creating some of the most famous actors and actresses in film history. In the early days Ruby Keeler and Dick Powell appeared in backstage Musicals such as *42nd Street* and *Gold Diggers of 33* (Mervyn LeRoy, 1933). Ginger Rogers also featured in these films, but became most famous for her pairing with Fred Astaire. Other classical stars from the Musicals include Mickey Rooney, Judy Garland and Frank Sinatra. Musicals fell in popularity in the 60s and 70s as discussed above. Barbra Streisand, Julie Andrews, Bette Midler,

John Travolta and Olivia Newton-John gained fame in spite of this. At the turn of the twenty-first century, Zac Efron and Vanessa Hudgens from the *High School Musical* franchise are more familiar to a contemporary audience.

It is interesting to note that Busby Berkeley is probably one of the most renowned Musical stars; he was not an actor but a choreographer. Berkeley is most famous for his kaleidoscopic dance routines, where he made abstract, geometrical formations using the bodies of the chorus line. His distinct style of choreography is still influential today and can be seen in the 'Be Our Guest' sequence in Disney's *Beauty and the Beast* and also in the Take That music video *Shine* (2007).

Iconography and hybridity

As with most genres, it is easy to identify recurring iconography in Musicals. When the narrative deals with putting on a show then you will typically see the following: stage, red curtains, an orchestra pit, piano, glamorous costumes, sequins and spotlights. Similarly the fairytale may include crowns and other royal regalia, objects with magical properties (wands, broomsticks, etc.). The folktale is more difficult to predict as these films are often a hybrid of genres.

The Musical, probably more so than any other of the traditional genres we have discussed so far, lends itself well to hybridity. This is because you can set any narrative to music. Below is a list of famous film Musicals that not only conform to conventions of the Musical genre but can also be considered as belonging to another category. One way of establishing whether a Musical fuses with another genre is to think about the iconography as this will alert you to other possibilities:

1 **Westerns**
   - *Annie Get Your Gun*
   - *Calamity Jane*
   - *Seven Brides for Seven Brothers*
   - *Oklahoma*
   - *Paint Your Wagon* (Joshua Logan, 1969)
2 **Gangster**
   - *Guys and Dolls* (Joseph L. Mankiewicz, 1955)
   - *Bugsy Malone*
   - *Chicago*
3 **Horror**
   - *The Rocky Horror Picture Show* (Jim Sharman, 1975)
   - *The Little Shop of Horrors* (Frank Oz, 1986)
   - *The Phantom of the Opera* (Joel Schumacher, 2004)
   - *Sweeney Todd*
4 **School**
   - *Grease*
   - *Hairspray* (John Waters, 1988 and Adam Shankman, 2007)
   - *High School Musical*
   - *Fame* (Alan Parker, 1980).

Cultural competency

The understanding of genre is dependent on the viewer's cultural competency. Bollywood is a fascinating case in point. India's film industry is located in Mumbai, previously known as Bombay. Because of the similarities with Hollywood, this centre for Eastern filmmaking became affectionately known as Bollywood. The term has since become synonymous with commercial filmmaking in India; a style of cinema that is fundamentally based on song and dance.

Recently Indian Musicals have become more and more popular with Western audiences. This is clearly evidenced by the emergence of Western-produced Bollywood films such as *The Guru* (Daisy von Scherler Mayer, 2002) and *Bride & Prejudice* (Gurinder Chadha, 2004). However, without the cultural knowledge it is difficult for Euro-American viewers to understand the cultural references and importance of Indian history and iconography. From 1757–1947 India was subject to the Raj (British rule). Britain colonized India in order to exploit its people and natural resources. On leaving, the British split the country in an attempt to separate Hindus and Sikhs from Muslims. Although the different religions had managed to coexist long before the British ever arrived, Hindus and Sikhs were made to relocate in India and Muslims were forced to move to Pakistan. The results were horrific, with 14.5 million people made refugees and massacres and riots ensuing.

Bearing this in mind, films such as the classic *Mother India* (Mehboob Khan, 1957) allude to the oppression suffered by Indians at the hands of the British. In the film a tyrannical landowner exploits a young family. The father is physically crippled while attempting to pay off his debt to the landowner. In an act of self-pity, he leaves his family, never to return. The mother struggles on, losing the youngest child in a storm. The great hardships suffered by the family over decades can be seen as a metaphor for the oppression Indians experienced under the Raj. Therefore the viewing experience has greater poignancy if the audience is aware of the historical allegories at play.

Iconography and Indian rituals are also of importance if you are aware of their semiotic coding. The number of times the female lead changes her sari in the love duet is supposed to indicate how long the lovers have been courting. More importantly, there are strict social rules in Indian society concerning relationships and this is similarly translated onto the screen; the lovers in Bollywood films do not kiss. There may be some rare exceptions to this rule but kissing is generally considered taboo.

Conclusion

Despite changing trends and the fact that critics often dismiss them as superficial, Musicals continue to attract audiences. Musical formats of storytelling can be found in all cultures, which may also account for the enduring popularity of the genre. Most recently the Abba-inspired musical *Mamma Mia!* (Phyllida Lloyd, 2008) became the highest-grossing Musical film to date. The film/stage play comprised of disconnected songs by the Swedish pop group and the structure should thus have shared similarities with the old-fashioned revue-style Musicals. However, the narrative cleverly interwove the familiar lyrics into a coherent romantic story. The success of *Mamma Mia!* has led to a new trend in Musicals of borrowing from the pop repertoire. Most Musicals begin life either on Broadway or in the West End and, depending on their popularity, make the transition onto the big screen. Yet many Musicals sink without trace. The use of popular music does not guarantee success but it can help as it appeals to a ready-made audience.

Reflect and respond

1   Consider the two generic case studies, Musicals and Swashbucklers. Do they appeal to the same audience? Explain your answer fully.
2   Do you agree that Musicals are escapist? Can you think of any that do not adhere to escapist ideology?
3   Have you seen any non-Western Musicals (world cinema)? In what ways are they similar and how do they differ?
4   What makes the Swashbuckling genre an easy vehicle for covert political messages?
5   In what way, if any, do modern Swashbuckling films differ from their older counterparts?
6   Are generic categories relevant considering the amount of hybridity and number of sub-genres?

Conclusion

In summary, Genre Theory creates passionate debate as it continues to fascinate and divide academics, critics and audiences alike. Theoretical models have been developed but should not be regarded as prescriptive. One of the main criticisms of Genre Theory is that critics and theorists appear to repeat the main concepts using different terminology to say similar things. This can be very confusing and frustrating when trying to evaluate its development. Further confusion may arise from the way in which genre theorists criticize each other's approaches without necessarily furthering the debate. Regardless of the conflicting debates, audiences enjoy genre films. Genre provides familiarity and repetition. Economically it rewards both the paying viewer and the film industry. The formulaic approach continues to dominate film production with genres experiencing peaks and troughs in popularity.

Bibliography

Altman, A. (1984) 'A Semantic/Syntactic Approach to Film Genre', *Cinema Journal* vol. 23 no. 3, pp.6–18.
Altman, A. (1987) *The American Film Musical*, Bloomington: Indiana University Press.
Buscombe, E. (1970) 'The Idea of Genre in the American Cinema', *Screen* vol. 11 no. 2, pp.33–45.
Chapman, J., Glancy, M. and Harper, S. (2007) *The New Film History: Sources, Methods, Approaches*, Basingstoke: Palgrave Macmillan.
Dyer, R. (1992) 'Entertainment and Utopia', in *Only Entertainment*, New York: Routledge, pp.17–34.
Kitses, J. and Rickman, G. (eds) (1998) *The Western Reader*, New York: Limelight Editions.
Neale, S. (1990) 'Questions of Genre', in B. K. Grant (ed.) (2003) *Film Genre Reader III*, 3rd edn, Austin: University of Texas Press, pp.160–84.
Staiger, J. (1997) 'Hybrid or Inbred: The Purity Hypothesis and Hollywood Genre History', in B. K. Grant (ed.) (2003) *Film Genre Reader III*, 3rd edn, Austin: University of Texas Press, pp.185–99.
Stam, R. (2000) *Film Theory: An Introduction*, Malden, MA: Blackwell Publishing.
Tudor, A. (1974) *Theories of Film*, London: Secker & Warburg.

Formalism

3

Formalism

1. a. The theory held by a Russian literary group in existence between 1916 and 1930 that technique and form are both the means to and the goal of artistic creation.
   b. Subsequently, a term often used pejoratively in Communist criticism to denote an artist's concentration on form at the expense of social reality and content.

Setting the scene

As with many theories, Formalism developed as a means of studying literary texts. It was an early attempt to theorize and draw attention to the way narratives are constructed. It was initiated by a group of progressive Russian critics who wanted to develop a formal way (hence the name) to produce an objective and scientific method of analysing literature. Vladimir Propp, Viktor Shklovsky, Yuri Tynanov and Boris Eichenbaum were key literary Formalists who were not interested in the content of a text, believing rather that its form was of prime importance. At this time also, cinema was in the process of establishing itself as a legitimate art and it provided the Formalists with an exciting arena in which to extend these 'scientific' ideas into the field of film.

In order to understand fully what the Formalists were trying to achieve, it is useful to be aware of the political and social climate they were working in. In 1917, the Bolshevik Revolution sought to overthrow the Tsarist regime in favour of a Communist state. After the uprising many commercial filmmakers fled Russia, taking with them equipment and film stock. Additionally, foreign blockades prevented celluloid from being imported. As a consequence, filmmakers experimented by recycling and editing footage from existing film stock to create new films. During this process they recognized the power editing held as a manipulative device and this led to a radical rethinking about film.

The key filmmakers associated with this practice were all Russian and accordingly their output became known as Soviet montage. The leading practitioners were Sergei Eisenstein, Dziga Vertov and Lev Kuleshov. Eisenstein became the figurehead in formalizing their methodology. In short the key ideas that underpin Formalism are:

- A concern with form over content at the expense of subject. The topic of a film was unimportant; instead the focus was on how the film was physically put together (editing, narrative structure, etc.).

- To find a scientific way of understanding and writing about an artistic form (using science to explain aesthetics).
- To undertake formal analysis across disparate texts as a way of assessing quality by recognizing similarities and differences (in aesthetics, narrative, cinematography, *mise-en-scène*, etc.).

Much of their work comprised detailed technical research, as they looked for an insight into art as a system of signs and conventions rather than as inspiration and aesthetic style. They saw art as a process to be studied, taking into consideration the forms and devices involved in making a film, writing a book or creating a painting. Their aim was to 'lay bare the device'.

'Laying bare the device' can be literally understood as showing the means of production. For example, the much-cited opening sequence of *The Player* (Robert Altman, 1992) includes a long shot showing the characters on screen discussing the impact of using such shots in the openings of films. A different example of 'laying bare the device' can be found in one of the final scenes of Jean-Luc Godard's *Breathless/À Bout de Souffle* (1960). Here the characters walk around the fictional set switching on lamps. However rather than domestic lighting, Godard uses industrial studio spotlights to once more remind the audience of the artificiality of cinema.

Drawing attention to cinematography and editing can greatly impact on an audience, especially when the editing process is made overt. The Soviet school of filmmakers was at the forefront of exposing the very nature of film construction by experimenting with editing forms and camera placement.

Cinematography and editing

One of the most important things specific to the discipline of film, which came out of Formalist debates, was a systematic approach to reading cinematography. In order to understand the methodology proposed by Formalists, it is necessary to be familiar with the traditional practices of film language. Prior to the Soviet school of filmmakers, which favoured a specific form of editing, Hollywood opted for a seamless style of filmmaking that had become uniform across the industry. This practice is known as continuity editing or the industrial mode of representation.

Continuity editing (industrial mode of representation)

Hollywood adopted a non-intrusive approach to film editing, as the intention was for the audience to remain entirely unaware of cuts. The industry introduced a series of cinematographic and editing devices in order to achieve this:

- **Establishing shot/re-establishing shot:** An opening shot to establish the location and distance between characters and objects within a scene; this helps orientate the audience. Typically shot from a distance (long shot), it provides spectators with important visual information. Following the initial establishment of this information, the camera typically cuts into the action. At certain points in the scene the camera may need to return to the original opening position, or establish a new point removed from the action, in order to redetermine spatial relations (re-establishing shot).

- **Eye-level shot:** The camera is placed at a height that is equivalent to that of the actors' eyes and the action is filmed from this point.
- **Reframing:** When action takes places in a scene, the camera moves (reframes) to keep key points of focus central to the frame.
- **Eye-line matching:** When a character looks off screen, the following shot reveals the object of their attention.
- **Shot/reverse shot:** To shoot dialogue between two characters, the camera alternates between two points. The first shot frames character A and is typically shot from character B's point of view, or over B's shoulder. This process is reversed with character B shot from character A's perspective. This model continues throughout a scene and is repeated as many times as is necessary.
- **180-degree rule (axis of action):** For purposes of continuity, it is important when shooting a scene that the cameraman imagines an invisible line cutting through the action. It is necessary that all shooting takes place on one side of this line, as to cross over would disorientate and confuse an audience. The diagram below shows a circle with a line through the centre. The camera 'C' must always be placed on one specific side of this line. It can shoot the action 'A' from any place within zone 'C' but it cannot cross into the opposite zone 'A'. The important thing is that the camera must stay in one zone only and not alternate between the two. To film the action from the other zone a new establishing/re-establishing shot would be required.

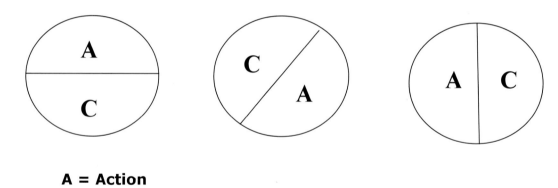

A = Action
C = Camera

A clear example of this is given in Bordwell and Thompson's *Film Art* (2004, p.312). They discuss the final shootout in a Western involving two cowboys. If the cameraman adheres to the 180-degree rule, the characters are depicted as walking towards each other. If the axis of action is broken, the same character shot from the opposite zone (camera angle) would appear to be walking away from his opponent.

When the methods above are enlisted, the audience is kept unaware of the technicalities involved in creating cinema. When editing does occur, it is typically to lead the viewer to certain conclusions. This approach has become standard practice across the industry and as a result the audience is often unaware of the manipulative power of editing.

Reflect and respond

1 To what extent were you aware of editing techniques in commercial filmmaking before studying film?
2 Can you think of any film examples where the 180-degree rule is broken?
3 Why do you think Hollywood repeatedly adopts the approach of continuity editing?

Montage

The terms montage and editing are often used interchangeably in Film Studies, but in this case we are referring to a specific style of film editing associated with Soviet filmmakers in the 20s.

Sergei Eisenstein

'Film Form' (1929)

The Soviet school was anti-bourgeoisie and accordingly sought to radicalize film and disassociate it from any elitist connotations. As a key member of this group Sergei Eisenstein strongly agreed with these political aims. One of the ways in which this political ideology became manifest was in his hiring of non-professional actors. Casting was based entirely on looks rather than ability. This process, known as typage, involved Eisenstein personally choosing members of the general public to star in his films. They were selected due to their physical resemblance to certain types even though they generally had little or no acting experience. The key stereotypes he looked for included sailors, factory workers, aristocracy, clergy, etc. Below (Figures 3.1 and 3.2) are examples of typage from the film *Battleship Potemkin* (1925).

Figure 3.1 *Battleship Potemkin* (Sergei M. Eisenstein, 1925)

Figure 3.2 *Battleship Potemkin* (Sergei M. Eisenstein, 1925)

Eisenstein looked to move cinema away from the traditional perspective of the static viewpoint offered in theatre. He saw montage as an exciting alternative to the conservative approach practised on the stage. He believed editing had a psychological dimension and advocated that, when an image is placed alongside another image, new meaning is created. Here he emulated the art of Japanese writing.

The Japanese model of writing recognizes that the combining of two symbols (words) creates a third concept (meaning); a concept that cannot be physically represented by a picture. For example the following 'hieroglyphs' are combined to create a third non-representational meaning (p.14). He cites the following examples:

The representation of water and of an eye signifies 'to weep', the representation of an ear next to a drawing of a door means 'to listen',

a dog and a mouth mean 'to bark'
a mouth and a baby mean 'to scream'
a mouth and a bird mean 'to sing'
a knife and a heart mean 'sorrow', and so on
[he concludes] But – this is montage!! (p.14)

Applying this linguistic approach to film, Eisenstein followed the same simple rule that an image juxtaposed with a conflicting image resulted in a third meaning. He saw 'montage as a collision' or as 'conflict' and he believed that conflict lay at the 'basis of every art' (p.19). This is summarized by David Cook as: 'Thesis + Antithesis = Synthesis' (1981, p.170). Although Cook uses the term 'antithesis', montage does not have to consist of opposing images, just two images that are different.

Eisenstein furthered his writings on film form by identifying sites of conflict which had previously been ignored in film analysis. He believed that the following areas of visual counterpoint (clashes on the screen) should be considered (p.28):

- graphic conflict
- conflict between planes
- conflict between volumes
- spatial conflict
- conflict in lighting
- conflict in tempo, etc.
- conflict between matter and shot (achieved by spatial distortion using camera angle)
- conflict between matter and its spatiality (achieved by optical distortion using the lens)
- conflict between an event and its temporality (achieved by slowing down and speeding up)
- conflict between the entire optical complex and a quite different sphere

For a detailed application of Eisenstein's visual counterpoint see the *Lola Rennt/Run Lola Run* (Tom Tykwer, 1998) case study on p.58.

Eisenstein famously identified five different types of montage (Cook, 1981, pp.172–3):

1   metric montage (length/duration of shot; builds suspense)
2   rhythmic montage (based on rhythm of movement within the shot; can enhance or contra-
    dict the image)
3   tonal (emotional content rather than duration of shots)
4   overtonal (synergy of metric, rhythmic and tonal)
5   intellectual montage (conceptual relationship between images/visual metaphor).

Each of the above categories offered directors a variety of tools when presenting information to
an audience. For Eisenstein intellectual montage held the greatest impact. He used it to great
effect in all of his films, especially *Battleship Potemkin*. Intellectual montage is reliant on the viewer
reading the juxtaposition of images to come to a new understanding. The stills in Figure 3.3
depict metaphorically the uprising of the working masses after years of laying dormant. Although
the images are of three different statues, when juxtaposed the seemingly inactive lion is stirred
to react.

Figure 3.3   *Battleship Potemkin* (Sergei M. Eisenstein, 1925)

This idea (Thesis + Antithesis = Synthesis) was exemplified in the unique experiment by Lev
Kuleshov. Taking an image of the actor Ivan Mozhukhin, Kuleshov juxtaposed the actor with
three poignant images, those of a bowl of soup, a woman dead in a coffin and a girl playing with
a teddy bear. On each occasion the image of the actor remained the same. However, the audience
interpreted his expressionless face as portraying the emotions of hunger, sorrow and joy respectively. This became known as the 'Kuleshov Effect'.

The long take

In complete opposition to montage, the long take remains focused on a scene as it evolves rather
than cutting into the action. After viewing the work of Orson Welles and the cinematographer
Gregg Toland in the film *Citizen Kane* (1941), André Bazin was one of the first to recognize the
importance of deep-focus photography. This occurs when both the foreground and background
of a shot are in focus. This technique was not new and had been practised in France by Jean Renoir
in films such as *La Grande Illusion/The Grand Illusion* (1937) and *La Bête Humaine/The Human Beast*
(1938). Bazin notes three implications behind the use of deep-focus composition:

1 Deep focus is similar to how an audience experiences the real world and could therefore be seen as a more natural way of viewing
2 With the long take the viewer has to be more active in deciphering information as the director is not guiding the audience.
3 'Montage rules out ambiguity' as the viewer is shown important images. 'Depth of focus reintroduces ambiguity' (p.50).

Continuity editing, montage and the long take offer filmmakers three radically different ways of telling stories. Deciding which approach to take is central as editing can manipulate an audience in various ways. It can be subtly leading, overt or non-existent. Although Soviet montage is most famously associated with Formalism, all three ways of composing a narrative involve selecting a form and applying it to a text.

Reflect and respond

1 Can you name any films where the editing is intrusive? Why do you think these decisions were made?
2 Make a list of five directors you associate with continuity editing and five directors you associate with self-conscious cutting.
3 Which of the following film movements do you associate with continuity editing and which with self-conscious cutting: Italian Neo-realism, French New Wave, German Expressionism and British Social Realism?
4 As a viewer, which style do you prefer and why?

Narrative traits of Formalism

Certain narrative forms are employed in film that we often fail to recognize due to their frequent use. These forms are more commonly known as genres (see Chapter 2, 'Genre Theory'). Below are narrative devices which gained common usage through the Formalist study of literature and are key to understanding narrative traits in film.

Fabula *(story) and* syuzhet *(plot)*

The Formalists identified two major elements in the study of narrative, which they called *'fabula'* (story) and *'syuzhet'* or *'sjuzet'* (plot).

- *Fabula*: (audience-led). This is the entire story; the full sequence of events. This includes sequences that are not visibly, or aurally, represented on the screen (characters eating, sleeping and going to the toilet). Here the audience is active as it must make assumptions based on the information given; it must fill in the gaps. On occasions reconstructing the *fabula* (making sense of the omissions) can help us gain a greater understanding. It is the entire sequence of events with nothing taken out.
- *Syuzhet*: (writer/director-led). This is the information and organization of material which is presented on the screen (the sequence of frames chosen by the director). The information

given cannot be changed as all viewers are privy to the same facts. However, in a suspense the director may have reconstructed the sequence of events, leaving the audience unaware that the character may have gained information unrevealed to us. This specific selection of events is especially useful in crime stories as the audience can be manipulated and led to incorrect assumptions to increase the suspense.

It is important to remember that the director can easily manipulate an audience as the information presented in the *syuzhet* may be purposely misleading. Consider the twist at the end of the film *The Usual Suspects* (Bryan Singer, 1995). In this example the director has manipulated the audience through the *syuzhet* and in turn it has jumped to the wrong conclusions about Keyser Söze and the entire story (*fabula*). Putting the *fabula* together constructs the bigger picture, so that all the events are present even when not physically or aurally represented on the screen.

Pulp Fiction (Quentin Tarantino, 1994) is a key text to deconstruct when exploring Formalist ideas. The film is renowned for its non-linear approach, with actions occurring out of chronological order. Accordingly, there are many versions of what is thought to be the 'true' linear time of the *fabula*. Below is our version of both the *fabula* and *syuzhet* for *Pulp Fiction*:

The fabula *for* Pulp Fiction

Day 1

- Morning: Vincent (John Travolta) and Jules (Samuel L. Jackson) visit young men in their apartment to collect Marsellus's (Ving Rhames) briefcase. Shot at by these young men, Vincent and Jules miraculously escape injury and kill three of the four youths. Jules believes that their survival is a sign that he should stop being a villain.
- The fourth man is accidentally shot and killed in the car by Vincent. Marsellus's henchman, Winston Wolfe (Harvey Keitel), organizes Vincent and Jules in the disposal of the body and the car; they then go for a late breakfast at a diner.
- Pumpkin (Tim Roth) and Honey Bunny (Amanda Plummer) plan to hold up the diner. They attempt to take Vincent and Jules's briefcase but the latter refuse to hand it over. They overpower the two robbers but allow them to leave with their loot. As a reformed man, Jules gives them $1,000 of his own money.
- Late afternoon: 'washed-up' boxer Butch (Bruce Willis) is bribed by Marsellus to throw his fight. Before the fight, Butch dreams about a gold watch left to him by his father, a war hero.
- Evening: Vincent buys heroin before taking Marsellus's wife Mia (Uma Thurman) to the club, Jack Rabbit Slims, where they win a dance contest. Back home Mia overdoses. Vincent takes her to his drug dealer where she is saved by an adrenalin injection.
- Late evening: Butch cheats Marsellus and wins his boxing match. He takes a long taxi journey to a hotel where he meets his girlfriend, Fabienne (Maria de Medeiros).

Day 2

- Morning: Butch discovers Fabienne has left his gold watch at their apartment. He returns there to retrieve it where he also finds Vincent, sent by Marsellus to kill him. Instead, Butch kills Vincent.

- Afternoon: Driving back to collect Fabienne, Butch runs over Marsellus; they fight but get taken prisoner by two perverts, Zed (Peter Greene) and Mason-Dixon. Marsellus is raped by Zed but Butch escapes yet surprisingly returns to save Marsellus, his nemesis. In return for this, Marsellus agrees not to kill Butch as long as he keeps quiet about the embarrassing events.
- Butch steals a chopper (motorbike), collects Fabienne and the two of them drive off to a new life.

The syzhet *for* Pulp Fiction

This is very complex. Tarantino has used a framing device for his story (in this case Pumpkin and Honey Bunny). The prologue shows the start of the diner robbery and the epilogue shows the robbery and its aftermath. All other events occur in a non-linear fashion and it is the audience's task to unravel these. Below is our version:

- Pumpkin and Honey Bunny hold up diner.
- Vincent and Jules are attacked but retrieve briefcase.
- Butch accepts Marsellus's bribe.
- Vincent and Mia (Marsellus's wife) go to Jack Rabbit Slims.
- Butch dreams of father's gold watch.
- Butch cheats Marsellus, wins fight and meets Fabienne at hotel.
- Butch discovers the watch has been left behind and goes to retrieve it.
- Vincent is sent by Marsellus to kill Butch. On finding Vincent in his apartment, Butch kills him.
- Butch encounters Marsellus on route to his hotel; they fight.
- Butch and Marsellus are taken prisoner. Butch helps Marsellus escape. As a result, Butch is granted his freedom.
- Butch steals a chopper, collects Fabienne and they leave.
- Vincent and Jules are shot at but not hit while retrieving the briefcase. Jules believes this to be divine intervention. They shoot the youths.
- Vincent accidentally shoots fourth youth in the car.
- Vincent and Jules dispose of the body with Wolfe's help.
- Pumpkin and Honey Bunny hold up diner. They leave with stolen goods and $1,000 given to them by Jules.

The *fabula* requires an active audience to construct and interpret the chronological order of the story, as much of the information is implied rather than being part of the diegesis. The *syzhet* is created by the director/writer as a form of shorthand, allowing stories to be told in a condensed manner. Being aware of these two devices enables viewers to understand the complex narrative forms that occur in numerous films including *Groundhog Day* (Harold Ramis, 1993), *Sliding Doors* (Peter Howitt, 1998), *Memento* (Christopher Nolan, 2000) and *Inception* (Christopher Nolan, 2010).

Reflect and respond

1   Take a film of your choice and attempt to identify moments in the *fabula* that do not appear in the *syuzhet*.
2   Discuss the *fabula* and *syuzhet* in relation to the following key figures involved in film production:

a   writer
b   director
c   actor
d   editor

3   Can you name any films where the *fabula* and *syuzhet* are identical?
4   When the above occurs, are any aesthetic traits frequently used?

In addition to the narrative-based theories of the Formalists, Vladimir Propp wrote about the recurring characters that appear in storytelling.

Vladimir Propp

Morphology of the Folktale (1928)

Vladimir Propp was a literary scholar who endeavoured to look beyond the traditional approach to studying folktales, which focused primarily on themes. He examined over 100 Russian folktales in order to discern common structures and elements which could then be broadened and applied to other genres. From this survey Propp maintained that traditional tales are based on the following:

Archetypes/spheres of action

Despite the confusing name 'spheres of action' refers to the recurring characters found in most stories in some form or other. Propp identified seven characters:

1	The Hero	A character who seeks something.
2	The Villain	Opposes or actively blocks the Hero's quest.
3	The Donor	Provides an object with magical properties.
4	The Dispatcher	Sends the Hero on their quest.
5	The False Hero	Disrupts the Hero's success by making false claims.
6	The Helper	Assists and rescues the Hero.
7a	The Princess	Acts as the reward for the Hero and the object of the Villain's plots.
7b	Her Father	Looks to reward the Hero for his efforts.

It is important to recognize that although these characters may seem dated they do translate to modern texts. *Casino Royale* (Martin Campbell, 2006) provides an interesting study for this. Unlike traditional Bond movies, *Casino Royale* plays with archetypal expectations. Some of the seven roles are easily identifiable as shown below:

1	The Hero	James Bond/007 (Daniel Craig)
2	The Villain	Le Chiffre (Mads Mikkelsen)
3	The Donor	????
4	The Dispatcher	M (Judi Dench)
5	The False Hero	Mathis (Giancarlo Giannini)
6	The Helper	Felix (Jeffrey Wright)
7a	The Princess	Vesper (Eva Green)
7b	Her Father	????

Whereas Bond and Le Chiffre epitomize our idea of a Hero and a Villain, other characters prove to be more problematic. Vesper may appear to be Propp's 'Princess' as she is the love interest for 007, but she could also be considered as the 'Helper' or the 'False Hero'. This is not unusual as often a character can fit into more than one archetype. In the case of *Casino Royale* the Princess's 'Father' is not evident in the narrative although Mathis is to some extent a father figure to Vesper. To complicate matters further, traditionally the 'Donor' in the Bond franchise is Q; however, in this film the gadget man who supplies the magical agents does not feature. Bond takes a proactive role in gaining the tools of his trade (he retrieves information from M's laptop and he wins the Aston Martin), therefore he adopts the role of the Donor. This shows that Propp's approach is not outdated and applicable only to fairytales. At first glance it can appear that Propp's archetypes do not feature, but with the aid of lateral thinking the seven characters can typically be found.

Functions

Propp noted that, in addition to recurring characters, similarities in plots were also evident. He described thirty-one key moments that occur in the majority of tales; he called these components 'functions'. Each function represents a different stage in the protagonist's journey. His approach was limited in that he only looked at the fairytale genre. Focusing on simple linear stories, he did not have to consider complex narratives with no neat resolution, like Truffaut's *Les Quatre Cents Coups/400 Blows* (1959).

On first glance Propp's work may seem somewhat dated. However, contemporary viewers can apply his functions to modern forms of storytelling. For example, while Propp envisioned tales ending with the 'marriage function', this did not have to be a literal marriage. Instead it could be read in terms of a satisfying outcome, which delivers resolution and allows the 'Hero' to return 'home', avoiding a traditional clichéd ending.

Although Propp's work is important, it does not provide a complete understanding of narrative but instead shows that there are underlying structures or patterns in narratives. The following table is based on Paul Simpson's (2004, p.73) Proppian reading of *Harry Potter and the Philosopher's Stone* (Chris Columbus, 2001).

Propp's functions	Harry Potter
1 One of the members of a family absents himself from home.	Harry Potter (Hero) (Daniel Radcliffe) has been orphaned and is forced to live in the home of his cruel aunt and uncle, the Dursleys (Fiona Shaw and Richard Griffiths).
2 An interdiction is addressed (Hero is told not to do a specific thing).	Harry is told by the Dursleys *not* to go to Hogwarts School of Wizardry.
3 The interdiction is violated (Hero breaks the command).	Harry goes to Hogwarts School of Wizardry.
4 The Villain makes an attempt at reconnaissance (searches for information).	
5 The Villain receives information about the Hero.	
6 The Villain attempts to deceive the Hero in order to take possession of him or his belongings.	Unknown to all, Voldemort (Villain) has taken over the body of Professor Quirrel (Ian Hart).
7 The Hero succumbs to deception and thereby unwittingly helps his enemy.	
8 The Villain causes harm or injury to a member of the Hero's family/One member of the family either lacks something or desires to have something.	Harry learns that Voldemort has killed his parents.
9 Misfortune or lack is made known: the Hero is approached with a request or command; he is allowed to go or is dispatched.	Harry embarks on a mission to recover the philosopher's stone.
10 The seeker agrees to or decides upon counteraction.	
11 The Hero leaves home.	
12 The Hero is tested, interrogated, attacked, etc., which prepares the way for his receiving either a magical agent or Helper (gift from Donor).	Harry receives (unexpectedly) a top-of-the-range broomstick, a Nimbus 2000.
13 The Hero reacts to the actions of a future Donor.	
14 The Hero acquires the use of a magical agent.	Harry uses the Nimbus 2000 in the Quidditch game.
15 The Hero is transferred, delivered or led to the whereabouts of an object that he seeks.	
16 The Hero and Villain join in direct combat.	Harry and Voldemort join in combat.

Propp's functions	Harry Potter
17 The Hero is branded.	Harry has acquired a lightning-shaped scar through an earlier encounter with Voldemort.
18 The Villain is defeated.	Voldemort is defeated.
19 Initial misfortune or lack is liquidated (resolved).	In the Hogwarts school competition, Harry's house Gryffindor is reinstated above cheating rivals Slytherin.
20 The Hero returns.	Harry leaves Hogwarts for the summer recess.
21 The Hero is pursued.	
22 Rescue of the Hero from pursuit.	
23 The Hero, unrecognized, arrives home or in another country.	
24 A False Hero presents unfounded claims.	
25 A difficult task is proposed to the Hero.	Harry is charged with retrieving the 'golden snitch' in a game of Quidditch.
26 The task is resolved.	Harry successfully retrieves the golden snitch.
27 The Hero is recognized.	
28 The False Hero or Villain is exposed.	Quirrel is exposed as the host of Voldemort.
29 The False Hero is given a new appearance.	Quirrel is transformed into dust during the combat.
30 The Villain is punished.	Voldemort is forced to leave the body of his dead host.
31 The Hero is married and ascends the throne.	

From: *Stylistics: A Resource Book for Students*, Paul Simpson, © 2004 Routledge. Reproduced by permission of Taylor & Francis Books UK.

Not all thirty-one functions have to be present in each tale but, according to Propp, those that do occur always appear in the same order. However if you are familiar with the original Harry Potter story, you will realize that the functions do not necessarily appear in this regulated order (see table). Both the film and J. K. Rowling's book conclude with Harry leaving Hogwarts for the summer holidays, function twenty in Propp's model; however, this structure paves the way for a sequel in the Harry Potter franchise.

Many scholars have attempted to construct theories around narrative structure, for example, Roland Barthes and Christopher Volger. Contemporary scholars have also been fascinated with identifying similarities in narratives. For example, Chris Booker in *The Seven Basic Plots: Why We Tell Stories* (2004) identified the following universal stories: overcoming the monster, rags to riches, the quest, voyage and return, comedy, tragedy and rebirth. However, alongside Propp, Joseph Campbell is most renowned for his writings exploring the hero's journey.

Joseph Campbell

The Hero with a Thousand Faces (1949)

The American scholar Joseph Campbell worked in the field of literature and mythology. He originally wanted to write 'the great American novel' and in order to prepare for this feat he decided to read as many classic novels and mythological tales as possible. Like Propp he began to recognize that stories, independent of national origin, adhered to the same common pattern. He identified that all religious tales, mythology and great works of fiction shared similar traits regarding the hero's journey. In the book *The Hero with a Thousand Faces*, Campbell mapped out the narrative of the hero who leaves behind a world of comfort and safety, guided by a mentor, to fight evil. The hero encounters many obstacles and battles but eventually overcomes the dark forces to return home, having grown spiritually. Campbell divided the progression of the hero into three sections: 'Departure', 'Initiation' and 'Return'. Each section was further subdivided into more specific moments of action. Campbell believed that the universal tale of the hero exists in all cultures. He further claimed that psychologically, the adventure coaches people in how to a live a fulfilled and morally sound life.

Joseph Campbell gained notoriety when George Lucas used his blueprint and applied it to his screenplay for *Star Wars* (1977). The table below demonstrates how Campbell's hero's journey can be applied to the character of Luke Skywalker (Mark Hamill) (see following table).

The journey of the hero	*Star Wars* (George Lucas, 1977)
I Departure	
1 The call to adventure.	Luke Skywalker receives a message from Princess Leia (Carrie Fisher) (R2-D2's hologram).
2 Refusal of the call.	Luke is fearful of leaving his old life.
3 Supernatural aid (mentor).	Obi-Wan Kenobi (Alec Guinness) saves Luke from the Sandpeople.
4 The crossing of the first threshold.	Luke leaves Tatooine after his home is destroyed.
5 The belly of the whale (hero nearly dies and is reborn ready for adventure).	Luke and his friends enter the Death Star (trash compactor – literal belly).
II Initiation	
1 The road of trials.	Obi-Wan teaches Luke how to use the lightsaber.
2 The meeting with the goddess.	Luke rescues Princess Leia.
3 Woman as the temptress/temptation away from the true path.	Luke is tempted by the 'dark side'.
4 Atonement with the father.	Luke and his father (Darth Vader) (David Prowse) are reconciled.
5 Apotheosis (the hero enters a new state of being).	Luke becomes a Jedi Knight.

The journey of the hero	*Star Wars* (George Lucas, 1977)
6 The ultimate boon (the hero's objectives are accomplished).	The Death Star is destroyed.
III Return	
1 Refusal of the return.	'Luke, come on!' Luke wants to stay to avenge Obi-Wan.
2 Magic flight.	The Millennium Falcon.
3 Rescue from without (forces from the ordinary world rescue hero).	Han Solo (Harrison Ford) returns to save Luke.
4 The crossing of the return threshold.	Millennium Falcon destroys pursuing TIE fighters.
5 Master of the two worlds.	Victory ceremony. Luke is both ordinary yet Jedi Knight.
6 Freedom to live.	The Empire is defeated.

Note: Much of the above table has been adapted from the work of Kristen Brennan (1999–2006), http://www.moongadget.com/origins/myth.html.

Reflect and respond

1 See if you can apply Propp's seven archetypal characters to three films of your choice (only one of your three examples should be a fairytale).
2 Identify a film that you think adheres to Propp's thirty-one functions.
3 Try to apply Joseph Campbell's 'Hero's Journey' to one of the following films: *The Lord of the Rings: The Fellowship of the Ring* (Peter Jackson, 2001) or *The Matrix* (Andy and Larry Wachowski, 1999)
4 How restrictive or inspirational do you find the narrative blueprints proposed by Propp and Campbell?

Formalists were also concerned with the way the everyday world was represented in texts. Viktor Shklovsky and Bertolt Brecht attempted to formalize how creative texts (literature and theatre) worked to make the mundane exciting and relevant.

Viktor Shklovsky

'Art as Technique' (1917)

Although Shklovsky was writing about language, his ideas can be applied to film. He suggested that there are two distinct ways of communicating information to an audience. Poetic forms appeal to an audience's emotions by using abstract metaphorical devices to reveal something in a new light. Alternatively, information can be given in a matter-of-fact way that is grounded in straightforward ideas and can be perceived as factual. To clarify, in Film Studies the terms 'denote' and 'connote' are frequently used. 'Denote' is the literal representation of a subject/object, whereas 'connote' is the symbolic representation. Shklovsky uses the word 'butterfingers' as an example:

> [T]o attract the attention of a young child who is eating bread and butter and getting the butter on her fingers. I call, 'Hey, butterfingers!' [...] Now a different example. The child is playing with my glasses and drops them. I call, 'Hey, butterfingers!' (1965, p.8)

Shklovsky's first illustration, of a child with butter on their fingers, is a literal representation and is therefore denotative. The second version is symbolic as the child has clean hands but is clumsy; in this case the term is connotative.

Shklovsky believed that the connotative/poetic approach had more impact. He argued that non-poetic forms cause our perceptions of familiar objects to become dulled out of habit. But poetic forms make us see ordinary things in a different way, to make the familiar strange (*ostranenie*). The way to do this was to make ideas and objects appear unusual or new to the viewer/reader. Shklovsky referred to this as 'defamiliarization'.

Defamiliarization

Film is a fantastical medium and therefore lends itself well to defamiliarization. This is where the ordinary is made extraordinary, where the viewer is invited to see the world through new eyes. This notion of 'seeing things anew' is a frequent trope found in film narratives. Defamiliarization can occur in various ways; below are a few examples:

- A foreigner arrives in a new country and experiences a new culture at first hand in *Lost in Translation* (Sofia Coppola, 2003), *The Last King of Scotland* (Kevin Macdonald, 2006) and *Avatar* (James Cameron, 2009).
- Characters become intoxicated or dizzy (alcohol, drugs, poison). This process is often emulated by the cinematography: shaky point-of-view shots, blurred images, etc. and occurs in *Vertigo*, *Trainspotting* (Danny Boyle, 1996) and *Requiem for a Dream* (Darren Aronofsky, 2000).
- The everyday world is transformed by magical, alien or scientific means, as seen in *The Wizard of Oz*, *Invasion of the Body Snatchers* and the *Harry Potter* franchise.
- The narrative takes an unexpected turn of events, leading the audience to reassess all earlier information. Examples are *The Crying Game* (Neil Jordan, 1992), *Fight Club* (David Fincher, 1999) and *The Sixth Sense* (M. Night Shyamalan, 1999).

All of the above are character- or narrative-driven examples of defamiliarization. However, the technique can occur within the cinematography and soundtrack. In the film *Apocalypse Now* (Francis Ford Coppola, 1979) the opening sequence juxtaposes a ceiling fan with the sound of helicopter blades. This device serves to initiate a flashback, but it also defamiliarizes the hotel room for the audience.

Bertolt Brecht

Verfremdung

These ideas were taken and developed by the theatrical practitioner Bertolt Brecht. He believed that audiences were prone to passively experience theatre. Rather than actively questioning the action being presented, the audience would be drawn into the fictional world of the stage narrative. Brecht felt that theatre needed to be more challenging. He therefore employed a number of techniques to make audience members aware of their setting and remind them of the fact that they were watching a play. *Verfremdung*, translates as 'to make strange', it is also often referred to as 'alienation' or 'estrangement'. Below are a number of devices he enlisted to create this effect.

- actors playing more than one character
- actors directly addressing the audience
- lighting rig and other technical equipment on view (reminding the audience that they are in a theatre)
- scene changes undertaken by cast in full view of the audience
- experimentation with new technology (conveyor belts, escalators, filmed images. etc.)
- advising the audience of what is about to happen before it occurs (narrator or intertitles).

The tactics above were adopted in an attempt to make the audience critically detached (active) rather than unthinkingly accepting (passive). Brecht's motives were political but ultimately he was concerned with laying bare the device – like most Formalists. A good example of *Verfremdung* can be found in Lars von Trier's *Dogville* (2003). The entire film is shot on a blank sound stage where the houses are represented by chalk outlines rather than fully formed sets.

Reflect and respond

1. Other than foreign travel, substance abuse and magic/alien encounters or scientific transformation, can you think of other narrative settings or components which cause characters to view the world from a new perspective?
2. Identify visual examples of defamiliarization other than that used in *Apocalypse Now*.
3. Looking at the techniques employed in the theatre by Brecht, think about how they can be translated to film.
4. Why do you think Brecht employed *Verfremdung* as a political tool? How successful do you think it would be?

Case study: *Lola Rennt/Run Lola Run* (Tom Tykwer, 1998)

Run Lola Run, written and directed by Tom Tykwer, won twenty-six awards. The film is highly acclaimed for its editing and unusual narrative, which sees the story repeated three times. However, subtle changes in the events that take place mean that the outcome is altered. The catalyst for this plot is Manni (Moritz Bleibtreu), Lola's (Franka Potente) boyfriend. In the opening scenes he phones to tell her that he has lost 100,000 Deutschmarks that belong to his gangster boss. He has twenty minutes to replace this or he will be killed. In her attempt to save Manni, Lola must run and run because her moped has been stolen. This is a poignant, romantic thriller where small changes in timing have an impact on Lola, and these random acts of fate alter the consequences for both characters.

Run Lola Run can be read as a fairytale. The fairytale genre permits the natural and supernatural to exist alongside one another. For example, Lola's scream can shatter glass and slow down a roulette wheel so that she can win the money she needs, and her touch heals the security guard who is suffering a heart attack. These supernatural powers occur at points in the narrative when all hope for a positive resolution is lost and only magical intervention can save the situation. To continue with the fairytale theme, the 'archetypal characters' and 'spheres of action' as identified by Vladimir Propp can be detected in this psychological crime thriller.

Lola is the Heroine and the Donor in this tale. She is given a dangerous quest that will take her through a number of seemingly impossible obstacles and tasks. As the Donor, she has been given 'magical' properties such as the scream and touch which assist in her quest. The Dispatcher is Manni, her boyfriend, who needs to be rescued from the Villain (the gangster boss). Hindered by the False Heroes (her alcoholic mother and her two-timing father), Lola and Manni are aided by their 'fairy godmother' (Helper), who appears in the guise of the blind woman. These familiar archetypal characters assist the narrative and draw the spectator into the plot as the audience cares about what happens to the couple. Lola's continual striving to save Manni is rewarded and furthermore the audience sees that people are prepared to help one another.

The 'fairytale' moral suggests that human endeavour can change things for the better and stir others to empathize and help. However, Owen Evans (2004, p.113) notes that, with the traditional German fairytales, known as *Märchen*, stories are often politically motivated. The protagonist is often a female who has to undertake trials alone. While acknowledging that *Run Lola Run* is in the fairytale form, Evans suggests that the political element is absent from Tykwer's work. He finds that Tykwer is 'simply intent on stimulating a sense of community between us and his characters' (p.113). As with all fairytales, there is a happy ending, with Manni retrieving the money from the tramp and avoiding reprisals from his boss. The money won by Lola is no longer needed to save Manni and the viewer is left to draw their own conclusions as to what this huge sum may be used for in Manni and Lola's future.

The above approach privileges the form the content takes. Yet for Formalists such as Eisenstein the formal aspects of editing held importance and are very relevant to a reading of *Run Lola Run*. On examination, the editing techniques in this film are appropriate for the psychological crime thriller, serving to heighten suspense and maintain the adrenalin-fuelled pace. Eisenstein believed that editing could add a psychological dimension to storytelling. In the opening sequences of the film it is made clear that time is of the essence. The images of Lola running down a spiral staircase and of a very ugly, angry-faced wooden clock symbolize that time is her enemy and is 'spiralling' out of control. The running image is then transformed into an animated cartoon figure of Lola, moving at incredible speed, immediately identifiable by her red hair. This gives way to splitscreen coverage of Lola running down the street, showing the same event from different angles. This is an example of what Eisenstein would call 'rhythmic montage' as the editing heightens the percussive motion of her feet. The key tracking image of Lola sprinting is accompanied by an insistent techno rhythm to emphasize the relentlessness of Lola's task.

From the outset, the audience knows that Lola's task has a time frame of twenty minutes (Manni's phone call is at 11.40 and his gangster boss will arrive at midday). However, each filmed sequence takes less than twenty minutes. The overall editing of the sequences lengthens some scenes and shortens others thereby increasing the tension and focusing attention on significant events or elements. For example, slow motion is mainly used when Lola is in a state of emotional conflict. When Manni phones and she first commits herself to helping him, the red telephone receiver is seen flying through the air in slow motion, to land on the telephone cradle. Lola's dilemma is how to help, what to do? Similarly, when she is ejected from her father's bank she stands outside holding her head, uncertain of the way forward. Again, when she is running towards the supermarket, calling out for Manni to stop the robbery, rather than magnifying the tension through fast edits, Tykwer chooses slow motion. This has the effect of showing Lola's frustration and desperation to reach Manni on time. This use of editing evokes how, when people experience an accident or other emotional trauma, time appears to halt and the action to shift into slow motion. Conversely, when Lola is running, these sections are often drawn out to increase the sense of urgency and time running out. Eisenstein called this 'metric montage' when the passage of time is manipulated for dramatic cause and effect.

Interestingly, aspects of Tykwer's quirky editing and the fairytale meld together when Lola encounters various minor characters on her journey. These interludes are told via flashforwards, which are inserted as freeze frames (this is accompanied by the sound of a click imitating the mechanics of a camera). If Lola narrowly misses bumping into the character, the action sequence stays the same. However, should she collide with the character the scene is transformed by a brief 'intellectual montage' (where the audience has to piece together the visual metaphors). In each instance the flashforward changes to depict either a positive future or an alternative negative one. For example, the woman with the pushchair is first shown as having abducted a baby and on the second encounter, winning the lottery. Finally the audience witnesses her taking up religion and doing charitable work. Similarly, the female employee at the bank is shown having a car accident, in hospital and dying. In our second encounter with her, she is going out with a male bank clerk, shown in a dominatrix relationship with him and then happily married. These aforementioned sequences imply that it is Lola's magical contact that changes their destiny.

This is a clear indicator of another major theme in the film, chaos theory. The opening scenes show a documentary of a domino rally, alluding to the domino effect, where an action sets in place a chain reaction. The notion is that one action generates consequences. In the overarching narrative, first Lola then Manni die. In Lola's final attempt they both survive. It appears that Lola 'rewrites' her future until she has her happy ending. Just as if playing a video game, Lola has the opportunity to restart her adventure, learning from past mistakes, until she is able to overcome all obstacles.

Referring back to Eisenstein's ideas on visual counterpoint, *Run Lola Run* illustrates an extensive use of rhythm, texture and tempo due to its nonconventional approach to editing and imagery. Below is a list of devices used by Tykwer that epitomize Eisenstein's ideas:

- 180-degree rule is ignored (Lola is seen running left to right, right to left, towards and away from the camera – confusing the physical geography of Berlin)
- disorientating techniques (jump cuts, whip pans)
- various visual effects (animation, film stock, video, black and white, colour washes, freeze frames, splitscreen)

- temporal experimentation (action is speeded up and slowed down; moments of frenetic activity are followed by sudden stillness).

Tykwer's editing calls attention to itself; it prevents the audience 'losing' themselves in the story. Eisenstein believed that editing was key to revolutionizing cinema. Accordingly, *Run Lola Run* gained a lot of critical acclaim due to its nonconventional approach, which also led to many Postmodernist readings of the film. However, the analysis above shows that Tykwer's use of editing, narrative and characterization is equally suited to a Formalist interpretation.

Reflect and respond

1   Do the fairytale and Propp's archetypical characters help you to understand the film?
2   Do Formalist editing techniques add to the excitement of a text or do they hinder your enjoyment?
3   Do you think *Run Lola Run* lends itself to a Formalist or Postmodern approach? Justify your answer.
4   Does Formalism still have validity in contemporary Film Studies?

Conclusion

Russian Formalists have left a vast legacy within film theory; in fact it could be said that modern theory started with the work of the Russian Formalists around 1915. Formalist theory was developed by linguists but became better known under the umbrella term 'Structuralism' (see Chapter 4, 'Structuralism and Post-structuralism'). We can see that the Russian Formalists were the first to critically explore the analogy between form and film. They took little interest in the way films looked, being more concerned with how they were constructed (narrative and cinematography). Above all it is important to remember that for the Formalists, form is privileged over content.

Bibliography

Booker, C. (2004) *The Seven Basic Plots: Why We Tell Stories*, London and New York: Continuum.
Bordwell, D. and Thompson, K. (2004) *Film Art: An Introduction*, 7th edn, New York: McGraw-Hill.
Brennan, K. (1999–2006) *Star Wars Origins*. Retrieved 18 June 2010. Available at http://www.moongadget.com/origins/myth.html.
Campbell, J. (1968) *The Hero with a Thousand Faces*, Princeton, NJ: Princeton University Press (first published 1949).
Carney, S. (2005) *Brecht and Critical Theory: Dialectics and Contemporary Aesthetics*, Oxford and New York: Routledge.
Cook, D. (1981) *A History of Narrative Film*, 3rd edn, New York and London: W. W. Norton & Co.

Eichenbaum, B. (1981) 'Problems of Cinema Stylistics', in H. Eagle (ed) *Russian Formalist Film Theory*, Ann Arbor, MI: Slavic Publications, pp.55–80.

Eisenstein, S. (1929) 'Film Form', in L. Braudy and M. Cohen (eds) (2004) *Film Theory and Criticism: Introductory Readings*, 6th edn, Oxford: Oxford University Press, pp.13–40.

Evans, O. (2004) 'Tom Tykwer's *Run Lola Run*: Postmodern, Post-human or Post-theory?', *Studies in European Cinema* vol. 1 no. 2, pp.105–15.

Propp, V. (1928) *Morphology of the Folktale*, Austin: University of Texas Press.

Shklovsky, V. (1965) 'Art as Technique', in *Russian Formalist Criticism: Four Essays*, Lincoln: University of Nebraska Press, pp.3–24.

Simpson, P. (2004) *Stylistics: A Resource Books for Students*, London: Routledge.

Structuralism and Post-structuralism

```
Structuralism
1. Theories concerned with analysing the surface structures of a
   system in terms of its underlying structure.
```

Setting the scene

Structuralism developed out of the work of the Formalists. At first glance it is hard to distinguish where one theory ends and the other starts so it is useful to think of Structuralism as a continuation of Formalist ideology. Formalism is concerned with the devices and rules that go into the making of cultural artefacts, with the author actively employing techniques to achieve specific ends. Structuralists, on the other hand, are concerned with the framework of meaning; how an audience reads and understands signs within a text. Their interest is focused on the workings of human perception, which moves us away from a particular text to the more general universal context. However, these signs are not always within the artist's control as the way they are read is dependent on each individual's interpretation. Structuralism can be seen as an attempt to understand texts in line with more traditional academic disciplines.

It is interesting that, almost simultaneously but without knowing each other, Ferdinand de Saussure (a Swiss linguist) and Charles Peirce (an American philosopher) were engaged in similar work. They used different terminology, with Saussure favouring the term sign and Peirce preferring the word symbol. Saussure adopted a scientific approach to discover what constitutes and governs signs (symbols), which he called the science of semiology, whereas Peirce undertook philosophical research into symbols (signs), which he considered to be the foundations of all thought and scientific ideas; he called this semiotics. It is important to note that the terms semiotics and semiology are interchangeable. At the outset 'semiotics' was favoured by American Structuralists whereas European academics preferred 'semiology'.

Ferdinand de Saussure

Semiotics – *Course in General Linguistics* (1915)

Saussure was a professor of Linguistics at the University of Geneva, where he often delivered lectures that were never committed to paper. After his death these lectures were reconstructed from students' notes and published in 1915 as *Course in General Linguistics*. His approach to the study of language was a scientific one, departing from earlier conventions that had looked at the historical development of language. The core premise of his research was to explore language as a series of signs. This line of enquiry is known as semiology. Saussure helped formalize the study of semiotics as a system of communication. He noted that:

- Language is comprised of two elements. He referred to these as *langue* and *parole*. *Langue* (language) is used to describe an entire vocabulary (and the grammatical rules that enable us to string words together in order to make sense). Whereas *parole* (speech) is the actual utterance of vocabulary (the spoken word).
- Language is a system of signs and these signs are arbitrary (unconnected/random) and defined by difference from other words. They can only be understood within a cultural system. The word 'dog' is not common to all languages; for example, the French for dog is *chien* and the German word is *Hund*, although all refer to the same animal. Furthermore, within each culture there has to be a consensus that certain letters in a particular order serve to represent a four-legged, barking, tail-wagging companion. However, the word 'elephant' could easily have been chosen in place of the term 'dog'. Saussure famously used to state that 'there are only differences'; that language is only a series of phonetic (sound) differences matched with a series of conceptual (image) differences. By this he means that each sign only has a meaning because it is different from others. 'Dog' has no inherent meaning; its meaning comes because of its difference from 'dug', 'dot', 'bog', etc.

This all becomes clearer if we look at Saussure's distinctions between what he called the sign, signifier and signified.

Sign

The sign communicates information. It can be anything; an image, a gesture, a word (written or spoken), a shape or a colour, etc. The sign is the first step in the process of interpretation. However, signs have no intrinsic meaning; meaning is given to them and established by universal and/or cultural conventions. A sign has to stand for something else. For example the '+' symbol in mathematics indicates that two or more numbers must be added together, whereas on the button of a remote control it can be used to increase volume or to switch to the next channel. In each instance the '+' sign indicates an increment either in sum, volume or channel. In this case '+' is synonymous with an increase.

The sign is comprised of two components: the signifier and the signified.

Signifier

The signifier is the form that the sign takes. It can be a word. It can take the form of a specific sound or marks on a piece of paper (a combination of letters or symbols).

Signified

The signified is the conceptual stage of communication. This is when the sign stimulates a mental idea/image.

To continue with the 'dog' example above, Saussure conceived that the signifier (the written or verbal word 'dog') and the signified (the mental image of this four-legged animal) were like two sides of a sheet of paper; together they make up the sign, dog. However this mental image can vary from person to person. It may suggest a golden, long-haired Retriever to one person or a black, short-haired Labrador to someone else.

In summary, semiotics is the study of the signs and symbols which make up our means of communication. At the most basic level the three components of semiology can be thought of in the following simplistic way: the sign (trigger/catalyst), the signifier (form) and the signified (concept). Semiotic coding features heavily in the marketing of films and industrial practices; consider the questions below.

Reflect and respond

1   Look at the use of logos associated with famous cinematic studios. Undertake a semiotic reading of two of the following: MGM, Disney, Rank, Pathé. What does the image tell you about how the studio chose to represent itself?
2   Identify two logos of your own choice associated with filmmaking and/or film distribution. Discuss how they work and why they have become so iconic.
3   Consider the following famous iconic images (Aston Martin car, ruby slippers, lightsaber and the Empire State Building). Identify the film associated with each icon and think about what these objects have come to signify culturally.

The syntagmatic and paradigmatic axes

Because of the power that semiotic coding exerts on audience response, filmmakers have to think carefully about choices made within a film. The linguistic idea of the syntagmatic and paradigmatic axes can help us evaluate these decisions.

The chart on page 66 is an illustration of the syntagmatic and paradigmatic axes that emerged out of Saussure's work on semiotics. This is a different way of understanding signs.

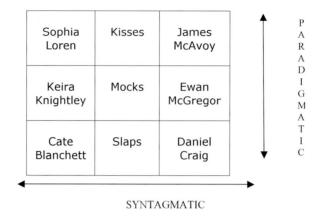

The paradigmatic axis

The paradigmatic axis should be read vertically. Paradigmatic relations are concerned with substitution. Taking our example, a production team can make a choice by selecting an element from each column. First an actress should be chosen, then the action she takes needs to be decided upon and finally an actor must be agreed on to interact with the sequence of events. These decisions are paradigmatic and any element could be substituted for an appropriate vertical alternative (you could not replace a Cate Blanchett with the horizontal 'kisses').

The film industry makes many paradigmatic decisions that relate to other aspects of film production (not just concerning narrative choices), for example:

- Who directs?
- Which actors are hired?
- Which character is played by whom?
- Which camera angles are used for each shot?
- Which technical crew is hired?
- Where is the film shot?

This list is not in any way exhaustive as all elements of filmmaking require a myriad of decisions. However, how the decisions relate to each other and impact on the overall picture can be understood via the syntagmatic axis.

The syntagmatic axis

The syntagmatic axis should be read horizontally. Syntagmatic relations are concerned with sequences. Once the paradigmatic choices have been made and fixed, the way in which all these decisions interact form a syntagmatic chain. Returning to our chart, Sophia Loren slapping Ewan McGregor is an example of a syntagmatic sequence. The chain would be very different if she had kissed him or if he had been kissed by Keira Knightley. Due to the age difference between Loren and McGregor, the audience may presume that there is generational conflict (a mother/child relationship). Alternatively, if Knightley slapped McGregor the audience might read it as a lovers' tiff. This is because each paradigmatic decision affects and informs the syntagmatic outcome.

Reflect and respond

1   Complete the syntagmatic and paradigmatic axes in the diagram below, by adding an actress to the first column and an actor to the final column.
2   Make paradigmatic choices for a fictional film.
3   How do your paradigmatic choices impact on the syntagmatic axis?
4   Make a minor adjustment to your initial paradigmatic selection. How does this affect the syntagmatic outcome?

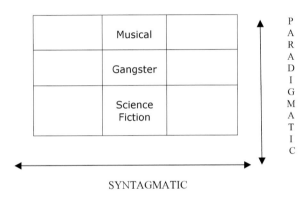

Formal semiotics

As viewers we develop the competency to read and interpret the formal elements of film (consciously or subconsciously). The aesthetic and technical choices made by filmmakers adhere to conventions adopted by the industry and established as standard practice over time. Below is a table listing technical devices and their popular semiotic meaning.

CAMERA

High-angle shot	A high-angle shot can often indicate the power relations in a narrative. When shot from above, objects or characters can appear small and inferior.
Low-angle shot	A low-angle shot inverts the aforementioned power structure. Here the camera points up and suggests a dominating force.
Zoom in	An incidence of importance has occurred and the audience is made aware of this.
Zoom out	This indicates that information outside the limited field of focus is necessary to the audience's understanding.

CAMERA

Close-up	Typically used to create empathy with the star vehicle or to provide detailed information for an audience.
Crane shot	This type of shot can indicate a transition from the particular to the general. It is often used to depict a change in focus to show the bigger picture.
Aerial shot	Often serves as an establishing shot in a big-budget film. Could signal the first in a number of spectacular shots that will feature throughout.
Deep-focus composition/Depth of field	Both the foreground and the background contain important information as they are both in focus. The audience must be active in reading the entire frame.
Framing	Where a character appears in a frame reveals a great amount of information. If they fill the screen this would suggest that they are important to the narrative. If they are pushed to the side of the frame this may reflect their state of mind or relationships with others (weak, confused, etc.).
Canted angle	This is when the frame is skewed in a lopsided manner. This will often reflect the fact that something is wrong (character's experiencing emotional turmoil or threat of crisis within a narrative, etc.). Alternatively it is often adopted by directors wanting to achieve a quirky aesthetic.

EDITING

Long take	Can be a badge of technical merit. Demonstrates the talent of either the director, actor and/or cinematographer. Makes the audience aware of the filmmaking process.
Fast cutting	A contemporary style of filmmaking that dictates pace. Accordingly the audience experiences heightened suspense.
Montage	A series of several shots, intercut to establish multiple perspectives. The audience is aware of the convention and happily accepts this cinematic shorthand for the passing of time, different geographical locations, etc.

LIGHTING

High-key lighting	Three-point lighting (key, fill and back) is used to achieve naturalistic light. The audience understands that the narrative is intended to be realistic.
Low-key lighting	Experimentation where one or more of the standard three light set-up is removed. The effect is known as chiaroscuro. The appearance of severe shadows typically indicates the darker side of nature (secrecy, horror and unease).

MUSIC

Major key	A combination of notes that adhere to a major key. The musical theme is interpreted by the audience as uplifting, heroic, joyful, uncomplicated, etc.
Minor key	A combination of notes that adhere to a minor key. Here the theme works to signify melancholy, heartache, regret, etc.

MUSIC

Modal scale	There are a variety of different modes that conjure specific mental images. For example, the Dorian mode evokes the Celtic countryside whereas the Phrygian mode suggests flamenco dancing and gypsy culture. Modes are often subconsciously read as a signifier of geographic locations.
Instrumentation	Certain instruments evoke filmic genres and/or national identities. For example the banjo, Jew's harp, honky-tonk piano are instruments associated with the American West. The accordion is linked to France whereas the bagpipes are synecdochical with Scottish culture.
Genre	Here specific genres of music are used to evoke historical and/or cultural periods. Rock 'n' roll is frequently played as a backdrop for the 50s, punk is suggestive of 70s class struggle and, more recently, rap is linked to African American gangsta culture.
Leitmotif	This occurs when a musical theme is employed to represent either a character, an emotion, a location or an object in a film. The leitmotif once established, recurs time and time again and is interpreted, either consciously or subconsciously, by an audience.
Rhythm and tempo	The rhythm of a piece of music can provide pacing or further depth. For example, dotted rhythms can be used for comedic effect or to suggest folk culture. Additionally the tempo can influence editing choices and is integral to the pacing of a scene.

Saussure formalized academic research into comprehending the mental mechanics of reading visual signs. Above we have examined a number of the ways in which signs are employed by the film industry. Working at the same time as Saussure, the American mathematician and philosopher Charles Peirce was addressing similar ideas.

Charles Sanders Peirce

Logic, Regarded as Semeiotic [sic] (1902)

Peirce's work differed from that of Saussure in that he identified three important elements for the study of signs. Rather than adopting the established idea of the sign, signifier and the signified, he introduced the following terms in his writings: iconic, symbolic and indexical.

Iconic

An icon is when a structure visually resembles what it is supposed stand for. For example according to Peirce, classical paintings and photographs are iconic as they share a likeness with the subject or object captured. Icons can also take the form of an illustration or diagram, for example a picture of a lit cigarette in a red circle with a line through it warns us that smoking is not permitted. This is iconic because the image represents a physical cigarette. However, the red circle is a good example of what Peirce refers to as symbolic.

Symbolic

There is no obvious relationship between symbols and their meaning. Here the link is arbitrary, learnt and understood by conventions and cultural upbringing. We are taught from an early age that a red traffic light means stop and a green light means go. The relationship we have with the coloured lights is symbolic.

Indexical

Here there is a direct connection between what is indicated and our understanding of that information. The easiest way to remember this indexical relationship is to think of medical symptoms; a rash indicates a virus. A bandage suggests an injury. Further examples include smoke as an omen of fire and a national anthem as an indication of patriotism.

Reflect and respond

1 Look at the cinema certification symbols below and decide whether they are iconic, symbolic or indexical. Explain how you arrive at your decision.
2 What do the certification symbols signify to you semiotically?
3 Consider the way that Lara Croft and Harry Potter have been marketed. Relate your answers to Peirce's categories.
4 Note and discuss some examples of indexical signs that feature in films you have seen.

Please note that these symbols are trademark and copyright protected. They remain the property of the British Board of Film Classification.

Whereas academics researching the field of semiology in the main came from a literary/linguistic background, Christian Metz was the first theorist to recognize the potential of this area and apply it to film as a discipline.

Christian Metz

The Imaginary Signifier: Psychoanalysis and the Cinema (1975)

French theorist Christian Metz is best known as the first theoretician to apply semiotics to the study of film, his ideas being published in *The Imaginary Signifier: Psychoanalysis and the Cinema* (1975). Metz believed that we should think of film as a kind of language and try to develop an understanding of this. In film, opera and theatre the signifier is different to that in literature because it appeals to both visual and auditory senses at the same time. However, in opera and theatre the experience is heightened by the fact that the performance is live. Conversely, film is unique in that the signs (actors, props, music, staging, etc.) are not physically present. When we watch a film what we see is an imprint (shadow, phantom, double, replica): once the action has been committed to celluloid/digital it is never again physically present. Metz talking of this absent/present phenomenon describes the physicality of film:

> [A] little rolled up perforated strip which 'contains' vast landscapes, fixed battles, the melting of the ice on the River Neva, and whole life-times, and yet can be enclosed in the familiar round metal tin, of modest dimensions, clear proof that it does not 'really' contain all that. (1982, p.44)

Film is like a mirror but with a major difference, the spectator's body never appears as a reflection. Instead it can be thought of as a glass window, with the spectator looking into an imaginary world. Metz develops Jacques Lacan's work on the 'Mirror Stage', a study based on the identification process of children (see Chapter 8, 'Psychoanalysis'). Because the spectators have already passed through this identification process they know that the images are not physically present on the screen and that their role as viewers is to consume information.

Spectators are fully aware that they are in a cinema because they sit at a distance from the screen. Because the auditorium is dark they feel that they are alone and that the image shown is only for them. Furthermore, due to the positioning of the projector behind the audience, the image appears to emanate from their field of vision. This in turn helps them to identify with the image on the screen more fully. Metz explores this idea in more depth using the terms 'projective' and 'introjective' (pp.49–51).

In the filmmaking process the camera records action, which is then transferred onto celluloid or video. Here the camera is projective and the celluloid or video that receives the imprint of the image is introjective (see Figure 4.1). When the above process is transferred into the act of watching film in a cinema (see Figure 4.2), the projector transmits the image (projective) and the screen relays the information (introjective). Metz likens these relationships to the mental procedure

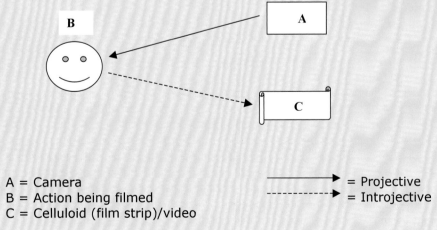

A = Camera
B = Action being filmed
C = Celluloid (film strip)/video

———————▶ = Projective
- - - - - - - ▶ = Introjective

Figure 4.1   Projective/introjective … in the filmmaking process

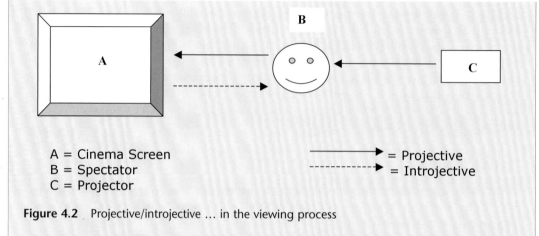

A = Cinema Screen
B = Spectator
C = Projector

$\longrightarrow$ = Projective
$\dashrightarrow$ = Introjective

Figure 4.2 Projective/introjective ... in the viewing process

humans undertake when recognizing visual information (see Figure 4.2). We look at an object (projective) and we decipher (often subconsciously) what we see (introjective).

Figures 4.1 and 4.2 illustrate the projective and introjective relationship between the filmmaking process and the screening/viewing process.

Although Metz's work is typically associated with Psychoanalysis, much of it was based on ideas of semiology. *The Imaginary Signifier* overlaps both Structuralist and Psychoanalytical perspectives. The above example is concerned with the way creative personnel and/or viewers read visual signs in a productive or cinematic environment. Similarly, Roland Barthes's in his critical writing is associated with more than one theoretical perspective (he was interested in Marxist ideology, Structuralism and Post-structuralism).

Roland Barthes

Mythologies (1957)

Roland Barthes, an eminent French intellectual and professor at the College de France, was connected with most of the main theoretical perspectives of French cultural life after World War II. Barthes's most important work is often considered to be a series of articles reflecting on contemporary French culture. These articles were originally written for the magazine *Les Lettres Nouvelles* during the period 1954–6 and were published under the collective name *Mythologies*. It is important to understand that Barthes's use of the term myth differs from the popular interpretation of a 'myth' as a fable, story or tale; something that could not really exist or have happened. However in his book *Mythologies* Barthes states that: '[m]yth is a system of communication, that it is a message. This allows one to perceive that myth cannot possibly be an object, a concept, or an idea; it is a mode of signification, a form' (p.109).

All signs can gain connotative meaning. Society may appropriate signs and through specific use these become laden with meaning. For example the white dove has become a symbol for peace and the fir tree has become synonymous with Christmas. All signs can be arbitrarily endowed with meaning.

In his article 'Myth Today' in *Mythologies*, Barthes demonstrates how seemingly neutral things can acquire multilayered meaning. The most quoted example of this idea from *Mythologies* is that of a photograph of a black soldier saluting the French Tricolour flag, which was featured on the cover of the magazine *Paris Match* in 1955. The image is a sign of that particular individual at a particular time and place. There is no focus on this soldier's personal history; instead he becomes a metaphor for larger sociopolitical issues. Myth ignores his past and the image becomes a sign that carries the concept of French imperialism: the myth of different nations living harmoniously together under one flag. For Barthes this image signifies that:

> France is a great Empire, that all her sons, without any colour discrimination, faithfully serve under her flag, and that there is no better answer to the detractors of an alleged colonialism than the zeal shown by this Negro in serving his so-called oppressors. (p.115)

Myths, in a Barthesian sense, function to make the constructed aspect of visual culture appear natural (the black soldier and the French flag were consciously put together to evoke an intended message). What distinguishes Barthes's analysis in *Mythologies* is his concentration on the apparently trivial; striptease, wrestling, soap adverts, etc. His non-elitist approach highlighted the fact that even the most frivolous of sources could be laden with possible meaning.

In addition to his work in *Mythologies*, Barthes identified two categories of text: the text of pleasure (*plaisir*) and the text of bliss (*jouissance*). Although he applied his ideas to the field of literature, these terms are very useful in analysing film.

Plaisir

This type of text is also referred to as the 'readerly' text because the focus is on pleasing the reader. The text is reassuring and comfortable. It typically confirms social beliefs and cultural identity. It is produced with audience enjoyment in mind. In film, generic texts adhere to audience expectations. Romantic comedies leave the viewer feeling uplifted and content. Commercial films in general can be regarded as texts of *plaisir*.

Jouissance

This is also referred to as the 'writerly' text because the author's intentions are imposed on the reader. The text is disturbing and challenging. It typically problematizes accepted social ideology. The text is produced to make the reader openly confront their beliefs. Applying this to film, avant-garde and experimental filmmaking often disrupts the viewing process. Similarly, much European filmmaking is not created with audience enjoyment in mind; instead it looks to unsettle and alienate the viewer. Consequently, its relevance to film is how much the viewer invests of themselves in the interpretation of the film text.

Whereas *Mythologies* is typically considered to be a Structuralist text due to the period in which it was written, on closer examination Barthes's ideas were concerned with deconstructing the sign and the text to find alternative meanings. Fundamentally this process of deconstruction lies at the heart of Post-structuralist debates; therefore *Mythologies* should be thought of as a link between Structuralism and Post-structuralism.

Reflect and respond

1 What is the key difference between Saussure and Peirce's approach with that of Barthes's way of reading a cultural sign?
2 Look at the following posters (Figure 4.3) advertising the film *The Day after Tomorrow* (Roland Emmerich, 2004). Attempt a Barthesian interpretation, in particular pay attention to any politically subversive connotations.
3 How difficult is it to undertake a Barthesian reading? What kind of information is required?
4 Identify films that fall into the categories of *plaisir* and *jouissance*. Discuss which kind of film-making you prefer and why?

Figure 4.3 Posters for *The Day after Tomorrow* (Roland Emmerich, 2004)

Post-structuralism

Post-structuralism

1. An extension and critique of structuralism, esp. as used in critical textual analysis, which rejects structuralist claims to objectivity and comprehensiveness, typically emphasizing instead the instability and plurality of meaning, and freq. using the techniques of deconstruction to reveal unquestioned assumptions and inconsistencies in literary and philosophical discourse.

It has been suggested that Post-structuralism started when Structuralists began to question the adequacy of the key theories. Post-structuralists were concerned with promoting the notion that texts have multiple meanings; interpretation is not fixed and can differ from person to person. So, Structuralism assumes stability, Post-structuralism looks for change and disturbance. This in itself appears an unusual idea, that a theory should stress problems with interpretation rather than attempt to make sense of the text. Post-structuralism took its lead from the work of Jacques Derrida.

Jacques Derrida

Of Grammatology (1967)

Jacques Derrida was an Algerian Jewish philosopher working in both France and America. Derrida took Saussure's ideas of the arbitrariness of the sign to extremes. Central to Derrida's work is the idea of what he calls '*différance*'. It is important to note that in French the word for difference is "différence' not '*différance*'. He changed the spelling from 'e' to 'a' in order to accentuate this.

Différance

Derrida claimed that language is an infinite chain of words. In order to explain this chain he introduced the concept of *différance*: words are defined by their difference from other words, and the interpretation is dependent upon the individual reader. There is no fixed meaning within a text and, due to the many possibilities, meaning is continually deferred (postponed).

    Différance is also of importance to Film Studies. Saussure claimed that:

Signifier + Signified = Sign.

Derrida on the other hand believed that:

Signifier + Signified = Sign
        Signifier + Signified = Sign
                Signifier + Signified = Sign

On first appearance Derrida's idea may seem unclear, but the formula above visually represents his notion of the deferment of meaning. Rather than the sign having a single meaning our individual interpretations allow for the sign to represent a continually evolving cycle.

In order to illustrate how this works consider the sequence in *A Clockwork Orange* (Stanley Kubrick, 1971) where Alex (Malcolm McDowell) and his Droogs break into a house and terrorize a couple. Here Kubrick has chosen to accompany the scene with the familiar Hollywood song 'Singin' in the Rain'. This track is universally associated with Gene Kelly's dance routine in the film of the same name, where he enthusiastically jumps in and out of puddles in a carefree manner. In Kubrick's version the song is juxtaposed with moments of extreme violence and sexual abuse. Whereas Kelly's routine was punctuated with the splashing of water, Alex emphasizes the beat by kicking and taunting his victims. What was originally an innocent, joyous celebration of love serves a darker, more horrific purpose here, the contrast between contexts maximizing the shock value. Therefore the sign is not stable in this case; it is invested with new meaning.

Deconstruction

Derrida's idea of '*différance*' led to the development of Deconstruction. Deconstruction is not a theory; instead it should be thought of as an interpretative attitude. It seeks to discover varied readings of a text rather than the accepted explanation. It looks for contradictions and conflicts that can destabilize traditional interpretations. It is often criticized for overcomplicating a text as it allows infinite possibilities. Furthermore, it questions and challenges traditional presumptions to reveal social and cultural leanings. Robert Hughes elegantly summarized this approach to analysis as 'cultural objects cut loose from any power to communicate' (1971). For example the final sequence of *Casablanca* (Michael Curtiz, 1942) is usually read as an allegory for people pulling together during the war, patriotism being more important than the personal happiness of Ilsa (Ingrid Bergman) and Rick (Humphrey Bogart). However, a Deconstructionist reading could interpret the relationship between Rick and Captain Renault (Claude Rains) as being homoerotic. This is suggested in Rick's final remark to Renault: 'I think this is the beginning of a beautiful friendship.'

Above is an example of a Queer reading of *Casablanca*. Although linked to Post-structuralism, Deconstruction can be applied as an analytical device to a variety of agendas imposed by other theories, including Feminist, Marxist and Postcolonial stances. Furthermore it can serve as an alternative to historical and national categories that allow for convenient divisions by movements, such as German Expressionism, Italian Neo-realism, French New Wave, etc. An important aspect to remember is that Deconstruction lends itself to a politicized reading as it questions established and accepted cultural hierarchies. This approach to reading texts is often referred to as 'reading against the grain' or 'reading the text against itself'.

In summary, Derridean Deconstruction requires that any analysis must be conducted from a sceptical position in order to call attention to alternative/marginal viewpoints. Deconstruction destabilizes textual meaning and challenges earlier semiotic hopes of identifying neat, 'scientific' systems to understand filmic codes.

Trace

From his studies, Derrida introduced the idea of 'trace' as a further textual device. Previously in this chapter it was noted how a film is created from signs that are not physically present (Metz,

1981). The object/subject is present at the time of filming but when the image/dialogue is trans-ferred to film all that remains is what Derrida called the 'trace' (in French this means footprint). So the sign is both there and not there. This idea is not only restricted to performances for the camera but can also be applied more generally to the history of cinema and/or other cultural forms of knowledge. For example, earlier films may influence filmmakers and audiences alike. This influence is once more both present and absent. Similarly our interpretation of a text is influenced by previous films we have viewed; we compare and contrast texts both consciously and subcon-sciously. Therefore trace impacts on every film we watch.

Graft

Often linked to the notion of 'trace', is the Postmodernist term 'graft'. Although Postmodern in origin, 'graft' developed out of Post-structuralist work on signs and meanings. Derrida's idea of 'graft' shows how a sign may change according to the context in which it is worked. For exam-ple, a star's image in a film carries, for the spectator, memories of earlier films in which they have featured. Logically these peripheral layers should not be considered in analysis. However, when the romantic comedy favourite Cameron Diaz took on the role of Lotte Schwartz in *Being John Malkovich* (Spike Jonze, 1999) audiences were shocked at her drab, unkempt appearance because they were used to seeing her play glamorous roles. This idea can be seen as a continuation of Saussure's 'syntagmatic axis'.

Of equal importance is the impact of real-life knowledge about specific stars that can inform our reading of a fictional film. It is near impossible to watch the Kubrick film *Eyes Wide Shut* (1999) with-out being aware of the media furore surrounding the breakup of Tom Cruise and Nicole Kidman.

Reflect and respond

1   Bearing in mind the previous movie posters for the film *The Day after Tomorrow*, look at the images on p.78 (Figures 4.4 and 4.5) and debate the idea of trace.
2   Try to recall stories in the media about famous stars. Did such tales impact on your viewing experience? Did your opinions about the real-life person (not the fictional character) change in any way?
3   To what extent are the terms 'trace' and 'graft' useful in the exploration of remakes? Illustrate your answer in reference to two films.

Case study: *Once Upon a Time in the West* (Sergio Leone, 1968)

Sergio Leone's name has become synonymous with the Western, but not in the traditional sense. His Westerns have a different quality stemming from his Italian heritage and the fact that the majority of his films were shot in Europe. Accordingly his style of Westerns have gained the affectionate term

Figure 4.4   Poster for *Cloverfield* (Matt Reeves, 2008)

'Spaghetti Westerns'. From a Structuralist point of view, Leone's epic film *Once Upon a Time in the West* provides rich pickings due to its playful approach to semiology.

One of the most famous sequences in the film is the McBain massacre. The iconic scene at the McBain homestead is a classic exercise in semiotics. The incident begins with the family preparing for the arrival of Jill (Claudia Cardinale), McBain's (Frank Wolff) new wife. The gingham, red-and-white-checked tablecloth signifies domesticity and functions as a trope throughout the entire film. At this point, the cloth represents hope and the future as the children get ready to greet their new step-mother. There is abundant food on the table and a joyful air of expectancy. However, this promise of family bliss is shortlived.

The first portent that something is wrong occurs when the cicadas stop chirping. This sudden silence is an example of what Peirce calls an 'indexical' sign. The insects are silenced by some unknown ominous force. The cause for concern is signalled further via a close-up showing McBain worriedly looking into wilderness. Although the cicadas begin calling to each other again, soon the stillness returns. McBain's anxiety is heightened as a flock of birds is disturbed and takes flight. His daughter Maureen (Simonetta Santaniello) watches smiling, unaware that the birds are an additional omen (indexical sign). Within seconds, a gunshot is heard and Maureen falls to the ground. McBain, then his eldest son, are killed in quick succession.

The final surviving member of the McBain family is the youngest child Timmy (Enzo Santaniello), who exits the house to find his family lying dead on the ground. It is at this point of heightened emotion that Leone introduces the foreboding soundtrack of his long-term collaborator Ennio Morricone; until now the scene had no music, instead the natural sounds were amplified, adding to the sense of danger. When the music begins it accompanies the gang that assassinated the Irish family. Yet, unlike the recognizable orchestral scores traditionally associated with Westerns, Morricone's theme is played on the electric guitar. This signifies

Figure 4.5   *Planet of the Apes* (Franklin J. Shaffner, 1968)

an end to the romantic, mythic Western frontier of old, as the edgy instrumentation connotes modernity. Rather than the glorified, nostalgic illustration of the West promoted by the founding fathers and the Hollywood studios, Leone offers a gritty and raw version. This is important as *Once Upon a Time in the West* was Leone's attempt to depict the end of the West, epitomized by the amplified guitar eerily resonating and reverberating across the familiar landscape. Furthermore, Morricone's score can be thought of as an example of defamiliarization (see Chapter 3, 'Formalism').

Returning to the plight of Timmy McBain, the musical theme accompanies Frank and his villainous men emerging from the undergrowth. The fact that the gang seem to magically materialize out of the terrain suggests that they do not adhere to the conventions of human society; there is something primitive about the men. This is reinforced by their attire. Once more Leone plays with the typical conventions of the genre: rather than depicting the cowboys in their stereotypical clean checked shirts and chaps, the Western characters here wear long, leather dust-coats. Once more there is a suggestion that Western expansion is coming to a conclusion as these men look like they have a lifetime of dirt and grime encrusted on their clothes and clogging their pores.

The leader of the gang is Frank, controversially played by Henry Fonda. The casting of Fonda as the villain of the narrative is probably one of the most memorable and shocking elements of the film. Fonda made his name playing all-American heroes. During his career he starred as Abraham Lincoln in *Young Mr Lincoln* (1939), Tom Joad in *The Grapes of Wrath* (1940) and Wyatt Earp in *My Darling Clementine*, all directed by John Ford. It is due to Fonda's past roles that he is cast as Frank. Leone was looking to destabilize the actor's on-screen persona, confounding audience expectations of the actor famous for his bright blue eyes, symbolizing hope for the Everyman. Therefore, when Fonda enters the frame as Frank, with chewing-tobacco oozing from his mouth, his blue eyes no longer indicate hope and American heroism. Fonda's iconic status is further shattered when he smiles as he pulls the trigger to shoot young Timmy.

Leone's decision to cast Fonda against type is indicative of changes occurring in the film industry at this point in history. Many genres were being revised in an attempt to attract audiences away from television and back into the cinema. Films of this era were far more violent, perhaps reflecting the problems that America was experiencing in Vietnam and closer to home, with the fight for racial equality. Accordingly, the violent act of killing a child could be seen as a critique of American society, the murder having far greater impact because committed by Fonda. Christopher Frayling points out, in the accompanying DVD commentary, that when the film was shown on American television, the shooting of Timmy was edited out as it was thought that American audiences would not be able to cope with such a horrific deed carried out by a star who had come to represent American ideology.

Here it is interesting to consider the syntagmatic and paradigmatic relation between the casting of Fonda and the role he was chosen to play (see figure on p.80). For example, the scene would not have been so controversial had the part of Frank been given to Lee Van Cleef, renowned for playing villainous characters in Westerns. Alternatively, if John Wayne had been given the role it would have been disconcerting to some extent, but Wayne had previously undertaken roles of dubious repute. In *The Searchers* (John Ford, 1956) Wayne starred as Ethan, an ex-Confederate soldier with a racist, violent streak. When that film was released, people were surprised to see Wayne playing a rogue rather than the traditional heroic lead. Therefore, Wayne would not have had the same impact as the blue-eyed, clean-cut Fonda. Considering other actors for the role of Frank is an example of a paradigmatic choice. A further paradigmatic decision would entail Fonda being cast in a different role. It is interesting to play with the paradigmatic alternatives in the chart as the syntagmatic outcome could lead to a very different film.

John Wayne	Saves the city	Is sent to jail with Clint Eastwood
Henry Fonda	Shoots a child	Kisses Marilyn Monroe
Lee Van Cleef	Robs a bank	Dies alone in the desert

PARADIGMATIC

SYNTAGMATIC

Another type of semiology employed in *Once Upon a Time in the West* is the leitmotif. The Morricone score is comprised of four main themes, each representing one of the four main characters. The musical themes are instantly recognizable due to their orchestration. The table below describes how the orchestration conveys information about the characters.

Character	Orchestration	Semiotic coding
Frank	Electric guitar over pizzicato strings. Wailing harmonica echoes in the background. Major key.	Foreboding doom. Powerful and dark, yet haunting harmonica always present.
Gill	Harpsichord opening gives way to soaring soprano melody accompanied by strings and brass. Minor key.	European presence (harpsichord). Beauty, melancholy, pride and hope.
Harmonica (Charles Bronson)	Solo harmonica played with lots of reverb. Becomes entwined with Frank's theme. Modal rather than major or minor.	Haunting sound, echoes of the past. Modal scale suggests non-Euro-American heritage. Theme is linked to that of Frank.
Cheyenne (Jason Robards)	Lilting honky-tonk piano and banjo. Dotted rhythm slowly driving tempo. Whistled melody. Major key.	Comedic tone. Weary traveller. Rhythm suggests horseback. The pause in the final rendition suggests Cheyenne's death.

As can be seen the music reveals a great amount of detail about the four characters. Interestingly, Frank and Harmonica's leitmotifs are connected. Whenever Frank is on screen, Harmonica is aurally present even if he is not seen. At the conclusion of the film the reason for this is revealed via flashback. At this point the viewer is privy to the importance of the musical instrument that gave Charles Bronson's character his name. Therefore, the Harmonica acts as a leitmotif, a moniker (name) and a narrative device.

Barthes's ideas of *plaisir* and *jouissance* can also be applied to the film. On one hand the text could be considered an example of *plaisir*, conforming as it does to the familiar generic conventions of the Western, fulfilling audience expectations. On the other hand, the text is laden with references to earlier classic Westerns, in particular those directed by John Ford. In this sense the film could be thought of as an illustration of *jouissance* because it subverts, challenges and questions the mythology of the West through its intertextuality. Although many of the instances cited in this case study could lend themselves to Postmodernism, it is important to recognize that these specific devices are not used in an attempt to parody the genre but are instead employed as a fond development of the Western. However, there are often numerous ways to approach a text and no single reading excludes another.

Reflect and respond

1   Using *Once Upon a Time in the West*, undertake textual analysis of the opening scene at the railway station. What do the formal semiotics in this sequence signify?
2   Can you appreciate how shocking it was to audiences in 1968 to see Fonda as a villain? Try to think of modern-day equivalents where actors are cast against type.
3   Would Henry Fonda's appearance in the film have had the same impact if he had played the role of Cheyenne or Harmonica?
4   How helpful is leitmotif as a semiotic device? Can you think of films that use repeating musical themes to convey information?
5   Two key visual motifs that recur throughout the film are water and the railway. What do you think they signify and why are they important to the narrative?

Conclusion

Structuralism is about trying to make sense of the world around us by investigating the way in which images communicate meaning. It looks at the relationship between language, image and concepts and recognizes that the way we interpret information is based on our cultural upbringing.

Post-structuralism questions the idea that meaning is fixed. Instead it looks at how our understanding of information is subjective (down to the individual). Furthermore Post-structuralists take the notion that meaning comprises of a continual cycle, with one meaning acting as a springboard to the next. Over time, Post-structuralist debates have become less reductive as they allow for the possibility of more than one reading, an approach favoured by Postmodernists.

Bibliography

Barthes, R. (1993) *Mythologies*, 2nd edn, London: Vintage (1957).

Derrida, J. (1976) *Of Grammatology*, Baltimore, MD and London: Johns Hopkins University Press.

Hughes, R. (1971) 'The Décor of Tomorrow's Hell', *Time* 27 December. Retrieved 26 July 2010. Available at http://www.time.com/time/magazine/article/0,9171,905637,00.html.

Metz, C. (1982) *The Imaginary Signifier: Psychoanalysis and the Cinema*, Bloomington: Indiana University Press.

Peirce, C. S. (1902) *Logic, Regarded as Semeiotic* (MS L75). Arisbe [electronic]. Retrieved 28 June 2010. Available at http://www.cspeirce.com/menu/library/bycsp/bycsp.htm.

Saussure, F. de (1983) *Course in General Linguistics,* London: Duckworth.

Marxism

5

Marxism

1a. The ideas, theories, and methods of Karl Marx; *esp.* the political and economic theories propounded by Marx together with Friedrich Engels, later developed by their followers to form the basis for the theory and practice of communism.

1b. Central to Marxist theory is an explanation of social change in terms of economic factors, according to which the means of production provide the economic base which determines or influences the political and ideological superstructure. The history of society can be viewed as showing progressive stages in the ownership of the means of production and, hence, the control of political power. Marx and Engels predicted the final revolutionary overthrow of capitalism by the proletariat and the eventual attainment of a classless communist society.

Setting the scene

Marxism was conceived as a revolutionary theory that attempted to explain and expose the relations of power in capitalist societies. It was jointly founded by Karl Marx, an editor and Friedrich Engels, a philosopher. Marx became interested in Communist ideology, which led him to join the Communist League (an international organization). It was here that he met Engels, who became a lifelong friend. After the League's conference in London, Marx and Engels were asked if they would write *The Communist Manifesto* (1848) which would become the foundation for Marxism.

Broadly, they were concerned with the apparent division between the ruling and the working class. They used the terms bourgeoisie and proletariat, the former referring to those with economic and political power, and the latter meaning those who are 'wage labourers' or dependent on the welfare system. They state that: '[s]ociety as a whole is more and more splitting up into two great hostile camps, into two great classes directly facing each other: Bourgeoisie and Proletariat' (Marx and Engels, 2002, p.220).

Accordingly, their aims in writing were to bring about a classless society. Although they did not write a systematic theory of culture, their influence on cultural theory cannot be underestimated because the Marxist theory of society and its historical development generated a significant body of work. Above all a Marxist approach to culture is concerned with the analysis of texts within their historical conditions of production.

It is important to note that the terms Marxism, Communism and socialism are often used interchangeably because they have many elements in common. However, of the three, it is Marxism that is most applicable to the field of Film Studies because it considers how power relations inform and impact on cultural artefacts.

Karl Marx

A Contribution to the Critique of Political Economy (1859)

Base and superstructure

In *A Contribution to the Critique of Political Economy* (1859), Marx sets out what he calls the 'base and superstructure' model. Although most people think of the 'base and superstructure' as a twofold relationship, Peter Singer correctly points out that it is more accurately described as threefold (2000, p.48).

The base comprises the two components; the 'forces of production' and the 'relations of production' (see figure below). The 'forces of production' relates to the materials, tools, labour and skills needed to produce goods. These forces dictate the 'relations of production'. Historically if a society has not advanced (to a point where tools and skills are available to the labour force) then the relations between people appear to be outdated. Marx writes in *The Poverty of Philosophy*: 'The handmill gives you society with the feudal lord; the steam-mill, society with the industrial capitalist' (1847, p.202).

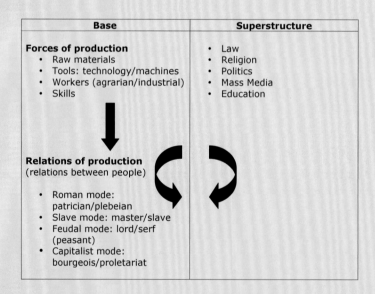

Base	Superstructure
Forces of production • Raw materials • Tools: technology/machines • Workers (agrarian/industrial) • Skills **Relations of production** (relations between people) • Roman mode: patrician/plebeian • Slave mode: master/slave • Feudal mode: lord/serf (peasant) • Capitalist mode: bourgeois/proletariat	• Law • Religion • Politics • Mass Media • Education

The skills available to the labour force change over time and this has a direct influence on how society is ordered. Singer clarifies this by stating:

> Feudal relations of production came about because they fostered the development of the productive forces of feudal times – the handmill for example. These productive forces continue

to develop. The steam-mill is invented. Feudal relations of production restrict the use of the steam-mill. The most efficient use of steam power is in large factories which require a concentration of free labourers rather than serfs tied to their land. So the relation of lord and serf breaks down, to be replaced by the relation of capitalist and employee. (2000, p.49)

As technology and skills progress, society adapts to cater for such advances. This leads to a complete restructuring of the economic class relations because the 'forces of production' determine the 'relations of production'.

The combination of these components, known by Marxists as the 'base', moulds the shape of the 'superstructure'. These terms relate to the way a society thinks and the way it rules its people (the ideology and institutions that are the foundation of any society: law, religion, politics, media, education, etc). Although the 'superstructure' is supposed to be determined by the 'base', many critics and scholars have debated this theory and once more we are left with a 'chicken-and-egg' dilemma. Does the economic grounding of a society inform the way people think or vice versa?

In order to apply the idea of the 'base and the superstructure' to the field of film, all cultural artefacts must be examined in relation to their historical mode of production. Marx and Engels believed that the dominant thinking of any specific time would display the ideas of the ruling class. It is those in positions of power who attempt to make the workers conform to their ideas. Accordingly, mainstream culture is infused with these dominant ideas and all other ways of thinking are considered to be marginal. Therefore, narratives that conflict with these prevailing modes of thought can 'bomb' at the box office or even fail to make it into production. For example, the film *Walker* (1987) directed by Alex Cox, was heavily influenced by Third Cinema. The narrative represented a brutal critique of US intervention in Central America. It was hated by the studio, underfunded and consequently not promoted. Cox's career was irreparably damaged and he never worked in Hollywood again. In the same way that the ruling classes exploit the labour force, dominant ideology serves to hide the fact that it is manipulating the masses. This is what Engels refers to as 'false consciousness', the notion that working-class people come to adopt the dominant class's ideologies. A naïve take on false consciousness can be seen in the film *They Live!* (John Carpenter, 1988). Here, the central character puts on the 'ideology sunglasses' and can suddenly see (through) ideology. For instance, he reads a billboard at the side of the road advertising 'Come to the Caribbean'; when wearing the special glasses the sign actually reads 'Marry and Reproduce!'

Reflect and respond

As outlined above, society has to constantly evolve to cater for technological advances, considering the film industry's new reliance on digital innovations look at the following questions:

1   Identify how the 'forces of production' have altered in traditional filmmaking; how have the skills and labour force changed?
2   Do you think the 'capitalist mode' (bourgeois/proletariat) is still relevant? If not, how should it be updated?
3   Has the 'superstructure' been affected by the introduction of digital technology?

Louis Althusser borrowed the term 'overdetermination' from the psychoanalyst Sigmund Freud to critique the idea of the 'base and superstructure'. In his study of dreams and their interpretation, Freud recognized that numerous factors determined the visions and images that we experience while asleep; hence 'overdetermination'.

Althusser openly rejected Marx and Engels's idea that the 'base' determined the 'superstructure'. Instead he believed that the relationship between the two was riddled with contradictions and therefore open to multiple readings. Film offers an interesting example when attempting to apply ideas of overdetermination. Althusser argued that films are relatively autonomous entities, not being solely influenced by financial implications but also affected by technical considerations and sociopolitical issues. The Frankfurt School promulgated this consideration of film in relation to industrial practice.

The Frankfurt School

In 1923 a group of academics based at the University of Frankfurt formed the Institute for Social Research. Here they combined Marxist thought and psychoanalysis in what came to be known as 'critical theory'. The key thinkers most associated with this group are Theodor Adorno, Walter Benjamin, Max Horkheimer, Leo Lowenthal and Herbert Marcuse. Collectively they were concerned with the changes in culture brought about by industrialization.

Culture industry

The 'culture industry' was a term coined by Adorno and Horkheimer in their discussions about popular productions (film, music, literature, etc.). Prior to the Frankfurt School, scholars had warned of the dangers of popular culture, fearing that it could lead to anti-authoritative behaviour and a breakdown in morality (see Chapter 12, 'Audience Research and Reception'). In contrast, Adorno and Horkheimer in the chapter 'The Culture Industry: Enlightenment as Mass Deception' (1947/1995), argued that popular culture was more likely to promote conformity. Rather than questioning the content of such artefacts, the audience passively absorbs information; this is often referred to as the 'hypodermic needle model'. It is important to note that they were writing in the early days of film criticism and expressed anxieties about the corrupting potential of this new technology. As exiled Germans, their worries were tied up with fears relating to the fascist engagement of cinema as propaganda.

Due to industrialization, films, books and music were by this time easy to reproduce, which, according to the Frankfurt School, changed culture into merely another commodity. In order to meet demand, production methods were adopted that generated goods which were formulaic in content (standardization); standardization leads to predictability: '[c]ulture now impresses the same stamp on everything. Films, radio and magazines make up a system that is uniform as a whole and in every part' (Adorno and Horkheimer, 1995, p.120).

When factory-line products flood the market, their easy availability may mean that consumers see and buy them unquestioningly. This allows industries to continue to produce items of their choice, knowing that the consumer will accept them without thinking. Therefore the purchaser is manipulated into buying the products that the manufacturers continue to deliver.

Ironically, the producers claim that these goods are being created to meet the needs of the public. The consumer is therefore given the illusion of choice, when in reality they are merely being offered the same product branded differently (different stars, director, location, etc.). Rather than artistic interests being the primary factor, large businesses are concerned with making money and perpetuating the capitalist economy. The working class has thus become depoliticized by the mass media, meaning that it accepts mainstream productions without question.

High art, on the other hand, has the potential to critique society. Unlike popular production, high art does not necessarily have to be commercial (it can be anti-capitalist) and is free to challenge and alienate its intended audience. Rather than representing dominant ideology, high art has the opportunity to present an alternative view.

Reflect and respond

1   A key criticism aimed at the productions of mass media was that they tended towards the formulaic. How is this uniformity shown in films?
2   The Frankfurt School was dismissive of mass entertainment, believing it depoliticized the general public. Can you think of any films that confirm and/or negate this?
3   To what extent do you agree with the argument that high art critiques society?

Herbert Marcuse was also interested in offering a different perspective and developed ideas which he called affirmative culture.

Herbert Marcuse

Affirmative culture

'Affirmative culture' (Herbert Marcuse), also known as 'autonomous' or 'authentic' culture (Max Horkheimer), is a term seeking to describe how art can affect people. Where in the past religion had offered a sense of refuge and a utopian view of a better world, affirmative culture propounds a similar premise: that art can equally promise optimism, albeit false, in times of hardship. Whereas in earlier times, the general masses would often be restricted in their access to high art, affirmative culture is concerned with art being openly available to all, independent of class status. Rather than being contained in elitist art galleries, libraries and concert halls, Marcuse called for open availability. Previously, art was created for and by the ruling classes; conversely, affirmative culture is informed by the ideas and values of the masses.

Instead of the alienation that high art tends to inspire, artefacts associated with affirmative culture offer people a sense of comfort because they are recognizable. For example, during World War II, Hollywood shelved plans to release its adaptations of hardboiled detective narratives (Film Noir) because they were deemed too pessimistic. Instead it saturated the market with song-and-dance movies, realizing that the optimism of Musicals helped relieve a period of darkness and hardship. A prime example of affirmative culture, Musicals adhere to a formulaic narrative where problems are created and solved easily, leaving the audience fulfilled and uplifted.

In summary, Marcuse is suggesting that culture can provide the feelgood factor when everything is going wrong, fulfilling a role similar to that of religion in the past. Affirmative culture works by making difficult times tolerable by offering a way in which 'the need for happiness [can be satisfied] in order to make such an existence bearable' (1968, p.119). Nevertheless, affirmative culture works along similar lines to false consciousness. Dominant ideology works by providing a diverting feelgood factor that disguises potential dissatisfaction with authority and its institutions. Its consumerist fantasies pacify and distract people from the real issues.

In addition to the utopian angle of affirmative culture, a further aspect needs consideration. As a powerful business, the culture industry can buy anything and turn it into a mass commodity. In doing this, an artefact that once started life as high or classical art can lose its impact or value through being mass-produced or applied and adapted to other ends. In 1964 Marcuse wrote *One-Dimensional Man*; here he stated that the high art shown in concert halls, opera houses and theatres can serve a variety of ends:

> [T]hey become commercials – they sell, comfort, or excite … the classics have left the mausoleum and come to life again … they come to life as other than themselves; they are deprived of an antagonistic force, of the estrangement which was the very dimension of their truth. The intent and function of these works have changed. If they once stood in contradiction to the status quo, this contradiction is now flattened out. (2002, p.67)

For example, many advertisements, television shows and films employ classical music. 'O Fortuna' from Carl Orff's *Carmina Burana* (1935–6) is played to introduce the judges on the hit show *The X Factor* (2004–) and Prokofiev's 'Montagues and Capulets' theme from the ballet *Romeo and Juliet* is used as the theme tune to the UK version of *The Apprentice* (2005–). Similarly in *2001: A Space Odyssey* (Stanley Kubrick, 1968) the appropriation of 'The Blue Danube' by Johann Strauss and 'Also Spracht Zarathustra' by Richard Strauss has made these refrains 'part and parcel' of our popular psyche. This appropriation of high art is not just applicable to the realm of music. The French novel *Les Liaisons Dangereuses* (1782) by Pierre Choderlos de Laclos would have remained an unknown classic if it had not been adapted for the screen by Stephen Frears in 1988. However, it was further popularized under the new title *Cruel Intentions* (Roger Kumble, 1999). Furthermore, its art-house credentials have been superseded by the hype surrounding the lesbian kiss between Sarah Michelle Gellar and Selma Blair. Another famous film example is Ingmar Bergman's Grim Reaper character from *The Seventh Seal* (1957) making a comedic appearance in *Bill and Ted's Excellent Adventure* (Stephen Herek, 1989). In all these examples the elitist signification is erased as cultural texts take on new life and meaning.

Reflect and respond

1 Are there any genres that lend themselves particularly well to the utopian aspect of affirmative culture? Why is this the case?
2 Does the film industry have a responsibility to entertain the masses and make 'feelgood' films? Do films have to be entertaining?
3 Can you identify characters, music, narrative tropes, etc. that have been appropriated from high art and inserted in popular film?

Working at a similar period to Marcuse, Louis Althusser and Pierre Macherey engaged with a very different approach to understanding texts. In their search for explanatory models to identify and interpret the gaps and ellipses that all texts would have, they attempted to encourage the reader to look between the lines in order to uncover conflicts and new meanings.

Symptomatic reading

One very useful idea posited by Althusser is that of 'symptomatic reading'. Writing in 1965 in *Reading Capital* (translated into English in 1979), he argued that, in order to fully understand a cultural text, the reader must look beyond the information presented to consider what has been omitted (1979). Rather than focusing on the questions asked, Althusser suggests that the reader should attempt to discern what is not being asked. Therefore in order to undertake a symptomatic reading, we need to identify holes, gaps, ellipses and silences; we need to look at what is being avoided or left unspoken in order to recognize problems.

In Film Studies this approach can be very helpful. In particular, mainstream, Hollywood productions will occasionally allude to wider political problems but refuse to engage on a deeper level for fear of alienating their paying audience. John Storey points out that the film *Taxi Driver* (Martin Scorsese, 1976) asks questions that are not addressed in the narrative, for example 'how does the Veteran return home to America after the imperial horrors of Vietnam?' (2001, p.97). A more recent example is the film *Iron Man* (Jon Favreau, 2008). This text touches on the issue of American corporate firms profiting from the sale of weapons to Middle Eastern nations. The film, however, does not ask pertinent questions about the West's responsibility in subsidizing terrorist activity in countries such as Iraq and Afghanistan.

The idea of symptomatic reading was developed further by Pierre Macherey in his book *A Theory of Literary Production* (1978). In the chapter 'Domain and Object', Macherey postulates that if a text is only afforded a single interpretation, believed to be that of the author, the text would remain incomplete. Alternative meanings, such as the readers' perspectives are of equal importance. This focus on the assumption that the author's intention is known is often referred to as 'interpretive fallacy' or 'authorial intention' (p.80). Macherey argues that meaning needs to be 'decentred' (p.79), taken away from the author as the sole source of intention.

He believed that texts have multiple explanations which engender discussion as sites of conflict. Put simply, critical analysis should 'read between the lines'. What is of interest is to explain why there is a silence and to recognize what is 'unspoken' (pp.85–9). To illustrate his point, Macherey draws on Freud's work on the unconscious (see Chapter 8, 'Psychoanalysis'). He suggests that attention needs to be paid to the gaps and ellipses. These spaces must further be read in the context of when an artefact was produced. For example, Orson Welles's *Citizen Kane* flopped when it was initially released due to the controversial similarities between its lead character and newspaper magnate Randolph Hearst. It was only when it was championed by the French New Wave critics that it gained iconic status. Taken out of its historical context when the narrative was no longer connected to Hearst, *Citizen Kane* received critical acclaim.

Reflect and respond

1   Looking at the examples above, can you think of other films where the unspoken subtext overwhelms the narrative to the point where it cannot be ignored?
2   How important is 'authorial intention' in filmmaking? Once a film has been released are the director's/screenwriter's intentions relevant?
3   Can you identify any films whose status has changed over time according to the socio-political climate?

As outlined earlier in the chapter, Louis Althusser's ideas are instrumental in undertaking a Marxist reading of film. His ideas concerning interpellation can also inform Film Studies.

Louis Althusser

Interpellation (1970)

Louis Althusser was interested in the way society worked and how, as individuals, we are all subjects within society. He recognized that from an early age we all learn how to conform and adopt social patterns of behaviour. He rejected the ideas of Engels as he considered 'false conscious-ness' a flimsy notion. Instead he saw ideology as an active thing; something we all take part in on a daily basis. Althusser suggested that dominant ideology seeks to indoctrinate everyone so that we all share the same beliefs, value system, desires and prejudices. This is achieved by two mechanisms:

1   repressive state apparatus: police, courts and judicial system
2   ideological state apparatus: church, education, politics, media and family.

The repressive state apparatus forces individuals in a society to adhere to rules and regulations in order to avoid punishment, whereas the ideological state apparatus manipulates in a far subtler way, pressuring individuals to conform to moral and ideological norms.

Althusser uses the term 'interpellation' or 'hailing' to describe how these unconscious processes work. As subjects we are all accountable for our actions, which can be called into ques-tion at any time. Althusser presents the example of a policeman shouting at a person in the street to stop. Whether innocent or not, our automatic reaction is to stop as we are programmed to obey the police. In stopping we become transformed into the subject. Yet Althusser claims that we are all ideological subjects before we are born. Here he cites the case of Christians who, in choosing to abide by the rules of God, become God's subjects (this would apply to all world reli-gions). As subjects we conform to societal rules.

In Film Studies, interpellation works when the viewer becomes the subject of the text. We, the audience, become interpellated when we become drawn into the narrative; when we empathize with the characters on screen. Laura Mulvey's work cites an instance of interpellation, claiming that women are typically encouraged to identify with the male protagonist rather than relate to the female star (see Chapter 9, 'Feminism'). Althusser's main aim in identifying interpellation was to make the audience aware that, although we often believe we are making decisions freely, the media manipulates us into a false state. We may not be aware that we are watching a film from a specific position (gender, political, class) because the ideological message is hidden (repressed).

Reflect and respond

1 Do you feel that our values and beliefs are informed by the repressive and ideological state apparatuses? Which do you think is more influential?
2 Althusser gives the example of how we are religious subjects. Can you think of any other examples where we perform a role as subjects in society?
3 The idea of interpellation is based on the premise that we do not have choices but are instead coerced into certain positions. Can you think of any other examples of how the film industry practises this?

Antonio Gramsci

Hegemony (1976)

Antonio Gramsci held a different view from earlier Marxists on the cultural and ideological relationship that existed in capitalist society. Conventional Marxist thinking held that the ruling classes enforced ideas on the 'rest'. Rather than the domination of one class over another, Gramsci saw ideology as a struggle or site of negotiation between the classes for hegemony (leadership, dominance, authority).

The ruling class seeks to replace the culture and ideology of the working class with its own. However, Gramsci argues that the ruling class can become hegemonic only if it finds space to appreciate and accept other class cultures and values. This concept appears to present agreement between the classes and implies that hegemony is desirable in offering the majority of people from all classes a safe and conflict-free society. Yet, to maintain harmony, hegemonic values are revised and reformed in an ongoing process. For example, in Wales there has been a collective move towards reinvigorating Welsh as the national language. This is illustrated by the establishment of the Welsh Assembly, Welsh-language road signs, BBC Wales and S4C, and the reintroduction of Welsh-language classes in all schools. This was achieved over time through pressure groups acting on behalf of the nation.

It is important to remember that, because hegemony results from negotiations within society, it is rarely imposed from 'above' (top down); the process allows for discussion and disagreement, therefore the outcome constantly changes. So ideas that are repeated and spoken become part of our day-to-day culture. Through this process, the government, ruling or dominant class can exercise strong guidance without appearing dictatorial. As with any system there are limitations to this inclusiveness. For example, in times of crisis such as war, the hegemonic process is suspended in order that the police, army, etc. (referred to by Althusser as the 'repressive state apparatus') can take the lead.

To summarize, hegemony takes shape from the struggle between the ruling class, which attempts to control ideology and the working class, which struggles to resist its hold. Accordingly, hegemony is not imposed; it is an area of negotiation between the two which allows for alterations. Gramsci has been influential in questioning this notion that culture emerges from ruling-class ideology in direct conflict with working-class culture. Hegemony, as a theory, allows for a more adaptable idea of culture.

Reflect and respond

1   Recently in cases where filmmakers planned adaptations of famous works, the production crew have actively sought fans, to seek their advice regarding the translation from book/comic to screen. Why do you think the industry has adopted this tactic?
2   Why does the ruling class care about what the masses think? Why not dismiss their views and produce elitist texts?
3   Does this ever work in reverse, where the masses attempt to appeal to the elite?
4   Is this battle between the classes still relevant today?

Mikhail Bakhtin

Carnivalesque (1968)

The philosopher Mikhail Bakhtin was an important figure in the development of Marxist thought. He is most well known for his writings on the Carnivalesque that feature in his book *Rabelais and His World* (1968). Carnivals have been recorded since the Roman and Greek empires and have long been positioned at the heart of folk culture. Carnival represents a time of celebration and revelry when normal conventions are overlooked and excessive behaviour reigns. Bakhtin's ideas concerning the festivities can be summarized as follows:

1   Law and order is suspended; rules, regulations and restrictions are lifted.
2   During the carnival traditional hierarchies no longer apply. Inequality between classes is temporarily abolished.
3   Carnival brings together all walks of life: rich/poor, old/young, learned/uneducated and the sacred/profane.
4   Celebration of blasphemy and obscenities is 'linked with the reproductive power of the earth and the body, carnivalistic parodies on sacred texts and sayings, etc.' (Storey, 2001, p.251).
5   Indulgence in colloquial language, euphemisms and *double entendre* is rife.
6   Laughter and parody are in essence what carnival is about; laughing at life, oneself and in particular laughing at authority. It is about not taking things too seriously, a theme often manifesting in spoof, satire and sending-up situations (parody).

The Carnivalesque often focuses on the grotesque and the ridiculous. For example, the *Carry On* films of the 70s epitomize this type of humour with their focus on bodily functions (burp and fart jokes) and sexual innuendo. Despite its comedic nature, Bakhtin related the Carnivalesque to Marxist ideology because once again it is concerned with subverting class distinctions.

Reflect and respond

1   Can you think of any films that take Bakhtin's notion of the Carnivalesque as the main trope for the narrative?
2   Why do you think the Carnivalesque lends itself to film as a format?
3   How would you apply Carnivalesque if you were writing a screenplay?
4   In what ways is Carnivalesque useful in terms of escapism?

Case study: Latin America: Third Cinema and Imperfect Cinema

The primary concern of Marxist theory is politics. So far we have focused on various Marxist ideas and devices, but now we will turn our attention to directors who have attempted to overthrow societal order through the medium of film. The Russian Formalist, Sergei Eisenstein, was one of the first filmmakers who believed that cinema had the capability to change the attitudes of the people. Accordingly he experimented with different types of editing to try to mobilize the masses to rise up against the controlling bourgeois forces (See Chapter 3. 'Formalism').

One of the main criticisms of Marxist film theory is that its preoccupation with narrative content makes it an arduous task trying to identify Marxist aesthetics within a text. However, in the 60s and 70s a group of filmmakers inspired by the post-revolutionary Cuban climate emerged in Latin America.

Third Cinema

Third Cinema is a term coined by Fernando Solanas and Octavio Getino, who were part of a radical Argentinian group of filmmakers known as the *Grupo Cine Liberación*. Collectively they made a film entitled *La Hora de los Hornos/ The Hour of the Furnaces* (1968), which looked at foreign imperialism and neo-colonialism in South America. The film was made secretly and then smuggled out of the country as it would have been heavily censored or even banned by national authorities. The film was designed to instigate debate:

We realized that the most important thing was not the film and the information in it so much as the way this information was debated. One of the aims of such films is to provide the occasion for people to find themselves and speak about their own problems. (Solanas, cited in Chanan, 1997, p.373)

Reflecting on the experience of making the film, Solanas and Getino aired their radical views in the seminal article 'Towards a Third Cinema: Notes and Experiences for the Development of a Cinema of Liberation in the Third World' (1969). This manifesto outlined three distinct types of filmmaking, the last being their approach to instil revolutionary change:

1 **First Cinema:** This is commercial filmmaking typically produced by Hollywood. The writers claimed that 'First Cinema' teaches bourgeois values. It is concerned with spectacle and entertainment; it positions the viewer as a passive observer.
2 **Second Cinema:** This is art-house filmmaking (typically European). Here the emphasis is on the director as auteur (individual expression). It challenges the conventions of Hollywood filmmaking yet directors are still forced to work within the same commercial/capitalist system.
3 **Third Cinema:** This is directly opposed to the hegemonic political and studio system. Solanas and Getino refer to '[M]aking films that the System cannot assimilate and which are foreign to its needs, or making films that directly set out to fight the System' (p.42).

The main goal of Third Cinema was to create a new cinematic language that would reinforce a new consciousness, a revolutionary consciousness which would effect change in society. Mike Wayne states 'For Third Cinema, one of the key areas of concern which needs to be explored is the process whereby people who have been oppressed and exploited become conscious of that condition and determine to do something about it' (2001, p.16). In order to achieve such politicized aims the group actively looked to reject traditional film aesthetics, stating that:

> The end product amounts to a militant poetic tapestry, weaving together disparate styles and materials ranging from didacticism to operatic stylization, direct filming to the techniques of advertising and incorporating photographs, newsreels, testimonial footage and film clips – from avant garde and mainstream, fiction and documentary. (Solanas, cited in Chanan, 1997, p.373)

This anti-Hollywood approach was influenced by an earlier movement of Latin American radical filmmaking known as 'Cinema Novo', which had emerged in the 50s and 60s. Its low-budget attitude to filmmaking was known as 'the aesthetics of hunger' or alternatively 'the aesthetics of violence' (Hayward, 2006, p.74). Its stripped-back working ethos was encapsulated by the phrase 'Uma câmera na mão e uma idéia na cabeça'/'a camera in the hand and an idea in the head'. Third Cinema's legacy was its influence on developing nations; in particular filmmakers from Africa took inspiration from its manifesto.

Imperfect Cinema

The term 'Imperfect Cinema' was invented by Julio García Espinosa. This Latin American director also sought to divorce film from any capitalist connotations and instead concentrate on providing political education. Espinosa's manifesto is in a similar vein to that of Solanas and Getino; it stipulates the ideological rules that filmmakers should adhere to. For example, he believed that directors should not strive to get their films screened in commercial cinemas: 'Imperfect Cinema rejects exhibitionism in both (literal) senses of the word, the narcissistic and the commercial (getting shown in established theatres and circuits)' (pp.81–2). Instead film should be taken to the people, to remote communities, village halls, etc. in order to politicize the masses against the system.

Espinosa further rejects the overriding assumption that filmmaking should be aesthetically pleasing. He claimed that films do not have to be created on traditional 35mm stock but 'can be created equally well with a Mitchell or with an 8mm camera, in a studio or in a guerrilla camp in the middle of the jungle' (p.82). Rather than attempting to create beautiful works of art, the film-maker should ensure that the message is of prime importance.

As we have seen, he believed that cinema should not be about 'good taste' or enjoyment but should instead have a political focus:

> Imperfect cinema is no longer interested in predetermined taste, and much less in 'good taste'. It is not quality which it seeks in an artist's work. The only thing it is interested in is how an artist responds to the following question: What are you doing in order to overcome the barrier of the 'cultured' elite audience which up to now has conditioned the form of your work? (p.82)

The critical engagement and theorized approach of these Latin American filmmakers enabled practitioners to take a more militant (Marxist) attitude to both narrative and aesthetic concerns. Interestingly, these ideas are the only theories associated with film as a discipline that do not originate from North America or Europe.

Conclusion

Collectively, this militant group of Latin American filmmakers was concerned with attacking the culture of neo-colonialism. Neo-colonialism refers to a major power exerting its influence over underdeveloped nations. For example, American ideology saturates the world through the media (Hollywood) so much that we are all familiar with US founding principles and national doctrine. The unease this generates perpetuates Marxist concerns. Whereas earlier Marxist writings were preoccupied with national class distinctions between the proletariat and the bourgeoisie, in more recent times this model has been applied on a global scale. Here the dominant force is America and Western assertiveness at the expense of the cultural annihilation of more vulnerable countries.

Stimulated by years of oppression under numerous dictatorships, these radical South American groups looked to invigorate cinema by infusing it with a political agenda. Their underlying belief was that film could stimulate political and social change. These ideals relate clearly to the Marxist belief that the system can be collectively changed from within.

Reflect and respond

1   How influential do you think the ideas of this radical group of Latin American filmmakers are?
2   How important is politics to filmmaking?
3   Can film aesthetics be political or can politics only form part of the narrative?
4   To what extent do you agree with this group's stance against Hollywood?
5   Would it be possible for Western filmmakers to adopt this revolutionary approach?

Conclusion

Marxism is primarily concerned with politics; this can make its usefulness in analysing film aesthetics appear questionable. However, a key Marxist approach is to examine the hierarchical order within a system. This is significant when exploring the relationship between the film industry and the viewing public. As highlighted above, the relationship between different sectors of society (masses, elites, institutions, government and judiciary) needs to be negotiated in order to achieve cultural consensus.

However, Marxist approaches to film can be restrictive as they tend to oversimplify relationships. In particular, there is an overriding focus on class (due to the legacy of Marx and Engels). Furthermore, people are typically (and to some extent blissfully) unaware that they are being manipulated by both society and the media. It is only when an awareness of this manipulation develops that wider questions can be debated. One of the main limitations of Marxism is that critics often favour narrative content over aesthetic concerns. It can be difficult to apply a Marxist reading to the aesthetics of a text but it is possible, as we have proven in looking at the Latin American filmmakers of the 60s and 70s.

There are often questions concerning the relevance of Marxism in today's global environment although the film industry is evidently still interested in exploiting the masses (financially and ideologically). However, there are some instances where filmmakers are striving to democratize the creative process. Buyacredit.com is the most recent example of an attempt to subvert the traditional financing of a film. Set up by three sixth-form students in the UK, the project is attempting to secure funding for a filmic adaptation of Jules Verne's *Dardentor*. Using social-networking sites such as Facebook and Twitter, the three youths have attracted publicity by selling credits to the general public at a starting fee of £1. This would make each contributor a producer on the film. Although a novel idea which may not come to fruition, it is ideologically rooted in a Marxist ethos. Alternatively, a capitalist take on this venture would expose it as a money-making scheme rather than an opportunity for the masses.

Over time the historical conditions of production change, as has been demonstrated in the Marxist model of the base and superstructure. As we now enter a digital era, the relationship between the creative forces and the consumers has shifted. Filmmaking is no longer completely reliant on studio funding, but instead can be achieved by a lone individual in their bedroom. Sites such as YouTube have democratized exhibition by providing a forum for marginal filmmakers. This could be seen as a strongly Marxist position because the control has been placed in the hands of the producers.

Bibliography

Adorno, T. (1991) *The Culture Industry: Selected Essays on Mass Culture*, London: Routledge.
Adorno, T. and Horkheimer, M. (1995) 'The Culture Industry: Enlightenment as Mass Deception', in *Dialectic of Enlightenment*, London: Verso (original work published 1947).
Althusser, L. (1970) 'Ideology and Ideological State Apparatuses', in *Lenin and Philosophy and Other Essays*, New York: Monthly Review Press.
Althusser, L. (1979) *Reading Capital*, London: Verso (1965).
Bakhtin, M. (1968) *Rabelais and His World*, London: MIT Press.

Chanan, M. (1997) 'The Changing Geography of Third Cinema', *Screen* vol. 38, no. 4, pp.372–88.

Eagleton, T. (1992) *Marxism and Literary Criticism*, London: Routledge.

Espinosa, J. G. (1979) 'For an Imperfect Cinema', in M. T. Martic (ed.) (1997) *New Latin American Cinema: Volume One*, Detroit, MI: Wayne State University Press, pp.71–82.

Gramsci, A. (1976) *Selections from the Prison Notebooks of Antonio Gramsci*, Southampton: Camelot Press Ltd.

Hayward, S. (2006) *Cinema Studies: Key Concepts*, 3rd edn, London: Routledge.

Hebdige, D. (2002) *Subculture: The Meaning of Style*, London: Routledge.

Macherey, P. (1978) *A Theory of Literary Production*, London: Routledge.

Marcuse, H. (1968) *Negations: Essays in Critical Theory*, Harmondsworth: Allen Lane the Penguin Press.

Marcuse, H. (2002) *One-Dimensional Man*, London: Routledge (1964).

Marx, K. (1859) *A Contribution to the Critique of Political Economy*, Moscow: Progress Publishers. Notes by R. Rojas (1977).

Marx, K. (1973). *The Poverty of Philosophy*. Moscow: Progress Publishers (original work published 1847).

Marx, K. and Engels, F. (2002) *The Communist Manifesto*, London: Penguin Classics.

Singer, P. (2000) *Marx: A Very Short Introduction*, Oxford: Oxford University Press.

Solanas, F. and Getino, O. (1969) 'Towards a Third Cinema: Notes and Experiences for the Development of a Cinema of Liberation in the Third World', in M. T. Martic (ed.) (1997) *New Latin American Cinema: Volume One*, Detroit, MI: Wayne State University Press, pp.33–58.

Storey, J. (1998) *Cultural Theory and Popular Culture: An Introduction*, 3rd edn, Harlow: Pearson Education.

Wayne, M. (2001) *Political Film: The Dialectics of Third Cinema*, London: Pluto Books.

Wayne, M. (2003) *Marxism and Media Studies: Key Concepts and Contemporary Trends*, London: Pluto Press.

Chapter

Realism

6

Realism
1. In reference to art, film, and literature: close resemblance to what is real; fidelity of representation, rendering the precise details of the real thing or scene: While realism in art is often used in the same contexts as naturalism, implying a concern with accurate and objective representation, it also suggests a deliberate rejection of conventionally attractive or appropriate subjects in favour of sincerity and a focus on the unidealized treatment of contemporary life. Specifically, the term is applied to a late 19th-century movement in French painting and literature.

Setting the scene

Realism describes a specific historical movement that preoccupied artists who were reacting against the Romantic movement of the late eighteenth and early nineteenth centuries. Their main concern was to attempt to show reality through art. Realism came to the fore in 1850s France in painting; this led to developments in the fields of both literature and theatre. Historically, the arts had focused on depicting gods and mythic tales (Classicism) and externalizing human emotions (Romanticism). Realism was an artistic attempt to re-create images as they appeared in real life or to describe them accurately in literature. These works tended to have contemporary subjects and commonplace themes that the viewer might recognize from looking out of a window onto the world.

In the 1870s in France, naturalism, an idea founded and developed by Émile Zola gained attention. Influenced by Charles Darwin, Zola advocated a 'scientific' approach to literature. He wanted characters who were formed by their social environment, accurately presented in the text through careful and extensive description. Furthermore, the topics were often unpleasant, harsh and pessimistic: poverty, racism, disease, sex and prostitution were dealt with in a frank manner. Naturalism, with its recording of minute detail and its desire to 'tell the whole truth', is often seen as an extreme form of Realism.

Before discussing Realism in film it is useful to think about the term 'realism' itself. Realism is a stylistic choice. It is the decision to use artifice in order to emulate reality. Realism can never be real. A good example is the famous series of paintings by surrealist painter René Magritte (1928–9). In these works he draws very accurate pictures of a pipe (Figure 6.1) and inscribes a title 'Ceci n'est pas une pipe' ('This is not a pipe'). Here Magritte is showing the viewer that the image is not reality but

98

the artist's representation of reality. In a similar manner, we can think of filmmakers as presenting the reality that they want us to accept.

This image raises questions concerning verisimilitude. Verisimilitude is a term adopted in Film Studies to mean 'the appearance of being true or real; likeness or resemblance to truth, reality, or fact' (OED online). It may help to think of the words 'very similar' as an explanation whenever you come across the term. For example, period dramas often provoke debates regarding verisimilitude. The authenticity of costume and props is often questioned. Furthermore, all films, even fictional narratives, have some elements of realistic representation (characters, location, etc.). Verisimilitude is one component in Realist debates, but in tracing the origins of Realism back to film we must look at the photographic work of Eadweard Muybridge.

Figure 6.1   René Magritte, *Ceci n'est pas une pipe* (1929)

Early experimentation

Eadweard Muybridge was one of the first people to experiment with still images and it was these experiments that enabled film to develop as a form of entertainment. In 1877, Muybridge entered into a bet to prove that when galloping, a horse lifts all four hooves off the ground simultaneously. He set about proving his point by lining up a series of cameras to capture the galloping motion on film. Whereas Muybridge was interested in freezing movement, his photographic experiments inspired pioneers to try and recreate action from still images. All early films in existence demonstrate a preoccupation with capturing real-life movement.

The first cinematic exhibition of real events occurred in the 1890s when the Lumière brothers showed *La Sortie des Usines Lumière/ Workers Leaving the Factory* (1895) and *L'Arrivée d'un Train à la Ciotat/Arrival of a Train at a Station* (1897). Although these films were silent, the realistic nature of the image of a train coming towards the audience caused many viewers to panic and flee the screening hall. These very short films made by the Lumière brothers were known as *actualités* as they documented actual events. It was not until Georges Méliès began making films that storytelling and artifice took centre stage. However, attempts to document real life became a strand of filmmaking in their own right.

Documentary tradition

When we think of Realism in film, the tradition of documentary filmmaking often springs to mind. Documentary originates from the French word *documentaire*, meaning a travelogue or illustrated lecture. However, the term 'documentary' was first coined by John Grierson in 1926 and is synonymous with the recording of facts and evidence. It is important that this filmic form is acknowledged as a construct. In the way that fictional film narrative is created through conscious choices in editing, lighting and content etc., documentary filmmaking is similarly assembled. The aesthetics and narrative trajectory may create a sense of the real, but are nevertheless fabricated.

Bill Nichols

Modes of documentary (2001)

Bill Nichols is a renowned academic working at the forefront of documentary studies. From his work he has identified six generic modes. These categories function as tools to assess Realism in documentaries, a form of filmmaking that is often considered to represent indisputable facts. The chart below summarizes his ideas.

Mode	Description
Poetic	Influenced by lyrical avant-garde filmmaking of the 20s. Disregard for continuity editing and temporal/spatial relations. Mood and tone (aesthetics) rather than knowledge and persuasion (information). Lack of psychologically developed characters. Strongly subjective (pp.102–3). Examples: *Koyaanisqatsi: Life out of Balance* (Godfrey Reggio, 1982) and *Powaqqatsi: Life in Transformation* (Godfrey Reggio, 1988).
Expository	Based on rhetoric and argument. Viewer is directly addressed. Expository documentaries often adopt a 'voice-of-god' perspective where the information is relayed to the audience (voice-over or titles). Constructs a forceful argument in need of a solution (pp.105–7). Examples: *Why We Fight* series (Frank Capra, 1943–4). Most news broadcasting takes this form.
Observational	Emerged through changes in technology (lightweight cameras). Camera follows the action, often resulting in shaky, amateur-style footage. Unobtrusive and non-interventionist as the filmmaker is regarded as a neutral observer (pp.109–15). Example: *The Last Waltz* (Martin Scorsese, 1978).
Participatory	Direct engagement between the filmmaker and subjects; this often takes the form of questions and interviews. The filmmaker becomes actively involved in the documentary as they instigate the action (pp.115–23). Examples: *Bowling for Columbine* (Michael Moore, 2002), *Living with Michael Jackson* (Julie Shaw/Martin Bashir, 2003).
Reflexive	This form of documentary aims to make the audience aware of the artifice of such filmmaking. It draws attention to editing, narrative construction, audience manipulation, etc. It challenges questions of Realism and truthfulness which are often associated with documentary (pp.125–30). Example: *Man with a Movie Camera* (Dziga Vertov, 1929).

Mode	Description
Performative	Personal, emotional and subjective concerns are the major traits found in performative documentary. It is often used as a vehicle for the marginalized (ethnic minorities, women, gays and lesbians). This personal approach is often used to explore wider sociohistorical issues (pp.130–7).
	Example: *Paris Is Burning* (Jennie Livingston, 1990) and *Tongues Untied* (Marlon Riggs, 1990).

Whenever studying documentary films it is important to question the information that is being imparted. You need to approach the genre with a level of caution and scepticism. We are conditioned to assume that documentaries are objective and free from bias whereas in reality this is frequently not the case. These films are produced via a process of selection and rejection of available material and are compiled to conform to a director's agenda.

Reflect and respond

1   Can you name any documentary films? How many of these were made before the year 2000?
2   Can you account for the rise in popularity of the documentary film in recent times?
3   Of the documentaries that you can name, which of Nichols's categories do they fall into?
4   Documentaries are often made to challenge public opinion. Can you think of any that you have seen that have influenced your ideas?
5   Can ideas of 'truth', 'objectivity', observation' and 'neutrality' be applied to documentary?

Realist filmmaking

As filmmaking became better established, key movements developed, with the underlying ethos of creating credible portrayals of daily life. Technological advances enabled filmmakers from different countries to achieve the appearance of Realism at different times. The national movements outlined below share many common traits, which include:

* location shooting
* naturalistic lighting
* long takes
* handheld cameras
* unscripted dialogue
* documentary influence
* focus on the working class
* a political agenda.

Below are three examples of national filmmaking movements that attempted to capture real-life experiences.

Poetic Realism

Poetic Realism describes the type of filmmaking that took place in France during the 30s. Famous directors emerging from this era include Jean Renoir, Marcel Carné and Julien Duvivier. Poetic Realists were influenced by naturalistic literature, in particular the writings of Émile Zola. However, it was not a visually recognizable movement like Soviet montage or German Expressionism; instead it consisted of a small group of filmmakers whose work displayed similar characteristics and themes. Poetic Realist films, rather than focusing on the bourgeoisie, tended to create stories about the masses and politicized the hard realities they faced. Jean Gabin was typically cast as the common man in many films of this period. Gabin became an iconic figure who epitomized the working-class Frenchman.

There were two distinct periods in French Poetic Realism: the Popular Front Period (1935–7) and the National Front Period (1937–40). The first period was informed by left-wing ideology. It was an optimistic era of filmmaking that depicted a bright future. However, in 1937 the liberals were overthrown in favour of a right-wing government, with power returning to the middle classes. The effect on filmmaking was an overbearing sense of pessimism as the shadow of fascism began to intrude.

Jean Renoir was the most noteworthy director associated with French Poetic Realism. He was the son of the famous Impressionist painter Auguste Renoir and in fact sold many of his father's paintings in order to finance his films. Although a narrative filmmaker and actor, he was interested in documentary films; accordingly his filmic style was rooted in a realistic aesthetic.

Renoir is often cited as the pioneering force behind the 'long take' (Bordwell and Thompson, 2003, p.292), because he believed that the camera should not manipulate the audience. The audience should be able to navigate their way around the frame rather than being visually led. This resulted in a filmic style that was reliant on framing, reframing, panning and tracking rather than editing. Aesthetically, Renoir wanted the camera to imitate the flow and motion of the human eye.

A further technique engaged by the French director was 'deep-focus photography'. Once more the camera reproduces the action of the human eye, with both the foreground and the background in focus. Figure 6.2, taken from the film *Partie de Campagne/A Day in the Country* (1936), shows two men inside a café watching women playing on some nearby swings outside. Here the depth of field is apparent as the audience can see action

Figure 6.2   *A Day in the Country* (Jean Renoir, 1936)

occurring clearly in both the foreground and background. This style of filming was revolution-ary, as technically it was difficult to ensure that subjects near and far from the camera remained in focus.

André Bazin identified the aesthetic impact of this style of filming. He observed that:

1   'Depth of field' is similar to the way we experience the real world. This device imitates our way of seeing (we decide what to focus on as we look around). Accordingly its 'structure is more realistic'.

2   With the long take the viewer has to be more active in deciphering information. This participation makes the experience more enjoyable as the audience is free to look anywhere within the frame.

3   'Montage rules out ambiguity'. The viewer's perspective is guided and there is no choice. Whereas '[d]epth of focus reintroduces ambiguity' as the audience must decide what to focus on. (1967, p.35–6)

When the Nazis came to power, Renoir fled to Hollywood. Here he worked on a number of films that failed to achieve the same critical acclaim as his European films. However, his stylis-tic approach inspired a number of directors and practitioners. His influence is seen most clearly in the work of Gregg Toland and Orson Welles. For example, their collaboration on the classic film *Citizen Kane*, is renowned for its deep-focus photography. In the image below (Figure 6.3), the young character of Kane can be seen through an open window as his mother signs over his guardianship to Thatcher. The use of deep focus makes the scene far more moving.

In addition to the influence of Poetic Realism in America, Renoir's work went on to inspire a new generation of filmmakers in France. The French New Wave directors were advocates of Renoir's attempt to create verisimilitude. However, they experimented with Realist forms in order to challenge spectators and make them aware of their position as viewers. For example, in Jean-Luc Godard's *Week End* (1967) there is a long take which lasts for around eight minutes. The scene is of a traffic jam and, poignantly as the single shot persists, the audience becomes frustrated, an emotion occuring in real life when trapped in the same situation. The technique of using long single takes was employed in one of the earliest French New Wave films *Les Quatre Cents Coups/400 Blows*. At the conclusion of the narrative, the camera tracks the young protag-onist as he runs and runs and runs.

Further viewing

*   *La Grande Illusion/The Grand Illusion*
*   *Pépé le Moko* (Julien Duvivier, 1937)
*   *Le Bête Humaine/The Human Beast*
*   *La Règle du Jeu/ The Rules of the Game*
*   *Les Enfants du Paradis/Children of Paradise* (Marcel Carné, 1945)

Figure 6.3   *Citizen Kane* (Orson Welles, 1941)

Neo-realism

Neo-realism was a label given by critics to a group of Italian filmmakers after World War II, during the years 1945–52. Vittorio De Sica, Roberto Rossellini, Luchino Visconti and Cesare Zavattini were the major figures in promoting this style of filmmaking and were strongly influenced by Poetic Realism. One of its main characteristics was that it centred on social and historical events and had political leanings. Italian Neo-realists sought a cinematographic language to deal aesthetically with the problems of war, partisan struggle, unemployment, poverty and social injustice. Their stylistic approach included on-location shooting, the use of non-professional actors, documentary effects (grainy film stock), handheld cameras and sequences with little or no editing. Although these filmmakers were renowned for their Realist tendencies, on further examination such verisimilitude can be questioned as these 'natural' sets were carefully contrived in a manner designed to highlight social issues.

The documentary quality of these films was an important feature. For example, in *Paisà/Paisan* (1946), Rossellini introduced each episode with an authoritative voice-over. He carefully mixed 'fact' and 'fiction' with actual newsreel footage, combined with grainy film stock and scripted narrative, to produce a seamless slice-of-life experience. The visual effects created by the quality of lighting and camera angles would reinforce the feeling of authenticity that viewers would expect from a newsreel of the 40s. Although Rossellini used non-professional actors in *Paisà*, they were supplemented with a handful of professional actors in crucial roles. For example, in the first Sicilian sequence the young Italian girl playing Carmela (Carmela Sazio) was discovered in her village by Rossellini, while Joe (Robert Van Loon), her American counterpart was a real GI. Allowing Germans, Italians and Americans to speak their own language heightened the authenticity of the dialogue. Furthermore, the apparently unscripted dialogue had in fact been worked on for months to seem natural and spontaneous.

The Neo-realists aimed to expose the harsh realities suffered by ordinary people and in particular women and children. The location shooting showed the post-war devastation that Italy was experiencing. Bombed-out tenement buildings documented day-to-day life as seen in the film *Roma Città Aperta/Rome Open City* (Roberto Rossellini, 1945). This documentary style made audiences think about and question the devastation of war. However, in many of these films, running counter to the Realist tendencies was the reliance on devices of melodrama such as the identification with central characters. The critic André Bazin famously noted, 'realism in art can only be achieved in one way – through artifice' (1971, p.26). So in spite of the use of some specific devices (professional actors, scripted dialogue, melodrama) a level of Realism is maintained which was unheard of in filmmaking at this time (grainy film stock and a conscious attempt to emulate newsreel footage, wartorn location shooting and members of the general public cast in roles).

Further viewing

- *Ladri di Biciclette/Bicycle Thieves* (Vittorio De Sica, 1948)
- *Germania Anno Zero/Germany Year Zero* (Roberto Rossellini, 1948)
- *La Terra Trema/The Earth Trembles* (Luchino Visconti, 1948)
- *Bellissima/Beautiful* (Luchino Visconti, 1951)
- *Umberto D* (Vittorio De Sica, 1952).

British Realist traditions

Realism in British filmmaking has had several reincarnations:

- 1940s wartime Realism
- 1950s–1960s New Wave
- 1980s Social Realism.

Britain has gained international importance for a film culture which focuses on social issues.

The forerunner and strong influence on British Social Realist films was the work by the documentary filmmaker John Grierson. Grierson's work emerged most strongly in the 30s. He stated that documentary should be the 'the creative interpretation of actuality' (Ellis and McLane, 2006, p.70). However, Paul Rotha noted that early British filmmaking lacked a sense of nationality. He believed that productions attempted to copy either the American or German stylistic models (1999, p.195).

As Britain moved towards war with Germany, government intervention in the film industry became more evident. The Ministry of Information (MOI) recognized the propaganda potential in films and accordingly invested and intervened in many productions.

1940s wartime Realism

After the outbreak of World War II, Realism became an instrument of propaganda. The MOI became heavily involved in approving scripts; especially those that emphasized British people united in a common cause. Films such as *Millions Like Us* (Sidney Launder and Frank Gilliat, 1943) combined documentary Realism with feature-film conventions. It starts with a montage sequence and voice-over that replicate newsreels of the time. These documentary scenes show wartime life with blackouts, air raids, troop manoeuvres, fortified beaches and the evacuation of children. In this and many similar films women are centre stage to encourage their participation in the war effort. They are seen undertaking male work in factories, which contrasts markedly with the usual preoccupation in Realist filmmaking with the white, working-class male. However, by the mid-40s the excessive use of factual footage and the heavily didactic government information inserted into the dialogue caused these films to lose popularity with audiences.

Further viewing

- *Target for Tonight* (Harry Watt, 1941)
- *Went the Day Well* (Alberto Cavalcanti, 1942).

After the war and into the mid-50s the Realist approach dwindled, with audiences favouring instead technicolour and escapist features such as those produced by Powell and Pressburger.

British New Wave (1959–63)

The products of British New Wave Cinema were also known as 'kitchen-sink' dramas and 'Angry Young Men' films. This movement is often thought of as a continuation of Free Cinema. The term

'Free Cinema' relates to a four-year project set up by Lindsay Anderson, Tony Richardson and Karel Reisz. Their films were produced using the following ideology: free from box-office pressures, free to choose their themes and free to develop filmmaking away from the mainstream commercial cinema.

Critics dubbed these films 'New Wave' due to the perceived similarities in the work of directors such as Anderson, Richardson, Reisz, Jack Clayton and John Schlesinger. Shot in black and white, with handheld cameras, their aesthetics arose partly from a lack of money, available technology and a desire to engage with 'real' Britain. Rather than the usual middle-class characters from London and the south, these directors wanted to present the northern working class. Emphasis was placed on regional accents as opposed to the Received Pronunciation (Queen's English/BBC English) prevalent in most films of this period. The narratives aimed to simulate the working-class experience instead of inserting workers for comic effect or as 'salt-of-the-earth' supporting caricatures.

Themes such as alcohol, sex, sport, abortion, prostitution, homosexuality, anger, depression, alienation, money and poverty were realistically portrayed in order to illustrate working-class communities breaking free from social conventions. This was new ground depicting England's angry, alienated youth in fresh and frank terms. Characters were typically factory workers, office juniors, dissatisfied wives, pregnant girlfriends and runaways. Moreover, a strong misogynistic element featured in these films as a backlash against women who had entered the male realm of work during the war .

Further viewing

- *Look Back in Anger* (Tony Richardson, 1959)
- *Room at the Top* (Jack Clayton, 1959)
- *Saturday Night and Sunday Morning* (Karel Reisz, 1960)
- *A Taste of Honey* (Tony Richardson, 1961)
- *A Kind of Loving* (John Schlesinger, 1962)
- *The Loneliness of the Long Distance Runner* (Tony Richardson, 1962)
- *This Sporting Life* (Lindsay Anderson, 1963).

The 70s saw a very troubled economic climate and a difficult time for British cinema as American finance for films ceased at the end of the 60s and their UK studios closed.

1980s onwards

It was not until the 80s and Margaret Thatcher's government that Social Realism experienced a revival. Thatcherism reduced state support for the arts. Channel 4 started in 1982 with the goal of appealing to minority groups. Accordingly, it commissioned works from independent production companies, resulting in a series of low- to medium-budget films between 1981 and 1990. Ken Loach and Mike Leigh are two notable directors from this time.

Loach came to public attention with his television dramas such as *Cathy Come Home* (1966). Throughout his career he has developed a certain naturalistic style and thematic traits, which make his films identifiable. He cast unknown actors, for example, in *Riff-Raff* (1991), set in the building industry, he found actors who had worked on building sites and for *Kes* (1969), he chose local children off the street to star in his film. Alongside the typical aesthetics expected of Realism, Loach's themes of social problems are explored in an overtly political style. He features soap-box speeches examining moral perspectives but offering no solutions (open-ended narratives).

Mike Leigh trained in the theatre and was influenced by the work of Samuel Beckett and Harold Pinter. Unlike Loach, Leigh has no overt political agenda. Instead he focuses on the impact that intimate relationships have on individuals. He is known for his unscripted/workshop-style rehearsal periods. His themes are presented in a tragi-comic world, a mingling of bleakness and humour developed in a claustrophobic manner. His films concentrate on embarrassing dynamics, which are often excruciating to sit through.

Ken Loach and Mike Leigh have inspired a new generation of directors who have continued in a similar vein. Shane Meadows is probably the most well known of these. However, there is one important distinction. Loach and Leigh, like the directors of the British New Wave, are middle class yet their films demonstrate a preoccupation with the working class as subjects. In contrast, Shane Meadows grew up on a council estate and therefore belongs to the community that features in his work. Geoffrey Macnab argues, that Meadows's observations are 'made from the perspective of a native insider rather than a sympathetic visitor' (1998, pp.14–16).

Meadows began his career making shorts and, along with a group of likeminded individuals, established a successful international video festival. His themes encompass the white working class, underclass, national identity, racism, xenophobia, patriotism, violence and comradeship. He favours a young and inexperienced cast. Music is important and is selected to reflect the urban location and youthful characterization of the films.

Unlike French Poetic Realism and Italian Neo-realism, the British Social Realist tradition is on-going. Samantha Lay speculates that as Britain becomes more and more multicultural, the term 'British' will come to encompass many different groups. Furthermore, she complicates the issue by asking in this 'post-devolution climate, will we be speaking of Welsh social realism, or Scottish social realism respectively?' (2002, p.121). This may provide a rich future for Realist debates.

Reflect and respond

1   Can Realist films help us understand society?
2   What are the problems with treating these films as 'historic' evidence?
3   Has the increasing trend to market these films with reference to specific directors (filmmaker as author), helped or hindered their promotion in the international market?
4   Do the images presented in these Social Realist films depict a biased portrait?

Method Acting

The term Method Acting describes a specific approach to performing a role. The idea originated from the teaching of Lee Strasberg, director of the Actors Studio in New York. Drawing from the work of Constantin Stanislavski, he developed an acting style informed by an individual's psychological connection with a particular role. In order to create believable/realistic portrayals, actors must unlock appropriate emotions from their own lives. Strasberg encouraged actors to recall tragic incidents and moments of ecstasy and grief. They would then remember how they felt and apply it to their characters on stage or on screen.

Method Acting was considered revolutionary as it signalled a move away from the traditional histrionic approach to acting. Histrionic acting involved actors externalizing their feelings through facial contortions and vocal intonation. This style of acting originated in the theatre, where large gesticulations were encouraged so that people at the back of the auditorium could see emotional gestures clearly on stage. Method Acting, on the other hand, was concerned with internalizing emotion. This psychological approach was deemed more realistic than the over-the-top theatrical performances of old.

Famous students who attended classes at the Actors Studio include Dustin Hoffman, Paul Newman, Marilyn Monroe, James Dean, Marlon Brando and Al Pacino. Sometimes Method Actors are criticized for taking their roles too seriously. There is a much-cited incident, of which there are two versions, alleged to have taken place on the set of *Marathon Man* (John Schlesinger, 1976). Dustin Hoffman supposedly stayed up for three nights in order to emulate the character he was playing and/or ran half a mile so as to be out of breath in a particular scene. Laurence Olivier, his co-star, asked him to account for his bizarre behaviour. Hoffman explained that he was attempting to embody the role he was playing. Olivier famously replied 'Try acting, dear boy.' Although this incident may be apocryphal, it illustrates the two schools of thought in preparing for a role.

Reflect and respond

1   Can you think of any modern-day anecdotes regarding Method Acting?
2   Do you believe that Method Acting is more successful in achieving a realistic performance?
3   Can you foresee any problems arising from Method Acting?
4   Which style of acting is most relevant today?

Temporal Realism

One of the challenges for early cinematic pioneers was to show the passing of time on screen. This was achieved through the use of various devices that drew attention to the artificial nature of film. However, technological advances have enabled directors to overcome this restriction and the 2000s have witnessed a number of films that have opted for real-time scenarios. This can be achieved by real-time narratives and/or real-time filmmaking.

- **Real-time narratives**: This means that the events of the film occur in the same time it takes the audience to watch them. *Phone Booth* (Joel Schumacher, 2002), *Timecode* (Mike Figgis, 2000) and the television series *24* (various, 2001–11) all follow this trend. Interestingly, all three examples, employ a splitscreen technique to tell their stories. This is similar to the deep-focus photography favoured by the Poetic Realists as the audience is left to navigate its own way through the events without guidance.
- **Real-time filmmaking**: The idea of incorporating real time into filming was taken to extremes by the Russian director Aleksandr Sokurov in the film *Russian Ark* (2002). The film is comprised of a single take. Filmed at the Hermitage Museum in St Petersburg with a cast of

2,000, *Russian Ark* was shot in real time on a Steadicam. It represents a landmark in the history of cinema, as a feature film running for ninety-six minutes with no edits.

Numerous other films have played with temporal continuity. For example, the film *Caché/Hidden* (Michael Haneke, 2005) starts with an image that we presume is an establishing shot. It is a single take of the outside of a house. As the take continues the viewer loses interest due to the length of the shot. However, they are soon shocked as the image suddenly freezes and rewinds. What they thought was a lengthy opening shot turns out to be a video being watched by the protagonists. Here reality becomes unstable, with the audience wrong-footed and accordingly ill at ease from the very onset of the film.

Experimenting with time in film can result in interesting ways of telling stories that go against the formulaic approach. The experimental methods taken by the directors mentioned were instigated in order to make the audience question notions of reality and perception. These ideas were considered much earlier by the German scholar Walter Benjamin.

Walter Benjamin

'The Work of Art in the Age of Mechanical Reproduction' (1936)

Walter Benjamin's seminal essay discusses how technological developments affect the arts. Art has always been manually reproduced through the available techniques of the time. For example, the Greeks replicated coins and the Victorians reproduced images through the means of lithography (printing using ink). These examples required manual involvement. However, with the development of the camera and photography, the process of creating images became more immediate; 'a film operator shooting a scene in the studio captures the images at the speed of an actor's speech' (Braudy and Cohen, 2004, p.792).

For Benjamin the development of mechanical reproduction had profound repercussions on how we view and understand art. He argues that original works of art contain an 'aura'; this means that the original retains a certain special significance that cannot be replicated during the copying process. Consider Leonardo da Vinci's famous masterpiece the *Mona Lisa*, a celebrated image that has been prolifically reproduced on t-shirts, pencil cases, posters, umbrellas, mugs, etc. According to Benjamin these imitations have been stripped of the aura found in the original: 'the masses seek distraction whereas as art demands concentration from the spectator' (p.808). To experience the essence of da Vinci's work you would need to visit the Louvre in Paris. The 'aura' that is integral to Benjamin's argument is connected to the idea of ritual; we seek out iconic images in museums and places of worship. Once taken out of this ceremonial context the work of art is devalued.

However, at the heart of Benjamin's thesis is a paradox. As a Marxist he endorsed the idea of wider participation, believing that the masses should have access to works of art. Yet in enabling this level of interaction the aura of the object is inevitably lost. In relating his ideas to film, he explores the role of the actor. In the theatre, players have one chance to deliver their lines. When performing to the camera, film actors are permitted multiple takes, which problematizes the idea of originality. Actors in a theatre can react with the audience to produce an 'original' performance because they are physically present. The film actor, on the other hand, loses the aura of authenticity, as the performance seen by the viewer is recorded rather than live. Benjamin's views are becoming more important as we embrace the field of digital technology and this in turn impacts on ideas of Realism.

Reflect and respond

1   Discuss Benjamin's ideas concerning 'aura' and ritual in relation to the opening night of a film.
2   Do you agree with the premise that when an image is over-reproduced it becomes devalued?
3   Can a film actor produce an original performance or does technology hinder its authenticity?
4   Are Benjamin's ideas still relevant?

Digital Realism

Digital methods have been adopted by many filmmakers in the last decade and this has fuelled debates about Realism. Previously, the industry utilized 16mm or 35mm film stock as standard, which always entailed a level of deterioration when the prints were copied. Digital video, on the other hand, can be reproduced without much depreciation in quality. This means that the image captured retains its clarity and therefore is more realistic.

It is still impossible to anticipate all the new developments that may arise with the advent of digital technologies. Neither can we predict the effects such progress will have on the way we interpret film. Stephen Prince began tackling this issue back in 1996.

Stephen Prince

'True Lies: Perceptual Realism, Digital Images and Film Theory' (1996)

Writing in *Film Quarterly*, Stephen Prince was one of the first academics to broach the question of how digital filmmaking would impact on film theory. He states that:

> The rapid nature of these changes is creating problems for film theory. Because the digital manipulation of images is so novel and the creative possibilities it offers are so unprecedented, its effects on cinematic representation and the viewer's response are poorly understood. Film theory has not yet come to terms with these issues. (p.27)

Prince identifies two broad categories of digital filming adopted by the industry.

1   Digital-image processing: this is when computer software is engaged to digitally remove or enhance items within the frame. For example, many stunts use wires and other machinery to achieve effects and this apparatus can be digitally removed from the scene in post-production.

2 CGI: Computer-generated images are produced using software to make drawings, models and landscapes appear as if in 3D. The latest technologies enable filmmakers to apply various devices (e.g. motion capture) to bring fantasy characters to life such as Gollum in *The Lord of the Rings* trilogy. Similarly, apocalyptic events can be simulated that cannot be filmed in real life, for example, the landscape that features in *I Am Legend* (Francis Lawrence, 2007) and *Cloverfield* (Matt Reeves, 2008). This kind of backdrop is achieved through the use of blue and/or green screens, with actors performing in a studio. Their performances are then super-imposed on the desired location in post-production.

One problem identified by Prince is that we often discuss these levels of digital trickery in relation to the term Realism. Here he refers to the work of Charles Peirce and Roland Barthes. Peirce explained that photographs have an indexical relationship with the referent: the photographic image should physically represent the subject. Although cinema's origins lie in photography, digital imaging challenges the notion of the indexical relationship between camera and subject. This is because reality can be manipulated, for example in the way that beings/animals that do not exist in reality can be brought to life in a seemingly realistic setting. Digital images are not restricted by the laws of physical photographs because they can be stretched and contorted to such degrees that they lose all relation to the original subject. However, some forms of manipulation are so subtle that they can pass unnoticed; for example, the digital process can illuminate scenes in ways that could never be achieved with standard lighting.

Bearing in mind the possibilities outlined above, Prince asks the question:

[If] digital-imaging possesses a flexibility that frees it from its referent [d]oes this mean, then, that digital-imaging capabilities ought not [to] be grouped under the rubric of a realist film theory? If not, what are the alternatives? What kind of realism, if any, do these images possess? (p.30)

Here he calls for a new attitude when reading films. Rather than dismissing production as non-realist, he explains that we should look at how the image corresponds to our own 'three-dimensional world'. Does the subject move in a realistic fashion? Does the hair blow as if being ruffled by the wind etc.? Prince calls this approach 'perceptual realism' (p.32) in that it enables filmmakers to apply realistic attributes to unreal subjects via 3D cues (light, space and movement).

Perceptual Realism is difficult to achieve as '[m]ultiple levels of information capture must be successfully executed to convincingly animate and render living movement because the viewer's eye is adept at perceiving inaccurate information' (p.35). As technology advances the audience demands an extra level of Realism despite the fact that movies are a form of fiction. These aspects raised by Prince highlight the need to readdress the debates surrounding Realism in order for theory to bring itself in line with industrial practices.

High Definition and 3D technologies

It is somewhat ironic that in this day and age of airbrushed celebrities, the industry is moving towards 'High Definition' (HD), a technology involving a higher resolution of pixels. Whereas magazines and advertising agencies 'photoshop' images to produce flawless film stars, television presenters shot in HD are seen to have blemished skin and other imperfections. Here we see how technology is pushing barriers at both ends of the spectrum, with heavily manipulated false representation on the one hand and genuine 'warts-and-all' depictions on the other.

More recently, the industry has seen an increase in the production of three-dimensional films (3D). Through stereoscopic photography and customized glasses, the audience experiences the narrative from an enhanced perspective. This perspective gives an illusion of depth, and could thus be considered more realistic. Yet it is important to note that this is another layer of artificiality attempting to replicate a sense of the real.

Although the technology for 3D filmmaking has been in existence since the 1890s it did not become a commercial possibility until the 50s. It gained further attention in the 80s, but it was not until the year 2009 with the release of *Avatar* that the 3D cinematic experience became a real option. How this technology will add to Realist debates is yet to be seen as the industry's usage is still in its infancy.

Reflect and respond

1 Discuss how computer-generated images have progressed in your lifetime.
2 In what ways have digital filmmaking enhanced or problematized debates concerning Realism.
3 Do you think Realism is important in fictional stories?
4 Consider the economic issues relating to digital filmmaking. Do these help or hinder the amateur filmmaker attempting to break into the industry?
5 In your experience, do you think 3D films are more realistic?
6 To what extent does 3D filmmaking lend itself to fantasy narratives as opposed to real-life stories?
7 How do you think 3D filmmaking will add to or complicate theories on Realism?

Case study: Dogme 95

The Dogme 95 movement emerged as a collaborative project between the two Danish directors, Lars von Trier and Thomas Vinterberg. Together the filmmakers listed all the things they hated about commercial cinema and then considered how they could counter the formulaic artifice associated with Hollywood. As a result, they came up with a set of rules known as the 'Vow of Chastity', which, if followed, would engender a new cinematic aesthetic. Von Trier and Vinterberg were soon joined by fellow Danish directors Kristian Levring and Soren Kragh-Jacobsen. Collectively, the group became known as the brotherhood and its aim was to revolutionize the industry, calling for a new avant-garde. This ideology was encapsulated in a manifesto, which ironically borrowed terminology from Truffaut's seminal 1954 text 'Une Certaine Tendance du Cinéma Français'. However, the intention was to highlight the fact that the revolutionary stance initiated by the French New Wave 'proved to be a ripple that washed ashore and turned to muck' (Dogme Manifesto, 1995). In summary, the intention of the Scandinavian group was to erase the cosmetic effects that proliferate in commercial filmmaking. Its members felt it to be their duty to encourage artists to strip film production back to its basics.

The 'Vow of Chastity'

Below is the set of ten restrictive rules known as the 'Vow of Chastity'. Each rule was proposed in order to purge filmmaking of its high production values and formulaic storytelling.

1   **Shooting must be done on location:** In specifying that filming must take place on location, the brotherhood tried to move away from the artifice of studio sets. Instead action should take place in a genuine environment. If props are needed then a location where such props are readily available should be sourced.
2   **Sound must not be produced apart from images:** Whereas many films accompany scenes of heightened emotion with a non-diegetic score and computer-generated sound effects, this rule stipulates that any sound occurring in a Dogme production must be captured during the shoot.
3   **The camera must be handheld:** Handheld cameras often result in images that have a documentary quality. Footage often appears shaky and somewhat amateur, which adds to the sense of Realism.
4   **Film must be in colour – special lighting is not permitted:** This rule was put in place to counter the black-and-white filmmaking often associated with art-house cinema (bourgeoisie). To represent the world accurately, colour must be used. This rule also inhibits filmmakers from trying to emulate earlier cinematic styles.
5   **Optical work and filters are forbidden:** Here the brotherhood was ensuring that filmmaking techniques remain simple and that footage captured is not manipulated during or postproduction.
6   **The film must not contain any superficial action:** Characters cannot die in Dogme films unless they actually die in real life; Dogme blood is real blood and only occurs if actors are injured on set. This means that the narrative avoids formulaic traits such as murder. Similarly, scenes of a sexual nature are actually played out in front of the camera. This represents an extreme approach to Realism.
7   **Temporal and geographical alienation are forbidden:** This rule guarantees that Dogme films are contemporary stories dealing with current issues as films cannot be set in the past or future. Additionally, the location chosen for filming must be where the story is set so that you could not write a script about the American West unless you physically filmed the production in that geographic locale.
8   **Genre movies are not acceptable:** This directive was designed to counter the formulaic nature of the film industry. Dogme films cannot be Westerns, Police dramas, Musicals or Romantic Comedies, etc.
9   **The film format must be Academy 35mm:** Of all the rules this is probably the most problematic as it negates the 'democratization of cinema' (Dogme Manifesto, 1995). Whereas

most of the regulations enable amateur filmmakers to participate in the Dogme movement, this rule is restrictive. Shooting on 35mm or transferring film into this format is an expensive procedure. However, the reasoning behind the rule was to pay homage to the early cinematic pioneers such as the Lumière brothers, Georges Méliès and Thomas Edison.

10 **The director must not be credited:** Acknowledging that film is a collaborative process was a key concern of the movement. Dogme members felt that the industry placed too much emphasis on the director of a production. Ironically, it was the Dogme films *The Idiots* (1998) and *Festen* (1998) that made von Trier and Vinterberg household names.

The Vow of Chastity, in looking to strip cinema back to its basics, exposes the artificial nature of cinematic storytelling. The brotherhood demanded that Dogme filmmaking should not include any superficial action (murder, traffic accidents, explosions, etc.). Whereas the examples cited act as typical plot devices in commercial filmmaking, Dogme called for a new approach, with the narrative only able to feature events that could be recreated live in front of the camera. Consequently, blood and violence in a Dogme film carry greater weight and impact. For example, at the conclusion of *The Idiots* when Karen's (Bodil Jørgensen) head is seen to be bleeding and in *Festen* when the brothers physically fight, this is not simulated blood and violence; it is real.

Additionally, the brotherhood dictates that manipulation and/or corrective procedures cannot be undertaken during post-production. They also disapprove of lighting setups. Therefore the visual appearance of Dogme films does not conform to commercial expectations; scenes are often underlit or overexposed. This enlightens the viewer as to the usual practice of extensive lighting setups and the doctoring of footage after it has been captured. Where scenes in mainstream cinema appear slickly produced, the Vow of Chastity ensures that much of the footage, shot within the stipulated restrictions, retains an amateur feel. Yet it could be argued that the aesthetic style achieved lends itself to realism because the footage captured during the live shoot is the same footage we see on screen. Ironically, we do not necessarily perceive Dogme stylistics as verisimilitude as we have become conditioned to the manipulated form that is presented by Hollywood.

Initially the movement was ridiculed by the industry as a joke, yet soon filmmakers began to experiment with the rules. Poignantly, in attempting to rid cinema of its customary genres, Dogme films began to develop stylistic signatures. In abiding by the rules, directors consistently told stories about damaged people and these bore aesthetic similarities due to the prescribed restrictions. Therefore, despite the original intentions of the brotherhood, Dogme has come close to becoming a genre in its own right.

Reflect and respond

1 To what extent does the 'Vow of Chastity' enhance or restrict filmmaking?
2 What are the ethical and moral implications of making a Dogme film?
3 Do you think imposing aesthetic parameters is an intellectual exercise or an innovative artistic approach?
4 Can you think of other Realist directors who adopt such extreme methods?

Conclusion

Realism tends to be a preoccupation in European cinema. That is not to say that American film-makers do not venture into this area. However, Realist filmmakers tend to consciously move away from American commercial filmmaking that is typically reliant on spectacle and high production values. Furthermore, Realist narratives tend to veer towards more politicized content, which does not necessarily translate into success at the box office.

Ideas of Realism evolve and develop over time as the sociopolitical climate changes. However, these narratives still tend to focus on the poor, disenfranchised and victimized, with Realist films championing the underdog while pointing the finger at the establishment and the bourgeoisie. Nevertheless, as technology advances, the way in which these stories are told similarly progresses. The industry consistently looks to improve our viewing experience with heightened sound and imaging technology. Yet, even with these available technologies, Realism is a stylistic choice because it is created through artificial means. Nevertheless, these innovations impact upon our understanding of Realism in film and ensure that theoretical debates continue.

Bibliography

Bazin, A. (1967) *What Is Cinema?* Vol. 1, Berkeley: University of California Press.

Bazin, A. (1971) *What Is Cinema?* Vol. 2, Berkeley: University of California Press.

Benjamin, W. (1936) 'The Work of Art in the Age of Mechanical Reproduction', in L. Braudy and M. Cohen (eds) (2004) *Film Theory and Criticism: Introductory Readings*, 6th edn, Oxford: Oxford University Press, pp.791–811.

Berthelius, M. and Narbonne, R. (1987) 'A Conversation with Lars von Trier', in J. Lumholdt (ed.) *Lars von Trier Interviews* (2003) Jackson: University of Mississippi Press, pp. 47–58.

Bordwell, D. and Thompson, K. (2003) *Film History: An Introduction*, Boston, MA: McGraw-Hill.

Braudy, L. and Cohen, M. (2004) *Film Theory and Criticism: Introductory Readings*, Oxford and New York: Oxford University Press.

Ellis, J. and McLane, B. (2006) *A New History of Documentary Film*, New York: Continuum International Publishing Group.

Lay, S. (2002) *British Social Realism: From Documentary to Brit Grit*, London and New York: Wallflower Press.

Macnab, G. (1998) 'The Natural', *Sight and Sound*, March, pp.14–16.

Mast, G. and Cohen, M. (eds) (1971) *Film Theory and Criticism*, Oxford: Oxford University Press.

Nichols, B. (2001) *Introduction to Documentary*, Bloomington: Indiana University Press.

Prince, S. (1996) 'True Lies: Perceptual Realism, Digital Images and Film Theory', *Film Quarterly* vol. 49 no. 3, pp.27–37.

Pulver, A. (2009) 'Reel Review: Antichrist: This Is a Film You Can't Afford to Ignore', *Guardian*. Available at http://www.guardian.co.uk/film/video/2009/jul/24/antichrist-von-trier-reel-review.

Rotha, P. (1999) 'The British Film (1930): From (The Film till Now)', in D. Petrie and R. Kruger (eds) *A Paul Rotha Reader*, Exeter: University of Exeter Press.

Truffaut, F. (1954) 'Une Certaine Tendance du Cinéma Français', in J. Hollows, P. Hutchings and M. Jancovich (eds) (2000) *The Film Studies Reader*, London: Arnold.

Postmodernism

The above is a dictionary definition of Postmodernism, yet it is important to remember that Postmodernism is almost impossible to define clearly. Postmodernism is not a unified movement but a site for debate. However, in popular or media terms, its use is often vague and it can stand as an umbrella term encompassing creative production in the arts. It should not be thought of as a distinct period of time but as an aesthetic movement that rejects Modernist ideology. In order to understand Postmodernism it is necessary to have some understanding of the key traits of Modernism.

Modernism

Peter Barry (1985) explains that Modernism was concerned with challenging and disregarding the 'fundamental elements' that customarily appeared in established artistic forms (pp.81–2). See table below.

Discipline	Rejected	Embraced
Music	Melody Harmony	Impressionism (Debussy) Atonality (Stravinsky) Minimalism (Satie)
Art	Perspective Realist representation	Cubism (Picasso) Surrealism (Dali) Dadaism (Duchamp) Futurism (Marinetti)
Architecture	Forms • Pitched roofs • Domes • Columns	Form • Plain geometrical shapes (art deco)

Discipline	Rejected	Embraced
Architecture *cont.*	Materials • Wood • Stone • Brick	Materials • Plate glass • Concrete
Literature	Traditional Realism Chronological plots Continuous narratives Omniscient narrators Closed endings	Stream of consciousness Non-linear plots Fragmented forms Multiple narrators Open endings

Modernism signalled a shift away from classical traditions. It stripped away any embellishments and unnecessary details in favour of new ways of seeing the world. It came about in the late 1800s as a move away from rural Romanticism as a source of inspiration, towards a grittier, urbanized mentality. Modernism can also be thought of as a reaction to the Russian Revolution (1905) and World War I (1914–18).

Reflect and respond

1   Why do artists often reject traditional creative practices?
2   Account for the Modernists' preoccupation with urbanization.
3   Why do you think the Russian Revolution and World War I were important in the emergence of Modernism?
4   Looking at the table above, how influential was Modernism as a movement?

Postmodernism

It is important to recognize that the beginning of Postmodernism did not signal the end of Modernism. Rather, Postmodernism should be acknowledged as a sensibility that emerged out of, and continues to develop, Modernist values. Although the two do not occupy distinct periods, the term Postmodernism first came into use in the 1980s (Barry, 1985, p.81). Yet Postmodernism as a term has a complicated history. As has been established, it has shifting, flexible and changeable meanings and its origins are unclear. Ihab Hassan believes it first appeared in or around September 1939 (1985, p.122), whereas for Tim Woods the term has been in use since the 60s (1999, p.10). The problematic nature of definition epitomizes the Postmodernist debate and its aesthetic concerns.

Postmodernism as a theory encompasses many different disciplines including architecture, art, literature, politics, philosophy and sociology, etc. Due to its interdisciplinary nature, you may come across the terms 'Modernisms' and 'Postmodernisms' and, although we are specifically dealing with film, the plurality here illustrates the diverse breadth of such schools of thought. Furthermore, in order to understand Postmodernism it is necessary to recognize that the terms

Postmodernism, Postmodernity and Postmodern are often used interchangeably to define a period (post-1980), a social condition (capitalism) and an ideological movement (aesthetic style). The quotes below illustrate this point.

Simon Malpas states:

> Postmodernity marks the transformation that has taken place in society during the last few decades with the rise of new forms of capitalism, the development of communications technology such as the internet, the collapse of the Soviet Union ... and the emergence of voices from different cultures to disrupt the traditional white male. (2005, p.3)

Fredric Jameson (see below) notes that the Postmodern:

> is not just another word for the description of a particular style. It is also ... a periodising concept whose function is to correlate the emergence of new formal features in culture with the emergence of a new type of social life and a new economic order. (quoted in Malpas, 2005, p.31)

Therefore when writing about Postmodernism it is important that you select the correct term and use it appropriately.

Key traits

There are many rich and diverse facets that are recognized as Postmodern. Listed below in the table are selected traits associated with the movement.

Ideas
• distinction between high and low culture challenged
• rejection of Grand Narratives (Lyotard)
• meaning of signs no longer stable
• originality questioned (Baudrillard)
• reality replaced by simulation (Baudrillard)
• self-reflectivity (aware of own artificiality)

Structure
• intertextuality and bricolage (art recycles ideas)
• eclecticism
• hybridity (generic conventions no longer fixed)
• non-linear/fragmented narratives rather than traditional formats

Aesthetic style
• pastiche (old styles reworked)
• parody (tongue-in-cheek humour)
• irony (playful challenge to seriousness of Modernism)
• camp and kitsch (celebration of naffness)

Characterization

- multiple and fractured identities
- traditional notions of good and bad blurred

Although this list of traits may appear extensive, many of the points featured follow a similar line of thought. There is an air of conscious playfulness interwoven into Postmodern texts; it can be thought of as the art of the 'nod and the wink'. For example, if watching a film you continue to notice references to other films, books, comics, etc., then it is highly likely you are watching a Postmodern film. The references you identify illustrate your level of cultural competency. Quentin Tarantino is famous for borrowing from other films and cultures which is evident in *Kill Bill Vol. 1* and *Kill Bill Vol. 2* (2003–4). This practice of borrowing, known as intertextuality, was formalized by the theorist Fredric Jameson.

Fredric Jameson

Fredric Jameson is an American Marxist theorist who writes about the Postmodern. His seminal articles, 'Postmodernism and Consumer Society' (1983) in Jameson (1998) and 'Postmodernism, or the Cultural Logic of Late Capitalism' (1991), attempt to analyse the role of cinema within these debates. Both articles cover similar ideas, but from slightly different perspectives.

'Postmodernism and Consumer Society '(1983)

In 'Postmodernism and Consumer Society', Jameson begins with the acknowledgement that the concept of Postmodernism is not widely understood or accepted because the works it covers are unfamiliar to many. His argument is that when Victorian and post-Victorian forms gave way to Modernism, this earlier generation thought that the works of Le Corbusier, Frank Lloyd Wright, James Joyce, Marcel Proust, etc. were shocking and scandalous. Yet by the 60s these were considered to epitomize Modernism and were accepted as part of the establishment.

This embracing of the 'new' (Modernism) then acted as a stimulus for the younger generation of the 60s, who wanted to move the boundaries by challenging traditions once more. This reaction against Modernism can be seen in the Postmodernist works of Andy Warhol (Pop Art). Similarly, the music of John Cage and composers like Philip Glass, along with punk and new wave rock (Talking Heads), the literature of Thomas Pynchon and the films of Jean-Luc Godard are all considered to be Postmodern (p.1).

For Jameson, this disregard for the past provides a plausible explanation for the emergence of Postmodernism and makes two things clear:

1   'Most of the postmodernisms mentioned [...] emerge as specific reactions against established forms of high modernism' (p.1).
2   There is a loss between the key boundaries of high culture and mass culture as many of the newer Postmodernisms are found in advertising, Grade-B Hollywood film, airport paperback genres (p.2).

A further significant feature of Postmodernist practice is pastiche. Modernism was predicated on the personal style of, for example, a writer or a film director. However, Jameson believes that we are now 'in a world in which stylistic innovation is no longer possible, all that is left is to imitate dead styles' (p.7). He offers an explanation through examples of what he calls the 'nostalgia film' or *la mode retro* which fall into three categories:

1   Historical films, set in the past and about the past: *American Graffiti* (George Lucas, 1973), *Schindler's List* (Steven Spielberg, 1993) and *The Young Victoria* (Jean-Marc Vallée, 2009).
2   Films that 'reinvent' the past: *Raiders of the Lost Ark* (Steven Spielberg, 1981), *Titanic* (James Cameron, 1997) and *Enigma* (Michael Apted, 2001).
3   Films that are set in the present but that evoke the past: *Sleepless in Seattle* (Nora Ephron, 1993), *Brick* (Rian Johnson, 2005) and *V for Vendetta* (James McTeigue, 2005).

These examples indicate that filmmaking looks to the past for inspiration, meaning that 'stylistic innovation is no longer possible'. Instead old genres are reinvigorated and hybridity becomes rife.

'Postmodernism, or the Cultural Logic of Late Capitalism' (1984)

As the title suggests, Jameson connects changes in culture with changes in economic structures (late capitalism). Jameson is concerned with keeping the Marxist heritage alive. Accordingly, in his Marxist account of society, the cultural superstructures of Postmodernism are connected to the economic base of society. Put another way, as economics change in the West so the culture which surrounds it is altered.

Consumption is no longer about purchasing useful products but is instead concerned with lifestyle choices and buying identities. This leads to a 'new depthlessness' (Natoli and Hutcheon, 1993, p.317). To illustrate this 'depthlessness', Jameson compares a painting by Vincent Van Gogh, *A Pair of Boots* (1887) with the work by Andy Warhol, *Diamond Dust Shoes* (1980). In Van Gogh's painting the boots are those of a peasant and are covered in dust; the image is contextualized. However, in the work by Andy Warhol, *Diamond Dust Shoes,* the image depicts many women's shoes floating in space; they appear to have no social context. For Jameson, Warhol's painting 'does not speak to us at all … [It has] a kind of superficiality … the supreme formal feature of all the Postmodernisms' (Natoli and Hutcheon, 1993, p.317). Here Jameson is highlighting the fact that contextlessness is a key trait of Postmodernism. Similarly the focus on commodities, such as the shoes, endlessly reproduced in the Warhol image, becomes another indicator of Postmodern consumer culture.

Jameson examines a variety of artists to demonstrate the diversity of Postmodernism and to further show that it is too chaotic and diverse a category to be a theory. To make his ideas plain, he sets out his discussions on what constitutes a Postmodern film with a focus on how he believes Postmodern culture has 'depthlessness' and a preference for the superficial, 'textual play' and 'multiple surfaces (what is often called intertextuality)' (p.318).

He sees Postmodernist works of art as 'a virtual grab bag of disjointed subsystems and random material … whose reading proceeds by differentiation rather than unification' (p.325). This requires a new way of looking and understanding. The example he cites is from the film

The Man Who Fell to Earth (Nicolas Roeg, 1976). Here Thomas Jerome Newton (David Bowie) watches 'fifty-seven television screens simultaneously' in order to understand the new and alien world around him (p.326). Rather than viewing a single cohesive work of art, he chooses to consciously deconstruct the many images to gain new meaning. At the heart of Jameson's argument is the contention that originality is no longer a possibility. In a way similar to that of Bowie's character, the Postmodern viewer must make sense of texts that borrow from many disparate sources. Jameson believes that creativity is inspired, developed and constructed from past traditions and/or contemporary sources. Postmodernism epitomizes this as an aesthetic style because its art is comprised from borrowing and reinventing the past and fusing it with new forms.

Reflect and respond

1   Can you identify directors and/or films that reference other cultural texts?
2   Do you believe the distinctions between high and low culture have become blurred?
3   Is original filmmaking possible?
4   Are all modern films Postmodern?

Metanarratives and micronarratives

'Metanarratives', 'grand narratives' and 'master narratives' are terms commonly found in the work of the French theorist Jean-François Lyotard. These terms are often used interchangeably but some theorists attempt to separate them, so be aware of this in order to avoid confusion.

Narratives are an intrinsic part of the world. They are written or spoken accounts of a connected series of episodes, recorded in a particular order and style appropriate to the practice of the discipline involved. The term narrative is usually associated with fiction, in particular in the fields of literature, theatre, film and television. However, narratives are equally important to the field of science, politics, law, philosophy, religion and so on (the way events are recorded). We understand the world through narrative structures.

Metanarratives/grand narratives

Metanarratives are totalizing narratives (big stories) that are deemed to be completely true, indisputable and unquestionable. Prior to the Enlightenment the idea that God created the universe was considered irrevocable until this was challenged by Charles Darwin. Metanarratives inform the decision-making framework in society and they influence the 'rules' by which society functions on a daily basis (law and religion). Metanarratives often inspired the work of Modernists whereas Postmodernists are dubious of such concrete ideas. Rather than embracing one definitive truth, Postmodernists prefer to draw upon a wide range of eclectic sources.

Micronarratives (little narratives)/petits récits

Micronarratives cover clear but limited areas of life; that is, we have lots of smaller roles that we perform from day to day. We can be parents, employees, sportsmen, musicians and students; any one of a number of roles. These roles each have courses of action within their limited contexts. We are classified by our effectiveness in these. For example, we may be good students but poor musicians. This fragmentation of life into many parts avoids the need for metanarratives. This concentration on details and experiences means that information is fragmented and partial.

In summary, metanarratives are concerned with big issues (religion, war, science, etc.) whereas micronarratives concentrate on personal stories.

Jean-François Lyotard

The Postmodern Condition: A Report on Knowledge (1979)

> Simplifying to the extreme, I define *postmodern* as incredulity toward metanarratives. (p.xxiv)

This work is considered to be one of the most important accounts of Postmodernism. It aims to examine the 'condition of knowledge in the most highly developed societies' (p.xxiii). Lyotard discusses what is understood by 'knowledge'; how it is generated, how it is communicated and how it is used by individuals, businesses, governments and society in general. More importantly he focuses on how knowledge is circulated via totalizing narratives (big stories). Lyotard believed that modern society had lost faith in metanarratives because they tend to be all encompassing (see above). Yet Lyotard cautioned that without such overarching, grand narratives, the basis for 'rule-making' would be challenged.

Here Lyotard draws on Wittgenstein's 'little narratives' (micronarratives/*petits récits*) (p.60). Sensing a general disillusionment with overarching explanations, he believes storytellers became preoccupied with smaller or single issues. For example, micronarratives can include incidents of NIMBY-ist (not in my backyard) protest, when locals object to road changes or a prison being built. Rather than being concerned with global issues (metanarratives), such as famine, war and global warming, modern society often becomes invested in issues that affect smaller communities (micronarratives). This change is clear as traditionally the film industry favoured epic storytelling, witnessed in *The Birth of a Nation* (D. W. Griffith, 1915) and *The Ten Commandments* (Cecil B. DeMille, 1956). But modern filmmaking is often more concerned with intricate, inconsequential details, for example, the discussion about McDonald's burgers in the opening of *Pulp Fiction*. Postmodernism enables a focus on the mundane, which has typically been disregarded in traditional storytelling as unimportant. It is the celebration of small moments rather than those of collective concern, that separates Postmodernism from earlier narratives.

Reflect and respond

1　To what extent are metanarratives dead or still existent?
2　Make a list of films that are based around grand narratives.
3　Do you agree with Lyotard's claim that modern society is more concerned with micro-narratives?
4　Make a list of films that are entirely based on micronarratives.
5　Using the list you compiled for the previous question, can you identify any grand narratives within the subtext of these films?

Jean Baudrillard's work went in a very different direction from other Postmodernists. Rather than looking to the past to interpret texts, Baudrillard questioned our understanding of truth and originality in light of media manipulation and modern technologies.

Jean Baudrillard

'The Precession of Simulacra' (1981)

The term 'simulacrum' comes from the Latin for similarity. To begin his writing on the idea of simulacra, the French theorist Jean Baudrillard refers to Borges's allegorical fable of cartographers drawing a map of the empire. As they become more preoccupied with details and scale, the map physically 'ends up covering the territory exactly' (Baudrillard, 1994, p.1). As the empire crumbles into ruins, the map too begins to fray until all that is left are small fragments that are still recognizable in the desert (1994, p.1). Baudrillard explains that:

> The territory no longer precedes the map, nor does it survive it. It is nevertheless the map that precedes the territory – *precession of simulacra'* […] it is the territory whose shreds slowly rot across the extent of the map. It is the real, and not the map, whose vestiges [traces] persist here and there in the deserts that are no longer those of the Empire, but ours. *The desert of the real itself.* (1994, p.1)

So the map which is a copy of the territory actually becomes more real than the physical landscape. The modern world is so filled with images, that the image which was once only a copy of a corporeal (physical) object is reproduced so many times that the simulation (image) gains more substance than the actual object it was attempting to copy.

It is important to understand the difference between 'simulation' and what Baudrillard calls 'simulacra/simulacrum'. To simulate is 'to pretend', 'to make believe'. Simulations are false images that manipulate viewers into believing they are experiencing reality. For example, trainee pilots will practise in a flight simulator before being entrusted to fly a real plane. Similarly, you may find a rollercoaster simulation at the fun-fair. Although it projects a life-like experience, it is clear that it is not real. Simulations work because there is an obvious connection between what is being simulated and real life.

Baudrillard claimed that in modern society, some simulations have gained another level of artificiality; he refers to this as 'simulacra'. This occurs when the simulation has lost its association with reality. It is the representation of something which has never existed. Baudrillard illustrates his point with the example of Disneyland. The theme park presents a nostalgic re-creation of smalltown America (Main Street, USA). However, this is NOT a re-creation. It is a simulacrum. This sentimental depiction is false because it is a fictional construct. It is not a faithful representation of America's small towns, but is instead an idealized romanticized myth. Therefore a simulacrum occurs when the simulation has no reference to reality, but instead gains a life of its own. It becomes 'hyperreal'.

You may recognize the phrase 'desert of the real' from the earlier quote, as it occurs in the Science Fiction film *The Matrix* (Andy and Larry Wachowski, 1999). In the film people are kept in a comatose state so that their bodies can be used as batteries. They are unaware of their condition because they are fed images of a simulated world that they believe to be real. They do not question this reality because they have only ever encountered the simulation. Only when Neo (Keanu Reeves) becomes conscious of his environment is he able to free himself. However, the world which he awakens to is an apocalyptic landscape where barely anything grows. Baudrillard warns: 'it is dangerous to unmask images, since they dissimulate the fact that there is nothing behind them' (1994, p.5). So, following his enlightenment, it is clear that the image of the world that was projected to Neo was in fact a simulacrum as it bore no reference to the desolate world to which he awakes.

Therefore, the thesis of Baudrillard's argument is that Postmodern society has become reliant on symbols, signs and models that simulate reality rather than reality itself. The mass-media industry can help illustrate Baudrillard's ideas. Due to print media, televisions, computers and other digital technologies, we are confronted with excessive visual material on a daily basis. Accordingly, reality and truth become confused as it is near impossible to separate truth from fiction. This is evident in the film *The Truman Show* (Peter Weir, 1998) and the Endemol programme *Big Brother* (1997–2010). Both productions were influenced by the George Orwell novel *Nineteen Eighty-Four* (1949); Big Brother is the name of the surveillance apparatus which acts as the eyes and ears of the ruling elite. *The Truman Show* is akin to the Disneyland example explained above, as the film incorporates a fictitious depiction of a utopian community. *Big Brother* is also a simulacrum. It was originally intended to be a simulation of real life with people living together in an environment where every moment of their lives would be recorded for viewing. However, over time the housemates became more aware of the cameras and worked to promote their own popularity. Furthermore, the footage that is aired has undergone severe editing to afford viewers an imposed narrative. Therefore, returning to Baudrillard's thesis, reality has been simulated.

The Gulf War Did Not Take Place (1995)

Jean Baudrillard wrote this influential piece concerning the First Gulf War of 1990–1 in three instalments; with the first article 'The Gulf War Will Not Take Place' appearing in *Libération* on 4 January 1991. The second instalment 'The Gulf War: Is It Really Taking Place?' followed on 6 February and the final part entitled 'The Gulf War Did Not Take Place' appeared on 18 February 1991.

The logic behind his writing points to the marked difference between modern-day warfare and the battles of the past. The premise of his work developed out of his preoccupation with ideas of simulation and simulacra (see above). Unlike in previous wars where soldiers would engage in one-to-one combat in the trenches, Baudrillard claimed that the Gulf War was fought from afar: important decisions were made in Pentagon boardrooms; information was gleaned from maps and satellite images; and military strategists gave advice without ever having set foot in the Middle East. Similarly, targets for air strikes were located from cockpits using computer screens and infrared imaging. Baudrillard questions how we know that the war in the Gulf ever took place when there was no physical contact with the enemy? The war was fought by the coalition in a comparable manner to the way we play interactive games on our PCs or other gaming platforms; it was simulated. The Iraqis, however, fought the war in a more traditional sense.

For Baudrillard the war was one-sided. His justification for such an argument was that the coalition forces did not suffer great losses: '[a] simple calculation shows that, of the 500,000 American soldiers involved during the seven months of operations in the Gulf, three times as many would have died from road accidents alone had they stayed in civilian life' (1995, p.69).

Therefore he asks, how could the conflict be called a war? The Iraqi military and Kuwaiti citizens, on the other hand, experienced countless casualties and deaths; their loss was so great that a number cannot be given. But, without concrete figures, how can we confirm that there were any casualties? He states that 'the non-will to know is part of the non-war' (1995, p.74).

Paul Patton, who translated the works into English and wrote the foreword to the published essays states that: 'Baudrillard's argument in *The Gulf War Did Not Take Place* is not that nothing took place, but rather that what took place was not a war' (1995, p.14). Baudrillard here turns his attention to the media and their role in the invasion. He suggested that the sensationalist style of reporting was akin to the spectacles witnessed in mainstream blockbusters. He believed that the television images of the Gulf War were so heavily edited for effect that they bore no correlation to the actual events, once more leading to the conclusion that the war was a simulation. Baudrillard justifies this belief by pointing out that after the conflict Saddam Hussein remained in power with his regime intact.

Reflect and respond

1 How far are Baudrillard's ideas informed by new digital technologies?
2 Can you think of any examples of simulacra? Maybe consider your experience of computer games.
3 Do you agree with Baudrillard's claim that modern culture's obsession with imitating reality blurs our understanding of truth?
4 Do you think the way the media report conflicts and war is similar to the approach taken by the film and gaming industry? Is this problematic?
5 In what ways is modern warfare less real?

As if Postmodernism is not complicated enough, there are certain critics who believe that it is not a new concept. Jürgen Habermas famously claims that it is a continuation of Modernism.

Jürgen Habermas

'Modernity versus Postmodernity' (1981)

The German sociologist and philosopher Jürgen Habermas is most famous for his critique of Postmodernism. Rather than following the cultural trend of embracing all things Postmodern, Habermas argued in favour of Modernity. In his widely recognized essay 'Modernity versus Postmodernity', also known as 'Modernity: An Unfinished Project', Habermas asserts that the 'relation between "modern" and "classical" has lost a fixed historical reference' (p.93). The term 'modern' was first coined by Christians in the late fifth century to distinguish their ways from those of the pagan Romans. More notably, it refers to a defining period associated with the Enlightenment and scientific progress. It has since been used throughout history to distinguish 'new' practices from traditional forms (p.92).

As has been established in this chapter, Postmodernism is often defined by its conscious break from the ideas of the Enlightenment but for Habermas this break is endemic of Modernism. He contends that the term 'Postmodernity' suggests a failure in 'Modernity' and claims that 'Modernity' still has credence as a way of understanding culture. Furthermore, he suggests that we should look at the failings of those who attempted to overthrow Modernity, meaning avant-garde and surrealist practitioners.

At this point, Habermas's argument becomes unclear because he does not openly discuss Postmodernists and their shortcomings but instead uses the term conservatives (young, old and neo) and refers to their 'terroristic' approach (p.101). His central premise is that Postmodernism purports to be anti-elitist yet those attempting to break with previous forms of artistic production are often pretentious in their cultural borrowing. Thus he believes that art has been removed from the Everyman and everyday life. It has to a certain extent become institutionalized and discussed by critics and academics rather than the general public.

Reflect and respond

1   Do you believe that Modernism as a movement is over?
2   Is Postmodernism an anti-elitist movement?
3   Is Postmodernism only of use to academics and critics? Does it have any value to the general public?

Case study: *Moulin Rouge!* (Baz Luhrmann, 2001)

The film *Moulin Rouge!* is often cited as a classic example of Postmodernist filmmaking. Baz Luhrmann opens the film with a CGI reproduction of Paris at the turn of the century in which he simulates an imaginary camera zooming through the streets of Montmartre. It is important to remember that this is not the real Bohemian district but a simulacrum as discussed in the works of Jean Baudrillard.

The film is a sumptuous exercise in artistic appropriation as the Parisian narrative is littered with references to both high and low cultural forms. The Australian director casts his cultural net far and wide with references as diverse as Indian Bollywood filmmaking and Greek mythology. The fact that the text is consciously camp and kitsch is evident in the homoerotic rendition of Madonna's 'Like a Virgin', with Harry Zidler (Jim Broadbent) and the Duke (Richard Roxburgh) paying homage to Hammer Horror while cross-dressed. *Moulin Rouge!* is a playful text featuring 'Carry On' style sexual innuendo. This mischievous attitude is also apparent in Luhrmann's approach to the musical as a genre. He parodies the generic conventions of the musical yet pastiches the formulaic narrative of the backstage show.

Operatic bricolage

The term 'bricolage' is used to describe a work that is made from combining existing materials (texts), independent of their original purpose, to form a new text. This relates to the Postmodernist notion that there are no original ideas (Jameson). *Moulin Rouge* provides a rich example of bricolage as the narrative draws from three famous operas:

1   *La Bohème* (Giacomo Puccini, 1897)
2   *La Traviata* (Guiseppe Verdi, 1853)
3   *Orpheus and Eurydice* (various renditions)

The most obvious references come from Puccini's *La Bohème,* based on Henry Murger's novel, *Scènes de la Bohème* (1845). The narrative is set in the Montmartre district of Paris at the turn of the century and follows the lives of a group of poverty-stricken artists. The table below illustrates how the characters in the film were inspired by Puccini's Bohemians.

La Bohème	Moulin Rouge!
Rudolpho – Poet	Christian – Poet
	Audrey – Poet
Marcello – Painter	Toulouse-Lautrec – Painter
Schaunard – Musician	Satie – Composer
Colline – Philosopher	The Argentine – Dancer
Mimi – Seamstress with consumption	Satine – Courtesan with consumption

Baz Luhrmann, and his writing partner Craig Pearce, skilfully introduce the real-life characters of Toulouse-Lautrec (John Leguizamo) and Erik Satie (Matthew Whittet). Both were famous residents of Montmartre associated with the *Moulin Rouge* nightclub and *Le Chat Noir* Café respectively. Therefore the script plays with notions of fiction and fact, blurring the boundaries between the two. The narrative of *La Bohème* revolves around the poet Rudolpho, who falls in love with the seamstress Mimi, who dramatically dies of consumption at the end of the final act. This trajectory is mirrored in the characters of Christian (Ewan McGregor) and Satine (Nicole Kidman), the main difference being that the heroine is a courtesan.

In casting Satine as a courtesan, Luhrmann takes inspiration from the Verdi opera *La Traviata* (1853).

La Traviata	*Moulin Rouge!*
Violetta – Courtesan	Satine – Courtesan
Alfredo – Lover	Christian – Lover
Germont – Alfredo's father	Harry Zidler – Father figure

As shown above, Violetta, the lead character of this opera, is also a courtesan and, like Satine, is hoping to leave her sordid affairs behind and settle down with her lover. Violetta's love interest is Alfredo. His father is embarrassed by their relationship due to her reputation as a woman of the night. So he convinces Violetta to pretend that she no longer loves Alfredo in an attempt to protect his family name. A similar scene occurs in *Moulin Rouge!* when Harry Zidler, the father figure, persuades Satine to profess that she never loved Christian, a gesture undertaken in order to save his life. Both narratives then depict the scorned lover following the courtesan back to Paris and humiliating her in public. Alfredo throws money at Violetta's feet declaring: 'Now I can pay the debt I owe. Now I can clear my honour. I call you here to witness. That I have paid my debt' (Act 2, Sc. 3). The same sentiment is uttered by Christian on stage just before the finale when he states 'This woman is yours now. I've paid my whore. I owe you nothing.'

La Traviata and the film both conclude with the lovers reuniting as the female dies of consumption. This is a traditional ending for women of ill repute; their bodies were consumed by men and thus it is poignant that they should contract the tragic disease of consumption. Grace Kehler highlights this play on words as, 'a problem designated by the multiple meanings of "consumption," which suggests her disease and profession' (2005). Ironically *Moulin Rouge!* is rightly considered Postmodern in its ethos, yet it conforms to the Victorian moral code of punishing the wicked.

The third opera providing an overarching framework for the film is that of *Orpheus and Eurydice*. This Greek myth has undergone a number of operatic treatments, the most famous being Gluck's *Orfeo ed Euridice* (1762) and Offenbach's *Orphée aux Enfers* (1858). Interestingly, Offenbach's version includes the 'Infernal Galop' from Act 2, Scene 2, instantly recognizable and more commonly known as the 'Can Can'. This musical interlude is more famously known as the signature theme associated with the real *Moulin Rouge* nightclub and its risqué performers.

The Greek myth informs the film, with Christian taking the role of the Orphean hero.

Orpheus and Eurydice	*Moulin Rouge!*
Orpheus – Hero	Christian – Hero
Eurydice – Doomed wife	Satine – Doomed love interest
Hades – God of the underworld	Harry Zidler – King of the underworld

Orpheus, according to legend, had the unique ability of being able to mesmerize those around him with his singing voice:

> Orpheus with his lute made trees,
> And the mountain-tops that freeze,
> Bow themselves when he did sing.
> (Shakespeare, *Henry VIII*, Act 3, Sc. 2)

Christian may be a penniless poet but when he sings 'My gift is my song', he is able to charm Satine. In the original tale, Orpheus's wife Eurydice is bitten by a snake and dies. Orpheus, beside himself with grief, travels to the underworld to win her back. Here, he sings to the god of the underworld Hades and is granted his wish to return home with his wife. However, Hades makes one condition: Orpheus must not look at his wife until he is safely above ground. Orpheus takes his wife's hand and begins to lead her out of danger. However, the temptation grows too much and he turns to look at his beloved whereupon she vanishes and is lost to him forever. In Luhrmann's film, Christian attempts to rescue Satine from the sordid world of Harry Zidler and the Duke. Similarly, as he takes Satine's hand to escort her from the stage, he turns to look at her face. At that point, with a sharp intake of breath, Satine collapses and dies in his arms.

It is clear that these three operas inspired the structure for the film and in borrowing and adapting these stories Luhrmann creates a universal tale of love. Ironically, although *Moulin Rouge!* is regarded as a Postmodern text, Luhrmann relies on love; a grand narrative. This raises questions as to whether the film should be classed as Postmodern. However, in spite of its traditional theme, the film borrows from both high and low popular cultures. Furthermore, the self-referential nature of the narrative and the conscious aesthetics employed confirm its Postmodern credentials.

Appropriating popular culture

Moulin Rouge! is knowingly self-referential because it plays with generic conventions. The musical has long been regarded as a camp genre and has accordingly been embraced as part of gay culture. Luhrmann relishes in this and adorns every aspect of the production in glitz and glamour. Additionally, he creates Christian's poetic verse from popular songs familiar to a contemporary audience. Playing with this association, the popular songs chosen are typically selected from gay icons and pop artists who are treasured by the gay community. Most obviously the music of Freddie Mercury and Elton John feature in the the score, along with that of other pop artists like Kylie Minogue, David Bowie, Dolly Parton and Madonna.

It is not just the music that references popular culture; there are numerous visual quotations in the film. For example, during the 'Elephant Love Song' melody, Christian leaps onto the elephant's head singing 'Love lifts us up where we belong' while recreating the famous 'king of the world' stance of Leonardo DiCaprio in the film *Titanic*. In the 'Your Song' sequence, as Christian and Satine dance across the Parisian sky, there are allusions to Gene Kelly's 'Singin' in the Rain' while Georges Méliès's animated moon from the 1902 *Le Voyage dans la Lune/A Trip to the Moon* is seen serenading the lovers.

The aesthetic style of the film is also recognizable to a contemporary audience. The film replicates the frenetic camerawork associated with MTV and music videos in general. Luhrmann employs high-speed editing techniques along with aggressive whip pans. The camerawork and editing choices imbue the film with a disorientating energy that matches the drunken locale of the nightclub. The stylized approach reflects the excessive lifestyle the characters lead. The simulated skyline, the consistent cultural borrowings and mischievous play with genre, all contribute to *Moulin Rouge!*'s Postmodern credibility.

Reflect and respond

1 Do you consider *Moulin Rouge!* to be a traditional love story or a Postmodern text? Justify your answer.
2 A number of reviewers found Luhrmann's excessive style alienating. Why do you think this was so and do you agree?
3 *Moulin Rouge!* blurs the boundaries between fact and fiction. Is this just a Postmodern trait?
4 Can you name any other films that comprise various cultural references?
5 Are Postmodern texts elitist? Can you only enjoy them fully if you are aware of the original texts from which they borrow?

Conclusion

It is difficult to draw a formal conclusion to Postmodernism as it is an ongoing practice. Furthermore, no apparent movements are emerging to replace it. Steve Best and Douglas Kellner summarize our present condition:

> Our contemporary situation thus finds us between the modern and the postmodern, the old and the new, tradition and the contemporary, the global and the local, the universal and the particular, and any number of other competing matrixes. Such a complex situation produces feelings of vertigo, anxiety, and panic, and contemporary theory, art, politics and everyday life exhibit signs of all of these symptoms. To deal with these tensions, we need to develop new syntheses of modern and postmodern theory and politics to negotiate the novelties and intricacies of our current era. (1998, p.298)

Bibliography

Barry, P. (1985) *Beginning Theory: An Introduction to Literary and Cultural Theory*, Manchester: Manchester University Press.

Baudrillard, J. (1994) 'The Precession of Simulacra', in *Simulacra and Simulation*, Ann Arbor: University of Michigan Press, pp.1–42.

Baudrillard, J. (1995) *The Gulf War Did Not Take Place*, Sydney: Power Publications.

Best, S. and Kellner, D. (1998) 'Postmodern Politics and the Battle for the Future', *New Political Science* vol. 20 no. 3, pp.283–99.

Habermas, J. (1981) 'Modernity versus Postmodernity', in J. Natoli and L. Hutcheon (eds) (1993) *A Postmodern Reader*, New York: State University New York Press.

Hassan, Ihab (1985) 'The Culture of Postmodernism', *Theory, Culture and Society* vol. 2, pp.119–32.

Jameson, Fredric (1991) 'Postmodernism, or the Cultural Logic of Late Capitalism', in J. Natoli and L. Hutcheon (eds) (1993) *A Postmodern Reader*, New York: State University New York Press.

Jameson, Fredric (1998) 'Postmodernism and Consumer Society' (1983), *The Cultural Turn: Selected Writings on the Postmodern, 1983–1998*, London: Verso.

Kehler, G. (2005) 'Still for Sale: Love Songs and Prostitutes from *La Traviata* to *Moulin Rouge!*', *Mosaic* vol. 38 no. 2. Retrieved 18 June 2010. Available at http://www.umanitoba.ca/publications/mosaic/issues/getissue. php?vol=38&no=2.

Lyotard, Jean-François (1979) *The Postmodern Condition: A Report on Knowledge*, Manchester: Manchester University Press.

Malpas, S. (ed.) (2001) *Postmodern Debates*, Basingstoke: Palgrave Macmillan.

Malpas, S. (2005) *The Postmodern*, London and New York: Routledge.

Natoli, J. and Hutcheon, L. (1993) *A Postmodern Reader*, New York: State University New York Press.

Shakespeare, W. (1957) *Henry VIII*, London: Methuen.

Woods, T. (1999) *Beginning Postmodernism*, Manchester: Manchester University Press.

Chapter

Psychoanalysis

8

1. A therapeutic method, originated by Sigmund Freud, for treating
   mental disorders by investigating the interaction of conscious and
   unconscious elements in the patient's mind and bringing repressed
   fears and conflicts into the conscious mind, using techniques such
   as dream interpretation and free association. Also: a system of
   psychological theory associated with this method.

Setting the scene

It is an interesting coincidence that in 1895 when the first films were being shown to the public, Sigmund Freud and Josef Breuer published *Studies in Hysteria*. This was the first Psychoanalytic text of Freud's on the study of the unconscious mind. As has been noted in other chapters, many theories that are used in film analysis had their beginning in literary studies or in political movements. Psychoanalytic Theory, on the other hand, emerged from the efforts that science and medicine were making to understand why people appeared to be 'mad'.

Historically people with mental problems (hysteria) had been burnt, exorcized, locked up or ridiculed. It was thought that they were, variously, liars, deviants and lazy who were not worth serious attention. In the later part of the nineteenth century, research aiming to gain a better understanding of mental illness began, with Professor Jean-Martin Charcot, who was to become Freud's tutor. Interest in studying the unconscious mind had gained momentum and credibility from the 1900s, more so with the general public than with the medical fraternity. Initial research into this field was known as neuropathology, which soon evolved into the now recognized Psychoanalysis.

The main purpose of Psychoanalytical research is to gain an understanding of the unconscious. Freud proposed that a person's awareness existed in layers within the psyche and that some thoughts lay just below the surface. In the manner that an iceberg has only one-tenth of its surface above sea level and nine-tenths submerged, only a small part of the mind represents the conscious while the rest (the preconscious and unconscious) is 'submerged'.

Psychoanalytic Theory has been a major influence on various academic disciplines other than psychology for example, literature, film, Marxism, Feminism and philosophy. Sigmund Freud, Carl Jung and Jacques Lacan are the most widely recognized practitioners of Psychoanalysis, their theories cover vast areas of the psyche (the mind) and for Film Studies they remain among the most relevant.

Sigmund Freud

Born in Moravia in 1856, Freud is commonly referred to as the 'father of psychoanalysis'. After studying under Charcot in Paris, he set up a private practice in Vienna. After the Nazis seized power in Austria he was forced to leave Vienna because he was Jewish. In 1937 he moved to London, where he died in 1939.

Freud's work covers vast areas which are impossible to explore in detail here. Therefore, this chapter will concentrate on areas that are appropriate to the understanding of film texts. His work has become so influential that a number of his ideas have entered common parlance. For example, the following terms will probably be familiar:

- 'Anally retentive' describes people who rigidly abide by rules and are excessively organized and fussy, those who find it hard to metaphorically 'let go'. It is commonly used in a derogatory manner: 'Oh you're so anal!'
- A 'Freudian slip' occurs when we inadvertently say the 'wrong' thing. This unintentional error is then regarded as revealing a subconscious feeling.
- 'Libido' is the psychic drive or energy, especially that associated with sexual desire.
- A 'phallic symbol' is an object that visually resembles an erect penis, for example, skyscrapers and monuments. It is often applied in an ironic sense to objects that symbolize power or male prowess (red sports car). This had become a joke even in Freud's own lifetime. As a constant cigar smoker, Freud once said, 'Sometimes a cigar is just a cigar', suggesting the danger of seeing connections where there are none.

Other terms of Freud's in common use are: 'repression', 'unconscious', 'ego', 'superego' and 'id'. These will be covered in greater detail in this chapter.

In his first, most widely recognized work *The Interpretation of Dreams* (1899), Freud describes a means of gaining access to the unconsciousness through dreams. Freud believed that dreams and dreaming represented a form of hallucinatory wish fulfilment; 'a dream is the (disguised) fulfilment of a (repressed) wish' (Wollheim, 1995, p.61). They were not nonsense as had been previously supposed as for Freud they were full of meaning. He noted that the logic in dreams was different to that of conscious thought and therefore needed interpreting. He states:

> [T]here is a causal connection between the obscurity of the dream-content and the state of repression (inadmissibility to consciousness) of certain dream thoughts, and that the dream had to be obscure so as not to betray the proscribed dream-thoughts. (Gay, 1995, p.164)

Freud claimed dreams were significant because they could reveal symptoms of illness and also act as a vehicle for creativity. On one hand, he believed that there was a link between dreaming and madness. On the other, dreams could also be seen as part of the cure.

Psychoanalysis relies on getting the patient to talk freely about concerns that they have repressed (hidden) over the years. Many of Freud's patients supposedly suffered from neurosis. He began treating what he called 'hysteria' with hypnosis. Later, he forswore hypnosis in favour of 'free association', a means of investigating a person's unconscious by inviting them to give spontaneous replies to questions. This method was famously dubbed 'the talking cure' by one patient (1895). The release of these buried problems, from the unconscious mind into the conscious, enabled the patient respond to treatment.

This therapy is illustrated in the plot of *Marnie*. Her husband (Sean Connery) attempts to help Marnie (Tippi Hedren) unlock the secrets of her past by encouraging her to talk them through. She vehemently rejects his 'psychobabble', insisting that she is not traumatized, that there is no problem. The narrative unfolds to reveal her as a liar, a thief and sexually inhibited, unable to bear a man touching her. The plot resolves when she finally 'lets go' and is prepared to talk about her problems. Her psychological problems can be traced to incidents in her childhood that she has repressed.

Although today the therapeutic value of the 'talking cure' is disputed, the impact of Freud's work on how we think of ourselves is incalculable. The best example of this is the way we now link the unconscious and hysteria to childhood events. Freud in particular focused on early relationships with parents, the drives of desire and the interest children show for different parts of the body (oral, anal and phallic). Indeed most of Freud's work is associated with sexual drives.

Reflect and respond

1 Nowadays we rarely hear the term hysteria. Why do you think this is?
2 Discuss your experiences of Freudian slips.
3 In pairs free associate from the following words, discussing differences in your responses.

   • hot chocolate
   • dentist
   • cinema
   • red
   • university.

4 Come up with some of your own terms and repeat the exercise.

In order to make sense of the information that surfaced through talking and free association, Freud looked to the workings of the mind. Taking a scientific approach, he proposed that a person's psyche can be understood as three interconnected layers (id, superego and ego).

The id, superego and ego (unconscious, preconscious and conscious)

Id

The id (also known as the unconscious) is the largest part of the mind that is beyond consciousness and has a strong influence upon our actions. It is associated with inherited, instinctive impulses linked with, for example, lust, sex and aggression. These range from straightforward desires for food, drink, warmth and sex, to those motivations of a more complex nature involving our memories. It is the irrational primitive part of the psyche; it stores our fears, wishes and needs (animal instincts). It is sometimes referred to as the 'pleasure-principle' as its objective is to seek pleasure and avoid pain. '[I]t may be said of the id that it is totally non-moral' (Gay, 1995, p.655).

In film the id is often associated with villains, who follow their desires irrespective of the hurt they may cause. Dracula and The Joker are examples of characters who are lawless, amoral and suffer no guilt or regret but allow the id to rule.

Superego

The superego (also known as the preconscious) dominates the ego in the form of a moral conscience able to impose guilt. It operates as an internal censor applying control to what it deems are unacceptable desires. It responds to rules set by society and those set by the father figure or authority. '[I]t may be said [...] of the super-ego that it can be super-moral' (Gay, 1995, p.655).

In film the superego is usually represented by a mentor, father figure or role model. For example, Jiminy Cricket (voiced by Cliff Edwards) in *Pinocchio* (n.a., 1940), Obi-Wan Kenobe and Yoda (voiced by Frank Oz) in *Star Wars* and *The Empire Strikes Back* (Irvin Kershner, 1980) respectively.

Ego

The ego (also known as the conscious or 'I') is the thinking part of our psyche, 'a coherent organization of the mental processes' (Gay, 1995, p.630). It is connected with reason because it learns from experiences in order to develop and become stronger. 'It goes to sleep at night even though it exercises censorship on our dreams' (Gay, 1995, p.630). It looks for ways capable of 'transforming the id's will into action' (Gay, 1995, p.636). The ego is responsible for understanding the real world and has mechanisms for suppressing and forgetting. It acts as a mediator or referee in finding a compromise between the id and the superego. '[I]t may be said [...] of the ego that it strives to be moral' (Gay, 1995, p.655).

In film the ego is typically represented by the hero. Most heroes work to overcome challenges in order to defeat a nemesis. They have to adapt to and learn from the situations that they find themselves in. The ego must suppress and control the id. Similarly, the hero battles and defeats the villain.

Reflect and respond

1   Applying Freud's notions of the id, ego and superego, explore these following famous characters: Frodo Baggins, Dr Doolittle, Frankenstein, Alice (in Wonderland), the Sheriff of Nottingham and Wolverine.

2   How do Freud's theories of the mind apply to characters in complete mental breakdown: for example, Dr Jekyll and Mr Hyde/Tyler Durden (Brad Pitt) and Ed Norton's character of the Narrator Jack, in *Fight Club* (David Fincher, 1999).

3   Can Freud's ideas of the mind help in understanding character development? How else might they be applied to film?

The id, superego and ego are interlinked. According to Freud, the mind can be seen to be in a permanent state of struggle due to the conflicting nature of the three layers of the psyche. This struggle, according to Freud, can be linked to his ideas of repression.

Repression

This is the forgetting or ignoring of past events that were traumatic in some way. These unpleasant memories are pushed out of the conscious into the unconscious. This process of repressing is a non-conscious act; you cannot actively choose to do this. Memories cannot be banished from the mind but they can be displaced. He states that repression: '[C]annot arise until a sharp cleavage has occurred between conscious and unconscious mental activity – that *the essence of repression lies simply in turning something away, and keeping it at a distance, from the conscious*' (Gay, 1995, pp.569–70).

As past traumas can be so damaging, the mind sometimes avoids processing the incidents. This is the mind's way of coping and can thus be seen as a defence mechanism. These defence mechanisms convert, redirect, sublimate or allow selective memory to act as a form of protection. Freud believed that when this happens, that which we repress can come back to haunt us. So for Freud the unconscious is both the cause and effect of repression.

The film *The Sixth Sense* (M. Night Shyamalan, 1999) epitomizes Freud's notion of repression. In the twist at the conclusion of the narrative, it is revealed that the psychologist (Bruce Willis), who has been counselling the child (Haley Joel Osment), is in fact a ghost. He has ironically repressed the fact that he was shot by one of his own patients. Only once he has recalled this information is he able to come to terms with his situation; a fitting act of repression for a psychologist.

Another famous component of Freud's Psychoanalytical work is the Oedipus complex.

Oedipus and Electra complexes

The Oedipus complex is one of the most overused Freudian concepts. The name is taken from the Greek tragedy *Oedipus Rex* by Sophocles, in which Oedipus unwittingly killed his father and married his mother. Freud used this model to explain the child's need for its parents and the change in the child's desires as it passes from infancy to adulthood where, along the way, it develops sexuality. Freud was mainly concerned with the male child here. He observed that as the child becomes older (three–six years) it recognizes that it is not the sole focus of the mother's attention, which is also bestowed on the father. Because the father is rightfully allowed sexual contact with the mother, the child supposedly hates the father for this. As part of this (Oedipal) rivalry between boys and their fathers, the boys fantasize (worry) that they will be castrated as punishment. Through this anxiety the boy comes to identify with the father as an ideal and love the mother as an object (no longer sexual).

For the female child, Freud suggests that the girl is similarly attracted to the mother. The girl, on the other hand, does not suffer from castration anxiety. At the point when she discovers that she lacks a penis, the girl becomes increasingly antagonistic and resentful towards the mother. She hypothetically believes that her mother has castrated her, resulting in what Freud calls 'penis envy' (this notion is now controversial in Psychoanalytic and Feminist Theories). The girl trans-fers her desires for the mother to the father. These give way in later life to the desire for a man like her father.

It was Carl Jung, Freud's student, who concentrated on female behaviour and developed what he termed the 'Electra complex', originating from the Greek myth in which Electra urges her brother Orestes to avenge the death of their father Agamemnon, who was killed by her mother Clytemnestra. Unlike Freud, Jung did not see the attachment children have for their parents as sexual, instead believing it to be spiritual. Freud not only disagreed with Jung, but he disliked the term 'Electra complex', preferring the phrase 'female Oedipus'. Furthermore, Freud deemed that to be fully socially developed all children must successfully go through this stage (Oedipal/Electra phase).

There are a number of films in which the concept of the Oedipus complex is incorporated into the narrative. In *Psycho*, Norman Bates (Anthony Perkins) kills his mother's intended husband because he sees him as a rival for his mother's attention. He then kills the mother who has mentally dominated him. Another example can be seen in *The Graduate* (Mike Nichols, 1967), where Ben (Dustin Hoffman) is seduced by a woman old enough to be his mother. She gives him the attention he desires before he turns his attentions to the daughter Elaine (Katharine Ross). In both these films the characters are shown not to have fully progressed in a balanced manner through the Oedipal phase.

Reflect and respond

1   Consider Freud's ideas of repression. What kinds of narrative would lend themselves to stories of repression?
2   How might repression result in mental-health problems?
3   Other than the examples cited, try to identify films that have Oedipal and Electra connotations.
4   Discuss whether Freud's ideas of repression and Oedipal/Electra relations are still relevant today.

The Uncanny

Many readers and spectators enjoy being indirectly frightened, by books, paintings or films. Freud's interest lay in the causes of this apparently masochist tendency, which often manifested itself in the unconscious through dreams. In his 1919 essay, 'The Uncanny' (Das Unheimliche/the unhomely/unfamiliar), Freud defined the Uncanny as, 'that class of the terrifying which leads back to something long known to us, once very familiar' (Sandner, 2004, p.76). The Uncanny occurs when everyday, seemingly normal objects are made unfamiliar. He noted that the Uncanny, in a way similar to dreams, provokes the mental anxiety in the spectator, arousing a feeling or sensation that is frightening, strange and yet secretly familiar.

Freud identifies three major elements that add to this odd feeling of unease. They are as follows:

1   ***Déjà vu***: This is a strange feeling of repetition. It is the illusion of having experienced something that in reality they could not have because it is happening for the very first time. This sensation of having been there before, yet knowing this is not possible, represents a clash between the familiar and the unfamiliar. This concept forms the foundation of the film *Groundhog Day*.

2   **The double:** Twins provide an illustration of doubling. They may appear identical because they look alike and this can create a sense of unease as we question whether we are seeing double. The device of spooky twins is a Hollywood staple as seen in *The Shining* (Stanley Kubrick, 1980). Doubling also occurs in the ghostly figure of the *Doppelgänger*. This idea originated from German folklore and seeing your *Doppelgänger* is supposed to be an omen of imminent death. The notion is also explored in the classic narrative *Dorian Gray* (Oliver Parker, 2009), based on Oscar Wilde's novel (1891).

3   **The automaton:** The viewer is left uncertain as to whether this character is real/human. This is the premise for the film *Blade Runner* (Ridley Scott, 1982) where replicants are created in the guise of human beings. It is also seen in the film *The Stepford Wives* (Bryan Forbes, 1975 and Frank Oz, 2004) with women replaced by robots looking exactly like them.

Any of these elements can intensify the Uncanny in a film. It is these incidents of confusion, which force us to question ourselves and our mental capacity that cause us to feel ill at ease. Furthermore, the Uncanny is a powerful device for filmmakers as it can disrupt viewers' sense of reality yet at the same time intrigue our sense of curiosity.

Surrealism and the Uncanny

In the 20s and 30s the Surrealists were one of the first artistic movements to understand the possibilities that blurring the boundaries between dream and reality could hold for cinema. They were hugely influenced by Freud's ideas on the unconscious and the Uncanny. For André Breton, founder of the Surrealist movement, the techniques of cinematography, in particular, dissolves, slow motion and the superimposition of images were ideal ways to express Freud's ideas. Salvador Dalí and Luis Buñuel collaborated on one of the earliest and best-known Surrealist films, *Un Chien Andalou/An Andalusian Dog* (Luis Buñuel, 1928). Buñuel stated their aim: 'No idea or image that might lend itself to rational explanation of any kind would be accepted. We had to open all doors to the irrational and keep only those images that surprised us, without trying to explain why' (Buñuel, 1983, p.103).

Unlike Freud, who attempted to understand the workings of the unconscious, Buñuel and Dalí embraced its elusiveness. Cinematic conventions encourage spectators to take spatial and temporal continuity for granted. When unable to do this, the viewer becomes disoriented and, as may happen in dreams, signs and signifiers become confused. This creates uncertainty. When the spectators' expectations are confounded, their ability to logically predict or interpret the narrative is affected. They then need to unravel the scenes for themselves.

Hitchcock explored the possibilities of the Surreal and the Uncanny in films such as *Vertigo* and *The Birds*. More recently directors such as Peter Greenaway, David Lynch, David Cronenberg, Terry Gilliam and the Coen brothers have found expression in experimentation with these elements. For example, Lynch's *Blue Velvet* (1986) renders the familiar mid-

American town exceedingly unfamiliar. The doubling in *Mulholland Drive* (2001) is also illustrative of Freud's Uncanny. Similarly, the disrupted narratives and exploration of strange and irrational mental states 'wrongfoot' the audience. Cronenberg's *The Fly* (1986) and *Crash* (1996) have a horrific dreamlike quality of irrational logic and concentrate on body transformations, which invest familiar incidents and objects with new and disturbing significance. Although all these directors utilize aspects of cinematic Surrealism it can be seen that they have no uniform style except that they all conform to the same agenda: to shock, confuse and disturb the audience.

Reflect and respond

1   The Uncanny is typically associated with the Horror/Suspense genre. Identify films that utilize these ideas from other genres.
2   What kind of aesthetics do dreams and the Uncanny necessitate?
3   Other than the directors and film examples cited above, list films that explore Freud's notion of the Uncanny.
4   To what extent is Surrealism a European preoccupation?

Despite Freud's overwhelming influence, enthusiasm for his ideas has declined in recent years. This is partly as a result of his mainly negative views on women and in particular what is seen as Freud's wilful misreading of a case known as 'Dora'. Here he insinuated that his client was hysterical and would be cured if she accepted a certain suitor's advances. He later admitted that he had omitted any consideration of her bisexuality (Gay, 1995, pp.172–239).

Freud was both revolutionary and controversial in his lifetime. Although derided by medical practitioners, his novel ideas prompted Psychoanalytic momentum throughout Europe and America. At his most popular Freud was the central figure among Psychoanalytic researchers. Another major influence was Carl Jung.

Carl Jung

The Archetypes and the Collective Unconscious (1959)

Carl Jung was a student of Freud and worked with him in investigating the unconscious. Their collaboration ended when Jung pursued his own path, feeling that there should be less emphasis on the libido and childhood sexuality. Jung believed that many of the symptoms of neurosis (hysteria) emerged when emotions became confused and irrational. Jung believed in a deeper level of unconsciousness. Like Freud, he divided the psyche into three parts:

1   **ego:** the conscious mind
2   **personal conscious:** holds our memories, including any we have suppressed
3   **collective unconscious:** is comprised of our inherited knowledge.

The third part, the collective unconscious, was the most groundbreaking component. According to Jung, it contains all the psychologically inherited knowledge that we share as human beings.

This refers to natural instincts that have unknowingly been passed down through the generations, knowledge that we are born with but are not directly conscious of. He believed that these inherent patterns structure our imagination and shape our minds (psyche). For example, most societies tell stories that have a hero; many countries recognize the image of a circle to represent wholeness; the sky generally symbolizes transcendence and so on. Our emotional experiences are influenced by this collective unconscious. For instance, all people experience a sense of wonderment when looking at the beauty of nature (sunset, solar eclipse, vast expanses of water, etc.). Jung identified this reaction as an inherently instinctual and spiritual element within the human psyche.

In order to investigate the collective unconscious, Jung carried out enquiries that, similar to Freud's, centred on dreams, myths and the soul. In this study, of his own and patients' dreams, he became aware that certain themes and symbols would reoccur. He formed the opinion that, in the way that all humans have a common physical appearance, there is a realm of unconscious collectively shared by all human beings.

> While the personal unconscious is made up essentially of contents which have at one time been conscious but which have disappeared from consciousness through having been forgotten or repressed, the contents of the collective unconscious have never been in consciousness and therefore have never been individually acquired, but owe their existence exclusively to heredity [...] the content of the collective unconscious is made up essentially of *archetypes*. (1969, p.42)

To explain and develop his new idea of the collective unconscious, Jung called the themes and symbols that occur in dreams and our imagination, archetypes. Jung's psychological models are strongly influenced by the Eastern ideas of opposites. Thus, for balance, the shadow archetype is opposite to the persona archetype.

Archetypes are universal associations to which everyone can relate (and not to be confused with Vladimir Propp's archetypal characters explained in Chapter 3, 'Formalism'). In film, archetypes can be both characters and themes. For example, we all have a mother and a father (character) and in life we encounter birth, marriage and death (themes). Simply put, all human beings share common associations related to human issues.

Jung explores the idea of archetypes from the point of six main figures: the persona, shadow, wise old man, earth goddess, anima and animus.

The persona (literally means 'mask')

This is the image that we show to the world, which masks or hides our shadow archetype (see over). It is the way we want to present ourselves to create a good impression. In dreams we typically play the role of our persona. Similar to the ego, the persona gathers knowledge from experiences. However, this can be a false image or a façade, because we can use our persona to manipulate or mask our true nature and pretend to be who we are not. The persona we present may not be real. We can often deceive in an attempt to fit in. The persona can be adopted for the benefit of others or self-advancement, to create a good or bad impression.

The shadow

The shadow is everything in us that is unconscious: repressed ideas, weaknesses and desires (sex and primal instincts). If we lose our temper we may say 'I don't know what came over me.' This would be the 'shadow' side of our personality, reflecting our uncontrollable impulses which we try to control and hide from others. In order to be accepted in society we conform to social and cultural expectations, hiding our shadow archetype behind the mask of our persona.

In the tale of Dr Jekyll and Mr Hyde, these characters are two sides of the same person, the outward representation (Dr Jekyll) and the repressed part (Mr Hyde). Mr Hyde wants to do everything that Dr Jekyll should not. In films such as *Black Swan* (Darren Aronofsky, 2010) these two characters are usually played by a single actor to convey the fact that they represent the outer and inner parts of the same person.

Jung believed that the shadow archetype is the most dangerous as it does not recognize boundaries. However, there is a positive side. The shadow exhibits tenacity, the ability to finish arduous work. Jungian writers believe that the shadow archetype can be responsible for creativity, energy and staying power. If the shadow element is rejected, the overall personality loses its drive.

The wise old man

Similarly to Freud, Jung believed that the male child would use a father figure as a role model. This model is symbolized by the 'wise old man', the archetype that possesses profound knowledge. He is typically an older male figure, a teacher or guru who represents wisdom and insight. Encountering 'wise old man' archetypes often enables people to overcome problems and lead a better life. In narratives these are frequently mentors: wizards like Merlin and martial arts masters like Mr Miyagi (Pat Morita) and Mr Han (Jackie Chan) in *The Karate Kid* (John G. Avildsen, 1984 and Harald Zwart, 2010).

The earth goddess/great mother

On the other hand, the female child would view the mother figure as a role model, symbolized by the earth goddess. Both nurturing and destructive, this archetype can give birth but can equally well destroy her young. Cate Blanchett's character of Galadriel in *The Lord of the Rings: The Fellowship of the Ring* embodies an excellent example.

Anima and animus

For most people their role is determined by their physical gender. However, Jung felt that we are all really bisexual in nature. When we begin our social lives as infants, we are neither male nor female in the social sense. Yet under the influence of society we are moulded into men and women. Women are expected to be more nurturing and less aggressive; men are expected to be strong and to ignore their emotional sides. He felt these expectations meant that we would develop only half of our potential. To achieve a balanced psyche, both the anima and animus are needed:

- **anima** is the unconscious feminine part in the male psyche
- **animus** is the unconscious masculine part of a woman.

A person who strongly identifies with their gender role (a man who is aggressive and never cries/a woman who is happy to remain in the domestic sphere and tend to her family) has not actively engaged with their anima or animus. This is illustrated in the traditional male and female roles found in classic American Westerns. However contemporary practitioners believe that everyone has both anima and animus present within their psyche. The characters of Superman and Lois Lane provide good examples here. Clark Kent is the more gentle, effeminate side of Supeman whereas Lois is quite masculine in her assertiveness and professional attitude. Interestingly, she is attracted to Superman rather than Clark Kent because he mirrors her own masculine attributes.

Jung did not believe that the number of existing archetypes was fixed. In his many volumes he recognized many other characteristics and these have been explored by countless critics. Joseph Campbell (see Chapter 3, 'Formalism') used Jung's work and, more recently, William Indick has applied Jung's archetypes when teaching screenwriting. He recognized that Jung's model provides a useful approach to developing conflict within a narrative. Consequently, Jung's work is still relevant to the film industry.

Reflect and respond

1   How can the collective unconscious be depicted on screen?
2   Give examples of Jungian archetypes in film (persona, shadow, wise old man, earth goddess, anima/animus).
3   Looking at the examples you identified for question 2, are any of them in foreign films? Discuss the universality of Jung's archetypes and whether they can be applied to other cultures.

Carl Jung's work in many ways has a similar trajectory to that of Freud. Yet, as has been shown, there are large areas of divergence. Likewise, Jacques Lacan was a student of Freud but, unlike Jung, most of his best-known work emanated from a Freudian perspective.

Jacques Lacan

'The Mirror Stage as Formative of the Function of the I' (1949)

Jacques Lacan, the French psychologist, developed his ideas from Freud's work but moved away from earlier preoccupations with sexual motivations. However, in a well-publicized turnabout, he returned to Freud's theories from an entirely new perspective and in 1964 formed his own school named *L'École Freudienne de Paris*. His new standpoint enlisted structural linguistics (utterance and grammatical rules) to examine the sense of identity (subjectivity) in isolation from his patients' sexual drives. His work redefined subjectivity by placing the emphasis on the role of language in culture.

His interest in the unconscious led him to speculate about how we learn to consciously perceive ourselves. According to Jean-Louis Baudry and Christian Metz, Lacan's essay, 'The Mirror Stage', is one of the most influential works in contemporary film theory. It gave Film Studies an account of the origins of subjectivity and was used by Metz in his exploration of the cinema as a 'technique of the imaginary' (see below). Whereas Freud's model of the psyche (mind) employs the terms id, ego and superego, Lacan's model of the psyche adopts the terms imaginary, symbolic and real. The imaginary, symbolic and real are not separable but are interdependent systems; if one is disconnected they all become disconnected. While both Freud and Lacan examined the unconscious, it is important to note that their terms are not interchangeable.

The imaginary

According to Lacan, before a child has a sense of who they are, (a sense of self-identity), they exist in what Lacan calls the imaginary. This stage begins before the child learns to speak. During this preverbal stage the child begins to develop a sense of separateness from the mother as well as from other people and objects. However, the child's understanding of this is incomplete.

In the first stage of the imaginary the child has no distinction between itself and 'Others'. Then between the ages of six to eighteen months (before it can walk or even stand unassisted) it may see its image in a mirror. At this point the young child enters into what Lacan calls the 'mirror stage'. The child playfully tries to understand the image in the mirror by testing the relationship of its movements against the reflected image. The child typically leans forwards and backwards, grabs the mirror, pulls faces and tries to lick or kiss the reflected image. The youngster gazes as if trying to take a photograph of itself, 'an instantaneous aspect of the image' (Lacan, 1977, p.2). This is the second stage according to Lacan.

Lacan explains this action as the formation of the ego, the first recognition of the child's own image. The child begins to see itself as a unified human being, as separate from the rest of the world. However, this first illusion of wholeness and the sense of 'that's me' is misrecognition. The child is in a state of helplessness, dependent on its mother, wobbly and in need of support, despite believing that what it sees is a complete, independent image. For Lacan this is an image of what might be; it is a myth, it is anticipation. The image seen by the child is a fiction (a *Gestalt*, a mirage) because it isolates the infant, concealing its lack of coordination and the fact that it needs physical support to stand upright.

This self-idealization is misrecognition because the 'imagined' real is always unattainable, a situation leading to frustration and aggression between the self and its image. Accordingly, the image can become:

- a double: a rival and the object of attack
- an ideal: something which needs to be defended or attacked as unattainable
- an opponent: once again to be attacked (Lacan, 1977, p.3).

The symbolic

At the age of six to eighteen months the child begins to learn to speak and to socialize. Socialization requires prohibitions (you mustn't do that) and restraints (often physical). Because language pre-exists the child, the child has to learn to abide by the rules. The male child now enters the Oedipal phase (Freud), which for Lacan is located in the language of the patriarchal figure (father) as the authoritative voice in the family. This Lacan refers to as the 'name of the father' (1977, pp.50, 150–3). In obeying this law the child represses desire and this repression brings about the unconscious. The child is now part of the symbolic order and realizes that it has misrecognized its mother as an object of desire and looks to find a female 'other' to fulfil the Oedipal path.

The symbolic realm is found in realist texts. It is the world of patriarchal order and logic seen in genres such as the Western and War movie. In a much more elaborate form these ideas became influential in explaining the psychic and political effects of cinema. The imaginary stage is largely focused on the mother, whereas when the child passes into the symbolic stage, the father becomes the focus of attention.

The real

This is the most intricate part of Lacan's system and for that reason we are dealing with it last. Lacan and his critics argue over whether the real order represents the period before the imaginary or after the symbolic. Similarly descriptions of the real differ greatly depending on what you read. In an attempt to summarize the majority of interpretations, the real is a state of existence that occurs during the first few months of life (neo-natal). At this stage there is no conception of language or the outside world. However, the infant does experience overriding sensations of need (food, comfort and sleep). More poignantly, the real can be thought of as 'nothing but need'. It is impossible to put into words, as once words are encountered we move beyond the real into the symbolic. Due to its elusiveness and indescribability, we experience a sense of anxiety and trauma because our levels of understanding fail to work. We cannot comprehend the real without returning to a state that existed before language. Consequently, this Lacanian stage is often found in academic writing on the Horror genre and is also linked to Freud's ideas of the Uncanny because it alludes to a sensation of fear.

Reflect and respond

1 Films often use mirrors to explore psychological issues. Can you recall scenes that illustrate this?
2 From the films you have identified, attempt to apply Lacan's ideas of the mirror stage (imaginary, symbolic and real).
3 Bearing in mind that the real order is impossible to describe, why has it influenced the Horror genre?

Lacan's psychological study of the mirror is useful to film scholars, with the screen substituted for the physical mirror. This raises questions about how the audience identifies (and misrecognizes) characters and situations on the screen. This idea was explored in greater depth by Christian Metz.

Christian Metz

The Imaginary Signifier: Psychoanalysis and the Cinema (1975)

Christian Metz is recognized as the first theorist to work on the relationship between film and spectator. In his seminal essay *The Imaginary Signifier*, Metz employed a scientific method to define the function and meaning of cinema. He asked 'what contribution can [...] psychoanalysis make to the knowledge of the cinematic signifier?' (1982, p.42).

Drawing from Lacan's work on the mirror stage, Metz formulates a connection between the ideas outlined in the mirror stage and the way we view film. In the cinema there is always an image on the screen but, unlike with the mirror, the reflection of the spectator is not there. Metz states: 'the activity of perception which it involves is real [...] but the perceived is not really the object, it is [...] its double, its *replica* in a new kind of mirror' (1982, p.45).

What the viewer sees and hears is not a fantasy (imagined) instead it is pre-recorded. Therefore, the spectator cannot identify with himself, but can only identify with the objects on the screen. The screen therefore ceases to be a mirror. Metz states:

I know I am perceiving something imaginary (and that is why its absurdities [...] do not seriously disturb me) and I know that it is I who am perceiving it. [...] I know that [...] my sense organs are physically affected, that I am not phantasising, that the fourth wall of the auditorium (the screen) is really different from the other three, that there is a projector facing it [the screen]. [...] I also know that it is I who am perceiving all this, that this perceived-imaginary material is deposited in me as if on a second screen. (1982, pp.48–9)

For Metz, watching a film necessitates identification, because without identification meaning cannot be understood. As Lacan suggested, identification takes place in the imaginary order, which is governed by the symbolic. This is true also for cinema (a system of signs that signifies an absent signified – see Chaper 4, 'Structuralism and Post-structuralism').

The most obvious idea is that the spectator identifies with a character, but not all films have characters (documentaries, abstract art films, etc.). Therefore, Metz concludes that the spectator also identifies with the cinematic apparatus itself (see Figures 4.1 and 4.2), which illustrates the relationship between the actor, camera, projector, screen and viewer and its re-creation of the act of looking. It is at this point that Metz's analysis utilizes aspects from semiology, explained in more depth in Chapter 4, 'Structuralism and Post-structuralism'. However, it is interesting to note that Metz drew from Lacan's idea of the child's misrecognition of self, and used it to explore the notion of identification in cinema and the false belief in its reality.

Reflect and respond

1   How can thinking of the cinematic screen as a mirror inform our reading of film?
2   Do we always identify with characters on screen? Cite examples to justify your answer.
3   Has the metaphor of the screen as a mirror been complicated by the emergence of digital technology?

Case study: *Oldboy* (Chan-Wook Park, 2003)

Chan-Wook Park was born in Seoul in 1963 and went to a Catholic university to study philosophy. As part of his degree he watched countless films, which led him to write critical reviews and essays. After university he worked as a translator of film scripts and became an assistant director. He made his directorial debut with *The Moon Is the Sun's Dream* (1992), a box-office failure. His big break came in 2002 with *Sympathy for Mr Vengeance*, which established him as one of the main directors in Korea. This was followed by *Oldboy* and *Sympathy for Lady Vengeance* (2005), which completed what has become known as 'The Vengeance Trilogy'.

Oldboy tells the story of an ordinary man, called 'Oh Dae-su' (Min-sik Choi) who disappears on his daughter's birthday and is imprisoned for fifteen years. While incarcerated he finds out that his wife has been murdered and that he is the main suspect. Then, without explanation he is released, given new clothes, money and a phone. A day after his release, Lee Woo-jin (Ji-tae Yu) (a former schoolfriend), phones to reveal himself as Dae-su's kidnapper. He offers Dae-su a chance to play a game; to discover Woo-jin's motive for imprisoning him. He has five days; if he fails, the girl that he has just met called Mi-do (Hye-jeong Kang) will be killed, if successful, Woo-jin will kill himself. The film is a powerful tale about a quest for vengeance and the aftermath once this aim has been achieved. The narrative lacks a conclusive ending, leaving the viewer to choose between multiple interpretations.

It is important to note that examining a non-Western film from the standpoint of European Psychoanalytic Theory could be deemed problematic. Different cultural backgrounds and societal structures could lead to misinterpretation, with the analytical tools not necessarily applicable to non-Western culture. However, Chan-Wook Park's knowledge of European philosophy and his strong interest in American and European films have enabled him to engage techniques and narrative tropes that span Western and Eastern cultures. *Oldboy* presents a wealth of elements that lend themselves to Psychoanalytic interpretation. Accordingly, the ideas of Sigmund Freud, Carl Jung and Jacques Lacan can furnish insights into the narrative and motivation of the characters.

From the outset of the film the audience is misled and manipulated. The main protagonist Dae-su says, 'I want to tell you my story.' This indication of a retrospective autobiographical tale is confirmed when the audience sees Dae-su imprisoned, recording what appear to be his memories. He hopes that this will lead him to discover who it is that wishes to do him harm. However, sequences follow that suggest a dreamlike state: gas is pumped into the room, injections are given and the audience witnesses, from Dae-su's point of view, a hazy image of a female hypnotist. Hypnosis plays a major role within the narrative and is instrumental in misleading the viewer.

Freud, Jung and Lacan encouraged patients to take part in what became known as the 'talking cure', so that repressed fears may surface. Coupled with hypnotism, this was thought to help people connect with their unconscious. Hypnosis is recognized as a means to 'free' and 'uncover' buried pasts and is typically engaged as a force for good. However, due to Dae-su's state of confinement, we need to question the intentions of the hypnotist. A major thread in this film hinges on which incidents are 'real' and which are drug-induced hallucinations. Furthermore, we question whether these memories are induced by hypnosis, or whether hypnosis, whose essential medical intent is curative, is being abused?

As spectators we witness what may be hallucinations or symbolic representations from Dae-su's unconscious as a result of hypnosis. Freud's Uncanny can be deployed as an explanatory method here. To depict these mind-bending states Park turns to Surrealism. For example, Dae-su is informed that he is to be released into a field. A shot of his cell is then juxtaposed with a close-up of grass. As the camera pulls back we see a field with a red suitcase in the centre. The suitcase begins to rock from side to side and surprisingly Dae-su tumbles out. This action unnerves the viewer in a manner reminiscent of the Surrealist tradition of filmmaking. It is then revealed that the protagonist is actually on a rooftop covered in grass. A man appears, clutching a dog and prepares to jump off the building. Dae-su prevents this suicide by holding onto the man's tie as he is suspended over the side. Without rational explanation, the next shot shows Dae-su in an elevator.

While all the images described above are familiar, the fact that there is no spatial or temporal continuity means that the audience cannot logically interpret these Surreal scenes. Shortly after this encounter, Dae-su meets a young woman called Mi-do who works in a sushi bar. Here, there are grotesque images of Dae-su gorging on a live octopus with flailing tentacles; he tears into the creature and ravenously chews it as Mi-do looks on, unconcerned. The action is shocking and unsettling to a Western audience, although this is accepted as a delicacy in South Korea. More importantly it could be illustrative of Freud's notion of the 'id', with primordial instincts being unleashed.

A further instance of the Uncanny is evident when a single ant is observed running up Dae-su's arm. This soon becomes three, then a dozen, until the camera shows his entire face teeming with ants, causing the audience to recoil. This can be read as a direct reference to Buñuel and Dalí's *Un Chien Andalou*. The only rational assumption is that this is the hallucination of a troubled mind. However, later in the film and without any context, Mi-do is shown travelling by train, late at night. A dark 'line' appears in close-up. As the camera draws back, it becomes clear that it is an insect's leg. Then, at the far end of the empty carriage, a human-size ant is seen calmly 'sitting' upon a seat. The use of ants is disorientating and hard to rationalize. Likewise, the examples of grass, suitcase and octopus avoid logical interpretation. In a manner similar to dreams, these Surreal incidents 'wrongfoot' the observer so that a sense of disquiet (the Uncanny) prevails.

These fragmentary and irrational glimpses of the main protagonist make it difficult to assess his character. Here, Jung's archetypes, in particular, the persona and the shadow, are pertinent to our understanding. Dae-su is frequently shown as unresponsive to others; he gets drunk on his daughter's birthday and fails to give her a present; steals a woman's sunglasses and laughs. Furthermore, Mi-do often pleads with him to follow a course of action; this he ignores, when, for example, he forces himself upon her sexually. It can be concluded that it is his shadow side that urges him to follow these impulses.

More importantly, the narrative goes back to Dae-su's time at high school when he is friends with Woo-jin and his sister Soo-ah (Jin-seo Yun). Here, Dae-su witnesses an incestuous act between Woo-jin and his sister. Dae-su spreads stories about this, which magnify to the extent that Soo-ah psychosomatically believes she is pregnant and, in a state of distress, commits suicide. Dae-su is apathetic to this outcome, yet at the conclusion of the film he recognizes what he has done and offers atonement. This could be illustrative of his persona attempting to learn from these events in order to assuage a sense of guilt.

The significance of the high-school trauma echoes throughout the film and explanations may be found in Freud's theory of the Oedipal phase. Although in this film the Oedipal stages are perversely engineered by a third party, they are nevertheless devastating. Both Dae-su and Mi-do have been conditioned to respond to hypnotic suggestion (what follows is a plot spoiler). It is this mind-changing dynamic that confuses and injures, causing untold suffering as they unknowingly perform incestuous acts. Their behaviour fulfils Woo-jin's catastrophic act of vengeance. Undeniably, the Oedipus complex sheds light on this outrageous aspect of the film.

Through post-hypnotic suggestion, Dae-su and Mi-do have been programmed to form a close sexual relationship. Woo-jin's vengeance is accomplished when he persuades Dae-su to open a box that contains a photo album of his daughter growing up. He is unimaginably shocked to discover that Mi-do is his daughter, and that he has been having an incestuous relationship with her. In Sophocles' *Oedipus Rex*, Oedipus blinds himself when he realizes what he has done. Similarly, Dae-su in a state of total repulsion, cuts out his own tongue, symbolizing his pledge of silence and plea to Lee Woo-jin not to reveal the dreadful truth to Mi-do. In 'silencing' himself, Dae-su shows recognition of the terrible wrong that he did to Soo-ah and Woo-jin. Furthermore, the removal of the tongue precludes any future use of the talking cure, denying Dae-su the possibility of ever mentioning what has happened.

In a final effort to control his 'shadow' personality, he asks the hypnotist to help him forget his secret. She tells him to imagine himself back at Lee Woo-jin's apartment where he cut off his tongue. Dae-su sees a reflection of himself in the window. The hypnotist urges him to acknowledge his reflection as the monster within (shadow archetype) and to let it walk away. He is encouraged to believe that with each step the monster takes, it will age a year, to die when it reaches seventy years' old. Initially the monster refuses to move as Dae-su battles with this part of his memory. Gradually he lets go and the shadow moves away. An awareness of Jungian archetypes facilitates a fuller appreciation of what may have contributed to this scene. The audience is led to believe that, in recognizing the 'shadow side' of his personality, Dae-su enables his persona (his public face) to take control. Therefore, hypnosis is presented as a positive way to help cure the protagonist's troubled mind. By confronting the two sides of his personality, his demons can be exorcized.

As we may expect in a film of such complexity, the ending is ambiguous. Once more there is little context for what follows. The epilogue is set in a wintry, snow-covered landscape. The audience sees a grey-haired Dae-su talking to the hypnotist in the snow. We do not have any sense of time passing. His grey hair could be a result of traumatic experiences or old age. Why the hypnotist is treating him in the snow is unclear and whether this meeting actually took place is uncertain.

The whiteness of the snow could be suggestive of a new page, a fresh start. Mi-do appears and says 'Oh Dae-su, I love you.' We know that she has no knowledge of his true identity (father). His tears and smile (forced or genuine?) may signify his hope for a sexual reunion or recognition of a bond between them. Whether he remembers 'the incestuous secret' and knows who Mi-do is is unclear. Whether the ending is positive or negative remains open to the viewer's interpretation. The end of the film is confusing, as it is not obvious whether Dae-su's character has been purged of the monster within or whether the beast has overcome the protagonist's persona. The conclusion is deliberately ambiguous and has thus generated much discussion.

The entire film is a game of vengeance. If you gain retribution, and that has been your life's motivation, what will happen to your life afterwards? What is the price for fulfilling your desires? The film ends with 'Thank you for listening to my story.' Knowledge of the analytic theories introduced by Freud and Jung makes it easier to appreciate the twists and turns of this thriller.

Reflect and respond

1 The ending of *Oldboy* can be interpreted in either a positive or negative light. Which do you favour and why?
2 Do the Surrealist images help or hinder a Psychoanalytical reading of the film?
3 Are the incidents of the Uncanny discussed only disconcerting for a Western audience?
4 How can we use Lacan's ideas of the mirror to understand Dae-su?
5 How helpful are Jungian archetypes of the shadow and the persona in understanding character motivation? Can you identify any of his other archetypes within the film?

Conclusion

Psychoanalytic interpretation is an ongoing science because our experiences continue to influence the way we read cultural texts. In undertaking a Psychoanalytical reading nothing is neutral; no feature or detail can be ignored as irrelevant as it can give rise to a multitude of meanings. However, we do need to guard against over-reading a film text (remember Freud's cigar).

It is important to note that a number of key aspects associated with Psychoanalysis are not covered in this chapter. This is because they are fundamental to the field of Feminism and so addressed in the next chapter (Chapter 9, 'Feminism'). For example, Freud's work on scopophilia, voyeurism and fetishism has been instrumental in underpinning Laura Mulvey's work.

Psychoanalysis has undergone many shifts in focus and certain ideas have been challenged. The work of Slavoj Žižek illustrates this point. Žižek, a Slovenian theorist, has questioned Lacan's concept of the imaginary in film theory (Žižek, 1989), as has Joan Copjec (2000). The combining of scientific thought with the arts continues to flourish and produce interesting ideas. As William Indick notes in his introduction to *Psychology for Screenwriters*: 'A thorough understanding of the unconscious mind – the birthplace of fantasy, dreams, and the imagination – is a fundamental point of departure for creating psychologically resonant scripts and films' (2004, p.xi).

Bibliography

Braudy, J. (2004) 'The Apparatus: Metaphysical Approaches to the Impression of Reality in Cinema', in L. Braudy and M. Cohen (eds) *Film Theory and Criticism: Introductory Readings*, 6th edn, Oxford: Oxford University Press.
Braudy, J. (2004) 'Ideological Effects of the Basic Cinematographic Apparatus', in L. Braudy and M. Cohen (eds) *Film Theory and Criticism: Introductory Readings*, 6th edn, Oxford: Oxford University Press.
Buñuel, L. (1983) *My Last Breath*, London: Jonathan Cape.
Campbell, J. (1968) *The Hero with a Thousand Faces*, Princeton, NJ: Princeton University Press.
Copjec, J. (2000) 'The Orthopsychic Subject: Film Theory and the Reception of Lacan', in R. Stam and T. Miller (eds) *Film and Theory: An Anthology*, Oxford: Blackwell.
Freud, S. (1919) 'Das Unheimliche (The Uncanny)', in D. Sandner (ed.) (2004) *Fantastic Literature: A Critical Reader*, Westport, CT: Praeger Publishers.
Freud, S. (1977) *Three Essays on the Theory of Sexuality*, Harmondsworth: Penguin.

Freud, S. (1999) *The Interpretation of Dreams*, Oxford: Oxford University Press.

Freud, S. (1999) *Totem and Taboo*, London: Routledge.

Freud, S. (2003) *Beyond the Pleasure Principle*, London: Penguin.

Gay, P. (ed.) (1995) *The Freud Reader*, London: Vintage.

Indick, W. (2004) *Psychology for Screenwriters: Building Conflict in Your Script*, Studio City, CA: Michael Wiese Productions.

Jung, C. (1969) *The Archetypes and the Collective Unconscious*, London: Routledge & Kegan Paul (first published 1959).

Lacan, J. (1949) 'The Mirror Stage as Formative of the Function of the I', in J. Lacan (1977) *Écrits: A Selection*, London: Routledge.

Lacan, J. (1977), *Écrits: A Selection*, London: Routledge.

Metz, C. (1982) *The Imaginary Signifier: Psychoanalysis and the Cinema*, Bloomington and Indianapolis: Indiana University Press (1975).

Sandner, D. (ed.) (2004) *Fantastic Literature: A Critical Reader*, Westport, CT: Praeger Publishers.

Stam, R. and T. Miller (2000) *Film and Theory: An Anthology*, Oxford: Blackwell.

Wollheim, R. (1995) *Sigmund Freud*, New York: Cambridge University Press.

Žižek, S. (1989) *The Sublime Object of Ideology*, London: Verso.

9

Feminism

Feminism
1. Advocacy of the rights of women (based on the theory of equality of the sexes).

Setting the scene

As far back as 1792, Mary Wollstonecraft (mother of Mary Shelley) published *A Vindication of the Rights of Women*, which is generally considered the first text on Feminism. During the nineteenth century, women started to campaign for equal rights and react against the suffocating Victorian image of the 'proper role' for women. Women were expected to care for the family above all and to be satisfied with domesticity and the patriarchal law. It was against this strongly patriarchal (male-led) society that the first Feminist movements emerged, although the term 'Feminism' was not coined until the 1890s. The development of the Feminist movement is recognized as having three stages, known as 'waves'.

The First Wave gained momentum around the 1900s. Writers such as Olive Schreiner, *Women and Labour* (1911) and Virginia Woolf, *A Room of One's Own* (1929) gave vivid portrayals of the unequal treatment of women. They felt that women seeking education and alternatives to marriage and motherhood were frowned upon. Therefore, Feminists campaigned for equal property rights, rights to higher education, to careers and later, women's right to vote (Suffragettes). During World War I (1914–18), women put their demands to one side to help with the war effort. In 1918, women were finally given the vote, providing they were thirty years of age, owned a property or held a degree. It was not until 1928 that women secured the vote on the same terms as men, at the age of twenty-one years.

The freedom afforded women during World War II, in undertaking what had been seen as male roles (factory work, farming the land, etc.), fuelled women's aspirations to remain in the public sphere. In 1949 Simone de Beauvoir wrote *The Second Sex*, a political and theoretical work that laid the foundations for subsequent Feminist research and incited women to question their position in society. De Beauvoir's book quickly became a classic and helped to inspire the next wave of Feminists.

This Second Wave of Feminism was known as the Women's Liberation Movement and lasted from the 60s–80s, with the term 'Women's Lib' passing into common usage, often with negative connotations. For example, it was implied that Feminists burnt their bras and disliked men. Importantly, these 60s Feminists were informed by the political, social and cultural climate of the time. They wanted to raise awareness of how the existing patriarchal ideology excluded, silenced and oppressed women. Rather than 'his-story', Feminists wanted 'her-story' to be recognized.

Feminists questioned the established order and encouraged radical reform. Germaine Greer's *The Female Eunuch* (1970) became an international success. Greer's main thesis was that 'traditional' society repressed women. She urged for change, which she believed would come, not from evolution but from revolution. Overall it was a period when Feminists fought for equal opportunities in the workplace and an end to sexual discrimination. It was at this point academics began researching women's literature and film.

The Third Wave Feminists, from the early 1990s to the 2000s, sought to address what they saw as the failures of the Second Wave. These later Feminists believed that the focus had been too concentrated on the upper-middle-class white woman. They saw that film theory could be employed as a radical act. As a result, there was a move to a more encompassing agenda which drew on Queer Theory, Race and Ethnicity Studies, Postcolonial Studies and so forth. These Feminists advocated a new definition of subjectivity. They highlighted issues that continued to oppress and limit women, such as the right to be able to access contraception and abortion. However, the Third Wave is often criticized for lacking a single objective.

Post 9/11, a movement has emerged that is recognized as 'New Feminism' or Fourth Wave Feminism. The main motivating issue for these Feminists is peace-making. It appears to be 'a fusion of spirituality and social justice that is reminiscent of the American civil rights movement and Ghandi's call for nonviolent change' (Peay, 2005). This is seen at popular conferences organized by women, spiritual and religious leaders. Peay notes:

> These gatherings share a commitment to a universal spirituality that affirms women's bonds across ethnic and religious boundaries. They're also exploring a new feminine paradigm of power that's based on tolerance, mutuality, and reverence for nature that have long been identified with women – values they now see as crucial to curing the global pathologies of poverty and war. (2005)

Meetings are attracting thousands of participants and celebrity speakers. For example, Jane Fonda spoke at the 'Women and Power Conference' in New York, September 2009. Currently, this 'Fourth Wave' has more credence and a greater following in America.

It is from these Second, Third and Fourth Wave Feminist aspirations that Feminist film critical theory developed. Early Feminist studies began to theorize on stereotypical images of female representations in film and the overt focus on the woman's body. The American Molly Haskell was one of the first academics to address these concerns. In her book, *From Reverence to Rape* (1974), she discusses how Hollywood's portrayal of women in conventional roles such as mothers and girls-next-door did not accord with women's real experiences. She noted a decade-by-decade shift from the respect afforded female characters in the silent era to a less deferential attitude in films of the 60s and 70s. Haskell argued that the American film industry 'manoeuvred to keep women in their place' by showing them to be socially inferior (Haskell, 1974, pp.2–3). She further maintained that women were stereotypically reduced to stock characters of glamorous sex goddesses, *femme fatales* or self-sacrificing mothers, all of which could be considered as traditional male fantasies (1974, pp.3–4). Haskell believed that the 'woman's film' emerged to compensate for the fact that women were excluded from most genres (Western, Gangster, etc). Overall her book implies that historically, films ignored the achievements women attained in real life, portraying them as submissive caricatures.

Psychoanalytic approaches to Feminism

Psychoanalysis has been readily adopted by Feminists as a means of understanding the way women are represented on screen. Claire Johnston and Laura Mulvey both produced seminal articles in the 70s, which were to have a huge impact on the study of film and media. Johnston's 'Women's Cinema as Counter-Cinema' targeted the processes of film production rather than concentrating on images alone. Johnston draws on Jacques Lacan, Roland Barthes, Michel Foucault and Louis Althusser in her investigation of film as a semiotic sign system. She focused on gendered and signifying contradictions to show how films maintained patriarchal order. She argued that films worked to preserve and perpetuate sexual inequality, and that 'the dominant ideology presented her [the woman] as eternal and unchanging, except for modifications in terms of fashion' (1973, p.32). Johnston stressed the importance of developing filmmaking in ways that would question and challenge mainstream dominant cinema and its patriarchal agenda.

At a similar time to Johnston's discussion of woman as a sign in patriarchal discourse, Laura Mulvey employed a Psychoanalytic approach to explain how cinema works at the level of the unconscious. In the male-dominated film industry, men had two widely differing roles: behind the camera, concerned with production and technology and as actors. In contrast, women would work in the costume and make-up departments (traditionally associated with the domestic sphere).

Before looking at Mulvey's groundbreaking essay, an understanding of the terminology that she appropriates from Freud is instructive:

- **Scopophilia:** This Freudian term denotes pleasure taken in looking. The scopophilic instinct occurs when people or images are viewed as erotic objects. For Freud scopophilia can become a perversion if it is connected with deviant behaviour as in the case of voyeurs (Gay, 1995, p.251).
- **Voyeurism:** Pleasure is voyeuristic when it is dependent on the object of the gaze being unaware. Someone spying on another is popularly known as a 'Peeping Tom'. To some extent both photography and film invite voyeuristic looking. It is the act of viewing the activities of others unbeknown to them. Therefore the act of looking can be seen as illicit or as having forbidden connotations. In the cinema we are voyeurs, watching people on screen who are 'ignorant' that we are watching them. We derive pleasure from this. The camera is also a voyeur.
- **Fetishism:** An object becomes a fetish when it is the focus of sexual desire. The fetishist idealizes an object associated with a woman to displace sexual anxiety. '[T]he normal sexual object is replaced by another which bears some relation to it. [...] what is substituted for the sexual object is some part of the body' (Gay, 1995, p.249). For example, images of shoes or hair can take on sexual connotations. In film, the audience may notice an excessive objectification of the female body, numerous shots of breasts and legs, say. The intense concentration on parts of the female body in the cinema is a prime example of fetishism.
- **Narcissism:** This is erotic pleasure derived from looking at one's own body. For both Freud and Lacan it was a natural stage in childhood. In film it is the audience's identification with the image on the screen and is often explained through the use of Lacan's 'mirror stage' (see Chapter 8, 'Psychoanalysis').

Reflect and respond

1 Can you think of any films that adopt scopophilia, voyeurism, fetishism and narcissism as plot devices?
2 From your examples, can you see any generic trends?
3 Can you speculate why Feminist film theorists were so preoccupied with scopophilia, voyeurism, fetishism and narcissism?

Laura Mulvey

'Visual Pleasure and Narrative Cinema' (1975)

Laura Mulvey is a Feminist film theorist. Her work signals a move from purely textual analysis towards an interest in the visual pleasure and identification found in the cinema. She employs Psychoanalytic Theory to discuss how popular cinema produces what she calls the 'male gaze'; here she appropriates theories from Freud and Lacan (see Chapter 8, 'Psychoanalysis'). In more traditional film theory, the spectator is assumed to be male; in light of this, Mulvey places the issue of sexual difference as central to her discussion. In order to do this:

> It [the essay] takes as its starting-point the way film reflects, reveals and even plays on the straight, socially established interpretation of sexual difference which controls images, erotic ways of looking and spectacle. [...] Psychoanalytic theory is thus appropriated here as a political weapon, demonstrating the way the unconscious patriarchal society has structured film form. (1975, p.34)

For Mulvey 'the gaze' is the main mechanism of control in film (1975, p.60). The image of the woman is first the object of male desire and second the signifier of the threat of castration.

Mulvey notes two 'pleasures', the first being scopophilia and voyeurism that are crucial to the sexual objectification of women. The second part of this pleasure is the narcissistic aspect that develops from scopophilia. This is discussed by Mulvey with the aid of Lacan's mirror stage as an explanatory model (see Chapter 8, 'Psychoanalysis'). According to Mulvey, elements of narcissistic identification with the person on screen occur because the projector is behind the spectator's head. This allows the spectator the illusion of controlling the image.

In her section, 'Woman as Image, Man as Bearer of the Look' (1975, p.62), Mulvey takes issue with the sexual imbalance of looking. It is Mulvey's contention that this gaze is always male because the 'look' in cinema (by the camera) is controlled by men and aimed at the female as an object. Furthermore, the male actors and the spectators (presumed male) voyeuristically identify with the camera and gaze at the woman in a fetishistic way. Mulvey selects films by Hitchcock as examples, *Rear Window*, *Vertigo*, *Psycho* and *Marnie*.

One of the key ideas that Mulvey promotes is that within traditional storytelling the female subject is always passive, whereas the male is active. For example, in fairytales the princess waits to be rescued by the dashing hero (knight, prince, etc.). Mulvey recognizes that these long-established tropes have carried through into filmmaking. She states:

In a world ordered by sexual imbalance, pleasure in looking has been split between active/male and passive/female. The determining male gaze projects its fantasy onto the female figure, which is styled accordingly. In their traditional exhibitionist role women are simultaneously looked at and displayed, with their appearance coded for strong visual and erotic impact so that they can be said to connote *to-be-looked-at-ness*. (1975, pp.62–3)

Mulvey has suggested that women have two roles in film, 'as erotic object for the characters within the screen story, and as erotic object for the spectator within the auditorium' (1975, p.63). Mulvey believed that filmmakers had been trapped into following certain codes and conventions in traditional Hollywood narrative. However, recent historical work suggests that the situation is much more complex than this. Women do undertake starring roles and increasingly make up part of the production team or are directors.

While Mulvey's article was groundbreaking and became the focus of debate and quotation, it was also criticized for its limited and essentialist focus in addressing only the male spectator. Variously, academics noted how she overlooked the important areas of women's voices, race and sexual preferences when looking at the male hero. Academics such as E. A. Kaplan (1976) contradicted Mulvey's findings, claiming that the male was not always a controlling force and that the female was not always a passive object. Furthermore, she believed that the female viewer could identify with both the passive and active positions. Nearly ten years later Mulvey responded to her critics.

'Afterthoughts on "Visual Pleasure and Narrative Cinema"' (1981)

'Afterthoughts' was inspired by King Vidor's *Duel in the Sun*. Here, Mulvey responded to critics who found her work essentialist and reductive (in her assumption that the gaze was solely male). After defending her position in the original article, this essay concentrates on Melodrama and on the woman spectator in particular. She develops two lines of analysis:

First (the 'woman in the audience' issue), whether the female spectator is carried along, as it were by the scruff of the text, or whether her pleasure is more deep-rooted and complex. Second (the 'melodrama' issue), how the text and its attendant identifications are affected by a female character occupying the centre of the narrative arena. (Mulvey, 1981, p.122)

Mulvey says that she is 'concentrating on films in which a woman central protagonist is shown to be unable to achieve a stable sexual identity, torn between [...] passive femininity and [...] regressive masculinity' (1981, p.123). She sees these as the dilemmas of the female spectator. Here, her work indicates a move away from how women are represented, towards studying female responses. She considers how women watch films and discusses the role of Melodrama (a genre traditionally considered female in orientation) in contrast with genres typically regarded as male (action movie).

Mulvey notes that the conventions cited by Freud on masculinity are deeply embedded in the structure of most popular narratives (Freud in Gay, 1995, pp.440–3). The male hero saves the female victim and any sexual desire is contained in marriage. Further, it is the hero's sense that 'nothing can happen to me' that drives him on. In contrast, the heroine is passive, waits to be saved and the narrative closes when this happens.

Mulvey then turns to Vladimir Propp's work on folktales (see Chapter 3, 'Formalism') to confirm how firmly these structures of active male/passive female are ingrained in storytelling. She notes that when a woman is introduced as central to the story, the structure and meaning of the narrative changes (as exhibited in *Duel in the Sun*). In this Western, the woman is faced with the conflicting desires of passive femininity or regressive masculinity. When the lead protagonist is female, the plot can be '*overtly*, about sexuality: it becomes a melodrama' (1981, p.127). Mulvey analyses the female position in this film in great detail and summarizes her findings. She suggests that female spectators need to be awoken to be '"pleasured" in stories' (1981, p.129).

Reflect and respond

1   To what extent do you think the tradition of the passive female and the active male is still prevalent in cinema today?
2   Discuss whether you agree or disagree that the camera adopts a male gaze?
3   Can we invert Mulvey's ideas and consider whether men adopt a female gaze when watching women's genres (Musicals, Romantic Comedies and Melodramas)?
4   Consider whether women are still objectified in contemporary filmmaking. Can the same be said of men?

Mulvey's 'Afterthoughts' in the early 80s recognized the change in mood among some Feminists. They wanted to focus the debate exclusively on political issues and indeed this remains a powerful line in Feminist thinking today. Accordingly, a number called for a counter-cinema to deconstruct the images associated with the patriarchal agenda of the film industry. There was a turn towards exploring the ideas of femininity and reconstructing lost or suppressed records of female experience.

Mary Ann Doane

'Film and the Masquerade: Theorising the Female Spectator' (1981)

The American theorist Mary Ann Doane explored the female gaze in relation to masquerade and drew insights from the work of psychologist Joan Rivière (1929). Rivière had observed that an 'intellectual' woman, when in a position of authority, donned a mask of 'Womanliness [...] to hide the possession of masculinity and to avert the reprisals expected if she was found to possess it' (Rivière, 1929, p.38). Doane introduces the term 'masquerade' to describe the way women often adopt a metaphorical mask; a way of behaving that is inscribed by gender expectations. She found that a common strategy was for women to act in an excessively flirtatious manner. This performance can then be manipulated for pleasure and this entails developing a new interpretative strategy (1981, p.137). Doane asks:

After all, even if it is admitted that the woman is frequently the object of voyeuristic or fetishistic gaze in the cinema, what is to prevent her from reversing the relation and appropriating the gaze for her own pleasure? (1981, p.134)

Doane combines Rivière's findings with Freud's lecture on 'Femininity', in which he maintained that issues in childhood paved the way for fetishism, and that this was an invariably male tendency.

Accordingly, Doane sees the male spectator as destined to be a fetishist, whereas the female finds it difficult, if not impossible, to take that position. Rather than absorbing the image, she is absorbed by it. She argues that the female spectator lacks the distance that voyeurism dictates. This has profound effects on women's leisure patterns and means that they will see adornment and consumption as inherently pleasurable activities. Women can indulge and inhabit their feminine identity. Doane refers to this as 'over-identification'. 'Womanliness is a mask which can be worn or removed' (1981, p.138).

Doane questions Christian Metz's work on apparatus and image in the cinema; she finds much of this theorizing untenable for a female spectator as it 'lacks the attribute of distance' (1981, p.143). Cinema has relied heavily on voyeurism, fetishism and identification with the ego, all in masculine terms. Thus it has encouraged theorists to see the female gaze as repressed. For Doane this shows that it is crucial to understand the woman's position in this in order for spectatorship theory to develop in a positive way.

Reflect and respond

1   Discuss whether femininity and masculinity are 'performed'?
2   Can you identify films where women deliberately adopt 'masquerade' as a plot device?
3   How far is the notion of 'over-identification' appropriate or useful?

Before moving on to consider Horror and the feminine, it is important to understand two crucial critical categories.

1   **Masochism**: Freud defines masochism as, 'any passive attitude towards sexual life and the sexual object [...] in which satisfaction is conditional upon suffering physical or mental pain at the hands of the sexual object' (Gay, 1995, p.252). For example, people who like to be whipped for sexual gratification can be termed masochists.
2   **Abject or abjection**: For the French Feminist Julia Kristeva, the abject is 'the place where meaning collapses' (1982, p.2). It is where we cannot explain what we see. It is being forced to face a traumatic event or object such as Kristeva's example of 'the museum that is now what remains of Auschwitz, I see a heap of children's shoes, or something like that, something I have seen elsewhere' (1982, p.4). Further, according to Kristeva this is '[e]ssentially different from "uncanniness", more violent, too' (1982, p.5). She explains: 'It is the infecting life. [...] It is thus not lack of cleanliness or health that causes abjection but what disturbs identity, system, order. What does not respect borders, positions, rules. The in-between, the ambiguous, the composite' (1982, p.5).

In summary, abjection comprises those ideas, images and objects that ignore borders and rules; they are disturbing because they question stable identity, systems and social order.

Barbara Creed

'Horror and the Monstrous-Feminine: An Imaginary Abjection' (1989)

Barbara Creed's contribution to Feminist critical analysis relates to the Horror film and the notion of the monstrous-feminine. Drawing on writers as diverse as Freud (fetishism, 1927), Joseph Campbell (primitive mythology, 1959) and Julia Kristeva (abjection), Creed examines 'horror as a perverse pleasure' (1989, p.253). She finds that the Horror film illustrates the way abjection works in the sociocultural arena.

Creed illustrates in great detail things that create the abject. First, there are countless images of corpses, 'whole and mutilated [...] bodily wastes such as blood, vomit' (1989, p.253). She records how spectators feel sick or experience fear within the viewing process. Yet watching Horror satisfies perverse desires and allows abjection to be encountered in the safety of the cinema. Second, the construction of the monstrous threatens to cross borders and threatens stability. Creed notes that the monstrous changes from film to film:

[B]etween the human and inhuman, man and beast (*Dr Jekyll and Mr Hyde*) [...] the border is between the normal and the supernatural, good and evil (*Carrie, The Exorcist, The Omen*) [...] or the monstrous is produced at the border which separates those who take up proper gender roles from those who do not (*Psycho, Dressed to Kill, Reflection of Fear*); or the border is between normal and abnormal sexual desire (*Cruising, The Hunger, Cat People*). (1989, p.253)

Third, Horror films frequently cast the maternal figure as abject. Creed draws on Kristeva again, who suggests that all babies face abjection when they try to break free from the mother who tries to resist this separation. This refusal to let go prevents the child from achieving its proper place in society. This is seen in Hitchcock's *Psycho*, *The Birds* and Brian De Palma's *Carrie* (1976), where the mother is presented as the monstrous-feminine (1989, p.254).

Furthermore, Creed draws on Kristeva's discussions on the rituals of defilement, the polluting substances of excrement and menstrual blood, 'Images of blood, vomit, pus, shit etc., are central to our culturally/socially constructed notions of the horrific' (1989, pp.255–6). Creed cites *The Exorcist* (William Friedkin, 1973) and *Carrie* as particularly representative examples of the 'gaping wound' and castration anxiety that are central concerns (particularly in Slasher films). Creed claims that historically, religion functioned as a means to purify the abject. However, this is no longer true because, 'the work of purification now rests solely with "that catharsis par excellence called art"' (Kristeva, 1982, p.17 and Creed, 1989, p.257).

Many of Creed's points are developed in her extensive analysis of *Alien* (Ridley Scott, 1979) in which she addresses the idea of the 'treacherous mother, the oral sadistic mother, the mother of the primordial abyss [...] the toothed vagina' (1989, p.258). This image of the 'toothed vagina' is present in many cultures and is frequently referred to as 'vagina dentata'. It can be read as a symbol of male castration anxiety. Creed argues that the function of the Horror film within a patriarchal culture is to evoke the monstrous-feminine. She also suggests that the blurring of gender boundaries in horror reveals a great deal about male fears and desires.

Reflect and respond

1   Why does the film industry rely on bodily fluids to instil feelings of abjection?
2   Why do you think the idea of 'vagina dentata' occurs in all cultures?
3   Can Horror be understood as the manifestation of male fears?
4   How does film deal with taboo objects such as bodily fluids and/or taboo practices such as necrophilia and incest?

Mulvey, Doane and Creed's work on the gaze, spectatorship and the monstrous-feminine utilizes Psychoanalytic theories to examine how the female spectator is constructed by the text. Yet there are other approaches that require attention, such as questions of audience response.

Feminist approaches to subjectivity

Annette Kuhn was concerned with the 'woman in the audience'. She felt that film theory had not examined the ways in which audiences have understood films within a framework of social contexts. To address this, she explores Soap Operas and Melodramas in her essay, 'Women's Genres: Melodrama, Soap Opera and Theory' (1984). Kuhn outlines three problems that she intends to address; first, the problem of gendered spectatorship; second, the historical specificity of gendered spectatorship; and third, the relationship between film and television texts (1984, p.21).

According to Kuhn, these problems have arisen because psychoanalytic theories have offered 'little scope for theorising subjectivity in its cultural or historical specificity' (1984, p.22). Kuhn advocated the notion that there was no fixed feminine text, although a text could become feminine when it was read. She looks at the relationship between text and context by concentrating on the differences between the spectator and the idea of the wider audience.

Kuhn notes that, 'Looking at spectators and at audiences demands different methodologies and theoretical frameworks, distinct discourses which construct distinct subjectivities and social relations' (1984, p.23). For her, it is important to question how large audiences of women identify with popular media texts. This will enable an assessment of 'the political usefulness of popular genres aimed at, and consumed by, mass audiences of women' (1984, p.27).

Teresa de Lauretis raised issues concerning subjectivity. In her essay, *Alice Doesn't. Feminism. Semiotics. Cinema* (1984), she examined the structural representations of 'woman' in cinema and discussed how narratives produce images of subjectivity. She points out that narrative structures are formed by desire. This desire is inherently Oedipal (men's control of women). To explain this, she cites many examples from Hitchcock, in particular the female characters in *Rebecca* (1940) and *Vertigo*. Here the females are made to conform to the ideal image that the male protagonist imposes upon them. In *Vertigo*, Scottie's (James Stewart) desire for the enigmatic Judy/Madeleine

(Kim Novak) drives the narrative of the film. The female subject is made to perform a specific feminine role. Yet for de Lauretis the performance of the female character is impossible, and the narrative tension is often resolved by the destruction of the female (Judy/Madeleine in *Vertigo* and the new Mrs de Winter (Joan Fontaine) in *Rebecca*). Furthermore, she finds that desire in narrative is intimately bound up with violence against women, and the techniques of cinematic narration both reflect and sustain the social forms of oppression of women.

De Lauretis writes about two different processes of identification in cinema. The first moves between a masculine and active identification with the gaze (Scottie) and a passive feminine identification with the image (Judy/Madeleine). This enables the female spectator to take up both the active and passive positions of desire. The second is simultaneous identification, which can be seen with both the new Mrs de Winter and with the imagined image of the first Mrs de Winter in *Rebecca*. For de Lauretis, feminist theory is built on the contradiction of the unrepresentability of woman as subject of desire.

> ### Reflect and respond
>
> 1 Discuss films in which female subjectivity is made central.
> 2 Account for the destruction of the female character when she is portrayed as an object of desire.
> 3 Identify other film texts where men manipulate women to conform to their expectations.

For Feminists, female spectators are seen as marginalized. In order to develop ideas from Mulvey and others into different directions, critical analysis began to focus on other 'marginalized' spectators (gay, black, etc.).

Feminist approaches to marginalized groups

Jackie Stacey's 1987 essay 'Desperately Seeking Difference' takes up the homosexual perspective to address critiques of homosexual spectatorship. Adopting the work of Doane and Kuhn, she notes that the pleasure of the female spectator has hardly been addressed, 'specifically homosexual pleasures of female spectatorship have been ignored completely' (1987, p.244). Although it needs to be noted that various writers, including de Lauretis (1984), have written on this, Stacey sets out to suggest some reasons for the general neglect.

She considers that the film text can be read and enjoyed from different gendered positions or, despite the masculine apparatus, spectators can respond differently to the visual pleasures of the text. Stacey examines *All about Eve* (Joseph L. Mankiewicz, 1950) and *Desperately Seeking Susan* (Susan Seidelman, 1985) to pursue ideas on the pleasures of desire and identification. From her work Stacey concludes that a focus on the 'distinction between *either* desire *or* identification, so characteristic of film theory, fails to address the construction of desires which involve a specific interplay of both processes' (1987, p.257) Of course, it is important to distinguish between the different spectator positions adopted by lesbians and male homosexuals.

Whereas Stacey acknowledged that Feminists had historically ignored the gay female audience, bell hooks raised concerns regarding black female spectatorship.

bell hooks

'The Oppositional Gaze: Black Female Spectators' (1992)

It is important to note that bell hooks, the African American feminist scholar, insists that her name appear in lowercase rather than with initial capitals. She believes it is the substance of her writing that is important, rather than who she is. hooks queried Mulvey's position on the 'male gaze'. She points out that black people have historically been punished for looking. Here she cites the incident when Emmett Till, a fourteen-year-old black boy, was murdered for looking and whistling at a white woman (p.118). She believes that Feminist theory ignores the issue of race in the same way that the film industry has historically struggled to represent black woman-hood on screen. Even when African American male filmmakers attempt to depict black women, they typically objectify them, which, for hooks, perpetuates the subtext of white supremacy (p.118).

hooks states that as a black woman she has a choice either to identify with the white woman or resist identification. The latter is the logical position, as black women do not recognize themselves on screen, since the film industry has tended to misrepresent or ignore them entirely. Accordingly, black women adopt an 'oppositional gaze' or what Manthia Diawara calls 'resisting spectatorship' (p.128). In embracing this attitude of rejection, black women can no longer be hurt by derogatory images of African American female identity. Rather than agreeing with Mulvey's concept of the female as passive and the male as active, hooks laments that, even when black women assume the role of director, black femininity is still victim to 'the white supremacist capitalist imperialist dominating "gaze"' (p.129).

Reflect and respond

1   Identify the difference in spectatorial positions between heterosexual and homosexual viewers.
2   Discuss whether hooks's notion of the 'oppositional gaze' can be usefully applied.
3   Have gay women and black females been under- and/or misrepresented on screen?

As has been noted here, much of the work from Feminist critics in the 80s has taken its lead from Mulvey. However, there are other approaches. Kaja Silverman is a Feminist critic who has focused her attention on the woman's voice. In 'Dis-Embodying the Female Voice' (1984), her analysis looks at the sound/image relationship in terms of gender, and concentrates on the noticeable absence of a female voice-over in classical cinema. She believes that this absence expressed the fact that the female subject was 'associated with unreliable, thwarted, or acquiescent speech' (1984, p.131). Silverman called for a re-analysis of Hollywood films with more attention focused on the construction of the soundtrack. She discussed the use of the 'disembodied' female voice-over in a number of films directed by women, especially Yvonne Rainer's *Journey from Berlin* (1971). She developed her ideas further in the book *The Acoustic Mirror: The Female Voice in Psychoanalysis and Cinema* (1988).

In the 90s there was a notable interest in Feminist theories on pornography, which took a wide-ranging approach to the issue of female objectification. Maggie Humm noted that Feminists were divided in their opinion. Some were anti-pornography, arguing that it was misogynist and dehumanized women, with Andrea Dworkin claiming that it encouraged violence against women (Dworkin in Humm, 1997, p.43). On the other hand, other Feminists such as Linda Williams took an anti-censorship stance, arguing that: '[P]ornography involves issues of fantasy and fetishism too complex to be reduced to any possible effects; and that pornographic representations could be an important, even creative, part of women's – not just men's – sexual pleasure' (Humm, 1997 p.43).

In her essay, 'Film Bodies: Gender, Genre and Excess' (1991) Williams succinctly summed up what she thought of pornography and Horror films,

> Alone or in combination, heavy doses of sex, violence, and emotion are dismissed by one faction or another as having no logic or reason for existence beyond their power to excite. Gratuitous sex, gratuitous violence and terror, gratuitous emotion are frequent epithets hurled at this phenomenon of the 'sensational' in pornography, horror, and melodrama. (1999, p.142)

In this chapter we have shown some of the ways in which Feminism has stimulated new debate for Feminist theory. Moreover, it can be seen that there is a lot of 'cross-fertilization' between Feminism as a political movement (female suffrage, a right to education and equality in the workplace, etc.) and Feminist film criticism. As Feminists they were working to the same agenda in the fight for female recognition.

Case study: *Mamma Mia!* (Phyllida Lloyd, 2008)

Mamma Mia!, based on the 1999 West End Musical of the same name, became the highest-grossing musical of all time in October 2008 (Bradshaw, 2008). Musicals are commonly considered to be 'women's films'; however for *Mamma Mia!*, the category takes on a new meaning. It can be seen as the most Feminist film of the year because it breaks with many Hollywood conventions. It is a 'woman's film' in terms of genre, production, female characters and narrative trajectory, which accordingly presents an ideal opportunity to explore Feminist issues. Its narrative inverts many of the standard perspectives, social and cultural expectations and psychological tropes of mainstream Hollywood films.

The story is set on a Greek island and is about the 1970s, where twenty-year-old Sophie (Amanda Seyfried) is to marry. To make her wedding day complete, she would like her father to attend. However, she does not know who he is. Finding three possible names in her mother's diary, she invites each of these men to her special day. The story unfolds as the daughter tries to keep the presence of the three men secret from her mother, while attempting to uncover the real identity of her father. As the community prepares for the big day, the mother is reunited with her female friends, who provide support when her three lovers appear.

Writing in the *New York Times*, Sylviane Gold comments on the rarity of female directors and writers in the film business. The figures are telling: in 2007, of the top 250 films only 6 per cent had women directors and only 10 per cent were written by women (figures not dissimilar to those of twenty years ago) (2008). Yet *Mamma Mia!* was directed by Phyllida Lloyd and written by Catherine Johnson. Furthermore, all the top positions connected with the production were held by women, including co-producer Judy Craymer, film editor Lesley Walker, casting, production design, art director, set director and costume design. Additionally, the production studio, Universal Pictures, had just appointed British Donna Langley as the co-chairman who gave *Mamma Mia!* the go-ahead. With this level of female input, both in front of and behind the camera, a shared aim that appears to question notions of femininity is evident. This is a film about women; their sexuality, ageing, lifestyles, male and female friendships.

In *Mamma Mia!, in* contrast to many films, the main characters are women in their fifties to sixties. Meryl Streep's character, Donna, a single mother who owns a hotel, is sexy and raunchy. Julie Walters plays Rosie, another single woman, who is a successful cookery writer and Christine Baranski is Tanya, an attractive, thin, rich, three-times married, surgically enhanced socialite. They are far removed from the more common film caricatures of older women, typically depicted as quiet grandmothers or feisty, but cranky, old crones. Molly Haskell has argued that the American film industry sought to 'keep women in their place', but that 'place' has been firmly rejected in this film (1974, p.3).

As has been shown in this chapter, much of the analysis in Feminist film theory has evolved from Laura Mulvey's work on the male gaze. Accordingly, it seems appropriate to start with her ideas in this case study. However, a theoretical position that employs Mulvey's argument, that all mainstream films are complicit in their favouring of the 'male gaze' and the objectification of women, would be difficult to sustain for *Mamma Mia!*.

Lloyd directs the scenes in order to show women as central and in control. The fifty- to sixty-year-old stars are rarely shot in tight close-ups, nor does the camera sexualize the women with an overt concentration on body parts. Indeed the notion of objectification is deployed in a playful way. There appears to be a deliberate mocking of the conventional 'male gaze'. During many of the song-and-dance routines, the characters appear to invite the lens to follow them in a 'come hither' fashion. Donna, Rosie and Tanya turn to face the camera and are seen moving enthusiastically towards it, shaking their upper bodies, gyrating their hips and, in a non-sexual fun manner, grabbing their own body parts in an act of ownership, while laughing. Their clothing is loose and to some extent shapeless. This is not about a voyeuristic camera, but one where the female character is actively empowered. Scenes are designed to laugh at and mock sex and lust, rather than offer a voyeuristic gaze at the women. What could have been problematic as a method of presenting female desire, in particular desire in older women, is skilfully deflected. Accordingly, possibilities of voyeurism or fetishization are neutralized and Mulvey's notion of the 'male gaze' is evidently not the mechanism of control in this film. Therefore, a blanket application of the 'Mulvey' position is not helpful in this case, as in these scenes the female characters are actively controlling the gaze.

It is clear that modern filmmakers (particularly if they are women) know that, in order to engage the audience, a point of view needs to be provided with which the audience can sympathize. Some feminist critics have worked extensively on the notion of narrative pleasure, identification and spectacle. Such ideas are very useful for accounting for the popularity of the text.

The film offers a historically precise window on the world. In addition to being popular with a young female audience, *Mamma Mia!* has been instrumental in appealing to the older female spectator. It is possible to speculate that many of the females in the audience would have lived through the 70s, either as single or married young women, meaning that the music would be well known to them, so that they can sing along, while also relating to the clothing and cultural references.

This nostalgia for a shared past supplies some of the many points of identification for the female audience. Yet, as Doane warns, comfort in the familiar may lead to an active 'over-identification' with the images. This is prominently displayed in the sing-a-long screenings where members of the audience dress up as their favourite characters.

Donna is a single parent who is unsure which of three men is the father of her daughter. This sexual freedom would have been almost unheard of prior to the 50s, considered promiscuous in the 60s, yet by the 70s had become more widespread and less shocking. Rosie has not married and is financially independent, achieving success as a writer. Although Tanya has followed the traditional route of marriage, she has nullified this by divorcing several times. Despite the fact that they have not followed the conventional paths of the time, there is no hint of reproach or stigmatism from the patriarchal society for their lifestyle choices. This represents a departure from de Lauretis's view (1984), whereby women are made to conform to male ideals or suffer violence. Here there is no question of punishing these women for stepping outside patriarchal boundaries. Lloyd's subjective approach is non-judgmental.

Doane's application of ideas of masquerade has a particular resonance within the film. The female protagonists have led successful independent lives. Yet all three are accomplished in assuming the guise of femininity, as displayed in their girly, frivolous demeanour. It is possible to see this as a mask to subsume their intelligence, independence and experience of life, which could mark them as unfeminine. Their metaphorical mask is provided by their colourful relaxed outfits, shared laughter and foolish reminiscences. However, this masquerade is complicated at the narrative's conclusion. In the form of an encore or epilogue, the three female friends sing a final Abba number, dressed in their glam-rock costumes from the 70s. The 'pantomime' of over-the-top costumes, strutting and gyrating is suggestive of the Carnivalesque (Mikhail Bakhtin). As this final scene finishes, Donna moves towards the camera and points in the direction of the assumed audience and shouts, 'Do you want more? Do You Want More?.' The question remains: is this a rock chick inviting further encores or a solidarity call to the women in the cinema or a veiled and light-hearted 'Siren-esque threat' to the men in the room?

Some of the writers examined in this chapter took the view that classical cinema can give inadequate or biased coverage of socially marginal groups, such as gays/lesbians, or non-white groups (hooks). It is certainly apparent that such groups are represented in an uneven way in *Mamma Mia!*. Colin Firth plays a gay character (although ironically he may have fathered the daughter). However, his portrayal has clearly been directed so as to minimize the traditional signs of gayness. There is no hint of camp in the performance and indeed the choice of Firth is noteworthy. He brings with him the baggage of his earlier famous heterosexual roles in *Pride and Prejudice* (Simon Langton, 1995) and *Bridget Jones's Diary* (Sharon Maguire, 2001). This problematically neutralizes the gayness of his character.

Additionally, the one 'token' black character, lusted after by Tanya, clearly performs the function of the objectified male. Also, although the film takes place in Greece, there are few signs of the authentic culture, other than a picturesque dilapidation. Furthermore, all the Greek characters are menial workers (kitchen hands, chambermaids, servants); thus both the 'character' of Greece and the Greek people are marginalized. Both these absences (of non-WASP and non-heterosexual characters in central roles) affect the texture of the film. Therefore it can be argued that, some Feminists' attention to the white and heterosexist bias of mainstream cinema can change our view of the film in alerting us to these absences.

Conclusion

Mamma Mia! evokes a nostalgic and escapist narrative of the 70s in a prescribed Musical fashion. It follows the light-hearted escapades of three women who have pursued their individual paths. Further, it celebrates womanly virtues of sisterhood, caring, sacrifice, empathy and so on. Yet, as shown above, on closer examination it is evident that many of the patriarchal and cinematic codes have been inverted. Lloyd's lightness of touch presents on the surface a seemingly neutral narrative. However, it is not neutral and the outcomes deny a straightforward reading. Throughout the story, the theme is one of freedom, living outside the typical conventions still prevalent in the 70s, the idea that women should marry and have children rather than pursue a career. These women were shown as being in control of their lives and free to follow their dreams.

However, the daughter's wedding does not take place: her mother Donna marries Sam (Pierce Brosnan); Rosie rejects her single status and throws herself into the arms of the Swedish writer (Stellan Skarsgård); and Tanya returns to her husband. The three older women interestingly turn their back on the 'free love' attitude of the 70s and choose to adhere to conventional patriarchal order. However, the daughter, who represents the younger generation, opts for freedom as she sails into the sunset with her former fiancé.

It can be concluded that not all Feminist positions will produce new insights on films. Some of them may give rise to new knowledge, some prove too restrictive. Clearly there is a need to be selective when deploying the theoretical ideas. Moreover, we need to take account of when a film was produced, since some films are made from a Feminist perspective, or take on board a Feminist agenda. *Mamma Mia!* is clearly one of these and, although a popular film, it undertakes a sophisticated exploration of Feminism.

Reflect and respond

1 To what extent is *Mamma Mia!* a female film? What does it have to say about masculinity?
2 Discuss whether the format of the narrative (Musical) enhances the film as a female text.
3 Consider the four main female characters (played by Streep, Walters, Baranski and Seyfried). Are they stereotyped in any way?
4 How far are the ideas of femininity informed by the seemingly 'all-female' production team?

Conclusion

Feminism can be seen as site of social and intellectual debate. There is a focus on women's experience of sexuality, work and the family. The Feminist movement recognized the patriarchal structure of society; that the world is organized on terms dictated by men to their own advantage. In order to challenge this, Feminists have worked to achieve rights for women, to promote women's artistic undertakings in order to challenge the stereotypical representation of women.

Feminism has no single vision; Feminist theory crosses borders of history, philosophy, anthropology, arts, etc. Furthermore, it utilizes other theories such as Structuralism and semiotics, Post-structuralism, Race and Ethnicity, Queer Theory and most importantly of all, Psychoanalysis.

Much has changed in Feminist film theory. The gaze is definitely no longer considered to be male; it can be homoerotic, oppositional and so on. Film could be engaged as an ideological tool, which can counteract stereotypical images of women presented in a male-dominated media. It can also raise women's awareness of their inferior position in patriarchal society, where they are generally relegated to a subservient role. These broader perspectives enable critics to see that film is a part of the cultural apparatus and that it relates in a complex way to the structure of patriarchy.

Bibliography

Beauvoir, S. de. (1984) *The Second Sex,* London: Penguin Books (first published 1949).

Berger, J. (1972) *Ways of Seeing,* London: British Broadcasting Corporation and Penguin Books.

Bradshaw, P. (2008) 'Mamma Mia!' *Guardian.* Retrieved 11 August 2010. Available at http://www.guardian.co.uk/culture/2008/jul/10/film.reviews.

Campbell, J. (1959) *Primitive Mythologies,* New York: Viking Penguin Inc.

Creed, B. (1989) 'Horror and the Monstrous-Feminine: An Imaginary Abjection', in S. Thornham (ed.) (1993) *Feminist Film Theory: A Reader,* Edinburgh: Edinburgh University Press, pp.251–64.

Doane, M. A. (1981) 'Film and the Masquerade: Theorising the Female Spectator', in S. Thornham (ed.) (1999) *Feminist Film Theory: A Reader,* Edinburgh: Edinburgh University Press, pp.131–45.

Freud, S. (1905) 'Three Essays on Sexuality and Other Works', in P. Gay (ed.) (1995) *The Freud Reader,* London: Vintage.

Freud, S. (1953) *The Standard Edition of the Complete Psychological Works of Sigmund Freud; Vol. 7 (1901–1905) A Case of Hysteria; Three Essays on Sexuality and Other Works,* London: Hogarth Press and the Institute of Psycho-analysis.

Gay, P. (ed.) (1995) *The Freud Reader,* London: Vintage.

Gold, S. (2008) 'The *Mamma Mia!* Factor Times 3', *New York Times.* Retrieved 11 August 2010. Available at http://www.nytimes.com/2008/07/06/movies/06gold.html.

Greer, G. (1970) *The Female Eunuch,* London: MacGibbon & Kee.

Haskell, M. (1974) *From Reverence to Rape: The Treatment of Women in the Movies,* New York: Holt, Rinehart and Winston.

hooks, b. (1992) 'The Oppositional Gaze: Black Female Spectators', *Black Looks: Race and Representation,* Boston, MA: Southend Press, pp.115–31

Humm, M. (1997) *Feminism and Film,* Edinburgh: Edinburgh University Press.

Johnston, C. (1973) 'Women's Cinema as Counter-Cinema', in S. Thornham (ed.) (1999) *Feminist Film Theory: A Reader,* Edinburgh: Edinburgh University Press, pp.31–40.

Johnston, C. (1982) 'Femininity and the Masquerade: Anne of the Indies', *Screen* vol. 23, pp.3–4.

Kaplan, E. A. (1976) 'Aspects of British Feminist Film Theory: A Critical Evaluation of the Texts by Claire Johnston and Pam Cook', *Jump Cut* vols 12/13, pp.52–5.

Kaplan, E. A. (ed.) (2000) *Feminism & Film,* Oxford: Oxford University Press.

Kristeva, J. (1982) *Power of Horror: Essay on Abjection,* New York: Columbia University Press.

Kuhn, A. (1984) 'Women's Genres: Melodrama, Soap Opera and Theory', in G. Turner (ed.) *The Film Cultures Reader,* New York: Routledge, pp.20–7.

Lauretis, T. de (1984) *Alice Doesn't. Feminism. Semiotics. Cinema,* Bloomington: Indiana University Press.

Metz, C. (1982) *The Imaginary Signifier: Psychoanalysis and the Cinema,* Bloomington and Indianapolis: Indiana University Press.

Mitchell, J. (1990) *Psychoanalysis and Feminism*, Harmondsworth: Penguin.

Mulvey, L. (1999) 'Afterthoughts on "Visual Pleasure and Narrative Cinema" Inspired by King Vidor's *Duel in the Sun* (1946)', in S. Thornham (ed.) *Feminist Film Theory: A Reader,* Edinburgh: Edinburgh University Press, pp.122–30.

Mulvey, L. (2000) 'Visual Pleasure and Narrative Cinema' (1975), in E. A. Kaplan (ed.) (2000) *Feminism & Film*, Oxford: Oxford University Press, pp.34–47.

Peay, P. (2005) 'Feminism's Spiritual Wave', *UTNE Magazine* March/April 2005. Retrieved 29 July 2010. Available at http://www.feminist.com/resources/artspeech/insp/spiritualwave.html.

Rivière, J. (1929) 'Womanliness as a Masquerade', in V. Burgin, J. Donald and C. Kaplan (eds) (1986) *Formations of Fantasy,* London: Methuen.

Rosen, M. (1973) *Popcorn Venus: Women, Movies & the American Dream*, New York: Coward, McCann & Geoghegan.

Silverman, K. (1984) 'Dis-Embodying the Female Voice', in M. Doane, P. Mellencamp and L. Williams (eds) (1984) *Re-Vision: Essays in Feminist Film Criticism,* Los Angeles, CA: University Publications of America, Inc.

Silverman, K. (1988) *The Acoustic Mirror: The Female Voice in Psychoanalysis and Cinema*, Bloomington: Indiana University Press.

Stacey, J. (1987) 'Desperately Seeking Difference', in J. Caughie, A. Kuhn and M. Merck (eds) (1992) *The Sexual Subject: A Screen Reader in Sexuality,* London: Routledge, pp.244–57.

Thornham, S. (ed.) (1999) *Feminist Film Theory: A Reader,* Edinburgh: Edinburgh University Press.

Williams, L. (1991) 'Film Bodies: Gender, Genre and Excess', in B. K. Grant (ed.) *Film Genre Reader III*, Austin: University of Texas Press, pp.141–59.

Woolf, V. (1929) *A Room of One's Own*, London: Hogarth Press.

Chapter

10

Masculinity

Masculinity
1. The state or fact of being masculine; the assemblage of qualities regarded as characteristic of men; maleness, manliness.

Setting the scene

Unlike some of the theories and critical perspectives addressed in earlier chapters, Masculinity Studies has a short history, despite the fact that most world cultures are founded on patriarchy. The male has historically been the authoritative force making the important decisions whether in the public or the private sphere. The dominance of patriarchal society was largely unquestioned as it was accepted as the natural order of things. This was reflected in academia and accordingly, theories concerning masculinity were largely ignored and therefore slow to gain momentum. In this chapter we intend to identify some of the main areas for discussion in order to provide the tools to assess theories of masculinity.

Film Studies as a discipline has typically addressed how certain groups have been depicted on screen. Academics have focused in particular on the way film represents women, homosexuals, different races and ethnicities. Interestingly, the one area of study that has traditionally been overlooked is how masculinity is embodied. Because men feature so predominantly in films, their presence is habitually accepted as a given. Men have traditionally been the heroes of the narrative with women most frequently relegated to the love interest (in need of rescuing). Laura Mulvey famously discussed male and female in terms of binary oppositions, with the woman as passive and the male as active (see Chapter 9, 'Feminism'). She noted that women in film were objectified by men because the camera (typically controlled by men) adopted a voyeuristic stance. Her seminal text opened the field for Gender Studies as it both highlighted and problematized the workings of gender relations on screen.

The reason why many scholars felt that women were subjected to the 'male gaze' was because the industry was run predominantly by men. Women would often gain employment working in the costume and make-up departments (traditionally associated with the domestic sphere), but the mechanics of the film industry were controlled by men. Men had two very differing roles, one as the filmmaker behind the camera and the other as the performer taking centre stage and this was the way the industry functioned. As a result of their influence, the role of the male on screen was simply ignored. His image saturated all aspects of filmmaking and so he became invisible. This idea of invisibility (the male accepted as the 'norm') was not addressed specifically until the early 80s, with Steve Neale's article 'Masculinity as Spectacle' instigating the debate.

Steve Neale

'Masculinity as Spectacle' (1983)

Steve Neale was one of the first academics to recognize that the field of gender, representation and sexuality in Film Studies had overwhelmingly focused on female identity. In his article 'Masculinity as Spectacle' Neale looked to redress the balance and initiate debate concerning men on screen. Taking John Ellis's book *Visible Fictions* as a starting point, he discusses how audience identification with images is never stable. As viewers we shift identification from one character to the next. One minute we may identify with the male protagonist and in the following scene we are rooting for the female. Ellis tried to understand our 'different forms of identification' through the terms 'narcissism' and 'phantasies and dreams' (Neale, 1983, p.278). Narcissistic identification occurs when we read some element of ourselves into a character; whereas phantasies and dreams involve 'multiple and contradictory tendencies'. Although neither Ellis nor Neale explain the latter term fully, it can be interpreted as daydreaming and fantasizing about stars and imagining ourselves in the diegetic film world in place of the original characters.

Neale states that narcissistic identification is concerned with 'power, omnipotence, mastery and control' (p.279). In identifying with the male hero the viewer experiences a sense of power. However he warns:

> While the ideal ego [powerful male] may be a 'model' with which the subject identifies and to which it aspires, it may also be the source of further images and feelings of castration, inasmuch as that ideal is something to which the subject is never adequate. (p.279)

In summary, identifying with Hollywood's representation of manliness often leaves the male viewer feeling inadequate as the eroticized image (well-toned six-pack, chiselled jaw, full head of hair) is rarely achievable.

Building on the work of Mulvey, Neale explores how the on-screen male is in control of the 'look'; we view the world through his eyes. However, he cannot function as an erotic image. Mulvey claims that 'in a heterosexual and patriarchal society the male body cannot be marked explicitly as the erotic object of another male look'; instead this look must be repressed. This repression is manifest in the way Hollywood tends to juxtapose stimulating images of masculinity and images of violence (p.281).

Willemen (1981) observes that the voyeuristic pleasure for the viewer in seeing the man on screen is frequently punished because the star is shown undergoing brutal masochistic trials. The sadistic treatment of the male star is a reaction to the erotic energy of the image. In order to divert any homophobic or homoerotic feelings, the male body is defaced in some manner as a way of relieving the sexual tension. This can also apply to male friendships on screen. When a male character is seen to be very close to a comrade of the same sex, the friendship is often terminated by death or disfigurement. This way any homoeroticism is avoided and traditional patriarchal order restored.

Thought needs to be given to the conclusion of narratives, as it is here that the male protagonist can also become a threat to social hierarchy. Vladimir Propp identified the fact that most narratives finish with the marriage of male hero and female love interest. In his article, Neale examines the archetypal heroes found in Westerns. Many Westerns will conclude with the cowboy hero turning his back on the happy ending (marriage), instead opting for the narcissistic trope of wandering into the sunset. Neale observes that, in cases where the male avoids the threat of castration by turning his back on marriage and domesticity, death will surely follow, as inferred in *Shane* and clearly depicted in the character of Billy the Kid in *Young Guns II* (Geoff Murphy, 1990).

The article concludes with Neale exploring how men can be photographed in a fetishistic manner. Women are represented by body parts and iconography in a fragmented way (hair, lips, nails and high heels) to displace fears of castration. Men are similarly depicted in a fragmentary, objective manner to represent fear, hatred and aggression (eyes, guns, chaps). Nevertheless, the male is really only captured in this way during combat, when the male body is acceptable as a spectacle. Even then, the images are cut to emphasize energy, action and pace, rather than a lingering sensual focus on the body. However, when the male body is displayed as a sight for voyeuristic pleasure, violence is absent. In these instances the body is typically feminized as often seen in Musicals (John Travolta in *Saturday Night Fever* and Zac Efron in the *High School Musical* franchise. This is very telling, as it shows the industry to be uncomfortable with the objectification of the male.

Reflect and respond

1   Do you agree with Neale that the male image has to be repressed and beaten up in order to deny the spectator the erotic gaze?
2   Do you agree that when the male body is celebrated it becomes homoerotic? (Consider the following stars famous for their bodies: Arnold Schwarzenegger, Sylvester Stallone, Brad Pitt, Vin Diesel.)
3   Why do you think there has been more academic research into the representation of women than of men?

The body

The image of the male in film has changed considerably over time. In the days of silent cinema, Rudolph Valentino was considered the archetypal romantic male. Women would swoon over his Italian good looks. However, with the advent of talking cinema, Valentino soon found himself unemployed because his effeminate voice contrasted with his seductive image. Learning from this, Hollywood sought new talent from Broadway as talking movies demanded a more rounded performance.

Consider some of the greatest Hollywood leading men; it is interesting to note how the idea of manliness was not initially associated with a muscular physique. Throughout the Great Depression, Humphrey Bogart with his craggy face and world-weary demeanour symbolized the Everyman to the American audience. Jimmy Stewart was similarly lacking in musculature, yet his comfortable manner put people at ease. And Clark Gable may not have been blessed with a muscular frame, yet women found his 'Frankly, my dear, I don't give a damn' attitude magnetic.

Figure 10.1   *Conan the Barbarian* (John Milius, 1982)

It wasn't until the appearance of Marlon Brando in *A Streetcar Named Desire* (Elia Kazan, 1951) that the male body took on new significance. In the film Brando's ripped t-shirt reveals his well-defined upper body. This image of raw physicality, coupled with his bad-boy, rebellious attitude, paved the way for a new generation of male stars.

The male body as spectacle was taken to extremes in the late 70s and early 80s with the arrival of stars such as Arnold Schwarzenegger, Jean-Claude Van Damme and Sylvester Stallone. The Austrian-born Schwarzenegger broke into movies following his career as a body builder (see Figure 10.1). He had been the youngest person to achieve the title of Mr Olympia (the highest accolade available in the sport). Similarly, Jean-Claude Van Damme, known as the 'Muscles from Brussels', made his name on the martial-arts circuit, winning numerous titles. As a result of their sporting prowess and their impressive bodies, both Schwarzenegger and Van Damme made the crossover into films. Sylvester Stallone, on the other hand, honed his muscular physique in order to secure the role of 'Rocky Balboa', the title character of *Rocky* (John G. Avildsen, 1976), for which he wrote the script. Such stars represented an exaggerated image of masculinity (hyper-masculinity). Typically shot with bare torso on display, they marked a significant departure from the classic male actors of the studio era. Instead of the traditional willowy, genteel, male frame the 'beefcakes' of the 80s were objectified for female viewing, inverting the normative voyeuristic depiction of women for male viewing.

However, alongside the macho musclemen, a softer image of masculinity was beginning to appear in the mid-80s. In the UK this was signalled by the iconic Spencer Rowell poster 'Man and Baby'. Here the well-toned male is pacified as he carefully cradles a small baby. In juxtaposing the heightened masculinity of the adult male with the vulnerability of the child, the meaning of the body is transformed from competitive machismo to one of refuge and protection. The idea of the sensitive male similarly featured in popular films of the 80s. Leonard Nimoy's *Three Men and a Baby* (1987) documented the impact of a baby being left on the doorstep of three confirmed bachelors in New York (Figure 10.2). The film was a remake of the French *3 Hommes et un Couffin/Three Men and a Cradle* (Coline Serreau, 1985), which fared equally well at the box office, suggesting that the phenomenon of the gentle male was a welcome change for the Western world. Other films continuing in this vein, well into the 90s, include *Curly Sue* (John Hughes, 1991) and *Léon* (Luc Besson, 1994). Even 'hard-man' 'Arnie' showed a lighter side to his manly persona when he starred alongside a cast of pre-school children in *Kindergarten Cop* (Ivan Reitman, 1990).

Figure 10.2   *Three Men and a Baby* (Leonard Nimoy, 1987)

Moving into the 90s and the twenty-first century, representations of masculinity became more diverse. The classic hero found in traditional literature and art gave way to a variety of male characters, ranging from the 'über' macho male to more effeminate personas. This shift reflects the social spectrum of manhood in society, as there is no single interpretation of what it means to be a man. Indeed, aspiring to emulate the cinematic, heroic figure could be responsible for male feelings of insecurity and unmanliness because the romantic, chivalrous stereotype is to a certain extent unachievable; the classic archetype having set up false expectations. Robert Bly in his book *Iron John* correctly points out:

> The male of the past twenty years has become more thoughtful, more gentle. But by this process he has not become more free. Many of these men are not happy. You quickly notice the lack of energy in them. They are life preserving but not exactly life-giving. (1991, pp.1–2)

Despite the developing representation of masculinity, below the surface there exist unresolved issues relating to social expectation.

Yvonne Tasker

Spectacular Bodies: Gender, Genre and the Action Cinema (1995)

Yvonne Tasker has written extensively about masculinity since the 90s, with particular focus on the male body. One of her aims, in the book *Spectacular Bodies,* was to rethink the role of the body in Action films. Whereas many scholars had ignored mainstream commercial filmmaking, Tasker looked to the populist Action movie genre of the 80s in order to examine what she felt was a new focus on the male body.

One interesting point that Tasker makes concerns the ageing male. Taking the familiar examples of Arnold Schwarzenegger and Sylvester Stallone, she considers how the once young and body-beautiful make a successful transition into mature, middle-aged actors. Once cast purely for their physique, securing roles becomes more problematic as actors age. Additionally, more mature actors often desire to be taken more seriously and seek to redefine their talents as substantial rather than superficial. Here, Tasker identifies a recourse to comedy and self-parody (p.83). Stripped of their macho façade, both Schwarzenegger and Stallone have often relied on comedy as a way of 'sending up' their former image in films such as *Twins* (Ivan Reitman, 1988) and *Stop! Or My Mom*

Will Shoot (Roger Spottiswoode, 1992). Tasker goes on to highlight the fact that the 'built body, both male and female, has often been the object of disgust and humour rather than admiration' (p.80), possibly an additional justification for trying to shed their former image.

Tasker also discusses other Action-movie heroes such as Bruce Willis, Harrison Ford and Clint Eastwood. Unlike 'Arnie' and Stallone, Willis, Ford and Eastwood's personas were not as reliant on body image as they were also known for their 'wise-cracking' one-liners. Tasker claims that Ford imbues the character of Indiana Jones with a different set of qualities to the typical action hero. His spectacle-wearing archaeologist, (p.75) a mature professional, goes completely against type. Similarly, all three actors have moved behind the camera to become producers, with Eastwood directing a number of critically acclaimed films. This can also be seen as an attempt to be taken more seriously. Tasker's focus on the ageing male arose from her realization that most writing on masculinity neglected the phenomenon, marking her work as groundbreaking.

Although much of her research is tied in with notions of class, race, gender and sexuality, more recently she has become preoccupied with the digital image of masculinity. She claims that CGI and special effects have resulted in extraordinary sequences of male performance. Using both *The Matrix* and *Crouching Tiger, Hidden Dragon* (Ang Lee, 2000) as examples, Tasker is looking into heightened displays of physicality and how these inform our contemporary understanding of masculinity (2002).

Reflect and respond

1   Consider the image of the male body. Do you think it has changed over time?
2   Do you think the film industry tends to promote an idealized physique only achievable through hard work and perseverance in the gym?
3   To what extent have CGI and special effects manipulated our ideas of masculinity?
4   Identify any male actors who have reinvented themselves as they have grown older. Why do you think they felt such adjustments were necessary?

Another scholar researching the topic of male bodies is Richard Dyer. Writing in 1997, Dyer's 'The White Man's Muscles' looks at the early Tarzan films, among others, as sites of colonial tension and white supremacy. He sees the story of the white male surviving in foreign lands as a metaphor for colonial rule. Typically pitted against hostile natives, the physically superior imperial character can be read as a signifier of wealth and prestige. Dyer points out that the actors cast to play such roles as Tarzan and Hercules were often famous sportsmen who had achieved notoriety in their chosen fields. Their physical appearance was indicative of their class status as they had the time and money to perfect their hyper-masculinized bodies.

Dyer points to the Greeks and Romans as a historical reference point to this male fixation on the toned body as ideal. In antiquity, the carefully chiselled marble statues were revered as epitomizing male heroism. This myth was perpetuated in the early colonial films in order to further the message of Western dominance over indigenous peoples overseas. According to Dyer, the white male body therefore represents a political message as well as performing a narrative function that can inform our reading of film.

Male anxiety

At certain times in world history the male image on screen has suffered lapses in confidence. In most cases, anxiety in the film narrative reflects wider social concerns. For example, men returning home following World War II found that women had taken over many traditional male occupations. Enjoying their new-found employment, many women were reluctant to return to the domestic sphere. As a result, gender roles were less clearly defined and these issues were brought to the fore through a new genre, later to become known as Film Noir.

Film Noir was based on the 30s hard-boiled novels of Raymond Chandler, Mickey Spillane, Dashiell Hammett and James M. Cain. The films were not made in the 30s, the genre being considered too pessimistic for an America in the throes of the Great Depression. After the war, however, America experienced a period of affluence and the film industry no longer needed to be cautious about screening films that did not necessarily promote escapism. A typical Film Noir narrative would involve a male protagonist being led astray by an overpowering *femme fatale*. The females in these films were stereotypically seductive and manipulative. The males, on the other hand, easily succumbed to their feminine charms, willingly breaking the law to win their affection. The moral message of these films was that women posed a threat unless they were pacified by a strong manly figure; males were at risk of being metaphorically emasculated. This served as a warning to women that they should return to the domestic sphere in order for patriarchy to be restored.

Decades later, the film *Fight Club* traces similar themes. The film is regarded as a critique of consumer culture, with the main protagonist Jack losing his sense of male individuality amid capitalist propaganda. The film's director argues that man has become displaced from his primal role as the hunter in modern-day society: '[w]e're designed to be hunters and we're in a society of shopping. There's nothing to kill anymore, there's nothing to fight, nothing to overcome, nothing to explore' (Smith, 1999, pp.58–66). In order to re-engage with his libidinal (sexual) masculine persona, Jack subconsciously calls forth his alter ego Tyler Durden. Whereas Jack is a non-confrontational insomniac, disillusioned with his job and relationships (emasculated), Tyler is a militant force, sexually overactive, who inspires a following of loyal devotees who make up the eponymous 'Fight Club'. It is interesting to note that in his quest to regain his lost masculinity, Jack resorts to his primeval instincts; violence.

Violence

Since prehistoric times, man has been associated with violence. The film industry is culpable in promoting this myth. Although many narratives feature the strong, protective hero, most films will also involve a violent nemesis to act as a counter-force. However, violence is not wholly reserved for the anti-hero, it has long been established as a generic trait capable of attracting a film audience.

Westerns, Gangster movies and War films all display elements of aggression, rivalry and combat. Although these genres are specifically linked to male audiences, Paul Willemen argues that everyone enjoys watching the male on screen.

The viewer's experience is predicated on the pleasure of seeing the male 'exist' (that is, walk, move, ride, fight) in or through cityscapes, landscapes or, more abstractly history. And on the unquiet pleasure of seeing the male mutilated (often quite graphically ...) and restored through violent brutality. (1981, p.16)

Willemen's thesis points to the sadistic enjoyment in watching the male body become disfigured. Paul Smith summarizes this idea simply in four key stages (1995, p.81):

1   eroticization
2   destruction
3   re-emergence
4   regeneration.

These stages can be applied to the character of Tyler Durden. Introduced to the narrative as a charismatic, well-toned Adonis, this physical appearance is quickly disfigured by scars and bruises. However, his damaged frame is as quickly restored by the conclusion of the film and his dominance reasserted at the expense of Jack's demise.

Reflect and respond

1   Can you identify any other periods in American history that have instigated changes in the way masculinity is perceived?
2   Can you think of any particular events in world history that have made us question the role of masculinity?
3   Why do so many genres traditionally associated with men include scenes of violence?
4   Do you agree that the male star has to be beaten and tortured as a sign of archetypal male strength?

Homoeroticism

Homoeroticism is typically dispersed through violence in most traditional mainstream films unless the narrative itself is concerned with homosexuality. As already outlined by Neale, homoerotic tension has to be banished in order to appeal to the wider heterosexual male audience. To some extent heterosexual men can experience a historical residual awkwardness because traditionally, homosexual encounters were frowned upon and indeed illegal in many countries. Thus, violence can serve to deflect any homoerotic connotations.

Staying with *Fight Club*, the complete obliteration of the character Angel Face (Jared Leto) is symptomatic of the need to suppress homoeroticism in any form. Angel Face, as the name suggests, is beautiful but in an androgynous way. Accordingly, Jack feels compelled to smash his features to a pulp, stating 'I felt like destroying something beautiful.' This is a strong example of displaced homoerotic tension. Jack is jealous of the youngster's boyish good looks yet at the same time repelled by his subconscious attraction to him. Interestingly, Leto went on to appear as Colin

Farrell's supposed lover in the film *Alexander* (Oliver Stone, 2004), a casting decision once more attributed to his androgynous look. Leto can be considered part of an emerging breed of actor to reflect the metrosexual style that came to the fore in the 90s.

The metrosexual male

The term 'metrosexual' was first coined by British journalist Mark Simpson in his article 'Here Come the Mirror Men' in the *Independent* (1994). He described how young men between the ages of eighteen and thirty-five had developed narcissistic tendencies. Whereas the cosmetic counter in most shopping outlets targeted women as prime consumers, many brands have now developed facial products and lotions specifically aimed at men. Simpson highlighted the fact that this shift signified a departure from the archetypal idea of masculinity:

> The metrosexual man contradicts the basic premise of traditional heterosexuality – that only women are looked at and only men do the looking. Metrosexual man might prefer women, he might prefer men, but when all's said and done nothing comes between him and his reflection.

Whereas the traditional male saw shopping as a necessary evil, the modern man, according to Simpson, has become a 'commodity fetishist'. David Beckham epitomizes the metrosexual male, launching his own fragrance and unafraid to be seen in public wearing a sarong and an Alice band (headband).

The film industry has also promoted the metrosexual image. This is evident when comparing the new generation of male stars with those of the studio era. For example the iconic Humphrey Bogart typically looked old, tired and unkempt. Modern-day icons such as Brad Pitt, Leonardo DiCaprio, Orlando Bloom and Jude Law offer a more clean-cut image of masculinity.

Reflect and respond

1 Can you think of any films that have a homoerotic subtext?
2 Do you think Hollywood actively avoids moments of homoeroticism? How and why does it do this?
3 Do you think the emerging trend of the metrosexual male is problematic?
4 Why do you think Hollywood endorses the image of the metrosexual?

Case study: Christian Bale

Actor Christian Bale affords an interesting case study for an exploration of masculinity in film. Born in Wales in 1971, he spent most of his early years travelling England, Portugal and America because his mother was a circus clown. He made his acting debut in the film *Anastasia: The Mystery of Anna* (Marvin J. Chomsky, 1986). Amy Irving, who played the title role, was so impressed with the youngster's talents that she recommended Bale to her then husband Steven Spielberg.

In the film *Empire of the Sun* (1987), Spielberg cast Bale as the schoolboy Jim. This harrowing tale, adapted from J. G. Ballard's semi-autobiographical novel, follows the journey of Jamie (Jim), a child of the elite British upper class in Shanghai. When war breaks out he becomes separated from his parents and ends up in a Japanese internment camp. Here he comes of age, learning to scrape a living in order to survive. The character of Jim presented a challenge, evolving from arrogant innocence to a haunted maturity beyond his years. Spielberg describes how he was drawn to the project:

> I was attracted to the main character being a child, [...] But I was also attracted to the idea that this was a death of innocence, not an attenuation of childhood. [...] This was the opposite of Peter Pan. This was a boy who had grown up too quickly, who was becoming a flower long before the bud had ever come out of the topsoil. (Forsberg, 2000, p.127)

Bale's performance was met with praise and he also succeeded in winning a number of low-profile awards. *Empire of the Sun* launched the actor into the limelight, leading to a number of juvenile roles including *Treasure Island* (Fraser Clarke Heston, 1990) and *The News Boys* (Kenny Ortega, 1992).

His transition from child star to adulthood was completed by the film *American Psycho* (Mary Harron, 2000). Playing the role of Patrick Bateman was a brave decision for Bale because the film was highly controversial for a number of reasons. It was adapted from the Bret Easton Ellis novel, which had attracted attention due to its violent and sexual content. In particular, Feminists were concerned about the descriptions of violence towards women. Therefore, when Mary Harron was brought on board to direct the production, many people were shocked. There were also rumours that Leonardo DiCaprio had been cast to play the role of Bateman. Harron resigned in protest as she had championed for Bale as her lead. However, DiCaprio's advisory team warned him against the serial-killer role, believing that it would be detrimental to his popularity with the young teen fanbase he had accrued following *Titanic*. Despite the media hype, the British star secured the role and went on to gain critical acclaim.

The character of Patrick Bateman provides a fascinating case study for masculinity. Daniel Mudie Cunningham states:

> Bateman, named after Norman Bates from Hitchcock's *Psycho* (1960), epitomizes all the ideals that attend straight white masculinity: he is exceedingly handsome, possesses a muscular body, attracts beautiful sexual partners, his career requires very little effort or work but makes him wealthy and powerful. He is in a position to indulge every materialistic desire, which includes a regular cocaine supply, a rigorous beauty regime, a spectacular apartment decorated with chic furnishings, and a wardrobe consisting of designer gear. (2009, p.42)

Bateman is an exaggeration of one aspect of the modern metrosexual male. When he makes love he ignores the women and watches himself as he poses in a full-length mirror. He is obsessed with commodities and breaks out in a sweat when he realizes his business card is inferior to those of his work colleagues. Cunningham builds on Richard Dyer's claims that the white male has become invisible due to his normativeness. Cunningham states: 'Instead of being noticed,

Figure 10.3 *American Psycho* (Mary Harron, 2000)

Bateman is one of countless white executives that live and work in an identical manner. All the white male characters are alike in that they share similar suits, haircuts, accessories, and even names' (2009, p.44). The narrative deals with modern man in crisis. Bateman longs to fit in yet at the same time is repulsed by the circles he moves in. The tale is a critique of consumer culture and one of the ways this is explored is through Bateman's well-toned physique.

In order to achieve the body required for the role, Christian Bale underwent extensive fitness training. Bale is known for being a Method Actor. Apparently while filming *American Psycho* the crew were amazed at how much time the actor spent in the twenty-four-hour gym on the set (Figure 10.3). Conversely, for the film *The Machinist* (Brad Anderson, 2004) Bale lost an enormous amount of weight in order to play the skeletal figure of Trevor Reznik (Figure 10.4). Reznik, an insomniac factory worker, is suffering from a mental breakdown following involvement in a hit and run. Bale adopted a diet of coffee and apples in order to achieve his emaciated figure; he also put himself through long periods of sleep deprivation. The actor bulked up once more in order to play the iconic caped crusader Batman in *Batman Begins* (Christopher Nolan, 2005) and John Connor in the film *Terminator: Salvation* (McG, 2009). He has since drastically lost weight to play Dicky Eklund, a boxer turned trainer, whose career was ruined by drug addiction in *The Fighter* (David O. Russell, 2010), a role which earned him an Oscar.

Figure 10.4 *The Machinist* (Brad Anderson, 2004)

This obsessive approach of toning and abusing his body in order to psychologically and physically connect with the characters he plays represents an extreme example of Method Acting. This could account for an incident that made the headlines in 2009. On the set of *Terminator: Salvation* Bale was captured on tape losing his temper with a member of the technical staff. The recording revealed Bale's foul language as he verbally assaulted Shane Hurlbut for ruining his concentration. The incident attracted a lot of media hype with people condemning Bale's outburst. He has since apologized, blaming his reaction on his total absorption in the emotion of the scene.

Method Acting, which seems to be more commonly practised by men, often attracts most attention when adopted to play aggressive, hyper-masculine roles. Famous examples include Robert De Niro's portrayal of the boxer Jake La Motta in *Raging Bull* (Martin Scorsese, 1980). Like Bale, De Niro changed his body shape, in his case gaining significant weight in order to become obese for the role. Likewise, Daniel Day Lewis in *Gangs of New York* (Martin Scorsese, 2002) worked as an apprentice butcher to prepare for his part as Bill 'The Butcher' Cutting. Whether Bale's intense approach to characterization will continue to secure him roles is yet to be seen. However, the demands he puts on his body may have adverse affects as he ages. Bale may have to readdress the kind of roles he accepts as all stars have to adapt to industrial constraints regarding maturity.

Reflect and respond

1   Is it possible to question ideas of masculinity when looking at male child stars?
2   Consider Mary Harron as the director of *American Psycho.* Is her role problematic and if so why?
3   Why do you think Method Acting is more associated with men?
4   To what extent does the film industry marginalize and stereotype ageing males? Do you think this will always be the case?

Conclusion

Throughout this chapter we have explored the many shifts and trends that the film industry has accommodated in its portrayal of masculinity. Depending on the historical context, men have been depicted as dominant, confident and brutal or conversely, sensitive, subservient and anxious. Many ideas relating to masculinity can be traced back to the primal incarnation of the hunter tribesman fending for his family and defending his land. Therefore a preoccupation with the body has typically saturated most cultures. This idea of looking to the ancient past in order to forge modern male identity can be seen in the film *300* (Zack Snyder, 2006) where CGI-enhanced figures exhibited a form of hyper-masculinity. Whereas actors once had to spend time and money working on their physique, new technologies have enabled stars to achieve a similar look through special effects. This can further alienate the male viewing public as the image on screen is even more unattainable.

Male identity in film and culture has traditionally also been accompanied with instances of violence and aggression. Recently this trend has been challenged to give a more inclusive perspective of masculinity representing the wider spectrum of male identity. At present it is difficult to consider ideas of masculinity progressing beyond the boundaries of the combative action hero and the more passive family man. However, the gradation of male identity is brought into question in the field of Queer Theory, which will help further this debate.

Bibliography

Adams, R. and Savran, D. (eds) (2002) *The Masculinity Studies Reader,* Malden, MA and Oxford: Blackwell.
Berger, M., Wallis, B. and Watson, S. (1995) (eds) *Constructing Masculinity,* London and New York: Routledge.
Bly, R. (1991) *Iron John: A Book about Men,* Shaftesbury: Element.
Cohan, S. and Hark, I. R. (1993) *Screening the Male: Exploring Masculinities in Hollywood Cinema,* London and New York: Routledge.
Connell, R. W. (1995) *Masculinities,* Cambridge: Polity Press.
Cunningham, D. M. (2009) 'Patrick Bateman as "Average White Male" in *American Psycho*', in E. Watson (ed.) *Pimps, Wimps, Studs, Thugs and Gentlemen: Essays on Media Images of Masculinity,* Jefferson, NC: McFarland & Co, pp.40–50.
Dyer, R. (1997) 'The White Man's Muscles', in R. Adams and D. Savran (eds) (2002) *The Masculinity Studies Reader*, Malden, MA and Oxford: Blackwell, pp.263–73.
Ellis, J. (1982) *Visible Fictions: Cinema, Television, Video,* London: Routledge.
Forsberg, M. (2000) 'Spielberg at 40: The Man and the Child', in L. D. Friedman and B. Notbohm (eds) *Steven Spielberg Interviews,* Jackson: University of Mississippi Press.
Neale, S. (1983) 'Masculinity as Spectacle', in S. Cohan and I. R. Hark (eds) (1993) *Screening the Male: Exploring Masculinities in Hollywood Cinema*, London and New York: Routledge, pp.277–87.
Powrie, P., Davies, A. and Babington, B. (2004) (eds) *The Trouble with Men: Masculinities in European and Hollywood Cinema*, London: Wallflower.
Propp, V. (1928) *Morphology of the Folktale*, Austin: University of Texas Press.
Silverman, K. (1992) *Male Subjectivity at the Margins*, New York and London: Routledge.
Simpson, M. (1994) 'Here Come the Mirror Men', *Independent*, 15 November. Retrieved 9 February 2009. Available at http://www.marksimpson.com/here-come-the-mirror-men.
Smith, G. (1999) 'Inside Out', *Film Comment* vol. 35 no. 5, pp. 58–66.
Smith, P. (1995) 'Eastwood Bound', in M. Berger, B. Wallis and S. Watson (eds) *Constructing Masculinity*, London and New York: Routledge, pp.77–97.
Tasker, Y. (1995) *Spectacular Bodies: Gender, Genre and the Action Cinema*, 2nd edn, London: Routledge.
Tasker, Y. (2002) 'Interview with Yvonne Tasker', *Velvet Light Trap* no. 49, 22 March.
Willemen, P. (1981) 'Anthony Mann: Looking at the Male', *Framework* vols 15–17, p.16.

Queer Theory

11

Queer Theory
1. An approach to social and cultural study which seeks to challenge or deconstruct traditional ideas of sexuality and gender, esp. the acceptance of heterosexuality as normative and the perception of a rigid dichotomy of male and female traits.

Setting the scene

Queer Theory first emerged in the 70s but did not gain recognition until the early 90s. It grew out of a number of new areas of critical discourse that were concerned with ideas of marginality (gender, race and ethnicity). Whereas Feminism looked to readdress the balance of patriarchal traditions and African American Studies contested the history of white supremacy, Queer Theory challenged the premise of heterosexuality as normative.

Terminology

On initial reading the term 'queer' may cause offense and therefore seem an inappropriate name for a field of study. Similarly, dictionary definitions of the word 'queer' are also problematic:

1. Strange, odd, peculiar, eccentric. Also: of questionable character; suspicious, dubious.
2. Out of sorts; unwell; faint, giddy. Formerly also (*slang*): drunk.

As can be seen, the term 'queer' is historically associated with unsavoury behaviour, leading to its adoption by homophobic individuals wishing to insult homosexuals and label them as different. The term was later reappropriated by the community as a celebration of gay sexuality. Rather than being ashamed, they vehemently invoked the term as a badge of pride. In adopting it for themselves they hoped to defuse all negative connotations.

The introduction to Benshoff and Griffin's *Queer Cinema: The Film Reader* explains that the term is not intended to label sexuality but instead to express an attitude of inclusivity:

The term was meant to gather together multiple marginalized groups into a shared political struggle, as well as fling back at mainstream heterosexist culture an epithet that had been used to oppress people for decades. (2005, p.5)

Approaching this area of study can be like entering a 'minefield' because labels go in and out of fashion. Care must be taken not to cause offence. The definitions below are an attempt to give an idea of how certain terms are interpreted. However, as has been proven, these definitions are not 'set in stone' and therefore should be used with caution.

- **Queer:** This overarching term encompasses a whole range of sexualities. However, it has specific political connotations associated with defiance. 'Queer' was initially linked to the activist groups ACT UP (AIDS Coalition to Unleash Power) and OutRage!, which emerged in the late 80s in the US and UK respectively. These groups were formed following the public outcry concerning the United States' response to the AIDS virus. Their aim was to instil gay pride and redress (or 'challenge') the effete stereotyping associated with homosexuality. Their political legacy can be seen in the many ways that the gay community continues to challenge discrimination. The term also serves to describe alternative approaches to sexuality; even straight people can adopt a queer lifestyle, and challenge heteronormative behaviour (e.g. reject monogamy; cross-dress; have sexual relationships with men and women). More recently the term 'queer' has begun to be used synonymously with the word 'gay', thus sanitizing the political ideology associated with it.
- **Gay:** Traditionally this term was used to describe male homosexuality. However, it has become a generic expression to categorize people who are attracted to the same sex. Unlike 'queer', 'gay' is a more neutral label and so has become a catch-all for homosexuals in general. In a more recent incarnation, it has, unfortunately, been colloquially adopted as a pejorative term.
- **Camp:** Camp is an attitude. It is a performance that a person may choose to adopt. Interestingly, campness is not exclusive to homosexuals as it can also be embodied by heterosexuals. For example, both Dolly Parton and Russell Brand can be considered camp due to their 'over-the-top' personas and their fondness for self-parody. Furthermore, it can be engaged as a strategy for reading gay films (see section on the camp aesthetic, p.188).
- **Lesbian:** Traditionally this term has referred to female homosexuality. However, it can be deemed as problematic due to cultural prejudice (male fantasies). Therefore many female homosexuals prefer the term 'gay'.

The choice of label comes down to the individual. It is about self-definition. Care and sensitivity must be taken regarding word choice when reading film from this theoretical perspective. Issues surrounding terminology initiated 'Queer Theory' as a new site for discourse. It was the French theorist Michel Foucault who made strides to formalize the debate.

Michel Foucault

The History of Sexuality: Volume 1 (1976)

Michel Foucault was one of the key thinkers of the twentieth century. His writings consisted of both historical and theoretical critiques, addressing a variety of social and cultural issues frequently concerned with power. Many writers and activists have been inspired by Foucault's pioneering bravado in opening up this area of Queer Studies. It is his major work of three volumes known as *The History of Sexuality* (1976–84) (and Volume 1 in particular) that is of interest here. The trilogy presents ideas that effectively challenged conventional notions of sex and sexuality. He did not document a history of sexual conduct or explore the topic from a religious, philosophical or scientific perspective, but looked at the development of sexuality and focused on how sexuality constructs the individual.

He notes that from the Ancient Greeks to the nineteenth century homosexual behaviour was evident, but the label of homosexuality as an identity only emerged later. As part of his focus Foucault charted the work of Victorian medical and scientific writers who wrote on sexual normality and abnormality. In 1870, Carl Westphal was one of the first professionals to recognize and acknowledge homosexuality. Westphal's medical article adhered to Victorian sensibilities and thus condemned homosexual acts, dividing them into 'psychological' and 'psychiatric' categories (Foucault, p.43). Foucault drew from Westphal's work and oversimplified it to declare 1870 to be the precise birth date of modern homosexuality (p.43).

Although the common conception was that sex was not openly discussed by the general public, Foucault observed that, as early as the seventeenth century, institutions had attempted to repress homosexuality. Same-sex relationships threatened the social and economic structure, which was based on marriage, patriarchy and monogamous households. He found that concerns for the public's health and morality led to the proliferation of 'a whole grid of observations regarding sex' (p.26). This produced discourses on sexuality in psychiatry, medicine, the legal system and social work.

In summary, the establishment condemned gays as either criminals or madmen. Foucault suggested that the aims of earlier writers in these areas were to define, diagnose and find a 'cure' for improper desires of same-sex love and other perversions. All these differing points caused Foucault to challenge the notion that discourses on sexuality had been previously repressed.

Foucault presented a case that the very institutions intending to suppress same-sex relationships did in fact unknowingly encourage them. In attempting to stigmatize homosexuality, the establishment actively labelled what they believed to be perverse forms of sexuality. In giving homosexuality and bisexuality a name, gay communities were able to adopt a formal identity. Therefore the medical and legal professions were in fact responsible for categorizing and making visible all forms of sexuality.

Reflect and respond

1   Why do you think medical and legal institutions chose to affiliate homosexuality with criminality and/or madness?
2   To what extent has the institutional need to categorize sexual preference led to stigmatizing behaviour?
3   Do you agree with Foucault that 'power' encourages what it attempts to repress? Why is this?

Nowadays the term 'queer', when employed in academic circles, covers a myriad of identities. Benshoff and Griffin state:

Queer was not only meant to acknowledge that there are many different ways to be gay or lesbian, but also to encompass and define other sexually defined minorities for whom the labels homosexual and/or heterosexual were less than adequate: bisexuals, cross-dressers, transgendered people [...] sadomasochistic sexualities, etc. (2005, p.5)

Judith Butler, the American philosopher who writes prolifically on issues of gender and sexuality, concurs with this account of the inclusive nature of the term:

My understanding of queer is a term that desires that you don't have to present an identity card before entering a meeting [sic]. Heterosexuals can join the queer movement. Bisexuals can join the queer movement. Queer is not being lesbian. Queer is not being gay. It is an argument against lesbian specificity: that if I am a lesbian I have to desire in a certain way. Or if I am a gay I have to desire in a certain way. Queer is an argument against certain normativity, what a proper lesbian or gay identity is. (Michalik, 2001)

Therefore the term is more complicated than it may first appear. It is not just used as a binary opposition to differentiate gay and straight. Sexual identities are not fixed; for example, a straight person may fantasize about having a homosexual encounter and vice versa. Therefore, the term 'queer' provokes much debate and these issues feature strongly when looking at Queer Studies.

Reflect and respond

1 What are your thoughts about the term 'queer'; is it offensive or celebratory?
2 Can you think of other words originally used as an insult that have later been reappropriated by those they were originally intended to offend?
3 Do you think it is an appropriate term for an academic theory?
4 Do you think as a term it will date?

History of gay filmmaking

Queer cinema, according to Benshoff and Griffin, incorporates three broad categories (2005, pp.1–2):

1 production: films made by gays or lesbians
2 content: films about homosexuality, with the narrative addressing queer issues
3 reception: films that are watched by gays and lesbians.

Queer Theory developed in response to the way homosexuality was portrayed in films. Vito Russo was one of the first writers to point out that gay characters were typically demonized and then killed off at the close of a film. He clarified this by including a 'necrology' in his 1981 book *The Celluloid Closet: Homosexuality in the Movies*.

One of the first films to explore homosexuality was the experimental avant-garde short

Fireworks (1945) directed by Kenneth Anger. The Surreal film comprises a homoerotic dream sequence of a young man who is physically beaten and molested by sailors. It concludes with the image of a sailor unzipping his flies to produce a Roman Candle. This landmark film is often cited as the starting point of queer cinema.

Prior to Anger's avant-garde approach, homosexuality more commonly appeared in film as a comedic element. Gay males were represented as effeminate and cowardly (sissy) and accordingly ridiculed throughout the narrative. The sissy stereotype became a staple character in early cinema. To some extent this appeased members of the gay community as they would rather be represented in some form on screen than be totally ignored.

With the introduction of the Hays Code in 1934, gay representation in cinema became heavily censored. Images of homosexuality and bisexuality were banned; the code referred to any such activity as 'sexual perversion', which problematically suggested deviancy. One of the films that managed to bypass the censors was Alfred Hitchcock's *Rope* (1948). Based on the true story of gay psychopathic killers Leopold and Loeb, the film made no mention of homosexuality. This was typical procedure within the film industry. Homosexuality was either restricted to avant-garde filmmaking or it was heavily coded within the mainstream. Gay audiences had to actively work to find themselves represented on screen. However, Stonewall signalled a welcome change.

Stonewall

In 1969, America was experiencing a period of civil unrest. Following the fight against fascism in Europe, African Americans demonstrated to the world that America was not the racial 'melting pot' it professed to be. At the same time, protests were rife among students and pacifists seeking an end to the conflict in Vietnam. These attempts to challenge attitudes motivated the gay community to fight for its freedom and Stonewall provided that opportunity.

Stonewall signalled a dramatic change within gay culture. The incident occurred in New York's Greenwich Village, home to a large homosexual population. In the early hours of 28 June 1969, the Stonewall Inn was raided by the police for serving gay clientele. Prior to Stonewall, gay dancing and drinking establishments had been outlawed and forced underground due to societal discrimination.

On the night in question, the police turned up at the mafia-owned bar and began arresting patrons. Raids were a regular occurrence in the district, but when the police became heavy-handed on this particular occasion, the patrons decided to take a stand. Typical procedures would involve officers lining customers up to check their identification to verify gender. Any men found dressing as women would be taken into custody. However, this time the patrons refused to comply with police demands and soon a crowd of local gays began to congregate outside the bar, significantly outnumbering the police.

As the skirmish ensued, police were taken hostage inside the bar as their cars and wagons were overturned in the street. The riot spread and bottles, bricks and garbage cans were thrown through windows. When police attempted to turn fire hoses on the demonstrators, the lack of water pressure only encouraged the mob. David Carter's book *Stonewall: The Riots That Sparked the Gay Revolution* (2004) quotes Bob Kohler, who witnessed the Tactical Police Force arrive to aid its colleagues:

The cops were totally humiliated. This never, ever happened. They were angrier than I guess they had ever been, because everybody else had rioted ... but the fairies were not supposed to riot ... no group had ever forced cops to retreat before, so the anger was just enormous. I mean, they wanted to kill. (p.175)

With their numbers strengthened the police attempted to push the crowds back. This led to the iconic response of the crowd cheering and starting an impromptu kickline, singing:

> We are the Stonewall Girls.
> We wear our hair in curls.
> We don't wear underwear.
> We show our pubic hair.

This openly defiant, yet camp display of resistance inspired the gay community. The riots continued for a number of nights before finally calming down.

Stonewall was a landmark episode that instigated the gay revolution and the fight for gay civil rights. Rather than shamefully hiding their sexuality, gay pride became the new slogan and the gay liberation movement was born.

Reflect and respond

1   Which, if any, aspects of the history of discrimination faced by homosexuals were you aware of?
2   Why was the political climate of 1969 important?
3   Consider the camp response of the protesters. Why did they react in such a manner?
4   Why was the Stonewall incident such a turning point?

Post-Stonewall

Stonewall acted as a catalyst. It incited many gay practitioners to openly embrace their sexuality and use it to inform their cultural work. Derek Jarman, the British director, was among the forerunners in promoting gay pride. Coming from an experimental background, akin to Anger and other gay filmmakers, Jarman produced the first positive, openly gay film *Sebastiane* (1976). This was closely followed by his famous work *Jubilee* (1978). In the 80s, Jarman became a figurehead for gay civil rights, openly contesting Clause 28. This was part of the British 1988 Local Government Act, which stated that local authorities 'shall not intentionally promote homosexuality or publish material with the intention of promoting homosexuality'. The film *Caravaggio* (1986) can be seen as an open assault on Clause 28. His final work *Blue* (1993) was created as he was dying from AIDS and can be seen as a testimony to his convictions.

Other gay filmmakers who emerged in the post-Stonewall period include Pedro Almodóvar, John Waters and Isaac Julien. It is important to note that Julien's work looks at issues of race as well as gay sexuality.

New Queer Cinema

B. Ruby Rich

'New Queer Cinema' (1992)

The phrase 'New Queer Cinema' was first coined by B. Ruby Rich in an article written for the *Village Voice* in 1992, reprinted in *Sight and Sound* later that year. In this seminal text she highlights the significant increase in gay films being shown at film festivals:

> There, suddenly, was a flock of films that were doing something new, renegotiating subjectivities, annexing whole genres, revising histories in their image. All through the winter, spring, summer, and now autumn, the message has been loud and clear: queer is hot. (p.15)

Rich was quick to point out that this new trend in filmmaking incorporated a diverse range of concerns. However she purports that films of 'New Queer Cinema' are recognizable due to a shared ethos:

> Call it 'Homo Pomo' [Postmodernism]: there are traces in all of them of appropriation and pastiche, irony, as well as a reworking of history with social constructivism very much in mind. Definitively breaking with older humanist approaches and the films and tapes that accompanied identity politics, these works are irreverent, energetic, alternately minimalist and excessive. Above all, they're full of pleasure. They're here, they're queer, get hip to them. (p.16)

Her defiant turn of expression is illustrative of the excitement experienced in gay communities as these films depicted homosexuality as celebratory. The films she discusses as integral to the emergence of New Queer Cinema include: Gus Van Sant's *My Own Private Idaho* (1991) and Derek Jarman's *Edward II* (1991). However, in spite of mainstream interest in gay filmmaking, Rich points out that it was the male filmmakers who were being acknowledged. Lesbian filmmaking was still marginalized although it featured strongly on the festival circuit.

Rich anecdotally summarizes the debates that ensued at a range of festivals she attended. She recalls Richard Dyer's comments that 'there are two ways to dismiss a gay film: one is to say "Oh, it's just a gay film": the other, to proclaim, "Oh, it's a great film, it just happens to be gay"' (p.21). Rich enthuses that this was not the case with the majority of the films screened in Utah:

> [T]hey were great precisely because of the ways in which they were gay. Their queerness was no more arbitrary then their aesthetics, no more than their individual preoccupations with interrogating history. The queer present negotiates with the past, knowing full well the future is at stake (p.22)

While B. Ruby Rich's article identified a new trend in gay filmmaking it was Monica B. Pearl who accounted for its emergence. Pearl boldly claimed that: 'New Queer Cinema *is* AIDS cinema' (2004, p.23). Her approach was to consider how AIDS drastically changed gay communities and attitudes towards homosexuality and how filmmaking became a way of understanding the disease:

> New Queer Cinema provides another way of making sense out of the virus, that does not placate and does not provide easy answers – that reflects rather than corrects the experience of fragmentation, disruption, unboundaried identity, incoherent narrative, and inconclusive endings. It is a way of providing meaning that does not change or sanitise the experience. (2004, p.33)

For Pearl, these notions of 'fragmentation' and 'incoherent narratives' mirror the way the illness takes hold of the body. She points out that AIDS is a retrovirus that attacks a person's immune system by becoming part of the body. 'When the immune system attempts to fight the foreign infection, it ends up battling the body that harbours it. The body's attempt to save itself is what kills it' (2004, p.24). Therefore traditional linear tales of illness and recuperation and/or death must be rewritten. Many films associated with new queer cinema explore AIDS and its devastating effects, yet Pearl uses the disease as a metaphor for reading the genre where AIDS is not the subject matter.

Reflect and respond

1 Why do you think New Queer Cinema veers towards excess?
2 Account for the rise in popularity of gay filmmaking in the early 90s?
3 To what extent does Postmodernism lend itself as a theory for understanding gay filmmaking?
4 Discuss your ideas on why lesbian filmmakers were overlooked during this period.
5 Do you agree with Pearl's idea that new queer cinema was born out of an attempt to understand AIDS?

Camp aesthetic

Another area that has become a key way of reading queer films and gay filmmaking is the use of camp as an aesthetic device.

Susan Sontag

'Notes on Camp' (1964)

In 1964 Susan Sontag initiated a debate concerning the term 'camp'. In the article 'Notes on Camp', she explains that camp is a sensibility and so is difficult to define:

> A sensibility (as distinct from an idea) is one of the hardest things to talk about; but there are special reasons why Camp, in particular, has never been discussed. It is not a natural mode of

sensibility, if there be any such. Indeed the essence of Camp is its love of the unnatural: of artifice and exaggeration. (1964, p.176).

In order to attempt an understanding of campness she then outlines fifty-eight 'jottings' which include:

- Camp is an artificial aesthetic.
- It is depoliticized/apolitical.
- It is subjective.
- Camp is typically exaggerated.
- Camp is intentional.
- Camp is either completely naïve or else wholly conscious.
- Camp is the spirit of extravagance.
- It attempts to be serious, but cannot be taken seriously.
- Bad movies are frequently camp.
- Ideas of camp change over time.
- Camp is the glorification of 'character'.
- The antithesis to camp is tragedy.
- The whole point of camp is to dethrone the serious. Camp is playful, anti-serious.
- Camp offers a comedic view of the world.
- Camp taste is, above all, a mode of enjoyment, of appreciation rather than judgment.
- The ultimate camp statement: it's good *because* it's awful … .

Jack Babuscio drew from Sontag's findings and attempted to formalize ideas of campness.

Jack Babuscio

'Camp and the Gay Sensibility' (1977)

In his article 'Camp and the Gay Sensibility' (1977), Babuscio observes that people often refer to films as being camp, but for gay filmmakers adopting a camp aesthetic can be a statement of sexuality. He starts his findings by defining what he means by a gay sensibility:

A creative energy reflecting a consciousness that is different from the mainstream: a heightened awareness of certain human complications of feeling that spring from the fact of social oppression, in short a perception of the world which is colored, shaped, directed, and delivered by the fact of one's gayness (p.121)

Babuscio explains that society is typically polarized as heterosexual (normal) and homosexual (abnormal) (p.121). One response to such essentialist delineations is the employment of camp. He points out that not all directors who incorporate a camp aesthetic are gay (naming Busby Berkeley as an instance in point). It is only when the aesthetic is achieved out of a gay sensibility that it becomes a trait of queer cinema.

Identified below are four specific applications of camp 'irony, aestheticism, theatricality and humor' which he discusses at length (p.122).

Irony

Here he puts forward 'incongruous contrasts' as a key trait of campness. In particular he looks at the binary distinctions of male and female. When these oppositions are blurred, ironic campness is achieved. As examples he identifies Greta Garbo in *Queen Christina* (Rouben Mamoulian, 1933), who pretends to be a man and Mick Jagger's androgynous qualities in *Performance* (Donald Cammell and Nicolas Roeg, 1970). Irony also occurs when distinctions of old and young are blurred in an inappropriate way. Consider Gloria Swanson's character refusing to age in *Sunset Boulevard* (Billy Wilder, 1950).

Aestheticism

Babuscio argues that camp aestheticism is dismissive of mainstream artistic practices in favour of the 'dissolution of hard and inflexible moral rules' (p.123). Rather than being preoccupied with contemporary issues, camp filmmaking embraces exotic and fantastical subjects: 'an emphasis on sensuous surfaces, textures, imagery and the evocation of mood as stylistic devices' (p.124). These elements can be inconsequential to the plot but add a distinctly camp flavour.

Babuscio uses the genre of Horror to explore how narratives may include camp aesthetics as a metaphor. Many monsters in Horror have to contend with oppression from society and experience 'pressure to conform and adapt' (p.124). It is important to recognize that Babuscio's argument is confused because these are narrative rather than aesthetic concerns and thus this section is somewhat flawed.

Theatricality

> To appreciate camp in things or persons is to perceive the notion of life-as-theatre, being [self] versus role-playing, reality and appearance. (p.125)

Babuscio explains that in real life, gays do not conform to traditional sexual expectations. Accordingly, many homosexuals choose to conceal their sexual leanings by pretending to be 'straight', a practice known as 'passing'. This can manifest in overt, albeit false, displays of heterosexuality. He states that passing can 'lead to a heightened awareness and appreciation for disguise, impersonation, the projection of personality, and the distinction to be made between instinctive and theatrical behaviour' (p.126). An example he cites is when Jayne Mansfield holds two milk bottles to her ample bosom in *The Girl Can't Help It* (Frank Tashlin, 1957), an overt example of female sexuality.

He also points out how camp theatricality can accrue over time. Although an acting style may be accepted as naturalistic when a film is produced, as it ages the performance may begin to look dated and overly stylized. Examples include Rudolph Valentino's iconic status as a romantic hero in early cinema and Marlon Brando's Method Acting in *A Streetcar Named Desire*. Additionally, stars may acquire a camp aesthetic due to the characters they play. Here, Babuscio discusses Judy

Garland, who intensely played herself no matter what the role. He suggests that Judy's intensity and integrity are attributes the gay community can relate to.

Humour

Here Babuscio points to the coping strategy of laughing when things get difficult. Although he labels this a gay trait, it is in fact also commonly associated with being British and is therefore quite a weak argument. Nevertheless, as homosexuals have been historically oppressed, Babuscio talks of 'laughter rather than tears' in order to create a positive identity. Humour can be a smoke-screen for the pain and alienation experienced by gay communities.

He concludes his article by highlighting the fact that the term 'camp' has often been misused 'to signify the trivial, superficial, and "queer"' (p.134). As can be seen, definitions of 'camp' are integral to Queer Theory and Sontag and Babuscio can serve as good starting points.

Reflect and respond

1   How useful is the category of irony in assessing campness?
2   Is there such a thing as a gay aesthetic?
3   To what extent is gay culture stereotyped through ideas of theatricality?
4   Why is humour important in gay culture? What purpose does it serve?

'Trannies': transvestites, transsexuals and transgender

Queer Theory challenges the depiction of heterosexuality as normative. However another facet of Queer Studies is a focus on people who do not conform to easy labels of male and female. Debates in this particular area cover the differences between sex and gender, often described by the trans community as 'Sex is between your legs; gender is between your ears.' In order to explore trans issues the following terms will be of use:

1   **Transvestites:** Transvestites are people who deliberately dress in clothes associated with the opposite sex. Men who dress as women are sometimes labelled as drag queens and women dressed as men adopt the term drag kings, although this term is less common. Both can also be referred to as cross-dressers or gender-benders.
2   **Transsexuals:** Transsexuals are people who choose to undergo medical procedures to change gender. This process is often referred to as gender reassignment. Most transsexuals believe that they are members of the opposite sex physically trapped in the wrong body. Two other terms also need to be considered: pre-operative and post-operative. These labels indicate whether a transsexual is awaiting or has undertaken gender reassignment.
3   **Transgender:** The term 'transgender' serves to define people who do not conform to the gender they were born with. It is problematic because trans people do not fit into the traditional neat categories of male or female and the term 'transgender' is a similar label: a third

category which is rejected by many as oversimplifying the complex nature of the condition. Marjorie Garber discusses the idea of thirdness, recognizing that the idea of a third sex or third term is problematic:

> The third is that which questions binary thinking [...] the 'third term' is *not* a *term*. Much less is it a *sex*, certainly not an instantiated 'blurred' sex as signified by a term like 'androgyne' or 'hermaphrodite,' although these words have culturally specific significance at certain historical moments. The 'third' is a mode of articulation, a way of describing a space of possibility. (1993, p.11)

The three terms above should not be considered as mutually exclusive. For example a pre-operative transsexual may choose to cross-dress (be a transvestite). In addition, a transgendered person may also cross-dress or opt to have surgery (transsexual).

Although issues facing the trans community can be challenging, it is often treated in a jovial manner by the film industry. Transvestites often feature in films for comedy value such as Tony Curtis and Jack Lemmon's characters in *Some Like It Hot* (Billy Wilder, 1959) and *Mrs Doubtfire* (Chris Columbus, 1993). Alternatively they feature in overtly gay narratives such as *La Cage aux Folles* (Edouard Molinaro, 1978) and *The Adventures of Priscilla, Queen of the Desert* (Stephan Elliot, 1994). Serious depictions of trans people can be found in *The Crying Game* and *Boys Don't Cry* (Kimberly Peirce, 1999). Furthermore, the Spanish director Pedro Almodóvar manages to find the correct balance between seriousness and humour in the film *All about My Mother/Todo Sobre Mi Madre* (1999).

Reflect and respond

1   How important are labels in defining gender and sexuality?
2   To what extent does society preach the doctrine of binary oppositions (male/female and heterosexual/homosexual)?
3   Do you believe the idea of 'thirdness' is a useful approach in understanding trans people?
4   Why do you think the film industry chooses to represent trans issues in a lighthearted manner?

Political oppression

Although homosexuality has historically been marginalized in mainstream Anglo-American filmmaking, its treatment overseas has often been far worse. Below are a few examples of directors who have attempted to confront homophobic attitudes in their own countries.

Spain

The Spanish director Pedro Almodóvar started his career as a member of the *La Movida Madrileña* group. The Madrid-based group was set up during the transitional period following the death of the Spanish dictator Francisco Franco in 1975. During Franco's reign homosexuals were often imprisoned and tortured because homosexuality was a criminal offence. The country adhered to a strict Catholic orthodoxy, which severely restricted many aspects of life.

La Movida Madrileña was an underground countercultural group that celebrated the newfound freedom following Franco's death. They prided themselves in exploring sexuality, recreational drugs and all things taboo. Almodóvar's early work was consciously camp and flamboyant. The camp aesthetic (see above) has continued throughout his oeuvre, along with transsexual and cross-dressing characters. He is mainly revered for his melodramatic narratives, which interrogate and celebrate ideas of femininity (whether it is biological or achieved through surgical augmentation). Although such stylistic signatures could be attributed to the director's sexuality, he does not welcome the label 'gay filmmaker' as he thinks of himself as a filmmaker who happens to be gay.

China

Homosexuality in China has often been forced underground due to a history of intolerance. However, the internet has been instrumental in connecting gay communities because it creates a space where people can voice their opinions. A good example of this was the novel *Beijing Story/Beijing Gushi*, which appeared on the internet in 1996. It was written anonymously: 'The author adopted the pseudonym "Beijing Tongzhi" – literally "Beijing Comrade", but the word *Tongzhi*, the traditional form of greeting between Communists, has latterly picked up the slang meaning of "gay"' (Lan yu, 2001). It is a tale of the gay relationship between a young student and a businessman, set against the backdrop of the Tiananmen Square Massacre. Both these subjects are prohibited in mainland China.

The novel was adapted for the screen by the openly gay director Stanley Kwan. The film *Lan Yu* (2001) caused controversy due to its subject matter and the inclusion of full frontal male nudity. Although the film gained critical acclaim abroad, it has been banned in China along with Western films that depict homosexuality.

India

Homosexuality has long been a criminal offence in India. It was not until July 2009 that it was finally decriminalized. Although the ancient Kama Sutra overtly depicts sexual acts, including homosexuality, prostitution and sadomasochism, Indian culture typically treats sexual subjects as taboo.

Traditionally Bollywood films have featured effeminate characters as lighthearted relief. However, when Deepa Mehta made the lesbian film *Fire* (1996), she suffered a backlash from conservatives attempting to ban the film:

> Members of the state-governing Right-wing party, the Shiv Sena, organised violent riots in Bombay (Mumbai), which spread across northern India. Theatres were forced to cease screening the film and it was sent back to the Censorship Board for review causing outrage amongst civil rights activists. Shouting matches broke out in parliament. Major Indian newspapers carried the unfolding developments of the *Fire* story as front page news every day for a fortnight, and the controversy was reported in the foreign press too. (Marsh, 2002, p.237)

The reason the film caused such outrage was because Indian society is founded on traditional patriarchal ideas and lesbianism challenges the fundamental premise of patriarchy. When the lesbian affair is discovered in the film, the husband is so ashamed of his wife's infidelity that he allows her to burn when her sari catches fire. However, she survives the flames and is reunited with her lover.

Interestingly, Mehta was born in India but now resides and works in Canada. The move overseas has allowed her to freely question her heritage as an Indian. *Fire* is part of Mehta's 'Elements Trilogy' and the other films caused similar controversies. In *Earth* (1998) she explored the rift between Muslims and Hindus during the partition of India; and in *Water* (2005) she explored the taboo subject of child widows.

These examples from Spain, China and India demonstrate how homosexuality is treated around the world. Depending on a country's religious, political and moralistic stance, gay filmmakers can, and often do, come up against resistance. Therefore, it is important when looking at Queer Theory that you consider national attitudes towards homosexuality as this may influence production, funding and marketing.

Reflect and respond

1   Do you think homosexuality is treated differently around the world?
2   Do you think that political and religious institutions should have the right to censor filmmakers?
3   In China, the internet has enabled gay communities to form a network. Can you think of any instances where the internet has been used to foster hatred and intolerance?
4   Has Deepa Mehta the right to critique Indian society when she no longer resides in the country?

In the closet

Whereas some directors have endangered themselves in order to speak out against the atrocities inflicted upon homosexuals, such openness is rarely practised by Hollywood actors. Rupert Everett, one of the few openly gay actors, has recently discussed this problem:

> The fact is that you could not be, and still cannot be, a 25-year-old homosexual trying to make it in the British film business or the American film business or even the Italian film business. It just doesn't work and you're going to hit a brick wall at some point. You're going to manage to make it roll for a certain amount of time, but at the first sign of failure they'll cut you right off [...] And, honestly, I would not advise any actor necessarily, if he was really thinking of his career, to come out. (Cadwalladr, 2009)

Despite Everett's comments, there does seem to be a more tolerant attitude to homosexuality within the British film industry. A number of successful British actors refused to remain in the closet (Sir Ian McKellen, Stephen Fry, Alan Cumming and Simon Callow). Although there are a few Hollywood stars who are openly gay (George Takei, Neil Patrick Harris and David Hyde Pierce), all of these stars made their name in television rather than in film.

The reason that many American actors keep quiet about their sexuality may be out of fear that they would no longer gain serious roles. Everett believes that being openly gay has hindered his career because the parts he was once offered began to wane after he 'came out'. His interviewer Cadwalladr affirms his argument by stating:

> In the past few years there have been films which featured gay characters – *Brokeback Mountain* and *Transamerica* – but they've been played by heterosexual men, and while a straight man can play gay, a gay man can't play straight (2009).

Interestingly, history shows us that a number of classic stars who forged careers out of playing iconic heterosexual males were in fact gay. It is only after their deaths that we learned the sexuality of actors such as Rock Hudson and Dirk Bogarde.

The film industry seems to be more accepting of female homosexuality. Ellen DeGeneres was one of the first lesbians to publicly 'out herself' in 1997. She chose *The Oprah Winfrey Show* (1986–) to make her announcement; this real-life announcement was mirrored in her hit television show *Ellen* (1994–8) when her character also publicly proclaimed her homosexuality. The incident was significant as it was the first time a gay character had appeared in a primetime show. The show, however, was cancelled soon after. DeGeneres was famously in a relationship with the lesser-known film actress Anne Heche and a media frenzy surrounding the two of them and their personal life ensued. Other famous Hollywood lesbians include Rosie O'Donnell, Sharon Gless and Lindsay Lohan (possibly bisexual). The acceptance of female homosexuality was evident much earlier as both Greta Garbo and Marlene Dietrich were both believed to have had relationships with women although this has never been confirmed.

Reflect and respond

1   Can you name any A-list celebrities who are rumoured to be gay? Why do you think they remain 'in the closet'?
2   It appears that being lesbian is more acceptable than being male and gay. Do you think this is true?
3   Why do you think the television industry is more accepting of homosexuality than the film industry?
4   Account for the difference in attitude between the British and American industry regarding homosexuality.
5   When actors are 'outed' posthumously does their work gain new layers of meaning?

Case study: *Brokeback Mountain* (Ang Lee, 2005)

The Western has a long tradition in filmmaking and is probably the genre most associated with America. Whereas classic Westerns featured rugged displays of heterosexual manliness, *Brokeback Mountain* dared to break with this convention by inserting a same-sex love story. The huge media hype surrounding the release of Ang Lee's *Brokeback Mountain* in 2005 arose due to the film's depiction of a homosexual relationship between two cowboys.

The film was adapted from a short story by Annie Proulx and shows the developing and enduring love between Ennis del Mar (Heath Ledger) and Jack Twist (Jake Gyllenhaal). While it is often referred to as the 'gay Western' or 'gay cowboy' movie, Erika Spohrer considers this generic reading to be incorrect because the film is set in Wyoming rather than the West, with the men tending sheep rather than herding cows (2009, p.28). Furthermore, Amy Andre claims that the film is not about homosexuality but instead features two bisexual men:

> *Brokeback Mountain* is a not a movie about gay people, and there are no gay people in it [...] Despite what you may have read in the many reviews that have come out about this new cowboy feature film, *Brokeback Mountain* is a bisexual picture. Why can't film reviewers say the word 'bisexual' when they see lead characters with sexual and romantic relationships with both men and women? I am unaware of a single review of *Brokeback* calling the leads what they are – a sad statement on the invisibility of bisexual experience and the level of biphobia in both the mainstream and gay media. (2005)

Spohrer also dismisses the generic categories of queer film and the Western, instead claiming that the film has more in common with conventional tragic Romances such as *Romeo and Juliet* and *Tristan and Isolde*. Here, she quotes Hoberman (p.28), who highlights the compositional similarities between the posters for *Brokeback Mountain* (Figure 11.1) and James Cameron's 1997 tragic romance *Titanic* (Figure 11.2).

One reason the film became so controversial is that it invites the viewer to subconsciously re-evaluate the history of the Western. This was evident at the 2005 Oscar awards ceremony when the host ironically commented that the film had 'tarnished' the macho tradition of the Western. He then showed a humorous montage of homoerotic moments from classic American Westerns.

Unlike many contemporary films concerned with representing gay culture, *Brokeback Mountain* does not deal with, or mention, AIDS. The narrative is played out between the years 1963–81; this predates the outbreak of the AIDS epidemic in America. This allowed for the men to have unprotected sex, this omission of condoms giving rise to the derogatory nickname 'Bareback Mountain' (Barounis, 2009, p.68). Barounis explains that this choice rewrites modern queer filmmaking:

> While barebacking has often been conflated with 'bug chasing' in a rhetoric that has sought to stigmatize homosexuality as an antisocial behavior motivated by the Freudian death drive, the film escapes these associations ultimately by a feat of geographical and temporal dislocation. In the context of the film, barebacking loses its contemporary urban stigma and its association with threats to public health; it is instead transformed into a life-affirming practice structured around a principle of rural able-bodied masculinity. (2009, p.68)

In spite of the film's overt sexual content, it is often dismissed by the gay community as being too straight. On one hand they applaud the lack of camp, effeminate stereotypes but on the other they feel that the characters of Ennis and Jack are 'too' straight. There is no indication of gay subculture, although it is inferred that Jack often heads to Mexico for sordid encounters with male prostitutes. The absence of gay clichés may account for its breakthrough status, as

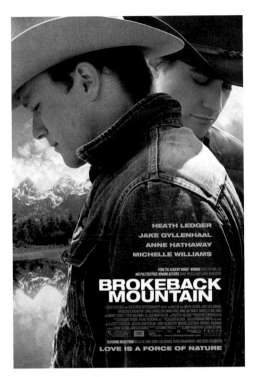

Figure 11.1   Poster for *Brokeback Mountain*
(Ang Lee, 2005)

Figure 11.2   Poster for *Titanic*
(James Cameron, 1997)

Brokeback Mountain did remarkably well considering its subject matter. Gay films often fail to attract mainstream audiences but, as Barounis notes, the film: '[H]arnessed the normalizing powers of masculinity, presenting a narrative of gender that helped to generate mainstream appeal in the box office and, more importantly, mainstream approval of a stigmatized social identity' (2009, p.55).

Reflect and respond

1   Consider the posters for *Brokeback Mountain* and *Titanic*. In what ways are they similar?
2   Make an argument for and against *Brokeback Mountain* as a Western, a gay film and a Romance.
3   Do you think the film was irresponsible in avoiding any mention of gay civil rights and the AIDS epidemic?
4   Why do you think *Brokeback Mountain* gained mainstream acceptance?

Conclusion

Queer Theory is mostly about identity politics and recognizing gay attributes within the *mise-en-scène* and narrative. It was born out of a history of oppression where gay people were made to feel marginalized. Filmmakers have been at the fore in challenging ideas of sexual acceptability and have been instigators in bringing gay issues into the mainstream.

On its initiation, Queer Studies was deemed controversial. As society has become more understanding of gay concerns the objectives of the academic field have expanded. Gay characters are typically no longer sidelined or purely introduced for laughs. Films like *Brokeback Mountain* and *Four Weddings and a Funeral* (Mike Newell, 1994) treated gay relationships as normal, challenging bigoted perceptions.

The focus in more recent debates concerns the representation of trans communities, be they transsexual, transgender and/or transvestite. Once more, as society becomes more embracing of alternative identities, Queer Studies may undergo another shift in direction.

Bibliography

Andre, A. (2005) 'Opinions: Bisexual Cowboys in Love', *National Sexuality Resource Center*. Retrieved 3 March 2010. Available at http://nsrc.sfsu.edu/article/opinion_bisexual_cowboys_love.

Babuscio, J. (1977) 'Camp and the Gay Sensibility', in H. M. Benshoff and S. Griffin (eds) (2005) *Queer Cinema: The Film Reader*, New York: Routledge, pp.121–36.

Barounis, C. (2009) 'Crippling Heterosexuality, Queering Able-Bodiedness: Murderball, *Brokeback Mountain* and the Contested Masculine Body', *Journal of Visual Culture* vol. 8 no. 1, pp.54–75.

Benshoff, H. M. and Griffin, S. (eds) (2005) *Queer Cinema: The Film Reader*, New York: Routledge.

Cadwalladr, C. (2009) 'I Wouldn't Advise Any Actor Thinking of His Career to Come Out', *Observer*. Retrieved 29 January 2010. Available at http://www.guardian.co.uk/film/2009/nov/29/rupert-everett-madonna-carole-cadwalladr.

Carter, David (2004) *Stonewall: The Riots That Sparked the Gay Revolution*, New York: St Martin's Press.

Foucault, M. (1976) *The History of Sexuality: Volume 1*, Harmondsworth: Penguin.

Garber, M. (1993) *Vested Interests: Cross-Dressing and Cultural Anxiety*, London: Penguin.

Lan yu (2001) Retrieved 29 March 2010. Available at http://lanyu.gstage.com/english/author.html.

Marsh, J. (2002) '*Fire*, the BJP and Moral Society', *South Asia: Journal of South Asian Studies* vol. 25 no. 3, pp.235–51.

Michalik, R. (2001) *The Desire for Philosophy: Interview with Judith Butler*. Retrieved 29 January 2010. Available at http://www.lolapress.org/elec2/artenglish/butl_e.htm.

Pearl, M. (2004) 'AIDS and New Queer Cinema', in M. Aaron (ed.) (2004) *New Queer Cinema: A Critical Reader*, Edinburgh: Edinburgh University Press, pp.23–35.

Rich, B. R. (1992) 'New Queer Cinema', in M. Aaron (ed.) (2004) *New Queer Cinema: A Critical Reader*, Edinburgh: Edinburgh University Press, p.15–22.

Russo, V. (1981) *The Celluloid Closet: Homosexuality in the Movies*, New York: Harper & Row.

Sontag, S. (1964) 'Notes on Camp', in D. Bergman (ed.) (1993) *Camp Grounds: Style and Homosexuality*, Amherst: University of Massachusetts.

Spohrer, E. (2009) 'Not a Gay Cowboy Movie', *Journal of Popular Film and Television* vol. 37 no. 1, pp. 26–33.

Audience Research and Reception

12

Empirical
1. Methods of practice on the results of observation and experiment, not on scientific theory.

Qualitative
1. Of or relating to quality or qualities; measuring, or measured by, the quality of something.

Quantitative
1. That is, or may be, measured or assessed with respect to or on the basis of quantity; that may be expressed in terms of quantity; quantifiable.

Setting the scene

The field of Audience Studies has long been a contentious one in academic approaches to film. The main reason for this is that Film Studies has a tendency to privilege the text rather than focusing on the viewers and the worlds they inhabit. However, looking at people, the places they lived, fashions they wore, leisure pursuits they chose and the social and political climates they experienced, can afford insights into the meaning of a text. More importantly, these facets bring history to life and enable us to appreciate the past.

The study of audiences has gone in and out of fashion over the years. As a result, Audience Research may also be referred to as Reception Theory, Response Studies and Spectatorship Theory, yet arguably these approaches do not actually study the audience. Unlike the previous chapters in this book, very few key academics have established theories concerned with Audience Research and Response. This is because studies on these topics are frequently empirically based rather than theoretically driven. However, a number of academics have worked extensively and developed ideas in this field, some of whom include: Robert C. Allen, Annette Kuhn, Richard Maltby, Janet Staiger, Katherine H. Fuller-Seeley, Martin Barker and Melvyn Stokes.

This chapter departs from the established format within this book because Audience Studies is based on empirical research. Rather than being founded upon individual theoretical perspectives, much academic work is undertaken through field study. Accordingly, this chapter offers a more methodological approach, yet still retains a historical overview of scholarly innovations.

Gathering information and codes of behaviour

Because Audience Research and Response is such a large and complex field, it is important that you approach your inquiry with specific questions in mind. There are so many potential avenues that it can be a daunting prospect choosing the most appropriate route. Remember that you will not be able to cover all aspects of research in this field. In order to help you limit your inquiry we have formulated four preliminary areas. Who, Where, How and Why. These are in no way exclusive and should not be undertaken in any specific order. All four criteria can be approached from either qualitative (relating to specific qualities: race, gender, class, etc.) or quantitative (relating to quantity: how many people saw a specific film, etc.) perspectives.

Who

It is very important to establish the demographics of your audience as this can reveal vital information. The past can become more vivid when we move beyond statistics on a page to consider the real-life experiences of spectators. It is useful to consider the following demographic information in determining evidence in a meaningful way:

- age
- gender
- race/ethnicity
- religion
- sexuality
- class
- employment
- location
- cultural subgroups.

Examples of Audience Studies that have taken this approach include:

- Richard Maltby's (1990) work on the 1927 film *The King of Kings* (Cecil B. DeMille). He discusses religious reactions to the scandalous image of Mary Magdalene and other moral issues.
- Jacqueline Bobo's work (1988–9) on *The Color Purple* explores African American female responses to Steven Spielberg's 1985 adaptation of Alice Walker's novel.
- Sue Harper's 'A Lower Middle-class Taste-Community in the 1930s: Admission Figures at the Regent Cinema, Portsmouth UK' (2004) undertakes close analysis of class at one specific cinema on the south coast.

Why

One of the main questions that preoccupies academics is why people choose to go to the cinema and what determines the films they see. There can be many factors influencing these decisions. Below you will find a number of examples that may affect audience attendance:

- escapism
- word of mouth

- cinematic experience (social)
- educational (children learning)
- franchise, sequel
- first date
- industry accolades (Oscars)
- marketing, promotional campaigns
- controversy
- star
- director
- genre
- content (political, historical setting, etc.)
- diasporic audience (connection to culture)
- financial implications (cinema vs other forms of entertainment).

Many academics have written about why certain films attract specific audiences; below are examples.

- Robert Warshow (2001) in 'The Gangster as Tragic Hero' (1948) considered audience response to the iconic figure of the gangster.
- Nandini Bhattacharya (2004) takes a broader view. She looks at how Bollywood films are consumed by non-resident Indians. She explores how Bollywood teaches younger generations in diasporic communities about their culture and heritage.

Where

Lots of academics have considered the spaces where film is consumed and this forms a great amount of the writing on audiences. Where a film is exhibited, the architecture of the building and the medium of projection and exhibition all affect the viewing experience. Different exhibition spaces are listed in the figure below.

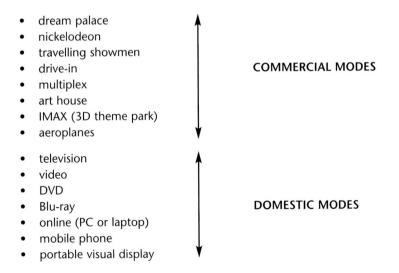

- dream palace
- nickelodeon
- travelling showmen
- drive-in
- multiplex
- art house
- IMAX (3D theme park)
- aeroplanes

COMMERCIAL MODES

- television
- video
- DVD
- Blu-ray
- online (PC or laptop)
- mobile phone
- portable visual display

DOMESTIC MODES

It is interesting to note how cinema has evolved from a communal experience into a more insular format. Whereas early studies in this field looked at film screenings as a collective activity, with the emergence of the television and home-video technology the watching process has become more intimate. For example, television screens cater for a domestic audience of family and friends. New media has led to film being consumed on an individual basis. Portable audio visual devices are designed to enable a solitary figure to 'plug-in' and watch irrespective of their surroundings. Accordingly, the traditional 'silver screen' has undergone a drastic reduction in size, being adapted to fit into the home and more recently into new digital formats. It appears that as time and technology progress, the collective viewing experience grows less and less common. In order to counteract the movement from the commercial sphere to the domestic, the film industry has invested in larger screen formats (IMAX) and three-dimensional technology (3D), a technology that has now been brought into the domestic sphere.

Academics who have written about the viewing experience include:

- Douglas Gomery has written extensively in the area of cinema consumption, in particular the exhibition business. One such article is devoted to the rise in national theatre chains in the US (1992).
- Jacqueline Stewart (2005) has researched viewing practices in custom-built cinemas, designed to cater for black American audiences.

How

Depending upon our environment, the way we consume film differs drastically. Society often dictates codes of behaviour; these codes are learnt from an early age from parents and social conditioning. Here are a number of examples:

Cinema

- **Silence (Western society)**
  In Western society there is an unwritten code that cinematic screenings be watched in silence. The cinema is treated almost like a temple. People are chastised for talking and eating loudly.
- **Interaction (world cultures)**
  Bollywood: Audiences throw coins if they appreciate a particular sequence. Long songs are worked into the narrative to typically allow for the male viewers to go and get refreshments for the family.
- **Singing**
  Certain films have gained a cult following and accordingly this has led to interactive screening experiences where the audience is encouraged to dress up and sing along. Such films include *The Sound of Music, The Rocky Horror Picture Show* and *Mamma Mia!*
- **Cosplay (short for costume play)**
  Here members of the audience dress up as their favourite stars. Particularly popular in Japan (anime and manga) and more recently in America and Canada (the *Star Trek* and *Star Wars* franchises are key examples).
- **Mother and baby screenings**
  These may occur in some venues. Here mothers can watch a film and not worry about young babies and children screaming and disturbing others.

Home

- Emotions: Viewing at home allows for the freedom to express reactions without feeling intimidated.
- Interaction with environment: If you watch a film in the domestic environment you can interact with your surroundings because you can move freely. A good example of this is when people use a cushion to hide behind when they become scared.
- Fragmented viewing (ffwd, rwd and pause): With the emergence of home-video technology it is now possible to pause, fast forward and rewind a film. This enables viewers to chat among themselves in response to the narrative or pause the action if the pizza-delivery man arrives.

Academic studies include:

- Jeffrey Richards and Dorothy Sheridan's *Mass Observation at the Movies* (1987).
- More recently Ann Gray looked at how home entertainment was consumed in *Video Playtime: The Gendering of a Leisure Technology* (1992).

Reflect and respond

1   Do you ever look at the other audience members when you go to the cinema? Do they tend to be of a similar age, class and gender to yourself? Can you think of any experiences where this has not been the case?
2   Does your viewing experience depend on who you attend the cinema with?
3   What influences you to go and see a film?
4   How important is the venue to your viewing pleasure?
5   Are there any other unwritten rules regarding cinemagoing or talking about films?

In order to undertake an audience-based research project, it is important to establish the questions of who, why, where and how. This will provide a firm starting point for your thesis. From here appropriate sources must be identified to provide evidence and original material to enrich and further your study.

Relevant sources

Historical audience research relies on primary sources (whereas contemporary research can be more dependent on empirical methods). Rather than focusing wholly on the film as text, it is important that researchers consider undertaking archival work to familiarize themselves with original historical material. This material is vast. Below we have included a number of potential primary resources, but be aware that this list is in no way exhaustive.

Nowadays resources are available in a number of different formats; you may be able to access physical hard copies of material, or online versions. Alternatively, you may need to take information from microfilm or microfiche. Most of the artefacts listed here can be accessed via library databases or special collections. Such collections are typically held by museums, studios or dedicated companies set up to house film-related material.

1 Newspapers

These are one of the first ports of call for information. Bear in mind that there are different styles of newspapers for different demographics. Broadsheets are written for a professional clientele and tabloids are more populist. Additionally, there are a number of trade newspapers dedicated to the industry. Newspapers boast a wealth of information, from film reviews and interviews with actors to feature-length stories, details of production histories and other promotional material.

2 Magazines

These adopt a more informal tone of journalism than traditional newspapers. From the early days of the industry, fan magazines became a staple for cinematic audiences. Magazines often feature interviews with celebrities and gossip columns, and they typically offer a more personal insight into the world of filmmaking. Specialist film magazines may include production histories and features. Early magazines included *Motion Picture Story Magazine*, *Photoplay* and *Bioscope*. More recent examples are *Empire* and *Total Film*. However, it is far easier to track down magazines aimed at specific audiences such as Horror, Science Fiction and Cult fans.

3 Posters and postcards

There is a growing market for film memorabilia, with posters and postcards ranking among the highly prized commodities for fans and academics. Images can say a lot about a film and the way it is promoted.

4 Theatre clippings

Box-office figures are an indicator of how well or poorly a film is received. This information can tell a researcher a lot about national and regional trends. It is important to note that a lot of this information can now be accessed online via sites such as IMDB or Mojo Box Office.

5 Industry records

Gaining access to data held by studios or distribution and exhibition companies can reveal a great amount of information. For example, you may uncover knowledge relating to censorship practices. You may also find financial records and other interesting facts concerning production history (script drafts, contracts, etc.).

6 Scrapbooks, diaries and personal papers

As the emphasis in this chapter is on the audience, it is paramount that personal artefacts and accounts are accorded similar importance to published material. This material needs to be handled sensitively; for example, should you unearth personal information about a public figure, you need to question whether it would benefit your research or whether to include it would merely be gratuitous and hurtful.

7   Interviews

Here you can attain specific insights into an individual's role and their opinions on what took place during and after the filmmaking process. This can offer an interesting perspective not readily available elsewhere. The key thing to remember is that both interviews and personal artefacts (see above) are highly subjective and therefore information should be taken with a 'pinch of salt' (or cross-referenced).

8   Government and local records

These records can be accessed in museums (local and national). Additionally, public record offices hold census records alongside geographical information. The Mass Observation project is a UK-based organization that holds a collection of data relating to all aspects of society. Film scholars have mined this archive to gain insight into regional patterns of behaviour. Similarly, there are numerous film-orientated collections held in the US.

9   Architectural surveys

If you are interested in the architecture of your local cinema, then you could seek out information from council archives or public record offices. This could reveal information regarding the kind of audience that would frequent the cinema, as a building that was renowned for its magnificent decor may attract a different class of spectator than a rundown 'fleapit'.

10   Fire insurance maps

This information can be revealing in relation to health and safety issues and more importantly as a way of gaining insight into periods of social reform. When cinemas were first established, little care was taken to ensure the safety of customers. However, journalists and temperance movements (especially in the US) exposed the dangerous environments through written articles and petitioning. Accordingly, delving into these records and noting changes reflects public concerns and legislation. Furthermore, they have helped scholars to identify where cinemas have been historically located.

11   Flea markets and antique stores

These may not come to mind when thinking about embarking on primary research, because not every stall or shop holds memorabilia relating to film. Nevertheless, a canny researcher could come across a cinematic treasure by chance. However, if you are in a position where you are able to spend lots of money, you need to ensure that any items bought are accompanied by official provenance documentation (written history).

12 *Internet auctions and websites*

These are fast becoming a new option for researchers. The wealth of memorabilia and promotional material available online is vast. Furthermore, you could monitor buying patterns in order to identify trends in popularity.

13 *Web ethnography*

This is another growing field of research. The internet provides a number of resources for academics to access opinions and criticism. Forums, chat rooms, blogs, personal websites, Twitter and social-networking sites are a way for fans to interact and form communities. The World Wide Web allows for anonymity, which may encourage participation. This offers a researcher understanding into how the film exists beyond the cinematic screen.

Reflect and respond

1 Consider the ways you undertake research. Which of the above sources have you accessed?
2 Are you surprised by any of the resources suggested. If so, why?
3 As a student, which of the above would you struggle to access?
4 Which resources do you think are academically more credible?
5 Using the table below, ✔ which resources you could use to locate the information listed. The numbers on top of the table refer to the sources recorded above.

	1	2	3	4	5	6	7	8	9	10	11	12	13
Studio's financial history													
Audience demographic for a specific film													
Intermission regulations in the 20s													
How many cinemas existed historically in a town													
Audience participation: singing and dressing up													
Cinematographer's criminal records													
Advertising for *Gone with the Wind* (Victor Fleming, 1939)													
Weekly takings for local cinema													
Censorship													
Online download figures for latest blockbuster													

Media effects

The very first Audience Research was concerned with what film does to people. In particular, it sought to expose the negative effects of film viewing on the general public. It is interesting that this initial research highlighted the negative rather than privileging any positive aspects of cinemagoing. Young children and women were considered vulnerable and easily susceptible to on-screen images. There was a fear that young minds were being corrupted by overtly violent and sexual images. Rather than concentrating on the educational and positive aspects of cinema, this field of research was initiated by the clergy, temperance movements and other groups hoping to cleanse society of its ills. Their motivation was to call for stricter regulation and censorship in the industry.

Payne Fund studies (1929–32)

The Payne Fund was established as a private foundation to examine the effect and influence of films on youngsters. The study focused on three main aspects in particular: the content of films, audience composition and the effects of cinema on children. In 1929, films were still considered a new form of entertainment that had grown in popularity in the early part of the twentieth century. Although moviegoing was all the rage, no censorship existed in the United States. It was up to individual cinematic establishments to decide what to show the viewing public.

The Payne Fund employed a number of specialists from the fields of sociology, psychology and education. This team of experts used a number of methodologies. Such methods included:

- questionnaires
- surveys
- personal interviews
- content analysis (1,500 films considered)
- personal diaries and autobiographies.

In addition to these investigations, they also undertook laboratory experiments. Here sample audiences would be subjected to filmic material and their responses recorded.

The foundation was also concerned with how films shape children's attitudes because cinema was integral in informing their ideas. Researchers also looked at children's sleep patterns after watching films to deduce whether there was any behavioural change. However, the main concern of the studies was to assess if film viewing was contributing to a growth in juvenile delinquency. The church, schools and local pressure groups were convinced that children's psyches were being damaged by the images shown in cinemas and as a result youngsters were becoming more violent and disruptive. Furthermore, it is important to remember that the Fund was established to confirm these worries and therefore its approach should be recognized as biased.

The Payne Fund published its results in over twelve volumes between the years 1933 and 1937. Among these is Herbert Blumer's *Movies and Conduct* (1933) and *Movies, Delinquency and Crime* (1933). The legacy of the experiment can still be felt today, with the issue remaining a concern that preoccupies academics, politicians and other social figures.

Categories of effect

Following on from the studies conducted by the Payne Fund, researchers have gone on to identify three ways in which the media influences viewers. They are as follows:

- **Cognitive:** Here, researchers are concerned with the way films influence what people think and believe. Film has often been associated with propaganda and questions should be asked as to whether film can impose ideology (a system of beliefs).
- **Psychological:** This category looks at individuals' emotional and mental responses after watching various film genres.
- **Behavioural:** Of equal importance is the possible copycat effect on the behaviour of spectators. This is the 'age-old' debate asking whether people can be influenced to replicate in life what they see on the cinematic screen.

Both the Payne Fund and the categories above assume that film viewers are passive. This idea led to what has become known as the 'hypodermic needle model'.

The hypodermic needle model

This idea developed out of debates at the Frankfurt School (a group of academics working in Germany from the 20s). Theodor Adorno and Max Horkheimer claimed that Hollywood filmmaking was dangerous because the films were not complex enough to stimulate thought. Because information is relayed in a simplistic manner, the audience does not question what it sees and instead subconsciously enters into the ideology of a narrative. The hypodermic syringe metaphor is powerful in illustrating how the audience passively receives information in the same manner that a patient would receive a medical injection. This metaphor also implicitly suggests that media can be a 'drug'. This model is frequently called upon in media-effects research but the most important thing to remember is that the approach presumes that the audience is passive (non-thinking or unable to resist information received).

Stuart Hall

'Encoding/Decoding' (1980)

Stuart Hall was one of the first people to challenge this idea of the passive audience. His work was more concerned with how meaning is created rather than how a text affected the audience. His seminal work suggested that people respond to a text in one of three ways:

1 **Dominant:** This is akin to the hypodermic needle model, where the audience passively accepts the dominant ideology of a text. This means that the viewer 'buys into' the intention of the director/screenwriter.
2 **Oppositional:** Here the audience actively works against the narrative and its messages. Taking an oppositional stance, it creates a new/different meaning.

3 **Negotiated:** This falls between the two readings (dominant and oppositional) and is the most common form of reception. Here the reader neither rejects nor accepts the ideology of a text. They may agree with some parts but may strongly disagree with others.

Hall acknowledges that an audience can be active as well as passive. British cultural studies of the 70s developed these ideas. They were interested in how societies produced and consumed culture and their research was based around film and television. This approach promoted a more objective and less biased perspective and it can still function as a device for reading modern films.

Reflect and respond

1 How influential do you think films are on the general public's behaviour?
2 Why do you think films have attracted criticism from religious and educational establishments?
3 Do you agree with the hypodermic needle model theory?
4 To what extent do you feel that some groups in society are more vulnerable than others when exposed to certain kinds of films?
5 Can you identify three films where you have experienced a dominant, oppositional and negotiated response?

Case study: Violence

As we have seen throughout this chapter, most academic work concerning audiences has been generated out of the fear that media can adversely influence vulnerable groups in society. Since its earliest conception, cinema has long been held responsible for society's ills. An ongoing debate concerns whether 'life reflects art' or 'art reflects life'. Put simply, are we influenced by what we see on the screen or are filmmakers inspired by real-life incidents?

A number of high-profile cases have witnessed specific films being blamed for inciting horrific events. In the 70s, the Stanley Kubrick film *A Clockwork Orange* (1971) caused controversy. Based on the novel by Anthony Burgess, the film was targeted as problematic due to its representation of mindless violence and rape. The film was named in the media as being responsible for inciting a number of supposed copycat incidents. These included a beggar being beaten to death and a schoolboy killing a classmate. Whether these acts of violence resulted from viewing the film has never been proven. Despite the fact that it passed the censors, Kubrick himself decided to withdraw the film in the UK after receiving threats. Following his decision, a Dutch tourist was raped by a gang of youths while they sang 'Singin' in the Rain' in direct reference to the film. The withdrawal of the film soon transformed it into a cult classic. After twenty-seven years out of circulation the film was re-released after the director's death. *A Clockwork Orange* still generates cult appeal, with fans wearing similar outfits to Alex and the 'Droogs', a high-profile example being the singer Christina Aguilera holding *A Clockwork Orange* theme party in 2008.

Controversies continued into the 80s surrounding the introduction of home video and the availability to youngsters of so called 'video nasties'. Two films that caused moral panic, but were not on the video nasties list, were *Straw Dogs* (Sam Peckinpah, 1971) and *The Exorcist*. Although made in the 70s, when the films were due for release into the home-entertainment market in the following decade, the BBFC refused to certify them. The BBFC (British Board of Film Classification) is responsible for classifying films in relation to age restrictions (U, PG, 12, 15 and 18). The concern was that violent and sexually inappropriate films could easily be watched by underage viewers in the home. Debates about censorship thus moved beyond the cinema to include home videos. The Video Recordings Act of 1984 sought to regulate videos offered for sale or hire without an official classification. It is important to note that, when videos were first introduced into the UK, they were not subjected to any form of censorship. Accordingly, the Video Recordings Act was a panic measure to try and defend against the perceived threats of the medium. Additionally, in 1985 the BBFC introduced new verbal descriptions on video boxes to indicate the content of films.

The 90s were marked by two events that shocked the world: the murder of Jamie Bulger and the Columbine High School Massacre. In 1993, toddler Jamie Bulger was abducted from a shopping precinct in Liverpool. His kidnappers, Robert Thompson and Jon Venables, were ten years' old. They tortured and then brutally murdered the two-year-old. The film *Child's Play 3* (Jack Bender, 1991), featuring a demonic doll, was named by the tabloid press as a possible influence on these horrific acts of violence. Equally shocking in 1999, Eric Harris and Dylan Klebold rampaged through the corridors of Columbine High School in Colorado with an arsenal of firearms and home-made explosives. In total they killed twelve fellow students and a teacher and injured twenty-one other pupils before turning the guns on themsleves. Harris and Klebold felt alienated from the popular group of students. Considered outsiders, they hung around with a group of likeminded individuals who adopted the name 'Trenchcoat Mafia'. The two wore long trenchcoats during the massacre, a detail that the media fixated on. They identified the film *The Basketball Diaries* (Scott Kalvert, 1995) as a catalyst for their actions. In the film there is a short dream sequence where Leonardo DiCaprio is seen entering a classroom wearing a long black leather trenchcoat. He kills his teacher and a number of other pupils; similarities can be drawn between this scene and the incident at Columbine. Similarly, a number of violent video games were named as having influenced the killers. Both these cases have been discussed in relation to copycat behaviour yet no links have ever been proven. It has been suggested that viewers, bombarded with a constant display of violence on screen, become desensitized to it. Youngsters are particularly vulnerable and can struggle to detach filmic violence from everyday encounters. Therefore the industry needs to self-regulate.

Whether film can be held responsible for acts of violence is a debate that will continue. So long as the film industry persists in simulating brutality and aggressive behaviour occurs in real life, then people will look for answers in order to attribute blame. Cinema often serves as a scapegoat, as it is easier to blame fictional characters than question how society influences individuals. Anthony Burgess, in defending Kubrick's *A Clockwork Orange*, was quoted as saying: '[n]o evidence has ever been adduced in a court of law to prove beyond a doubt that a work of art can stimulate anti social behavior' (Bugge, n.d.). More controversially, he claimed: '[t]he notorious murderer Haig who killed and drank their blood said he was inspired by the sacrament of the Eucharist – does that mean we should ban the Bible?' (Bugge, n.d.). In today's digital era, new questions concerning censorship of unsavoury material have arisen due to sites such as YouTube. This free website allows anyone to access material that has been uploaded by the general public. This includes films that may have carried specific age restrictions and featured scenes of violence and other inappropriate content. Although there is an option to flag and report offensive material, the open-access nature of the site is a 'minefield' regarding issues of censorship. However, it is key to be aware that YouTube is owned by Google and that they are keen for legitimate companies to advertise on the site. Therefore problematic content is swiftly dealt with.

Reflect and respond

1 Think of recent films that have caused controversy due to their content. Why was this?
2 To what extent do you believe youngsters are influenced by what they see on screen?
3 Looking at your own experience, identify any instances where you have been influenced by films.
4 What problems are specific to the home-entertainment market?
5 Consider online content. Who should be responsible for censoring offensive material?

Conclusion

Many criticisms have been levelled at Audience Studies. One of the most fundamental is that research projects were often designed with the aim of exposing the negative effects of films rather than exploring the positive and educational influence of cinema. In presuming that the audience passively consumes a film text, no attention is paid to the complexity of film narratives and their ideology.

Another problem with Audience Research and Response is that most of the work conducted has focused on large, urban centres. In particular a great deal of academic work has looked at New York, Chicago and other large American cities. Timothy Gilfoyle has referred to this phenomenon as 'Gotham-centric' (1998). In concentrating on the metropolis, academics fail to acknowledge rural communities whose residents also go to the movies. Richard Maltby, in the terminology of the early 30s, states that: '"metropolites", "deluxers", and "big keys" were at the center of an imagined universe of moviegoing, and "hicks", "dime houses", and the "Silo Belt" were located on the periphery' (1999, p.37). This has been rectified over the past few decades with more and more academics researching film screenings in rural areas. However, it is important to note that the majority of research in this field is concerned with America and Europe. Intensive studies of film-viewing practices around the world are still few and far between.

Bibliography

Allen, R. C. and Gomery, D. (1985) *Film History: Theory and Practice*, Boston, MA: McGraw-Hill.
Bhattacharya, N. (2004) 'A "Basement" Cinephilia: Indian Diaspora Women Watch Bollywood', *South Asian Popular Culture* vol. 2 no. 2, pp.161–83.
Bobo, J. (1989) 'Sifting through the Controversy: Reading *The Color Purple*', *Callaloo* vol. 39, pp.332–42.

Bugge, C. (n.d.) *The Clockwork Controversy*. Retrieved 11 June 2010. Available at http://www.visual-memory.co.uk/amk/doc/0012.html.

Gilfoyle, T. J. (1998) 'White Cities, Linguistic Turns, and Disneylands: The New Paradigms of Urban History', *Reviews in American History* vol. 26 no. 1, pp.175–204.

Gomery, D. (1992) 'The Rise of National Theatre Chains', in *Shared Pleasures: A History of Movie Presentation in the United States*, London: BFI, pp.34–56.

Gray, A. (1992) *Video Playtime: The Gendering of a Leisure Technology*, London: Routledge.

Hall, S. (1980) 'Encoding/Decoding', in S. Hall *et al.*, *Culture, Media, Language,* London: Unwin Hyman, pp.128–38.

Harper, S. (2004) 'A Lower Middle-class Taste-Community in the 1930s: Admission Figures at the Regent Cinema, Portsmouth UK', *Historical Journal of Film, Radio and Television*, vol. 24 no. 4, pp.565–87.

Kuhn, A. (2002) *An Everyday Magic: Cinema and Cultural Memory,* London and New York: I. B. Tauris.

Maltby, R. (1990) '*The King of Kings* and the Czar of All the Rushes: The Propriety of the Christ Story', *Screen* vol. 31 no. 2, pp.188–213.

Maltby, R. (1999) 'Sticks, Hicks and Flaps: Classical Hollywood Generic Conception of Its Audiences', in M. Stokes and R. Maltby (1999) *Identifying Hollywood's Audiences: Cultural Identity and the Movies,* London: BFI, pp.23–41.

Maltby, R., Stokes, M. and Allen, R. C. (eds) (2007) *Going to the Movies: Hollywood and the Social Experience of Cinema*, Exeter: University of Exeter Press.

Richards, J. and Sheridan, D. (1987) *Mass Observation at the Movies,* London: Routledge.

Staiger, J. (1992) *Interpreting Films: Studies in the Historical Reception of American Cinema*, Princeton, NJ: Princeton University Press.

Stewart, J. N. (2005) *Migrating to the Movies: Cinema and Black Modernity*, Berkeley: University of California Press.

Stokes, M. and Maltby, R. (eds) (1999) *Identifying Hollywood's Audiences: Cultural Identity and the Movies*, London: BFI.

Warshow, R. (2001) 'The Gangster as Tragic Hero (1948)', in *The Immediate Experience: Movies, Comics, Theatre, and Other Aspects of Popular Culture*, Cambridge, MA: Harvard University Press, pp.97–104.

Chapter

13

Stars

Star

1. A person of brilliant reputation or talents. An actor, singer, etc. of exceptional celebrity, or one whose name is prominently advertised as a special attraction to the public.

Setting the scene

Star Studies, in a similar way to many other theoretical approaches, emerged out of literary criticism. Academic interest focused on narrative structures and the function of characters within a specific narrative. In the field of Star Studies, the emphasis is on the actor and their ability to inhabit a role (also known as Acting Studies). Historically, actors were first recognized by traditional theatre touring companies. They acknowledged actors' 'star power' and often promoted their productions on the basis of the popularity of one performer. To attract an audience, publicity materials would highlight the most successful actors. However, this practice did not carry through to the early film industry, which often failed to appreciate the importance of actors.

Whereas theatrical actors were revered for their talent, early film actors were often dismissed due to their clichéd performance style. Film actors were often stereotyped; the male as hero and the female as pure and beautiful or alternatively as sex goddess or vamp. The advent of sound led to some character development, with male roles, in particular, becoming more varied. Female roles, however, remained stereotypical. In spite of the archetypal roles, the general public showed huge interest in film performances.

In the early years of cinema, this fascination with actors broadened to include their off-screen lives. This was fuelled by fan magazines and gossip columns. Film companies, fearful of bad publicity, attempted to control negative press, as they came to understand the huge part that stars played in the overall industry. By the mid-20s, the Hollywood studios established a system of managing stars in order to protect all concerned from disrepute. Restrictive contracts were put in place tying stars to specific studios for many years and enabling production companies to control every aspect of the actors' lives. These measures helped to uphold the reputation of the studios in the field of entertainment.

The recognition of the part played by successful actors in the system of production was ignored as research privileged Auteur and Genre Theory (see Chapter 1, 'Auteur Theory' and Chapter 2, 'Genre Theory'). What needed to be acknowledged was that a more complete understanding of film could be achieved if research into stars were part of the overall investigations, and if perspectives from cultural studies, economics, psychology and semiotic frameworks were appropriated, and applied to popular actors.

The star system

Stars sell films. Within the industry actors function as high-value commodities to encourage producers and financiers to back film projects. Equally, stars are instrumental in attracting an audience; casting Hollywood 'A-list' stars such as Brad Pitt, Angelina Jolie and Robert Pattinson can ensure that people will buy tickets. The importance of the star vehicle was initially dismissed when the industry was being established. However, the late 1900s marked a cultural shift as the very first star was cleverly cultivated and marketed by Carl Laemmle, the founder of new studio IMP (Independent Moving Pictures of America).

Florence Lawrence, also known as 'The Biograph Girl' was the first person to be considered a movie star. Lawrence worked for the Vitagraph Company as an anonymous actress in numerous films before moving to the Biograph studios. Although Lawrence was popular with the viewing public, actors at this time received no accreditation for their roles. Carl Laemmle sought to tempt Lawrence away from Biograph, having recognized her appeal with audiences.

In order to garner public adulation, Laemmle concocted a publicity stunt. He spread the word that 'The Biograph Girl' had been killed in a streetcar accident. He then went on to place advertisements in newspapers announcing that she was in fact alive and about to star in a new film produced by IMP. He also revealed her real name, which was important in establishing Florence Lawrence as the world's first movie star.

Richard de Cordova

'The Emergence of the Star System' (1991)

De Cordova writes about the emergence of the 'star system' and why people became interested in individual performers. He claims that the film studios were responsible for the creation of stars and achieved this by disseminating information about actors. Here, De Cordova identifies three 'systems' or criteria that were imperative in establishing an individual as a recognizable name. They are 'discourse on acting', 'picture personality' and 'the star' (p.17).

Discourse on acting

Prior to 1907, the general public were not familiar with the names of film actors. Stardom was reserved for the more legitimate art form of theatre. The film industry was more interested in the latest technical innovations that could enhance the cinematic experience. When journalists focused on individuals involved in filmmaking, attention was given to the producer, cinematographer and the screenwriter, rather than the actor. De Cordova points out that appearing on screen was thought of in the same way as posing for a photograph (p.19). However, as technology advanced, filmmakers moved away from filming short documentaries to comedies and dramas, in which actors were required to undertake roles. Yet performers in early films were cast due to their talent for telling stories through clear theatrical gestures (histrionic acting style) or because they looked like a specific social type (typage). Once more this differentiated what they did from the more sophisticated style of acting (voice control and psychological development), which was important in the theatre. Pathé was one of the first film companies to engage performers renowned for their reputation on stage. This trend soon caught on and serious actors began to star in films. As a result cinema became accepted as a more respectable art form and began to attract middle- and upper-class audiences.

Picture personality

De Cordova explains that there is a difference between the 'picture personality' and 'the star'. He claims that the former emerged in the year 1909 whereas the latter was not established until 1914. In order to create a 'picture personality', three forms of knowledge were required. First, the 'circulation of the name' was of utmost importance (p.24). This would involve the studio concealing and then revealing the name of an actor. Early fan magazines would further the relationship between its readers and players by devising quizzes for people to identify an actor who appeared in more than one film, etc. Acquiring intertextual knowledge (being able to note an actor's performance across a number of films) was the second stage in establishing the 'picture personality'. The third and final stage, according to De Cordova, was the 'professional experience of the actor' (p.26). This would involve awareness of a performer's work in both film and theatre.

The star

The star is different from the 'picture personality' in that there is public interest in the performer's private life. Stars were expected to be morally sound and there was pressure for them to be heroes both on and off screen. Whereas many theatrical actors were tarnished by scandal, film stars were manufactured to lead 'squeaky-clean' lives in order to act as strong role models. Accordingly, 'the star system worked to support the same ideological project as the films of the day' (p.28).

Reflect and respond

1   To what extent do you think stars are manufactured? Consider how stars change their names, their appearance, etc.
2   Can you think of any publicity stunts that have boosted or damaged an actor's image?
3   How reliant is the industry on stars when marketing films?
4   Do you think that there is still a hierarchy within the star system? Are some stars deemed to be better performers than others?
5   Who do you think has more power in today's film industry: the stars or the studios?

In order to fully understand the Star System, knowledge of the studios and how they operated in the golden era of Hollywood is also of importance.

The studio system

The studio system is usually credited with having started in the 20s, although similar systems were in operation in France around 1910 and Thomas Ince, producer/director, actually established the practice in America in 1912. Ince encouraged the new studios that were forming in Hollywood to adopt methods utilized in industrial factory production to enhance efficiency.

Frederick Winslow Taylor developed a system known as *Taylorism*, which was concerned with work allocation, in particular subdividing tasks into smaller areas of responsibility. These ideas were famously developed by Henry Ford for the production of the Model T Ford car. His application involved the introduction of the conveyor belt to increase the output of the assembly line (Fordism). This influenced the film industry as key individuals became responsible for specific areas of filmmaking, that is, the producer oversaw the financial and logistic components; and set designers would no longer work solely on one film but instead create sets for all productions.

The emerging studios in Hollywood wanted to control all aspects of the film industry. The most powerful of these corporations looked to monopolize the market in order to dominate other studios. Known as the Big Five (Major Five), MGM, Warner Brothers, Paramount, Twentieth Century-Fox and RKO held controlling interests in all three phases of cinema. These were production, distribution and exhibition, collectively known as vertical integration. This allowed studios to regulate supply and demand of films through their own distribution and exhibition networks. The important factor in vertical integration was control over exhibition. Block-booking became a practice that allowed studios to sell main feature films along with lesser-rated B-movies. In some cases theatre owners were unaware of the content of these B-movies, which was referred to as blind-booking. These practices were manipulative and commercial ploys to extract money from theatre owners and control what the general public saw.

The Little Three (Minor Three), Universal, Columbia and United Artists, on the other hand, were not completely vertically integrated studios. They were heavily engaged in the business of production and distribution, but the five majors had complete domination of exhibition. In essence, this meant that the Big Five were able to establish an oligopoly (overall control of the market by a few companies). This oligarchy, along with the Little Three, became known as the 'studio system', which lasted about twenty-five years before being gradually phased out in the 50s. This period of filmmaking was known as the studio era.

However, in 1938 the US Department of Justice sued the Big Five for this unfair monopolizing of the industry. The studios agreed to amend their practices but did not keep to this. In 1942 the Society of Independent Motion Picture Producers (IMPP) sued the Paramount Detroit theatres and won its case to change the oligarchy of the Big Five and the Little Three. Furthermore, in 1948 the Supreme Court forced these companies to sell their movie-theatre chains (*United States* v. *Paramount*).

Hollywood stars and the marketing of them were an important part of this controlled system. Actors were seen as a capital commodity on which finances could be secured. Star contracts stipulated very restrictive terms, binding actors to a specific studio for up to seven years. Any release to make a film with another studio would entail tough negotiations. As part of their terms, actors were not only limited in the films that they made but also in how they were presented to the media. This included press releases and articles in fan magazines; all images were 'tailor-made' to suit what the studio wanted. In an effort to resist this exploitation, actors attempted to form unions but these often proved ineffective due to the individual requirements of the members. The way forward was for each actor to negotiate better terms on an individual basis but this was only really an option for the most successful stars.

In summary the studio system was all about control by the major studios:

- control over the business
- control over the production, distribution and exhibition process
- control over key individuals.

Reflect and respond

1 How aware are you of different studios and how they operate?
2 What role do studios play?
3 Do you think studios today have as much control as they did in the past?
4 How has globalization and the onset of digital technology changed the workings of studios?

The breakthrough in Star Studies came in 1979 with the publication of Richard Dyer's work, *Stars*. Dyer used a semiotic framework to obtain a close analysis of star performance on screen and to investigate promotional publicity material.

Richard Dyer

Stars (1979)

Dyer's *Stars* is a canonical text, a critical approach to the study of stars and stardom. Martin Barker notes that, although critical investigation in this area did not start with this book, it remains a highly influential text (Austin and Barker, 2003, p.5). Dyer states that his aim was to 'survey and develop' work on film stars. He raised new questions about stardom, particularly exploring the relationships between celebrity and star images. He achieved this by conducting in-depth case studies of famous actors. However, we should remember that the main focus of his work is on the classical Hollywood period.

Dyer's book is divided into three parts:

1 **'Stars as a Social Phenomenon'**
   Here he questions the social impact of stars, inquiring why they exist, what their value is and assessing their position within other social structures. He also considers 'why they signify' (why do we endow stars with meaning)?
2 **'Stars as Images'**
   Here Dyer shifts attention away from thinking about the star as a person to the analysis of the textual materials. Additionally, he raises issues of how stars differ from the general public. He talks about the importance of particular stars as types (typecasting, and how they represent society on screen); that is 'what do stars signify'?

3 **'Stars as Signs'**
Inquires into ideas of 'character' and performance, 'how do stars signify'?

These are all concerned with ideology, which for Dyer means, 'a set of ideas and representations in which people collectively make sense of the world and the society in which they live' (p.2).

Heavenly Bodies, 1986 (2004)

In *Heavenly Bodies* (1986), Dyer looks to expand his work on stardom as an ideological system. A central position of Dyer's is how stars articulate ideas about appearance. He discusses stars as a phenomenon of production and consumption, with a particular focus on the way they are consumed. What we know about celebrities stems from what we see, hear and read. He considers how over time stars can reinvent themselves, yet the new persona will always exist in context with their old image.

He develops this contextualizing by assessing who controls the star image. He identifies the following four influences (p.4):

1   Control 'produced by the media industries' (promotional releases).
2   Control attributed to 'who got to interview a star' (how the interview is edited).
3   Control in 'what clips were released' (what media critics say).
4   Control over audience choice: 'Audiences cannot make media images mean anything they want to, but they can select' (we choose what we view and we make our own conclusions about material).

Furthermore, he suggests that stars' off-screen personalities are as important as their on-screen ones in forming spectators' opinions. However, these real-life personalities are as constructed as the characters they play. Ultimately, Dyer points out that, 'stars are made for profit' and that stars have an input into turning themselves into commodities (p.5). They are dependent on how both the controlling forces and their own behaviour combine to impact on audiences' perceptions.

Dyer had a strong impact because he had fostered an approach for producing contextual readings of star images, which appears to have influenced many readings since. Paul McDonald summarized Dyer's approach as an investigation of 'how cinema circulates the images of individual film performers and how those images may influence the ways in which we think of the identity of ourselves and others' (in Dyer, 1998, p.176). McDonald points out that Dyer showed little interest in political economy, screen acting/performance and empirical audience research which is where interest now lies.

Paul McDonald

'Reconceptualising Stardom' in *Stars* (1998)

More recent editions of *Stars* contain a supplementary chapter by Paul McDonald. It is an interesting survey, setting out and challenging some of the main ideas and texts of earlier critics. The chapter is divided into headings of: 'Stars and History', 'Star Bodies and Performance', 'Stars and Audiences' and 'Stardom as Labour'. McDonald starts by acknowledging that the text *Stars* was written in an effort to 'address questions around the social significance of film representations' (p.177). He notes that, in a move away from an ahistorical approach, academics chose to re-examine the early star system in America within a social historical context.

In a section on locating stars, McDonald finds Marian Keane's criticism of Dyer's approach in reading a star's image without the context of society, problematic. Keane suggests the solution is to use philosophical works. However, as McDonald rightly points out, philosophy is about universal notions of identity, which ignores the fact that such ideas change over time. For example, in the studio era actors would not openly discuss their sexuality, despite media speculation. However, nowadays it is generally accepted, more so in Britain than America, if a star 'comes out' as being gay. Similarly, identity can be read via more than one perspective, that is, race, gender, sexuality, class, etc. McDonald also explains that the field of philosophy can be elitist and likely to alienate the typical moviegoer.

Taking issue with Yvonne Tasker in his section on 'Star Bodies and Performance', McDonald finds her work *Spectacular Bodies* (1993) limiting. The identification of muscles as a sign, without discussing how these muscles move in a certain action, obscures a full reading. Stars need to be studied as 'moving bodies' combined with an 'analysis of acting and performance' (p.182). Using the examples of Meryl Streep and Arnold Schwarzenegger, McDonald discusses their different approaches to performance. Streep through her 'impersonatory skills' is able to convince an audience of her acting ability. Arnie frequently plays the same stereotypical character (himself) from film to film. Accordingly, his acting talents are often considered inferior to those of Streep. His 'brawn' associates him with the manual worker whereas in the field of culture, star performances equated with intellectual input carry more esteem.

In his section on 'Stars and Audiences' McDonald includes the idea of 'identification'. Here he explains that meaning is not just reliant on the content of films but is also influenced by the way viewers regard particular performers. McDonald looks to the work of Jackie Stacey (1994) who coins the term 'cinematic identificatory fantasies' (McDonald, 1998, p.191). Her research has investigated how stars inform childhood games and how some people chose to emulate their favourite icons in the way they dress and act.

In his final section entitled 'Stardom as Labour', McDonald discusses how 'only a few players actually become stars' (p.196). It is out of an actor's control as stardom is attained by gaining the affection and respect of the general public. All performers have the potential to achieve star status but only those who are successful are able to join the 'democratic elite' (p.197). Levy adds to this by identifying that it is often those stars who epitomize the American Dream, that is, 'rags to riches' who are favoured by an audience.

Concluding, McDonald proffers four areas for subsequent study that arise from his reconceptualizing:

1   The tendency to study each star in isolation fails to consider the role of other factors, in particular those of other stars, their differences and distinctions.
2   It is important to recognize that more work is required on how the star image may change over time, both historically and culturally. It is also important to consider whether other celebrities such as sportsmen and popstars have become more significant as role models. The inclusion of other national cinemas needs to be addressed as well.
3   'Instead of asking, "what does stardom mean?", a new question would be "what does stardom do?"' (p.200). The focus has been on the star as a text (like the novel or a film). Consideration is given to writing and debating the text rather than concentrating on the star as a performer and their talent.
4   Finally, McDonald advocates that, as these changes take place with a move from the text to the performance, then a 'rethinking of identity' is required (p.200). However, we do not all read and interpret a performance in the same manner. We each bring our own individual experience to our understanding. Ultimately, both the star and the audience are responsible for creating meaning.

Reflect and respond

1   Identify stars who have been typecast throughout their careers. Why do certain actors lend themselves to playing similar roles?
2   To what extent do actors have to reinvent themselves? Why is this so?
3   In what ways are our ideas about a star affected by what we read and see in the media?
4   Does a star have a say in the way that they are represented?
5   How important were stars in forming your ideas as a child?

Star/celebrity debate

Not all actors gain star status and there is a big difference between being a star and being a celebrity. However, it must be noted that the media industry uses the two terms interchangeably. Furthermore, the term star is always attached to the film industry, although celebrities originate from other fields, such as music, sport and the world of fashion. Richard Maltby writing about 'the star' states: '[s]tar performances place the most explicit emphasis on the person of the actor. The commercial imperatives of the star system require that stars are always visible through their characters' (2003, p.384).

Nick Lacey (2002, p.72) points out that for the star, the film is the primary text, whereas the celebrity relies upon secondary texts (songs and videos, sporting events and advertisements, etc.). It is also important to note that there is a great deal of interest in a star's off-screen life, which distinguishes them from the countless actors working in the industry. In addition to stars and celebrities there are also personalities (not to be confused with De Cordova's use of the term). This category of fame relates to people who are recognized for no real reason other than being famous. For example, Paris Hilton became well known due to her father's wealth and success in the hotel business. Similarly, siblings and partners of prominent media personas can attract media coverage.

Reflect and respond

1   Look at the table below and decide whether the figures in the first column are stars, celebrities or personalities. Tick the appropriate box and explain your answers.

Name	Star	Celebrity	Personality
Paris Hilton			
Madonna			
Arnold Schwarzenegger			
David Beckham			
Ice Cube			
Kelly Osbourne			
Joanna Lumley			
Russell Brand			

2   Can you think of people who do not easily fall into one category?

Fandom

One area of Star Studies that has attracted attention recently is the importance of fandom. As we have already established, fans are integral in making or breaking an actor's reputation and star status. Nevertheless, the audience was often overlooked in early debates concerning stars as academics tended to focus on the actors. It wasn't really until Jackie Stacey published her book *Star Gazing* in 1994 that the field began to consider the role of the spectator.

Jackie Stacey

Star Gazing: Hollywood Film and Female Spectatorship (1994)

Jackie Stacey's work was unusual in the field of Star Studies in that she was one of the first academics to carry out empirical work. Coming from a background in Cultural Studies, her approach combines Feminism with sociological and ethnographic audience research. In her book *Star Gazing*, Stacey looks at how British women of the 40s and 50s regarded Hollywood stars such as Bette Davis, Joan Crawford, Rita Hayworth and Doris Day. In order to undertake such a project Stacey corresponded with over 300 women after placing an advert in two British-based magazines, *Woman's Realm* and *Women's Weekly* (p.16). Here she asked women for their recollections of cinema during wartime Britain. She also asked them to reflect on advertisements from that period so she could gain an understanding of how women were influenced by images of celebrity and glamour.

The main premise of Stacey's work was to challenge the psychoanalytical foundations of Feminist theory. In order to do this, she placed the onus on the people that mattered, the audience. Rather than reading the film text from a theoretical point of view, she gained insight into how Hollywood stars influenced and informed the day-to-day lives of women. To make sense of her findings Stacey divided her book into three subcategories:

1 **Escapism:** Here she questioned the use of the term 'escapism' as it had long been associated with women and their tendency to fantasize about a life different from their own. Stacey put the term into historical context by explaining that her targeted audience was viewing films during World War II. At that time the concept of escapism had different connotations.
2 **Identification:** Stacey interrogated the traditional stance adopted by academics, in particular Laura Mulvey's notion that identification is fixed. Instead, Stacey explored the complex relationship between British women identifying with American actresses.
3 **Consumption:** In this final category, Stacey explored the complex nature of how stars are consumed by both the audience and the industry. More importantly, she asked the everyday consumers taking part in her study (empirical research) about the ways they consumed cinematic stars on and off screen.

The above categories relate to female desire and pleasure. Her work is now regarded as pivotal in the field of Star Studies because she moved the focus away from the star to the spectators and therefore it remains the only substantial work on the star/audience relationship.

Reflect and respond

1 Why do you think that stars are used to promote products? How successful is this?
2 Have you ever been tempted to buy an item due to star endorsement?
3 Discuss instances where you have tried to emulate a star's image (hair, clothes, make-up, etc.).
4 If Stacey were to undertake the same project today, which contemporary female stars do you think she would choose as case studies?
5 Consider Stacey's work. Would it have had the same impact if she had looked at male stars?

Since Stacey's work, the role of the spectator has been examined from many different perspectives. This overlaps greatly with Audience Research and Reception (Chapter 12). Chris Rojek's work on stars set about exploring the role of fans and the reciprocal, yet problematic, relationship with actors.

Chris Rojek

'Celebrity and Religion' (2006)

Chris Rojek approaches Star Studies from an unusual perspective. He equates the act of fandom as being akin to the practice adopted by devout followers of religion; the difference is that the temple is replaced by the multiplex. Rojek coins the term 'para-social interaction' to describe how the media simulates intimacy between the viewer and the star (p.390). We may not meet our favourite on-screen personalities face to face, but we feel that we know them due to the wealth of information available via DVD extras, television interviews, magazine articles and websites. He likens this 'para-social interaction' to the way in which deities are worshipped from afar, but he also points out that modern-day celebrities are often ascribed 'God-like qualities by some fans' (p.390).

Rojek accounts for the mass transition from communal spiritual worship to star adulation as a response to a shift in social attitudes. He states that:

> In secular society, the sacred loses its connotation with organized religious beliefs and becomes attached to mass-media celebrities who become objects of cult worship. Magic is often associated with celebrities, and powers of healing and second sight are frequently attributed to them. Rock concerts can generate ecstasy and swooning in the audience, which is comparable to some rites of magic. (p.390)

Here Rojek writes of how the sacred has somehow become lost as interest has been transferred from the deity to the celebrity. It is the audience that empowers the star; this idolization of the actor lifts the performer to a higher plane.

Rojek borrows from the work of Durkheim, who predicted the decline of popular religion, claiming 'the growth of moral individualism is bound to reduce the significance of organized religion' (p.392). Similarly, Neal Gabler also strengthens Rojek's ideas. He writes: 'Celebrity culture is now ubiquitous, and establishes the main scripts, presentational props, conversational codes and other source materials through which cultural relations are constructed' (p.393).

Whereas devout spiritualists would once travel the world to catch a glimpse of holy relics, people are now more interested in the discarded artefacts of the famous. Rojek points out that cemeteries where famous people have been buried are now considered tourist attractions. For example, people undertake pilgrimages to Gracelands to see the final resting place of Elvis Presley.

Rojek also discusses the 'St Thomas Effect', which refers to the biblical character of 'doubting Thomas'. Thomas was the only one of the disciples who was sceptical about Christ's resurrection. It was only when he touched Jesus's wounds that he was able to truly believe. Rojek controversially aligns this story with the excessive behaviour of stalkers. These obsessive fans feel the need to be in close proximity to their idols, knowing the star's every movement and diligently following them in order to prove their devotion.

The main premise of Rojek's discussion is that society is more secular nowadays and so the public need to fill the void once satisfied by religion. However, he admits that for the majority of fans, star worship is lighthearted escapism:

> Fans are attracted to celebrities for a variety of reasons, with sexual attraction, admiration of unique personal values and mass-media acclaim being prominent. Hardly any believe that celebrities can 'save' them in an orthodox religious or quasi-religious sense. But most find comfort, glamour or excitement in attaching themselves to a celebrity. (p.403)

Interesting as Rojek's ideas are, it is important to note that his work offers no empirical proof to support his assertions.

Reflect and respond

1   To what extent do you agree or disagree with Rojek's findings?
2   Have you ever travelled to see your favourite stars/celebrities? Would you consider doing so?
3   Where do you draw the line between fans, obsessive fans and stalkers?
4   Are stars different from the general public and if so should they receive special treatment?
5   Discuss whether stardom has become more important than religion?

Endorsement: commodities, politics and social causes

Many stars lend their image to endorse products. Commercial companies are aware of the selling power a star endorsement can unleash. Their promotion implies that if you purchase their commodity, you will in some way replicate the star's lifestyle and/or their image. For example, the cosmetic company L'Oréal relies on celebrity endorsement to promote its brand. Over the last few years contemporary stars have included Andie MacDowell, Jennifer Aniston, Beyoncé Knowles, Aishwarya Rai and Matthew Fox.

Similarly, films often incorporate product placement. Here, the characters within the narrative are seen to use specific brands and, by association, the audience is encouraged to acquire these items to emulate their star status. The Bond franchise is particularly guilty in this respect; the use of the Sony Viao laptop in *Quantum of Solace* (Marc Forster, 2008) and Ray-Bans in the 80s classic *Top Gun* (Tony Scott, 1986) epitomize such deals.

Stars do not capitalize on their value just for commercial gain; some stars also engage in charitable and political activities. Many actors become involved in supporting charities. Both Ewan McGregor and Nicole Kidman are ambassadors for UNICEF while Vanessa Redgrave has done charitable work for both UNICEF and Amnesty International. Furthermore, some stars become openly embroiled in political matters. During the aftermath of Hurricane Katrina, Sean Penn travelled to Louisiana and personally helped to rescue around forty people. Many sceptical media reporters dismissed his behaviour as a publicity stunt. Spike Lee, the African American director/actor incited fury at the Bush administration's failure to deal with the hurricane's devastation in his documentary *When the Levees Broke: A Requiem in Four Acts* (2006). All of these are positive examples of stars getting involved. Their status calls attention to the wider political cause, which otherwise may not have attained such a high profile. Alternatively, political involvement can backfire on a celebrity's image; consider the media circus that surrounded Madonna's controversial approach to adopting children from Malawi.

Reflect and respond

1 How persuasive do you find celebrity endorsement of commodities? Can you think of any examples where you have been influenced to buy a product due to the marketing by a star?
2 Is product placement in films ethical?
3 Why do you think stars lend their support to charitable causes?
4 There are advantages and disadvantages to star involvement in causes. Make a list of the 'pros and cons'.

Case study: Amitabh Bachchan

Bollywood star Amitabh Bachchan is probably the most famous Indian actor of all time. Yet, despite his celebrity status in Asia, he remains unknown to many people across Europe and America. In his homeland, Bachchan is often referred to as a 'demigod'. This was confirmed in the BBC1 documentary *Imagine: Bollywood's Big B: Amitabh Bachchan* (2007), where famous Indians reflect on the actor and what he means to the people: '[h]e is almost God to millions of people. People worship him […] We believe in him; there's a kind of faith in him […] He's blessed; he is the chosen one' (Lockhart, 2007). Amitabh Bachchan clearly epitomizes Chris Rojek's idea that film stars are revered in the same way that people worship religious figures. This adulation of the Delhi-born actor has developed over the years as his career encountered severe highs and lows.

Born in 1942 to the famous Hindi poet Dr Harivansh Rai Bachchan, Amitabh came to prominence in the early 70s. Casting Bachchan was a risk because the industry was convinced that he would not succeed. He was tall compared to traditional Indian actors and had a deep voice, which similarly went against convention. More importantly, he was very dark-skinned at a time when Bollywood tended to favour light-skinned actors. Even with the odds stacked against him, Bachchan came to symbolize a new type of Indian male: the angry young man.

In the 70s, India was experiencing political unrest. The country was at war with Pakistan, the government had been exposed as corrupt and there was a severe drought. In such turbulent times, Bachchan embodied the national resentment towards a corrupt system and disillusionment with the establishment as a whole. It was the film *Zanjeer* (Prakash Mehra, 1973), that first saw Bachchan cast in the role of the angry young man, courageously standing against moral injustice. He reprised this role in numerous films throughout the 70s and 80s.

Bachchan's most famous performance was in the classic 1975 Bollywood film *Sholay* (Ramesh Sippy), an Indian version of Akira Kurosawa's *Seven Samurai* (1954). This became the highest-grossing Indian film to date. Bachchan wasn't just known for his angry everyman roles, he also showed versatility by taking on comedic characters such as the role of Anthony Gonzales in the film *Amar Akbar Anthony* (Manmohan Desai, 1977). This film follows the plight of three brothers separated at birth and brought up by a Hindu policeman, a Muslim tailor and a Catholic priest respectively.

In 1982, Bachchan's career suffered an unfortunate setback when he was injured on the set of the film *Coolie* (Manmohan Desai and Prayag Raj, 1983). The accident occurred during the filming of a fight sequence, during which a blow to the stomach ruptured his spleen. Bachchan spent months in hospital; at one point he technically died but was revived by medics. The reaction from fans was unprecedented. Many offered their limbs and body parts in order to try to save the actor's life, while others rushed to temples to pray and shrines were erected in honour of the star. There were even rumours of some fans taking their own lives. News of the actor's near-death was reported around the globe, in spite of Bollywood films only being of interest to the diasporic, non-resident Indian audience.

Following his near-death experience many of Bachchan's films flopped so he took a break from the film industry in order to pursue a career in politics. This was due to his friendship with the Gandhi family. After the assassination of Mrs Indira Gandhi, he felt that he should support her son Rajiv who was also involved in politics. However, he failed miserably because he lacked the knowledge to be a politician. In fact his foray into politics left him tainted as his rumoured involvement in an arms scandal obliged him to spend a good number of years attempting to clear his name.

Bachchan is not the first actor to venture into politics. Famous examples include Clint Eastwood, Arnold Schwarzenegger and Glenda Jackson. Francesco Alberoni's 'The Powerless Elite: Theory and Sociological Research on the Phenomenon of Stars' critiques this course of action, stating:

> The racing cyclist who is a demi-god in the eyes of the enthusiastic admirer does not necessarily show competence in other fields. The specificity of charisma should be understood as a specificity relating to one class of actions, all requiring the same kind of skill. This is why the great racing cyclist can also be a great athlete. Specialization lies at the heart of any particular field. (2006, p.111)

In attempting to move beyond a specific 'specialization', in this case acting, Alberoni claims that the star becomes powerless. This was definitely the case for Bachchan although the other examples cited have carved successful careers in politics.

In the 90s, Bachchan turned his hand to the world of business. This too led to more misery as his corporation nearly went bankrupt. It was in the year 2000 that Bachchan finally resurfaced in public, as the host of the Indian version of *Who Wants to Be a Millionaire?* Here, he would finish each episode by delivering a personal message to his viewers. These messages were typically didactic, preaching the importance of education and staying out of trouble. This personal approach soon won him the affection of the audience and consequently led to his re-emergence on the Bollywood scene. When Bachchan returned to the film industry he was more successful than anyone could have ever imagined. His new status enabled him to secure leading roles and challenge filmic traditions. For example, he was the first actor to kiss on screen, which caused huge controversy because Bollywood films are known for their conservative narratives.

Amitabh Bachchan and his wife Jaya have been happily married since 1973 after starring opposite each other in the film *Zanjeer*. More recently, they appeared as an on-screen couple in the hit film *Kabhi Khushi Kabhi Gham* (Karan Johar, 2001). The general public celebrates this relationship because its longevity symbolically upholds traditional Indian values. Their son Abhishek is also a famous Bollywood star and pinup in his own right, who has appeared opposite his father in the film *Kabhi Alvida Naa Kehna* (Karan Johar, 2006). Abhishek married Aishwarya Rai in 2007. She is probably the most famous female Bollywood star, known for her beauty and global film hits, which include endorsing Gurinder Chadha's *Bride & Prejudice* (2004). She is also recognizable for L'Oréal mascara. It thus appears that the Bachchan dynasty is attempting to challenge the first family of Bollywood, the Kapoors, who almost single-handedly founded the Bollywood industry.

Amitabh Bachchan's career has seen many peaks and troughs but in his final reinvention he has increased his popularity beyond that of any other Bollywood star. Every Sunday people gather outside his house in Mumbai waiting to see the man in person in hope of a blessing. This is why he is often discussed in the media in terms of a religious icon. In response to this accolade Bachchan replies:

> It's someone else's invention; they love these words. The media loves to classify any event, give it a title, home and epithet. It makes writing for them a lot easier. They construct these wonderful words and then subject us to the idiocy of it. (Lockhart, 2007)

Amitabh Bachchan is a fascinating case study because throughout his career he has had to reinvent himself and fight to regain his popularity. The devotion he attracts from his fans is unprecedented but the actor himself refutes the claims, that he is revered as a god, as merely media hype.

Case study: Dame Judi Dench

Born in 1934, the British actress Judi Dench had her first professional engagement at the Old Vic Theatre in 1957. Since then she has appeared and starred in film, television and theatre, gaining numerous awards. In total her career spans over five decades, this longevity is an admirable achievement in such a fickle business. However, Dench resists stereotypical notions of star and celebrity status because she was in her sixties when she attained a heightened level of fame. Before this she was often referred to as a British 'national treasure'. Even with her newfound global acclaim, Dench is still regarded as being quintessentially British and is accordingly revered and loved by the general public.

Her early career, working with the Old Vic Company from 1957–61 and subsequently with the Royal Shakespeare Company, gave her the opportunity to undertake many classic roles, including Ophelia, Hermia and Juliet. Her television debut came in 1959 in ITV's popular series *Play of the Week*. Alongside her theatre and television work in the 60s, Dench was one of many classically trained actresses such as Glenda Jackson, Maggie Smith and Vanessa Redgrave who entered into film. She worked with director Charles Crichton, appearing in *The Third Secret* (1964) and *He Who Rides the Tiger* (1965). However, it was the role of Wife, a married woman whose baby is repressing her life, in *Four in the Morning* (Anthony Simmons, 1965) that won her her first BAFTA award as most promising newcomer. This was the first of many challenging characters that Dench undertook; rather than accepting safe, stereotypical female roles she sought out difficult and not necessarily likeable characters. In these first ten years, she established herself as a serious actor. Her roles were intellectually demanding and to some extent considered 'edgy'. Dench sought recognition as a serious actor rather than as a 'pretty face'.

In 1968, Peter Hall's stage production of *A Midsummer Night's Dream* was filmed, affording Dench the opportunity to combine her love of Shakespeare with a screen appearance as Titania. The cast included Diana Rigg and Helen Mirren (both now Dames). However, it was Dench's unforgettable performance, in which she appeared semi-naked and green, that caused a stir. This link between stage and film was to set a trend, as many of her screen appearances in the 70s sprang from theatrical successes. For example, her Adriane in *The Comedy of Errors* was televised in 1978 and her portrayal of Lady Macbeth in 1976 was later shown on television.

In 1971, she married fellow Royal Shakespearian actor Michael Williams. It was with Williams in the early 80s that Dench reached new audiences in the sitcom *A Fine Romance* (Bob Larbey, 1981–4). It was highly popular, telling the story of two people thrust together by the woman's well-meaning sister and friend. The sitcom follows the on/off romance of these two lonely and ill-matched people in an affectionate comic portrayal that is often stirring and poignant. This gave her the opportunity to show the fun and cheeky aspects of her character (and herself). It widened her fanbase from the audiences that followed Shakespearian productions to those entertained by light comedy. Such a move placed her more firmly in the public eye and, in keeping with De Cordova's ideas, stimulated public interest in her private life, with fans keen to know where fact and fiction intermingled.

Throughout the 80s, 90s and 2000s, Dench played character-driven roles adapted from novels. These included a flamboyant novelist in *A Room with a View* (James Ivory, 1985) and a social-climbing, outspoken mother in *A Handful of Dust* (Charles Sturridge, 1988). More recent appearances include a feisty Newfoundland widow in *The Shipping News* (Lasse Hallström, 2001), and a sixty-plus virgin who falls for a young foreign sailor in *Ladies in Lavender* (Charles Dance, 2004). In 2006, Dench portrayed the unlikeable Barbara Covett in *Notes on a Scandal* (Richard Eyre, 2006). This performance as the vengeful, lesbian schoolteacher confirms her determination to take on challenging roles even if the characters have no redeemable features. While Dyer's work notes the increasing demands from the public for personal information, Dench manages to avoid public scrutiny of her private life. Interestingly, Dyer suggests that, the 'bigger' the star, the more removed they become from the general public. He claims that this distance between their life and ours is what cements their popularity. Ironically, Dench retains the 'woman-next-door' persona in spite of her success.

Moving away from characters in literary adaptations, Dench accepted numerous biographical parts. In John Madden's *Mrs Brown* (1997), she portrayed Queen Victoria as a lonely person in need of friendship and support as a woman, not as a queen. Dench won a BAFTA for this and an Oscar nomination. The following year's witty and shrewd portrayal of Queen Elizabeth in *Shakespeare in Love* (John Madden, 2008) won her an Oscar. Further challenging roles include the role of Iris Murdoch, the novelist and philosopher who died of Alzheimer's disease in *Iris* (Richard Eyre, 2001) and the title role in *Mrs Henderson Presents* (Stephen Frears, 2005). Here Dench plays the resourceful owner of the Windmill Theatre in London, whose proud boast during the war was 'We never close.'

Her work has been honoured by the establishment and by her profession. She received an OBE in 1970, became a Dame in 1988 and was awarded the Companion of Honour in 2005. The industry has recognized her extraordinary talents, bestowing her with numerous prestigious awards. It is important to note that many of these awards were voted for by the public. Here we return to the notion of identification. Dench's star status is not only based on her acting ability, but her intrinsic 'niceness', fun and comfortableness; the audience want her as a friend.

Despite her more recent filmic success, 1995 signalled a turning point in Dench's career. In accepting the role of 'M' in *GoldenEye* (Martin Campbell), she became the first woman to play this iconic character. This immediately launched her as an international star and extended her fanbase to include young teenage boys, typically drawn to the James Bond franchise. However, this comes after forty years in acting. While Dench is seen at Bond premieres taking part as a star on this world stage, she still maintains her status and epithet of 'national treasure'. This unofficial accolade is awarded to few figures in Britain. Currently, Joanna Lumley, Julie Walters, Victoria Wood and Stephen Fry may be considered in this select group. However, stardom is not courted by Dench; indeed she appears embarrassed by it.

In this chapter we have considered the difference between star and celebrity status, but these two case studies have further complicated debates regarding terminology. On the one hand, Amitabh Bachchan is revered as a deity by some in India, while on the other, Dame Judi Dench is cherished as a British 'national treasure'. Such labelling is always subjective and the media use terms interchangeably as a shorthand to manipulate our emotions. Classifying Dench as a 'national treasure' is highly emotive as it evokes a sense of national pride. As a symbol of national identity, Dench epitomizes an image that we would wish to promote to the world. She has a certain warmth and eccentricity (something the British are renowned for). She has a comfortable familiarity and is not 'precious' about who she is or how she appears. Furthermore, there is the sense that she enjoys life to the full (she has a reputation for practical jokes and uncontrollable laughter). More importantly, she is able to appeal to the Everyman. This is ironic as Dench courageously inhabits unpleasant and loathsome roles. However, the audience can see beyond the repellant screen characters because Dench's real-life persona remains untarnished. Her ability as an exemplary actress enables her to totally immerse herself in a character, yet in interviews her larger-than-life charm will redeem any flaws in her fictional characters. The more risks she takes, the greater she is esteemed.

In an interview with Tim Teeman regarding her status as 'national treasure', Dench states:

I hate that. Too dusty, too in a cupboard, too behind glass, too staid. I don't want to be thought of as recognizable – I always want to do the most different thing I can think of next. I don't want to be known for one thing, or having done huge amounts of Shakespeare and the classics. I hate speaking as myself. I could never do a one-woman show. But I love being part of a company. On stage I am not trying to be myself, I'm trying to be someone else, the more unlike me the better. I remember someone who saw me in *Juno and the Paycock* said I was completely unrecognizable. How marvellous. I've done two sitcoms, lots of films. Look at my character (an obsessive, damaged stalker) in *Notes on a Scandal*. You wouldn't want to ask her around. (Teeman, 2009)

The attitude expressed in the above quotation stands testament to why she is applauded as an iconic figure; she does not take herself too seriously. Nevertheless, her body of films demonstrates her multifaceted talents as she can lend herself to serious drama or comedy. She can sing and dance and she excels, whether in classic or contemporary genres.

Tanya Gold, writing for the *Guardian*, questions what makes a 'national treasure'. Here she alludes to the idea that in the public's eye 'they can do no wrong'. Once more she identifies that the term is highly subjective, with certain people achieving this status while other similar performers do not:

> Dawn French is an acknowledged national treasure, but Jennifer Saunders is not. Why? Could it be that Dawn French is fat and Jennifer Saunders is not? Ronnie Corbett is absolutely a national treasure but Bruce Forsyth is not. Why? Does height come into it? David Mitchell will obviously become a fully smelted national treasure but Robert Webb, never. Why? Because Mitchell is possibly riven with shuddering self-doubt while Webb smiles like a lover at the looking glass. National treasure rank is not always born in physical or mental abnormality. Personal tragedy will swing it too. Stephen Fry became a national treasure when it was revealed he has manic depression; Judi Dench when her husband, Michael Williams, died. (Gold, 2009)

The implication here is that 'national treasures' arise out of public sympathy. This notion is far too simplistic and dismisses the talents of the aforementioned stars/celebrities. Gold ignores the fact that people who gain the status of 'national treasure' have forged careers over many, many years. In the case of Judi Dench, it is her longevity paired with her versatility and charisma that have earned her this status.

Reflect and respond

1 Can you think of any Western stars who have been worshipped in a similar manner to Amitabh Bachchan?
2 List stars who have fallen from grace. Which ones manage to reinvent themselves successfully and which sink without trace? Can you offer reasons for this?
3 How useful is the term 'national treasure'?
4 Is Judi Dench's late fame unusual? Can you think of any other stars who gained international acclaim later in life?

Conclusion

There are many problems with Star Studies as a critical perspective. First and foremost, academics tend to focus their attention on Hollywood stars and so the field is determined by a 'Hollywood-centric' attitude. Very little research has been undertaken on stars outside the dominant American industry, although some scholars concentrate on European stars, with actors in world cinema recently gaining recognition.

One main concern with trying to analyse stars is that most lines of enquiry necessitate the use of other more established theoretical approaches. For example, when Dyer looks at Marilyn Monroe as a case study, his research inevitably asks questions concerning gender, sexuality, Psychoanalysis, Audience Reception, etc. Therefore, Star Studies is reliant on other theoretical concepts because as a stand-alone approach, it lacks a clearly defined methodology. Star Studies borrows from many other theories and critical perspectives.

Bibliography

Alberoni, F. (2006) 'The Powerless Elite: Theory and Sociological Research on the Phenomenon of Stars', in P. Marshall (ed.) *The Celebrity Culture Reader,* New York: Routledge.

Austin, T. and Barker, M. (2003) *Contemporary Hollywood Stardom,* London and New York: Arnold.

De Cordova, R. (1991) 'The Emergence of the Star System', in C. Gledhill (ed.) *Stardom: Industry of Desire,* London and New York: Routledge.

Dyer, R. (1998) *Stars,* new edn, London: BFI.

Dyer, R. (2004) *Heavenly Bodies: Film Stars and Society,* 2nd edn, London and New York: Routledge.

Gold, T. (2009, 15 December) 'Sorry, Dame Judi, But There's No Escape from Being a National Treasure' [Electronic version], *Guardian.co.uk.* Retrieved 3 June 2010. Available at http://www.guardian.co.uk/commentisfree/2009/dec/15/judi-dench-tanya-gold.

Lacey, N. (2002) *Media Institutions and Audiences: Key Concepts in Media Studies,* Basingstoke: Palgrave.

Lockhart, C. (director) (2007, 30 October) *Imagine: Bollywood's Big B: Amitabh Bachchan* [television broadcast], London BBC1.

Maltby, R. (2003) *Hollywood Cinema,* 2nd edn, Oxford: Blackwell.

McDonald, P. (1998) 'Reconceptualising Stardom', in R. Dyer, *Stars,* new edn, London: BFI, pp.175–211.

McDonald, P. (2000) *The Star System: Hollywood's Production of Popular Identities,* London: Wallflower.

Rojek, C. (2006) 'Celebrity and Religion', in P. Marshall (ed.) *The Celebrity Culture Reader,* New York: Routledge.

Stacey, J. (1994) *Star Gazing: Hollywood Film and Female Spectatorship,* London: Routledge.

Tasker, Y. (1993) *Spectacular Bodies: Gender, Genre, and the Action Cinema,* London and New York: Routledge.

Teeman, T. (2009, 11 December). 'Dame Judi Dench: "I am very un-divaish"' [Electronic version], *Times Online.* Retrieved 3 June 2010. Available at http://entertainment.timesonline.co.uk/tol/arts_and_entertainment/film/article6952074.ece.

Race and Ethnicity

Chapter

14

Race

1. a. A group of people belonging to the same family and descended from a common ancestor; a house, family, kindred.
   b. A tribe, nation, or people, regarded as of common stock. In early use freq. with modifying adjective, as *British race*, *Roman race*, etc.
   c. A group of several tribes or peoples, regarded as forming a distinct ethnic set.

Ethnic (Ethnicity)

1. Pertaining to nations not Christian or Jewish; Gentile, heathen, pagan.
2. a. Pertaining to race; peculiar to a race or nation; ethnological. Also, pertaining to or having common racial, cultural, religious, or linguistic characteristics, esp. designating a racial or other group within a larger system; hence (*U.S. colloq.*), foreign, exotic.
   b. *ethnic minority* (*group*), a group of people differentiated from the rest of the community by racial origins or cultural background, and usu. claiming or enjoying official recognition of their group identity.

Setting the scene

As can be seen in the dictionary citations above, attempting to define the terms 'race' and 'ethnicity' is problematic. Often used interchangeably, their meanings have also changed over time. Writing in the *Dictionary of Race and Ethnic Relations* (1984), E. Ellis Cashmore traces the usage of the terms and makes the following observations.

Race

In his first perspective (pp.214–16), Cashmore observes that the term has been used 'primarily to refer to common features present because of shared descent'. By this, he means physical attributes, outward appearances, which set one body of people apart from another. Cashmore links this to Charles Darwin and scientific thought regarding breeding and the isolation of specific racial groups from others. He considers the social function of race, using the example of census information to illustrate the point. In America if you have any African ancestry in your family lineage, you are officially considered black (even if you physically appear white). Conversely, in Latin America people are regarded as white despite any black ancestry. Therefore race can be thought of as a social construct.

His second perspective (pp. 216–18) explores the historical approach of classifying race into biological subspecies. This refers to the anthropological division of man into three distinct groups: Negroid, Mongoloid and Caucasoid (Caucasian). However, these terms are now deemed outdated because groups have migrated and, as a consequence, interbreeding means that these racial distinctions can no longer be upheld. Returning to the social implications of race, he discusses the term as a way of socially classifying groups of people due to 'physical markers such as skin pigmentation, hair texture, facial features, stature, and the like' (1984, p.217). The term 'black' is used to describe certain people in Africa and Australia and, although they may share similar social status, they do not necessarily share genetic make-up. He concludes:

> Societies that recognize social races are invariably *racist* societies, in the sense that people, especially members of the dominant racial group, believe that physical phenotype is linked with intellectual, moral and behavioural characteristics. Race and racism thus go hand in hand. (1984, p.218)

Ethnicity

Deriving from the Greek word *ethnikos*, ethnicity 'refers to a people or nation' (1984, p.85). In its modern sense, it functions to describe a group of people who are connected by shared cultural heritage. For example, groups that have migrated from one nation to another, maybe due to political or religious persecution, find solidarity in their collective experience. Similarly, groups that have had their homelands taken by dominant forces pull together to find strength and form an identity based on their hardships. Cashmore points out that future generations may feel alienated from the experience of their ancestors so that ethnic groupings can become less valid over time. Ethnicity can be regarded as divisive in that it can promote a sense of 'us' and 'them' that can anger dominant groups. Cashmore claims that ethnicity is typically rooted in class divisions and inherently connected to working-class identity. More importantly, he states:

> Ethnicity is basically reactive: it is elicited and shaped by the constraints and limits on opportunities imposed on the people who seek to be ethnic. Those people perceive that they are up-against something and organize themselves (survive) or advance themselves (achieve). (1984, p.89)

In summary, race is typically associated with physical, biological differences (skin colour and facial features). Race can often dictate social status and is thus inherently tied up with power relations. Ethnicity, on the other hand, relates to shared experiences and beliefs. Ethnic groupings can be dependent upon religion, language, nationality, tribal affiliations, customs and traditions. Racial difference is often visual whereas ethnic difference is not always apparent.

Reflect and respond

1   Discuss whether it is important to classify people according to racial and ethnic groups?
2   Consider your own heritage; how do you classify yourself?
3   Have ideas of race and ethnicity changed in your lifetime?

Stuart Hall

Race, the Floating Signifier (1997)

Stuart Hall, the British-Caribbean theorist, has written prolifically on the subject of race. In the documentary *Race, the Floating Signifier* he asks that people adopt a discursive approach in order to deconstruct 'the metaphors, the anecdotes, the stories, the jokes that are told by culture about what physical racial differences mean'. He claims that racial identity is never stable but consistently changes over time and for that reason he refers to it as a 'floating signifier'.

Hall begins his lecture by outlining the problematic historical practice of classifying people in accordance with their biological heritage. He explains that it is part of human nature to attempt to classify and group together objects and people. However, this act of classification inscribes that certain people are treated one way, while another group is treated differently. It is a way of maintaining social order; identifying which groups are deemed superior and which are classed as inferior. Hall claims that it is when these boundaries of classification are challenged that society grows ill at ease.

Here, he borrows from the work of the social anthropologist Mary Douglas and her idea of 'matter out of place'. Hall explains her theory using the analogy of a piece of dirt. Dirt is fine when it is in the garden where it belongs, but once dirt is found in the bedroom, where it does not symbolically belong, then we react differently: 'You cleanse it, you sweep it out, you restore the order. You police the boundaries. You restore the hard and fixed boundaries between what belongs and what doesn't (inside/outside, cultured/uncivilized, barbarous and uncultivated and so on).' Douglas recognized that all cultures adopt a social order that promotes stability, based on the clear demarcation between leaders and lower ranks. Once these distinctions are questioned, social order becomes disturbed.

Hall maintains that these ranks of classification signify information that has been culturally embedded. Here he turns to the age-old question of whether intelligence is connected to race. In answer, he exposes the power structure of classification:

> You don't need to have a whole argument about 'are blacks intelligent'? The moment you say they're blacks, already the equivalences begin to trip off people's minds: blacks – sound bodies, good at sport, good at dancing, very expressive. No intelligence; never had a thought in their heads. Tendency to barbarous behaviour.

He propounds this stereotypical view to highlight the truth, that race as a signifier is not fixed. People cannot be put into neat categories and therefore racial classification is futile.

Hall's work is innovative because he rejects the age-old argument that race is dependent on biology. Instead, he purports that race is a signifier; it is a language that is learnt. He insists that, 'racialized behaviour and difference needs to be understood as a discursive, not necessarily as a genetic or biological fact'. Drawing from Saussure's work on semiotics (see Chapter 4, 'Structuralism and Post-structuralism'), Hall lectures that race can only be understood in relation to differences and similarities with other races. Meaning is relational and not essential (not based on the essence of a group). Therefore, meaning cannot be fixed as it is 'redefined and appropriated' in accordance with other cultures and subject to change over time; it is constantly being re-signified.

Hall acknowledges that people may be concerned with his conclusion that race is an empty signifier, due to the historical reality of racism. In response, he puts forward three approaches:

1   The realist position: Real genetic differences are the basis for racial classification.
2   The linguistic position: There are no real differences between 'races'. The differences are created by humans in language and culture.
3   The discursive position: Differences exist in the world. But what matter are the systems of thought and language we use to make sense of those differences.

In summary, the 'realist position' is concerned with biological difference; the 'linguistic position' is based on cultural assumptions; and the 'discursive position', favoured by Hall, seeks to interrogate race on the premise of difference.

Historically, religion, anthropology and science have attempted to fix racial classification and this has resulted in an uneven distribution of power. Nevertheless, race continues to be an issue because it is visibly on display. Hall cites W. E. B. Du Bois' phrase 'color, hair and bone' to illustrate the signifiers of race (Bell *et al.*, 1996, p.23). These three signs are beyond dispute, they are biological fact. They indicate that people are genetically coded in a specific way, but ironically we cannot physically see the code, so we attempt to classify human groups based on visual appearance. This can be misleading as some people may have features that are clearly identifiable as black, but other features that indicate Caucasian heritage. However, the process of reading the body is an example of semiotics; we read the body as a text; 'we are readers of race'.

Reflect and respond

1   Discuss whether you consider race to be a biological or cultural phenomenon.
2   Make a list of physical signs that signify race. Are any of your findings problematic?
3   Are Hall's ideas outdated? How can we use his ideas to understand race in contemporary film-making?
4   Can Hall's theories on race be applied to understanding ethnicity? Identify physical signs that signify ethnicity in order to justify your answer.

Historically, racial and ethnic groups have been subjected to oppression, servitude and genocide. Groups of people have been dispossessed of their land and left disenfranchised. Ironically, religion and science have served to justify racist behaviour and horrifying acts. In light of such attitudes, racism has often been inherently accepted as the natural order of things. For centuries man has attempted to control genetic qualities, a practice known as eugenics. This advocates selective breeding in order to rid the human race of attributes considered undesirable. Racial and ethnic groups have often been victim to atrocities. The Holocaust, for example, resulted from the Nazis' determination to strengthen the Aryan (blond, blue-eyed) race by incarcerating and exterminating those who did not fit this desired profile. Consequently, as a result of historical evidence, it is necessary to scrutinize how racial and ethnic minorities are depicted in order to expose, and make sense of, underlying power structures.

Stereotyping

Representing racial and ethnic groups in film has historically been a political minefield. The film industry relies upon stereotyping as shorthand because there are only so many minutes within a film to establish characters clearly. Accordingly, race and ethnicity are often depicted through iconography and fetishization.

Iconography

Iconography involves symbolic meaning being bestowed upon items or images (semiotics). It is a popular recourse for filmmakers because it offers an instant association for the viewer. The lists below provide examples of iconography engaged to depict three different ethnic groups.

1   Jewish iconography
    - Star of David
    - Menorah (seven-branched candelabrum)
    - Tallit (prayer shawl with tassels called tzizit)
    - Kippah/Yarmulke (skullcap)
2   Native American iconography
    - Wigwam/tepee
    - Totem pole
    - Feather headdress
    - Tomahawk (axe)
3   Rastafarian iconography
    - Dreadlocks and rasta hat
    - Marijuana leaf (cannabis)
    - Bongos
    - Red, green and gold (African symbolism, lion).

These objects, whether connected with religion, fashion, custom or tradition, all afford a quick signifier of either Jewish, Native American or Rastafarian ethnicity. The use of iconography to represent a people can be misleading, for example, Hollywood has consistently depicted Native Americans wearing feathered headdresses yet only a handful of tribes traditionally wore them. While the examples cited above are not harmful, the film industry has been guilty in depicting Jews as penny-pinchers and Native Americans as predatory animals. It is this damaging essentialization that is problematic. A further derogatory form of representation can be seen in the use of fetishization.

Fetishization

This is where parts of the body or objects are selected to represent the whole. For example, in Feminist readings of films, Laura Mulvey discusses the way that women are objectified through the imagery of painted fingernails, long hair, high heels and lipstick; all signifiers of female sexuality. Fetishization is often employed to stereotype racial and ethnic groups. Jewish people are frequently stereotyped as having large, hooked noses. African Americans have been deeply offended by the way they have been represented on screen; early images exaggerated large lips. Western society has historically been fascinated with physical difference. For example, when the Western colonists arrived in Africa, they interpreted the nakedness of the black Africans as a signifier of insatiable sexuality. This is a key example of the objectification of the exotic Other.

The case of the Hottentot Venus is a much-cited example of Western fetishization of the exotic Other (Figure 14.1). Saartje (Sarah) Baartman was an African woman who was kidnapped and brought to Europe to be exhibited like a wild animal in 1810. She was stripped naked and put on display to be viewed by scientists and the general public, who were amazed by her large breasts, pronounced buttocks and genitalia. She was nicknamed 'the heavy-arsed heathen' (Hall, 1997, p.265). This is a prime example of fetishization, where Baartman is discussed in relation to her body parts, rather than as an individual (whole). Even though she died in 1815, it was not until 2002, that Baartman was finally returned to Africa for a traditional burial. Prior to this, her body parts had been kept on display in Europe for anthropological studies.

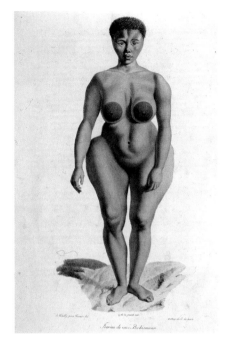

Figure 14.1   Venus Hottentot (Saartje Baartman)

As can be seen, stereotyping can be damaging because, rather than dealing with people as individuals, it reduces them to essential components, in an attempt to express the essence (through iconography and fetishization). The result is a two-dimensional caricature that teaches prejudice and discrimination rather than representing cultural authenticity and understanding.

Consider the following dialogue taken from the film *Do the Right Thing* (Spike Lee, 1989) and spoken by actors Spike Lee, John Turturro, Luis Ramos, Rick Aiello and Steve Park, respectively:

MOOKIE: You dago-wop, guinea, garlic breath, pizza slinging, spaghetti bending, Vic Damone, Perry Como, Luciano Pavarotti, Sole Mio, non-singing motherfucker.

PINO: You gold teeth, gold chain wearing, fried chicken and biscuit eating, monkey, ape, baboon, big thigh, fast running, high jumping, spear chucking, three-hundred-and-sixty-degree basketball dunking, titsun, spade, Moulan Yan. Take your fucking pizza-pizza and go the fuck back to Africa.

STEVIE: You little slanty eyed, me-no-speaky-American, own-every-fruit-and-vegetable-stand-in-New-York, bullshit, Reverend Sun Myung Moon, Summer Olympics '88, Korean kickboxing son-of-a-bitch.

OFFICER LONG: You Goya bean eating, fifteen-in-a-car, thirty-in-an-apartment, pointed shoes, red wearing, Menudo, meda-meda Puerto Rican cocksucker. Yeah, you!

SONNY: It's cheap, I got a good price for you, Mayor Koch, how-I'm-doing, chocolate egg cream drinking, bagel and lox, B'nai B'rith Jew asshole.

This dialogue of racial and ethnic slurs highlights the hurtful nature of stereotyping. In this instance, the characters spout insults based on unfounded cultural assumptions. The racist insults are chosen to demean and humiliate each group in an attempt to exert a sense of superiority in each spokesperson.

One of the most well-documented examples of stereotyping can be attributed to the cinematic depiction of African Americans. Donald Bogle identified six key stereotypes that reoccur throughout cinematic history in the book *Toms, Coons, Mulattoes, Mammies and Bucks: An Interpretive History of Blacks in American Films* (1973):

The Tom

Originating from the Harriet Beecher Stowe novel, the Uncle Tom character was the kindly slave who was happy working for white folk. Bogle states that: 'Even when chased, harassed, hounded, flogged, enslaved and insulted, they keep the faith, n'er turn against the white massa, and remain hearty, submissive, stoic, generous, selfless and oh-so-very kind' (1973, p.6). Uncle Remus (James Baskett) in the now deleted film *Song of the South* (Harve Foster and Wilfred Jackson, 1946), epitomizes this role. Interestingly, the term 'Uncle Tom' has become a modern-day insult directed at African Americans thought to have sold out.

The Mammy

The Mammy refers to the strong, matriarchal figure responsible for serving the white household and caring for the white children. Typically depicted wearing an apron and headscarf, she has an ample figure and is a feisty force to be reckoned with. Hattie McDaniel's character in *Gone With the Wind* is probably the most famous Mammy in cinematic history.

The Mulatto

A Mulatto is someone of mixed racial heritage with skin pale enough to pass as white. Although some films feature male Mulattos, they are typically female. Mulattos are tragic figures in that they belong to neither black or white society, when they try to pass as white the results are dire (see 'Narrative of Passing', p.241 below).

The Coon

The Coon is the lazy, good-for-nothing, stupid male who would rather sit in the sun, or entertain the white folk with funny skits. Lincoln Perry epitomized the archetype in his iconic roles under stage name Stepin Fetchit.

The Buck

This was the most damaging of all the stereotypes perpetuated by the film industry. This is where the black man is depicted as a potential rapist; primitive, savage and lustful for white women. Unlike the other stereotypes that were loyal and comical, the Buck posed a threat to white society. The character of Gus (Walter Long) in *The Birth of a Nation* epitomizes the problematic nature of the Buck. Gus, played by a white actor in blackface, chases after Flora (Mae Marsh), a young white girl. He wants to marry Flora but, rather than be touched by the black man, she leaps to her death off a cliff.

Bogle explained the subtext of power relations present in African American stereotyping as follows: '[a]ll were character types used for the same effect: to entertain by stressing Negro inferiority. Fun was poked at the American Negro by presenting him as either a nitwit or a childlike lackey' (1973, p.4). This inferred inferiority (stupidity, lustfulness and violence, etc.) has also been assigned to other minority groups depicted in a stereotypical manner. Bogle's work on black representation set a precedent for other academics to consider the depiction of other racial and ethnic groups. For example, numerous academic studies look at the way Jewish, Native American, Arabs, Mexicans, etc. have been stereotyped by the film industry.

It is important to note that such sweeping generalizations do not always have to have negative connotations. For example, think of the assumption that Italian men are good lovers (the Italian stallion). This is a positive attribute but completely unfounded. Similarly, the film industry needs to be careful that it does not, in an attempt to be politically correct, avoid casting marginalized racial or ethnic groups as villains. However, when the same group is consistently vilified, this becomes a problem (see Chapter 15, 'Postcolonial and Transnational Cinemas').

Reflect and respond

1   List iconography associated with the following ethnic groups: the Irish, Londoners, Chinese and those from the Middle East.
2   Look at the list of icons you have identified. Are any of them considered offensive?
3   Think of your status as students. How could you be stereotyped? Does this general categorization upset you?
4   Identify other examples of fetishization.
5   Discuss the political implications of stereotyping.
6   Can you think of any positive examples of stereotyping?

One of the first people to formalize writing about the problematic subject of race relations was the African American W. E. B. Du Bois.

W. E. B. Du Bois

The Souls of Black Folk (1903)

W. E. B. Du Bois was an author, a civil rights activist and a sociologist. Writing in 1903, he was one of the first people to realize that racial relations were going to have a profound effect upon modern politics and society. He declared that 'the problem of the twentieth century is the problem of the color-line' (1995, p.54). At a time when discussions on race were very rarely aired, Du Bois' writing was groundbreaking. The book *The Souls of Black Folk* is a collection of essays exploring race.

Being a black man in America, he understood that his people were in a position of duality. He referred to this notion of twoness as 'double consciousness'. He explains:

> The Negro is a sort of seventh son born with a veil, and gifted with second sight in this American world – a world which yields him no true self-consciousness, but only lets him see himself through the revelation of the other world. It is this peculiar sensation, this double consciousness, this sense of always looking at one's self through the eyes of others. [...] One ever feels his twoness, – an American, a Negro; two souls, two thoughts, two reconciled strivings; two warring ideals in one dark body, whose dogged strength alone keeps it from being torn asunder. (1995, p.45)

For Du Bois, African Americans were conflicted as they did not see themselves as American, nor did they feel wholly African. This position of struggle was a result of slavery, which existed from 1680–1865. Africans were kidnapped from their homeland and forced to work in the US. Unlike other immigrants who voluntarily left their homeland in search of the New World, the relationship African Americans have with America is a battle between affection and rejection. On arrival, they were treated with disdain and had their freedom taken from them. Therefore, black Americans are caught between their African heritage, of which they have little or no knowledge, and the New World that mistreated them. Du Bois acknowledges this predicament by stating:

> He [the black man] would not Africanize America, for America has too much to teach the world and Africa. He would not bleach his Negro soul in a flood of white Americanism, for he knows that Negro blood has a message for the world. He simply wishes to make it possible for a man to be both a Negro and an American, without being cursed and spit upon by his fellows, without having the doors of Opportunity closed roughly in his face. (1995, pp.45–6)

Du Bois proposed that this element of 'twoness', 'double consciousness' infiltrates all aspects of life for the black American. This idea of double consciousness is a useful tool for reading texts where race and ethnicity are key.

Racial and ethnic groupings are comprised of minorities that are pitted against the majority. Identity is typically fractured as they are, on the one hand, alienated from the dominant group due to their biological or shared heritage yet, on the other hand, rooted within a wider community. Hence most groups tend to hyphenate or conflate their identity, for example British-Jew (religion), French-Canadian (language), American Cherokee (tribe), Latin American (continent/region). As a result race and ethnicity can be understood through Du Bois' ideas of double consciousness.

One of the ways in which to apply this idea of duality to a film text is to look for hidden meanings, subtext or underlying tensions. If a black actor is seen playing a two-dimensional role, then we need to ask whether the stereotype is being reworked in any way. Bert Williams the early blackface minstrel actor provides a good example here. Williams was the most famous of all the minstrel actors. On stage, he pretended to be thick and lazy, adopting a Southern drawl. Off stage, people were surprised that he sported a Caribbean accent and was highly intelligent. The irony is that, while Williams was performing, white folk would laugh at his stupidity. Upstairs, because coloured folk were not allowed to sit in the stalls, the black audience would laugh at the white audience for believing that Williams was stupid. Therefore, it is a matter of agency; Williams was consciously adopting the false persona in order to make money and this is an example of double consciousness.

Reflect and respond

1 Can you think of any examples of double consciousness in films?
2 Should double consciousness be regarded as a survival technique, tongue-in-cheek humour or a rebellious act?
3 Double consciousness can be adopted by minority racial and ethnic groups. Discuss whether it can be applied to everyone (white British, white European, Anglo-Indian, Turkish-German, etc.).
4 To what extent can the idea of double consciousness reveal political and social power structures?

This notion of duality can be employed as a narrative device. Being caught between two cultures, yet belonging to neither, forms the premise of the genre known as the 'narrative of passing'.

The narrative of passing

As a result of the historical oppression of racial and ethnic groups, 'passing' has long been an inevitable option. The term 'passing' serves to describe a person who attempts to disguise their cultural or biological heritage and 'pass' themselves off as being part of the dominant group (white, Christian). The narrative of passing has had a long history in both literature and film. Traditionally, such stories focus on the character of the tragic Mulatto. The protagonist, who is usually female, is of mixed parentage (one black parent, one white); her light skin enables her to pass as white as she typically rejects her black ancestry. However, it is the presence of the distinctively dark-skinned mother (Mammy) that reinforces the Mulatto's true identity.

These tales tend to make moral judgments, with the protagonist frequently punished at the conclusion of the story. Their true identity is often discovered and they are physically beaten; many cannot cope with having to turn their backs on their family and friends, which leads to a life of misery and sometimes suicide. Such harsh treatment could also be read as a warning against miscegenation (interracial marriage or relationships). Famous examples of the narrative of passing include *Showboat* (James Whale, 1930 and George Sidney, 1946), *Pinky* (Elia Kazan, 1956), *Imitation of Life* (John M. Stahl, 1934 and Douglas Sirk, 1959) and *Sapphire* (Basil Dearden, 1959). More recently, passing has been explored from a male perspective in the film *The Human Stain* (Robert Benton, 2003).

It is important to note that 'passing' is not just a Hollywood plot device; it was a reality for many pale-skinned African Americans and other racial groups. Once slavery had been abolished, America became segregated. This meant that there were separate facilities for blacks and whites. There were separate churches, schools, swimming pools, restaurants, etc. Furthermore, African Americans were unable to gain well-paid jobs; therefore 'passing' became a way to overcome racism. Writing in 1963, James E. Conyers and T. H. Kennedy undertook a survey examining the motivations for passing as white; the responses included the following reasons (p.217):

1 lack of identification with other Negroes
2 fallen in love or married into the white race

3   to secure economic advantages
4   to hide one's past life
5   to secure equal social, cultural and recreational advantages
6   to have something to feel important about among other Negroes
7   to obtain some psychic thrill in fooling the white man.

The list can also be applied to other minority groups that 'pass'. One justification that does not appear is when people 'pass' in order to avoid danger. During World War II, many Jews with Aryan features (blond hair and blue eyes) denied their Jewish heritage to avoid being sent to concentration camps. The most famous case is the real-life story of Edith Hahn Beer, an Austrian Jewish woman who married a Nazi officer.

Interestingly, Jewish stories of passing are not frequently brought to screen. Hollywood was established and controlled by a handful of Jewish studio bosses. Accordingly, at a time when black actors were placed in subservient roles such as waitress, maid or butler, it was the Jewish stars, under newly Americanized names, who took the leading roles. Many famous actors consciously chose to erase their Jewish-sounding names in order to gain acceptance with a wider audience. For example, Tony Curtis was originally named Bernard Schwartz, Gene Wilder changed his name from the Jewish-sounding Jerome Silberman and Charles Buchinsky is better known as Charles Bronson. It is also surprising to learn that Woody Allen and Mel Brooks, who are renowned for incorporating their Jewish heritage into their films, once went by the names Allen Konigsberg and Melvin Kaminsky respectively.

The narrative of passing in relation to Native American identity takes an unusual twist. Whereas a number of African American and Jewish people have looked to erase their ancestry due to racism and anti-Semitism, conversely, there have been incidents where individuals have falsely professed to be Native Americans. Archibald Bleaney was born in England and emigrated to Canada, where he worked as a trapper and forest ranger. As a child he had been fascinated with cowboys-and-indians stories and, while living in the forest, he adopted the fictitious identity of Grey Owl. He accounted for his European features by claiming that his father was Scottish and his mother was an Apache. Under this assumed identity, Grey Owl successfully published several books about conservation and the environment. Even after his true identity came to light, his books remained popular. The story was brought to the screen by Richard Attenborough in the 1998 biopic *Grey Owl*. Similarly, the actor Iron Eyes Cody appeared in over 200 films playing Native American characters. However, near the end of his life it was revealed that his real name was Espera Oscar de Corti. Due to hostility towards Italians when he was growing up in Louisiana, he felt an affiliation with the Native American people and as a result chose to adopt that identity. Therefore, unlike other groups that have worked to hide their roots, Native American culture holds an exotic, mystical appeal.

Reflect and respond

1   Is the film industry making a political statement in punishing characters who pass?
2   Other than African Americans, Native Americans and Jews, can you think of any other examples of minority groups attempting to pass?
3   What kinds of genre would suit these films?

4 Can you recall ever being shocked when an actor's race or ethnic background has been revealed? Are they right in hiding this information?

5 The narrative of passing has dwindled in popularity in recent times. Can you account for this and can you think of any contemporary versions?

Looking at race from a different angle, Richard Dyer's seminal text *White* highlights the anonymity afforded white Caucasians.

Richard Dyer

White (1997)

Richard Dyer's book *White* signalled a groundbreaking approach to academic writing on race. He was one of the first scholars to point out that 'whiteness' is typically ignored in Western history. He believes that whiteness has effectively come to mean 'non-raced':

> The sense of whites as non-raced is most evident in the absence of reference to whiteness in the habitual speech and writing of white people in the West. We (whites) will speak of, say, the blackness or Chineseness of friends, neighbours, colleagues, customers or clients, and it may be in the most genuinely friendly and accepting manner, but we don't mention the whiteness of the white people we know. (p.2)

Dyer claims that when the term 'white' is employed, it is predominantly to signify ethnicity, based on 'cultural origins such as British, Italian or Polish, or Catholic or Jewish, or Polish-American, Irish-American, Catholic-American and so on' (p.4). Rather than employing the term 'white' as an indicator of race, universal terminology is applied such as 'people' and 'human race'.

The premise of Dyer's thesis is that Western history is told from a white, heterosexual, male perspective. Consequently, marginalized groups have had to actively fight to be heard (women, homosexuals, non-whites, etc.). White is accepted as 'the norm'; it is unquestioned as the dominant voice. Accordingly, whiteness has become invisible. He asserts:

> Whites must be seen to be white, yet whiteness as race resides in invisible properties and whiteness as power is maintained by being unseen. To be seen as white is to have one's corporeality registered, yet true whiteness resides in the non-corporeal. The paradox and dynamic of this are expressed in the very choice of white to categorise us. White is both a colour and, at once, not a colour and the sign of that which is colourless because it cannot be seen: the soul, the mind, and also emptiness, non-existence and death, all of which form part of what makes white people socially white. Whiteness is the sign that makes white people visible as white, while simultaneously signifying the true character of white people, which is invisible. (p.45)

In order to examine race relations fully, Dyer maintains that white people need to be made aware of their whiteness; 'whiteness needs to be made strange' (p.10). Only once the invisible power structures of whiteness are made evident can a true understanding be gained.

However, he does warn against the emergence of 'white studies', as white people have never struggled to be represented. He also cautions that too much focus on whiteness could be a step in the wrong direction, prompting a misled resurgence in white supremacy. Another problem he identifies is that issues of whiteness are inherently tied to guilt. Historically, the white man has oppressed non-white people and so it is necessary to recognize that whiteness is tied to issues of culpability regarding the legacy of racism. Dyer purports that this sensation of guilt can detract from efforts to interrogate whiteness as an ideology.

One of the ways in which Dyer explores the historical connotations of whiteness is through a detailed investigation of how the word has been used. Drawing from a range of extensive resources, he lists symbolic meanings associated with whiteness. These include (pp.72–3):

- innocence/chastity/purity
- advanced civilisation
- spiritual cleanliness/holiness/divine power
- honour/truth
- triumph
- light
- simplicity
- joy/happiness
- regeneration
- gaiety
- peace/transcendence
- modesty
- femininity/beauty
- delicacy.

All the words that feature in the list above have positive connotations. Conversely, Dyer demonstrates that negativity is associated with darkness (non-white). He discusses how it is associated with dirt, uncleanliness, sin, sex, sweat, semen, secretion and excrement (p.76). In the clearest sense, Dyer points out the problematic history of terminology:

We have a moral vocabulary such that white = good and black = bad we thus necessarily equate white people with goodness and black with evil. [...] However profoundly mixed up and various the actual representations of black and white people are, the underlying regime of dualism is still in play. (pp.63–4)

As an example of this binary relation of light and dark, he references Clyde Taylor's analysis of the original *Star Wars* trilogy. Here Luke Skywalker (Mark Hamill), 'a WASP of ancient biblical lineage', is pitted against Darth Vader (David Prowse), the 'dark invader [...] who is clad from head to toe in shiny black armour' (p.65). His study continues with an analysis of how the film industry has lit its subjects, both white and non-white and how traditional practices have favoured the

Caucasian. He carefully deconstructs iconic images of male and female in literature, on screen and in the media. He explores these, discussing the subtext of race in relation to lighting.

Dyer's text acknowledges that whiteness is laden with historical and political agency. Nevertheless, it is typically ignored as ordinary, commonplace and all-encompassing. Yet, it does not include everyone and should be acknowledged as a signifier of dominance over others. Thus whiteness should never be excluded from debates on race as it is central to ideas of identity.

Reflect and respond

1 To what extent are your ideas of dark and light rooted in childhood?
2 Do you think that the historical bias of good being associated with light and darkness equating to evil is in part responsible for racism?
3 Make a list of films where white is linked to positivity and black denotes negativity.
4 List films where these ideas are subverted.
5 Is whiteness a useful tool for reading race on screen?

Case study: *Rabbit-Proof Fence* (Philip Noyce, 2002)

In 1770, James Cook claimed Australia for the British with no consideration for the indigenous people, known as the Aborigines. Prior to this time, it was estimated that somewhere between 315,000–750,000 Aborigines populated the country. From 1788, around 80 per cent died either in the violent dispossession of their land or from European diseases from which they had no immunity. In spite of being the native race, the indigenous people of Australia were, and to some extent still are, treated as second-class citizens.

Accordingly, Aboriginal people have since been embroiled in what have been dubbed the 'History Wars'. This is not a physical battle but instead the fight for native Australians to tell their story of colonization, as the history of their land is typically written by the white European settler. The term 'black armband' has been used to describe Australia's past because it is a tale of mourning, guilt, dispossession and cultural genocide. Geoffrey Blainey, who coined the term, believes that modern accounts of Australian history have become too negative, tending to focus on the bad points of colonization. This argument is countered by those who say it is better to wear a black armband than a white blindfold (Macintyre and Clark, 2004, p.131).

When Australia was claimed by the British, they cited the ideology of *terra nullius* as justification of their entitlement. This Latin phrase translates as 'land belongs to no one'. In 1992, the 'Mabo' decision was passed, overturning the concept of *terra nullius*. So the founding ideology, which enabled the British to take Aboriginal land, has now been rejected (Macintyre and Clark, 2004, p.126). This historical background sheds light on the political and social power structure existing between the two groups and is thus relevant to any reading of Aboriginal people in film.

Whereas Aborigines comprise a racial group, it is important to acknowledge that native identity needs to be read in context with white Australians. Furthermore, white Australians also share ethnic traits: they originate from Europe (typically Britain), they all speak the same language and they adhere to the same cultural beliefs (predominantly Christian). Between 1869 and 1970, half-caste Aboriginal children, the result of miscegenation, were taken from their homes and placed in Christian settlements, with religion used as justification. This was done out of a fear that inter-racial relationships would lead to a third racial group that would not be black or white, but instead mixed. The authorities believed that if these mixed-race children were to breed with whites, then by the fourth generation all Aboriginal features would be eradicated, enabling them to effectively 'pass' as white. It is estimated that 10–30 per cent of all interracial children were forcibly removed. Those who were taken are now referred to as the 'Stolen Generations'.

The film *Rabbit-Proof Fence* relates the real-life story of three young half-caste girls, Molly (Everlyn Sampi), Gracie (Laura Monaghan) and Daisy (Tianna Sansbury). It is based on the biographical novel *Follow the Rabbit-Proof Fence* (1996) by Doris Pilkington Garimara (daughter of Molly). The film depicts the children being taken against their will to a Christian missionary camp called Moore River. Here they are taught how to serve white folk in order to become house servants. Unable to settle and suffering from homesickness, the girls escape and set off on the 1,500-mile long journey back to their family. A journey made possible due to a fence that was erected across the interior of Australia in an attempt to contain the disease Myxomatosis which infected the rabbit population. Although Gracie is recaptured, Molly and Daisy successfully make it back to Jigalong to be reunited with their Aboriginal parents.

The film was met with both praise and criticism. It was praised for breaking with the traditional stereotypes associated with indigenous Australians. From the earliest example of *Coorab in the Isle of Ghosts* (Francis Birtles, 1928), Aborigines have been depicted in films as the exotic Other. Representation of Native Australians tends to fall into two camps. The first is the mysterious, tribal elder with an instinctual knowledge and understanding of the land and the second is attached to issues of social deprivation.

The first category of stereotype has given rise to the figure of the 'tracker', seen in numerous films. This stock Aboriginal character is typically hired by whites to navigate the unrelenting terrain. As a result, he is conflicted between his heritage and the people he works for. Probably the most famous example can be seen in the classic text *Walkabout* (Nicolas Roeg, 1971). Here, David Gulpilil helps a young brother and sister who find themselves stranded in the outback. In these stories, the landscape acts as a character in its own right; in Peter Weir's *Picnic at Hanging Rock* (1975) the landscape acquires mysterious and dangerous connotations. Macintyre and Clark identify lost children as a familiar narrative device in Australian filmmaking. Their studies trace the origins back to the anxiety felt by the European settlers, who struggled to survive in the unfamiliar territory (2004, p.141). The Aboriginal tracker guides the children to safety. It is typically a genre of interaction where the white outsider gains a glimpse of traditional Aboriginal heritage. However, Macintyre and Clark claim that it is the Aboriginal that is truly the lost child. They illustrate their point by citing the conclusion of *Walkabout* when Gulpilil's character kills himself because he is unable to survive when taken out of his environment (2004, p.143).

The second group of stock caricatures is less traditional and to some extent Postcolonial. It is the depiction of the indigenous people as disenfranchised. The Australian media has in the past vilified Aboriginal communities, portraying them as uneducated, unemployed and prone to substance abuse and violence. More importantly, Aboriginal people have been subject to different social policies, laws and sanctions that help enforce such derogatory stereotypes. Recently, filmmakers have engaged their storytelling to record the harsh poverty and living conditions of the Aboriginal people. *Samson and Delilah* (2009), is directed by Aboriginal filmmaker Warwick

Thornton. The film attempts to humanize the social problems that plague many native communities. The narrative raises issues such as substance addiction, violence, sexual abuse and boredom but, unlike earlier depictions, this story is an attempt to increase awareness of such problems.

Returning to *Rabbit-Proof Fence*, the entire narrative of the film seeks to highlight social ills; therefore it does not focus too heavily upon the stereotype of the dispossessed. However, this caricature is present in the form of Mavis (Deborah Mailman), the mixed-race servant who is repeatedly raped. Interestingly, it is the white male abuser who is fetishized, the predatory male represented via the unzipping of his flies. This inverts the conventional fetishization of the racialized woman.

Noyce's story revolves around the more traditional caricature of the spiritual native with a natural connection to the land. *Rabbit-Proof Fence* once more includes the familiar trope of lost children, but Molly and Daisy rework its traditional trajectory. They are not European children, ignorant of their surroundings. These young girls, and in particular Molly, are driven not necessarily by an unconscious, almost supernatural understanding of the terrain, but instead by the desire to be reunited with their family. Standing in opposition to their challenge, David Gulpilil returns to his archetypal role of the tracker. His character, Moodoo, is hired to track down the missing children. He plays the silent force bearing down on the girls, yet as time passes he learns to respect Molly. In spite of trying to move away from two-dimensional caricatures, the film does at times evoke the age-old image of the 'exotic Other'. This is evident towards the conclusion of the narrative, where Molly's mother and grandmother are shown at night wielding sticks almost like spears. Yet, for the best part, the script does tend to avoid such clichéd portrayals.

The film also conforms to the formulaic genre of the Road Movie, typically associated with Hollywood. This could be down to the fact that Noyce, although Australian, had spent many years in Hollywood previous to making the film. Noyce was criticized for being overly sentimental; in particular, he was attacked for introducing the removal scene too early. Rather than establishing the relationships within the Aboriginal community and attempting to depict its day-to-day traditions and customs, the harrowing scene that epitomizes the experience of the Stolen Generations occurs within the first few minutes. The most vehement condemnation of Noyce's treatment relates to the ending of the film. The cinematic adaptation of Molly's journey visually concludes with the reunion of the family. However, Molly's own real-life voice-over tells a more tragic tale. On her return to Jigalong, she was captured and taken back to Moore River on two occasions and therefore she had to retrace her journey along the Rabbit-Proof Fence twice more. More poignantly, her own child was then taken and placed into the system, never to be seen again. The film mentions this in an epilogue delivered in Molly's own voice, accompanied by subtitles. Filming this real-life conclusion would have detracted from the girl's amazing achievement of navigating the outback, also painting a far worse picture of white Australians. Furthermore, classical Hollywood narratives require closure in the form of resolution. Yet Molly's true story was marginalized in favour of the Hollywood-esque happy ending.

It is important to note that the destructive image of Christian ethnicity is not trivialized in the film. Kenneth Branagh, who plays the real-life figure of A. O. Neville, skilfully captures the conflicted persona of the paternalistic racist. Ironically, Neville acquired the title of 'Chief Protector of Aborigines' although it was his job to oversee the removal of half-caste children. Whiteness in this text is not made invisible, yet it does not function as a signifier of the norm. Instead white race and Christian ethnicity tend to signify guilt. Their shameful endeavour, to secure white supremacy in the name of religion, is not dealt with lightly. Instead, white Christians are depicted as hypocritical and even the most sympathetic are vilified within the film.

The film was successful in managing to bring the plight of the Stolen Generations to global attention. Consequently, in a historically groundbreaking move, Kevin Rudd the then Prime Minister of Australia issued an apology to the Aboriginal people of Australia (2008):

[T]oday we honour the Indigenous peoples of this land, the oldest continuing cultures in human history. [...] We reflect in particular on the mistreatment of those who were Stolen Generations – this blemished chapter in our nation's history. The time has now come for the nation to turn a new page in Australia's history by righting the wrongs of the past and so moving forward with confidence to the future. We apologise for the laws and policies of successive Parliaments and governments that have inflicted profound grief, suffering and loss on these our fellow Australians. We apologise especially for the removal of Aboriginal [...] children from their families, their communities and their country. For the pain, suffering and hurt of these Stolen Generations, their descendants and for their families left behind, we say sorry. To the mothers and the fathers, the brothers and the sisters, for the breaking up of families and communities, we say sorry. And for the indignity and degradation thus inflicted on a proud people and a proud culture, we say sorry.

The above section from Rudd's speech is a clear signal to the world that Australia recognizes the harm and distress caused to native families. However, Aboriginal people continue to campaign for reparations in compensation for the way they were treated. The film *Rabbit-Proof Fence* can be seen as a catalyst in provoking this formal acknowledgment of wrongdoing. The significance of the film should not be underestimated, as Collins and Davis point out:

Rabbit-Proof Fence offers a powerful image of Aboriginal survival of colonial violence and subjugation. In doing so, it inverts two centuries of the representation of Aboriginal people as a doomed or dying race, a group of people who have no place in modernity. More specifically, it reorients the peculiar sense of loss and belatedness associated with the lost child narrative away from the settler anxieties of belonging to the post-*Mabo* issue of how the nation can best face up to the shame of the Stolen Generations. (2004, p.143)

Reflect and respond

1. Consider Philip Noyce's role as director. Why would it be problematic?
2. How would the film have differed if the entirety of Molly's story had been brought to the screen?
3. To what extent should *Rabbit-Proof Fence* be seen as an Aboriginal tale of rebellion and survival or a story of white Australian guilt?
4. Race and ethnicity are often emotive subjects. Discuss whether filmmakers have a responsibility in how they represent such issues.
5. Can you think of any other films that have affected public opinion and/or brought about political change?

Conclusion

Race and ethnicity continue to be of importance when reading film, as the industry still relies on stereotyping. This practice is in part due to time restrictions within the narrative and stereotyping establishes character traits quickly. Yet it is important to deconstruct the hierarchies of power that give rise to offensive caricatures and sweeping generalizations. These problems can only be addressed if the industry adopts a more inclusive approach and afford racial and ethnic minorities a chance to represent themselves.

Bibliography

Bartov, O. (2005) *The 'Jew' in Cinema: The Golum to Don't Touch my Holocaust*, Bloomington: Indiana University Press.
Bell, B. W., Grosholz, E. R. and Stewart, J. B. (1996) *W.E.B. Du Bois on Race and Culture: Philosophy, Politics and Poetics*, New York: Routledge.
Bial, H. (2005) *Acting Jewish: Negotiating Ethnicity on the American Stage and Screen*, Ann Arbor: University of Michigan Press.
Bird, S. E. (ed.) (1996) *Dressing in Feathers: The Construction of the Indian in American Popular Culture*, Boulder, CO: Westview Press.
Bogle, D. (1973) *Toms, Coons, Mulattoes, Mammies and Bucks: An Interpretive History of Blacks in American Films*, New York: Viking Press.
Cashmore, E. (1984) *Dictionary of Race and Ethnic Relations*, London, Boston and Melbourne: Routledge.
Collins, F. and Davis, T. (2004) *Australian Cinema after Mabo*, Cambridge: Cambridge University Press.
Conyers, J. E. and Kennedy, T. H. (1963) 'Negro Passing: To Pass or Not to Pass', *Phylon* vol. 24 no. 3, pp.215–23.
Du Bois, W. E. B. (1995) *The Souls of Black Folk*, New York: Signet Classic.
Dyer, R. (1997) *White*, London and New York: Routledge.
Eren, P. (1984) *The Jew in American Cinema*, Bloomington: Indiana University Press.
Hall, S. (1997) *Race, the Floating Signifier*, Media Education Foundation.
Hall, S. (ed.) (1997) *Representation: Cultural Representation and Signifying Practices*, Milton Keynes: Open University Press.
hooks, b. (1992) *Black Looks: Race and Representation*, London: Turnaround.
Macintyre, S. and Clark, A. (2004) *The History Wars*, Melbourne: Melbourne University Press.
Rudd, K. (2008) Apology Transcript. Retrieved 11 August 2010. Available at http://australia.gov.au/about-australia/our-country/our-people/national-apology-to-the-stolen-generation-video.

Chapter

Postcolonial and Transnational Cinemas

15

Postcolonialism

1. The fact or state of having formerly been a colony; the cultural condition of (a) post-colonial society.

Setting the scene

Postcolonialism is a collection of theories from many disciplines including literature, science, geography, politics, philosophy and film. It emerged in response to the legacy of colonial rule. Colonialism refers to the period when the Spanish, Portuguese, Dutch, French and British were expanding their territories overseas. These Western nations travelled to distant lands to set up colonies for a number of reasons, including the development of trade routes, to increase political power and to spread the word of God. Furthermore, exploitation of natural resources and local people was a common occurrence. In order to create colonies, native people were colonized; they were subjected to Western oppressive rule and disinherited from their land. In the expansion of European empires (imperialism), indigenous people suffered both materially and mentally.

Although the 'post' prefix suggests that this debate concerns only the aftermath of colonial rule, after colonized countries regained their independence (decolonization), Postcolonial Studies actually encompasses the relationship between imperial forces and oppressed nations from the onset of colonization to the present day. As such, Postcolonial Theory is concerned with the immediate and long-term effect of enforced occupation on the psyche and culture of native people.

Most historical accounts are written from a Western perspective, with the native voice remaining unheard. Postcolonial Studies aims to reinsert the indigenous voice yet, at the same time, deconstruct cultural artefacts for traces of colonial domination. Poignantly, Salman Rushdie, the Anglo-Indian novelist, famously coined the phrase 'the Empire Writes Back to the Centre'. Although a direct parody of *The Empire Strikes Back* (Irvin Kershner, 1980), Rushdie was describing the process of authors from former colonies rewriting their history from the viewpoint of the oppressed. The word 'centre' refers to the colonial powers while natives are often identified through opposing terms such as 'marginal' or 'peripheral/periphery'.

Western artefacts from the colonization period are of equal importance because they often reveal racist attitudes. Here the terms 'Otherness' or 'Othering' are appropriate. Western language and imagery, concerning the representation of native inhabitants, exaggerate ideas of primitive savagery or exotic fetishization (see Chapter 14, 'Race and Ethnicity'). At the heart of Postcolonial Theory there is a struggle for power (the historical struggle for land and possessions and the legacy of cultural annihilation and reappropriation). In order to liberate their culture, marginalized people had to assert their opinions and consequently denounce the paternalistic agenda of the tyrannical Westerners. One of the earliest writers to air views regarding the detrimental effects of colonization on the non-Western psyche was Frantz Fanon.

Frantz Fanon

Black Skin, White Masks (1952)

Frantz Fanon was born in Martinique in 1925. The Caribbean island was then a French colony and it was Fanon's experiences growing up under a colonial power that informed his writing. His work examined the psychological impact of colonization. In particular, he sought to expose the detrimental nature of colonial power structures on the psyche of the oppressed. He recalled that from an early age he was taught that whites were superior to blacks. 'There is a fact: White men consider themselves superior to black men. There is another fact: Black men want to prove to white men, at all costs, the richness of their thought, the equal value of their intellect' (1986, p.12).

Fanon's father was descended from African slaves and his mother was mixed race. His upbringing as a black man in colonial Martinique had an overwhelming impact on how he viewed himself and how he was viewed by others. These views were compounded by the time he spent in France. He described this experience as a kind of amputation; when he began to think of himself as an object rather than a subject. This sudden shift in perception followed an incident when white strangers pointed at him, saying 'look, a negro' and 'dirty nigger':

> On that day, completely dislocated, unable to be abroad with the other, the white man, who mercilessly imprisoned me, I took myself far off from my own presence, far indeed, and made myself an object. What else could it be for me but an amputation, an excision, a haemorrhage that spattered my whole body with black blood? But I do not want this revision, this thematisation. All I wanted was to be a man among other men. I wanted to come lithe and young into a world that was ours and to help to build it together. (1986, pp.112–13)

Fanon was instrumental in asking questions concerning the psychology of colonialism. He developed this line of argument further in his next book.

The Wretched of the Earth (1961)

The Wretched of the Earth is probably Fanon's most famous text. It was written as a response to the French occupation of Algeria and the struggle for independence faced by the oppressed. He once more considers the negative effects of imperialism on the psyche of the indigenous people and put forward his opinions on how these ideological shackles should be severed.

Fanon urged for a break with the cultural heritage of the colonial past. He warned that if the emerging middle classes took over government once the colonial powers had been removed, then the country would be at risk of perpetuating the power relations previously set in place. He further cautioned that establishing commercial ties with Western businesses rather than breaking ties with imperial powers, would ultimately lead to a new version of colonization. This continued dependency on former colonial powers became known as 'Neocolonialism'. It is important to note that the term 'Neocolonialism' is typically associated with America, which had no overseas colonies, but still managed to exert its power over other nations.

Regarding culture, Fanon made similar claims. He believed that it was important for native texts to depart from European traditions. He recognized that an indigenous voice was important in establishing a cultural identity separate from that of the West. He counselled that these forms of culture should not be a nostalgic look to the past but should strive forwards in a new direction.

Reflect and respond

1   To what extent is the relationship between the colonizer and the colonized a psychological one? In what other ways can we understand this pairing?
2   Do ideas of superiority and inferiority continue today? Are they still relevant in black culture? Can you think of examples where they occur?
3   Consider the legacy of colonial history. How far is colonial thinking ingrained once the controlling forces have left?

Fanon's work was rooted in psychology and Marxist thinking. His writing was instrumental ideologically in liberating the colonized from colonial power structures (economical, political and psychological). His work went on to inspire a number of Postcolonial scholars. In particular the damaging effects on the psyche of the oppressed was a site of discourse continued by Edward Said.

Edward Said

Orientalism (1978)

Edward Said was one of the first academics to expose the biased way the West depicted the East in literature and other forms of culture. The literary theorist gained academic acclaim when he controversially claimed that Oriental Studies is inherently linked to imperialist ways of thinking. He chose the ancient term 'Orient' to distinguish the Middle and Far East from the 'Occident' meaning Europe and America. His work explores the West's long-held fascination with Eastern culture. He maintains that the 'Orient' and 'Orientalism' do not exist but are instead a construct of Western imagination: '[t]he Orient was almost a European invention, and has been since antiquity a place of romance, exotic beings, haunting memories and landscapes, remarkable experiences' (p.71).

Said was motivated to write his study because he felt that the depictions of the East circulated in the West gave a very different impression to his own experience as an Arab. The Orient, for Said, is a mythic land conjured by Westerners. The romanticized image depicted in stories such as *Kubla Khan* (Samuel Taylor Coleridge, 1816), One *Thousand and One Nights* (Richard Francis Burton, 1885–8) and the Verdi opera *Aida* (1871) are key examples of what he terms 'Orientalism'. These examples are founded on stereotypes, where texts foreground exotic beauty and savage violence, rather than being based on fact and authentic cultural representation.

Said identifies three forms of Orientalism in his work:

1   **Academic**
Anyone who teaches, writes about, or researches the Orient – and this applies whether the person is an anthropologist, sociologist, historian, or philologist – either in its specific or general aspects, is an Orientalist, and what he or she does is Orientalism. (p.72)

2   **Style**
Orientalism is a style of thought based upon an ontological and epistemological distinction made between 'the Orient' and (most of the time) 'the Occident.' Thus a very large mass of writers, among whom are poets, novelists, philosophers, political theorists, economists, and imperial administrators, have accepted the basic distinction between East and West as the starting point for elaborate theories, epics, novels, social descriptions, and political accounts concerning the Orient, its people, customs, 'mind,' destiny, and so on. (p.72)

3   **Ideology**
Orientalism can be discussed and analyzed as the corporate institution for dealing with the Orient – dealing with it by making statements about it, authorizing views of it, describing it, by teaching it, settling it, ruling over it: in short, Orientalism as a Western style for dominating, restructuring, and having authority over the Orient. […] In brief, because of Orientalism the Orient was not (and is not) a free subject of thought or action. (p.73)

To summarize Said's findings, the first form of Orientalism is concerned with academic study. Due to scholarly interest in the mythic/fictionalized lands, the Orient continues to exist. Second, it can be thought of as a source for stylistic inspiration, typically manifesting in works based on binary distinctions (the East seen through Western eyes). The final form of Orientalism is the most troublesome as it exposes the history of Western supremacy and domination over the East. This ideological attitude of Western superiority served as a justification for the colonization of distant lands. Furthermore, this overbearing approach often seeps into filmic representation. Identifying racist and biased traits, informed by the legacy of colonial imagination, is key to undertaking a Postcolonial reading of a film.

Orientalism in film

For many Westerners, their only knowledge of the East, and in particular the Middle East, comes from images in the media. Sut Jhally, in a documentary entitled *Edward Said: On Orientalism* states that:

> Many people believe the way that Americans understand the Muslim world is very problematic. Indeed, Anti-Arab racism seems to be almost officially sanctioned. You can make generalized and racist statements about Arab peoples that would not be tolerated for any other group. At the heart of how this new American Orientalism operates is the threatening and demonized figure of the Islamic terrorist that is emphasized by journalists and Hollywood. (1998)

The fictional image of the Orient, that Said discusses in his writing, has consistently provided inspiration for the film industry due to its rich iconography. Vast deserts, camels, sheiks, scimitars, veils, dancing girls, whirling dervishes, etc., are just a few examples of why the Orientalist cinematic tradition continues. Film is a visual culture and caricatured representations of the East result in tales of mystery, exotic locales and people. More problematically, there does tend to be a leaning towards negativity and violence.

Take, for example, the Disney film *Aladdin* (Ron Clements and John Musker, 1992), which is often cited as an Orientalist text. When the film was originally released, the opening song 'Arabian Nights' contained the following lyrics:

> Oh I come from a land, from a faraway place
> Where the caravan camels roam.
> Where they cut off your ear
> If they don't like your face.
> It's barbaric, but hey, it's home.

After receiving complaints from the American-Arab Anti-Discrimination Committee (ADC) for violent and racist content, the lyrics were adapted in time for the video release in 1993. The new edition replaces the brutal image of butchery with a less offensive version:

> Oh I come from a land, from a faraway place
> Where the caravan camels roam
> Where it's flat and immense
> And the heat is intense.
> It's barbaric, but hey, it's home.

Another example can be found in the Spielberg family favourite *Indiana Jones and the Temple of Doom* (1984). Set in India, the story sees Indiana Jones (Harrison Ford) become embroiled in the happenings of a remote village. A precious jewel has been stolen by a local group of religious Thuggees. The name Thuggee was historically used to describe groups of robbers and assassins in India; it is now more commonly shortened to the colloquial term thug. In addition to stealing the gem, the occultists also kidnap the village's children. Kaizaad Navroze Kotwal warns of the imperialist messages contained in the film. In particular he identifies the colonial subtext relating to the missing children:

> By presenting the leader of the Kali cult as a child-enslaver, the filmmakers argue that Indians are incapable of treating their children with dignity and compassion. It presents the need of a more benevolent father in the guise of colonialists, ignoring the fact that many of the precepts of colonialism gave rise to virtual slavery (Kotwal, n.d.)

Figure 15.1 *Gunga Din* (George Stevens, 1939)

The villagers are depicted as primitive and superstitious, while the Thuggees are shown to be evil cannibals (Figure 15.2). This racist stereotyping is indicative of Western colonial legacy.

Kotwal points out that the film follows in the tradition of *Gunga Din* (George Stevens, 1939), which was produced when the British Empire was thriving. Based on a poem by Rudyard Kipling, the narrative features an Indian water-carrier who aspires to fight for the British army. Gunga Din is an 'untouchable' (lowest rank of the traditional Indian caste system) regarded as a social outcast. However, at the conclusion of the film Gunga Din sacrifices himself in order to save the white colonial forces. Poignantly, the character of Gunga Din was played by Sam Jaffe, a white man wearing dark make-up to appear Indian (Figure 15.1).

Although nearly half a millennium passed between the making of *Gunga Din* and *Indiana Jones and the Temple of Doom*, the pictures here (Figures 15.1 and 15.2) expose the continued stereotypical approach to Eastern representation. The character of Gunga Din inhabits the subservient role of loyal follower while the Thuggees, more problematically, epitomize the aggressive stereotype associated with Eastern culture. The films adopt a stance of Western superiority and accordingly force the Indians to perform the role of the exotic 'Other'.

Despite Disney's attempt to appease controversy and Spielberg's silence regarding the film, the semiotic coding in these films of the 80s and 90s suggests that people from the East are violent and barbaric. Such films reveal the distorted lens with which the industry frequently views the Arab world. Jack G. Shaheen explored this hateful depiction in the book *Reel Bad Arabs: How Hollywood Vilifies a People* (2001). The book looked at fifty films, only twelve of which contained positive portrayals.

Following the attack on the World Trade Center in New York on September 11 2001,

Figure 15.2 *Indiana Jones and the Temple of Doom* (Steven Spielberg, 1984)

vilification of Arab peoples has escalated. Shaheen developed his work in the light of the post-9/11 climate. His new book *Guilty: Hollywood's Verdict on Arabs after 9/11* (2008) continues in the same vein as his earlier works but also poses difficult questions regarding anti-Islamic dogma and media responsibility:

> Hate rhetoric, the war on terror, the conflicts in Afghanistan, Iraq, and the Middle East have generated damaging new media stereotypes and new government law enforcement policies. Congress approved the PATRIOT Act; the Department of Homeland Security launched 'Security Level Alerts,' profoundly affecting citizens worldwide. Whether they lived in the US or in the 25-nation European Union, after 9/11, bearded, dark-looking men and women wearing head-scarves were perceived as menacing threats to world security. (p.7)

Writing in 2008, Shaheen states 'The total number of films that defile Arabs now exceeds 1,150' (p.xiv). Over 100 of these were produced post-9/11. He describes derogatory filmic examples such as: 'gratuitous slurs and scenes that demean Arabs [and] villains [that] do dastardly things [...] (mostly gunning down or blowing up innocent people)' (p.xiv). He then lists the key negative archetypes as (pp.xiv–xv):

- ugly sheiks
- dense, evil, over-sexed caricatures
- unsavoury Egyptian characters
- not-so-respectable images of maidens
- stereotypical portraits of Palestinians.

Within the 100 films discussed, Shaheen does note that a handful of films champion Arabs and show them to be 'decent folk' (p.xv). So there is a glimmer of hope that, even in periods of extreme political unrest, Hollywood is beginning to abstain from its practice of Orientalism.

Reflect and respond

1 Drawing from films you have seen, discuss the way Western filmmaking has stereotyped East Asia, India and the Middle East.
2 How influential is film in informing our ideas about other nations?
3 Have these representations changed within your lifetime? If so, when did this happen and why did it occur?
4 Should the film industry be more sensitive in its depiction of the East? Is it just harmless fiction or are the political connotations important?
5 How could the film industry depict the East in a more authentic way?

Fanon and Said's work was instrumental in laying the foundations for Postcolonial thought. Gayatri Chakravorty Spivak furthered debates by investigating the stories and opinions of the subaltern.

Gayatri Chakravorty Spivak

'Can the Subaltern Speak?' (1988)

The Indian literary critic Gayatri Chakravorty Spivak's essay 'Can the Subaltern Speak?' is a seminal text in the field of Postcolonialism. Whereas Said looked at Western accounts of the Middle and Far East, Spivak aimed to reinsert the indigenous voice. More poignantly, she questions whether native people have ever been in a position to tell their version of history and if their voices are ever heard?

The term 'subaltern' literally refers to a person in a subordinate position and is used by the military to denote rank. However, in Spivak's writing she attributes it to everyone with limited or no access to Western colonial culture. Therefore the term cannot be used interchangeably with 'oppressed' or 'minorities' because these can refer to people who live within the Western world. Instead, it specifically encompasses those who are socially, politically and geographically alienated by hegemonic power structures (legal, education and judiciary systems).

Spivak adopts the term 'episteme' to denote these hegemonic power structures. She then introduces the phrase 'epistemic violence' to describe how the subaltern is subjected to imposed Western/European structures of learning (law, religion, economics and politics, etc.). Building on this idea, Spivak explains that history is told from the point of view of the West. Due to the imperialist historical narrative, the subaltern's account is suppressed.

> Let us now move to consider the margins (one can just as well say the silent, silenced center) of the circuit marked out by this epistemic violence, men and women among the illiterate peasantry, the tribals, the lowest strata of the urban proletariat. (p.25)

Spivak makes the point that even when indigenous people are afforded a voice, it is important to acknowledge the social hierarchy present in such accounts. The version of history contained in seemingly authentic native records would in fact be produced by the middle classes; the reason being that the middle classes and rich peasants would be in a better position to air their views.

In order for the real subalterns to have their say, they would have to adopt the language and procedures of the domineering or 'dominant' Western forces. Therefore, in order for the subalterns to criticize the imperial regime and initiate an insurgency, they would have to assume the ideology and politics of the West. In simple terms, in order to be heard, subalterns must step outside their own community or tribe and conform to Western structures. Spivak problematizes the plight of the subaltern further by stating that female subalterns are historically made invisible:

> Within the effaced itinerary of the subaltern subject, the track of sexual difference is doubly effected. … It is … both as object of colonialist historiography and as a subject of insurgent, the ideological construction of gender [that] keeps the male dominant. If, in the context of colonial production, the subaltern has no history and cannot speak, the subaltern as female is even more deeply in shadow. (p.28)

One of the main criticisms of Spivak's argument is not concerned with content. As can be seen, Spivak adopts a high-brow academic tone, meaning that her work is often deemed inaccessible. This is ironic because, although making a case for the voiceless who are forced to assume Western forms of language, her own writing alienates the very people she seeks to defend.

In order to apply Spivak's argument to the field of filmmaking it is beneficial to think of the 'episteme' (hegemonic power structure) as Hollywood. Non-Western filmmakers can face great hardships trying to get their films into circulation in part due to the Western modes of film production, distribution and marketing. One way to attract both funding and an audience is to conform to mainstream, commercial, formal traits. For example, employing continuity editing, a linear narrative, clear cause and effect, could all help promote their films in the West. Like the subalterns in Spivak's essay, non-Western filmmakers have to implement dominant models in order to tell their stories. In doing so, they risk diluting their own economic, political, social and cultural message.

Reflect and respond

1   Do you agree with Spivak's observation that any native representations of 'Otherness' are told from a middle-class perspective?
2   Why do you think the female subaltern is historically silenced more than her male counter-parts?
3   In your experience of non-Euro-American filmmaking, do films conform to dominant modes of production?
4   How important is it for non-Western filmmakers to retain their own cultural forms (language, narratives, aesthetics)? Is it possible if they want their films to gain a worldwide audience?

Postcolonial Studies offers a way of understanding global power relations and the history of oppression, exploitation, negotiation and reappropriation. One criticism aimed at Postcolonial approaches is that they often view native culture from an idealistic position. Postcolonial readings tend to ignore problematic cultural practices in favour of the binary argument of colonizer and colonized. Interestingly, Marxist and Feminist thinkers point out that social structures within indigenous populations may not necessarily have been harmonious before the arrival of the imperial forces. For example, India has a strict class system based on caste (social position), with specific members of society ostracized by their social status. Furthermore, women are considered inferior to men in many cultures. In light of this, knowledge of native cultural traditions and patterns of behaviour must be taken into consideration before exploring the impact of colonial conflict.

Transnational Cinemas

Transnational
1. Extending or having interests extending beyond national bounds or
   frontiers; multinational.

Setting the scene

A new area of Film Studies, which has developed out of Postcolonial discourse, is that of
Transnational Cinema. The term 'transnational' emerged in academic film writing around the
mid–late 90s. Deborah Shaw notes that:

> The notion of the transnational in Film Studies has developed in response to an increasing
> awareness of the limitations of conceptualizing film in terms of national cinemas, and an
> acknowledgment of the changing nature of film production and distribution as a part of wider
> patterns of globalization. (forthcoming, p.1)

When Film Studies was in its infancy, it was concerned with ideas of nationality, in part due to
academics working in language departments. This focus has now shifted as a result of a number
of key factors: the relaxation of national borders, the increase in political and social collaborations
(the end of the Cold War and the formation of the European Union), global co-productions and
wider circulation of films via new technologies.

Consequently, scholars have adopted 'transnational' as a solution to the inadequacy of
'national'. Transnational often acts as an umbrella term, evident from the broad description
below: 'The transnational comprises both globalization – in cinematic terms, Hollywood's domination of world film markets – and the counterhegemonic responses of filmmakers from former
colonial and Third World countries' (Ezra and Rowden, 2006, p.1). To date much of the academic
writing within this field is concerned with the problematic nature of the term 'transnational' and
whether it is appropriate. Shaw asks:

> Which films can be categorized as transnational and which can't? Does the term refer to
> production, distribution and exhibition, themes explored, aesthetics, nationalities of cast and
> crew, audience reception, or a range of these? Are mainstream Hollywood films transnational
> as they are distributed throughout the developed world? What about films with smaller budg-
> ets made in other national contexts that challenge Hollywood domination and explore the
> damaging effects of globalization? (forthcoming, p.1)

In answer to these central questions, there have been attempts to deconstruct the term further.
Will Higbee and Song Hwee Lim are among a number of academics recently endeavouring to
dissect this all-encompassing label.

Will Higbee and Song Hwee Lim

'Concepts of Transnational Cinema: Towards a Critical Transnationalism in Film' (2010)

In their article Higbee and Lim identify three ways in which the term 'transnational' has been used historically:

1 **Binary approach**
   Transnational readings of film often adopt a binary perspective (national/transnational). More recently there has been a shift towards a much broader remit in order to understand the global workings of the industry. Higbee and Lim problematize this approach, arguing that it is concerned with production, distribution and exhibition (how films and filmmakers cross borders and nations and how films are received by audiences outside 'indigenous sites of production') (p.9).They state that the drawback to this approach is that it obscures 'the question of imbalances in power (political, economic and ideological) as it ignores the issue of migration and diaspora' (p.9).

2 **Regional phenomenon**
   Here they look at academic work that examines films grouped together due to geopolitical and cultural similarities. They cite the following examples: 'Lu's work on transnational Chinese cinema (1997), Nestingen and Elkington's collection on transnational Nordic cinema (2005) as well as Tim Bergfelder, Sue Harris and Sarah Street's study of set design in European cinema of the 1930s' (p.9). However, they dispute the use of the term transnational here and suggest 'regional' or 'pan-European' as being more appropriate.

3 **Diasporic, exilic and postcolonial cinemas**
   They describe this approach as aiming

   > through its analysis of the cinematic representation of cultural identity, to challenge the western (neo-colonial) construct of nation and national culture, and, by extension, national cinema as stable and Eurocentric in its ideological norms as well as narrative and aesthetic formations. (p.9)

   They recognize that undertaking such a reading is difficult, as these films tend to exist outside Western film culture. Therefore it is difficult to assess the impact of such films on commercial filmmaking.

The main problems they find with these three historical approaches are that (p.10):

- 'Transnational becomes shorthand for international or supranational modes of film production whose impact and reach lies beyond the bounds of the national.'
- National loses currency when it is still important to transnational filmmaking.
- The term is used to 'indicate international co-production or collaboration between technical and artistic personnel from across the world' with no 'consideration of what the aesthetic, political or economical implications of such transnational collaboration might mean'.

- The term is used so often as a catch-all that it has potentially become an 'empty, floating signifier'.

In light of the problematic usage of the term, they urge for a new understanding and consequently adopt the phrase 'critical transnationalism' (p.10). They then identify how the field should be broached by academics as a site for thorough debate in order to counter the sweeping generalizations outlined above. They recommend the following areas of focus:

- film narratives
- production processes
- industrial workings
- academic practices
- cultural and financial policies
- questions regarding Postcolonialism, politics and power
- interrogation of national/local/global.

They conclude their assessment with the question, 'Can transnational film studies be truly transnational if it only speaks in English and engages with English-language scholarship?' (p.18). This signals a return to the warnings issued by both Said and Spivak. The label 'transnational' demands a global perspective but, in order to emulate the ethos proposed, it is important that we learn to view and discuss films in a similar manner to the way in which transnational films are produced.

In summary, the new field of Transnational Cinema enables a multilayered approach that interrogates industrial and ideological power relations within a global culture of exchange. It offers the opportunity for extensive research in a wide range of areas. The fifteen categories identified by Deborah Shaw illustrate the eclectic and diverse nature of the field (p.6):

1   transnational modes of production, distribution and exhibition
2   transnational modes of narration
3   cinema of globalization
4   films with multiple locations
5   exilic and diasporic filmmaking
6   film and cultural exchange
7   transnational influences
8   transnational critical approaches
9   transnational viewing practices
10 transregional or transcommunity films
11 transnational stars
12 transnational directors
13 the ethics of transnationalism
14 transnational collaborative networks
15 national films.

The scope that transnational research presents is vast yet it is illustrative of the way cultural and industrial practices now operate. Therefore transnational readings are innovative and indicative of a new trend in academic study.

Transnational filmmaking

The 2008 film *Slumdog Millionaire* (Danny Boyle) provides an illustration of a transnational production. At first glance, the film could be mistaken for a Bollywood production. Yet consider the following facts regarding the national status of this film:

Indian
- Based on a novel by an Indian author: *Q & A* (Vikas Swarup, 2005).
- The narrative is set in the Juhu slums of Mumbai (formerly known as Bombay).
- Uses Hindi dialogue for one-third of the film.
- The characters are all Indian.
- The majority of the actors are Indian.
- It conforms to Bollywood aesthetics in places (song-and-dance routine over closing credits).
- Most of the crew are Indian (composer: A. R. Rahman, co-director: Loveleen Tandan).

British
- The director Danny Boyle is British.
- A large part of the dialogue is in English.
- The lead character, Jamal, is played by a British Asian actor (Dev Patel).
- It was produced and part-funded by two British production companies: Celador Films and Film4.
- It was adapted for the screen by the Yorkshire-born Simon Beaufoy.

American
- The remainder of the funding came from the American company Warner Independent Pictures.
- The film was distributed by Fox Searchlight Productions, another US-based firm.

France
- The overseas distribution rights were owned by Pathé Pictures International, a French company.

Based on the evidence outlined here, despite initial assumptions that *Slumdog Millionaire* is a Bollywood production, on closer inspection it is a good example of Transnational filmmaking. It combines both Western and Indian cultures due to its Transnational production history.

The film does not necessarily conform to the political agenda of many productions associated with the field. However, a number of Indian critics did raise concerns. Some of the most outspoken objections came from the famous Bollywood star Amitabh Bachchan. In his personal blog he stated:

If SM [Slumdog Millionaire] projects India as [a] Third World dirty under belly developing nation and causes pain and disgust among nationalists and patriots, let it be known that a murky under belly exists and thrives even in the most developed nations. Its [sic] just that the SM idea authored by an Indian and conceived and cinematically put together by a Westerner, gets creative Globe recognition. The other would perhaps not. (2009)

His concerns echo those of Said and Spivak: first, that Indian culture is depicted as stereotypical and second, that if it were not for the Western backing, the novel may never have reached a global audience. He later backtracked and came out in support of the film on his blog.

Further controversy was aimed at the title 'Slumdog'. Members of the Slum-Dwellers' Welfare Group filed legal objections as they felt the word 'dog' was demeaning. Additionally, it has since been suggested that the child stars who feature in the film still live in the slums of Mumbai, despite their fame. Boyle defended his treatment of the children, explaining that he had set up child trust funds and provided transport to enable them to attend school. In 2009 the slums were ripped apart and Boyle bought a house for Azharuddin Mohammed Ismail and his family ('Slumdog Actor Given New Home', 2009). Boyle's act, although undoubtedly well-meaning, can be read as a continuation of the paternalistic attitude adopted by his colonial forefathers.

Reflect and respond

1   Make a list of films that initially appear to be national productions but in fact are Transnational productions?
2   In your opinion is the film *Slumdog Millionaire* predominantly a British, Indian or American production?
3   Was Danny Boyle acting appropriately when he bought a house for the young Indian star?
4   How useful is the term 'Transnational' in assessing both contemporary and older movies?
5   What are the limitations of a Transnational reading?
6   What information do you need to assess whether a film should be considered Transnational?
7   Discuss the relationship between Postcolonial and Transnational Theory. List their similarities and differences.

Case study: *Avatar* (James Cameron, 2009)

The 2009 film *Avatar* made cinematic history due to its use of 3D technology and its overwhelming success at the box office. Although the film is renowned for its innovative approach, *Avatar* tells an ancient tale that has long been a staple in Hollywood filmmaking. It is the story of Western colonization; the attempt to exploit the natural resources of foreign lands and subjugate their peoples.

Like so many narratives before, *Avatar* explores the customs, rituals and beliefs of a foreign race through the eyes of the white, Western male. The film follows the same familiar narrative trajectory seen in *Dances with Wolves*, *Ferngully: The Last Rainforest* (Bill Kroyer, 1992) and *Pocahontas* (Mike Gabriel and Eric Goldberg, 1995). In *Avatar*, the white American character, Jake Sully (Sam Worthington), enters the exotic world of Pandora. Being a stranger to the land is an obstacle soon overcome as he discovers an affinity with the terrain and the indigenous people. This is usually signalled in these stories by a sudden ability to communicate with the locals. As respect and friendship ensue, he soon becomes sympathetic to the natives' needs and is accordingly pitted against his own people and Western heritage. Furthermore, he undergoes the Na'vi rite of passage in order to become a warrior and gain acceptance. Predictably, Jake manages to 'out-native' the natives, gaining almost messiah-like qualities, demonstrated by his taming the legendary *Toruk*. As we can see from this summary, the story of Jake Sully is not new, but the narrative has been transported to a different planet.

Although Pandora is depicted as an alien planet, the inhabitants are represented through the semiotic coding of developing nations. For example, the soundtrack accompanying the scene where Jake learns to fly includes vocal intonation that bears a striking resemblance to the sounds of African or Indian chanting. This is further enhanced by the rhythmic beating of the tribal drums. So despite the otherworldly setting, it becomes apparent that *Avatar*'s plot is a metaphor for Western colonization of Eastern territory.

Interestingly, the film can be understood as either an anti-colonialist text or alternatively as a colonial fantasy. The first approach is probably the most obvious. The film typically depicts the majority of Americans as gung-ho mercenaries with no thought for the indigenous people of Pandora, epitomized in the character of Colonel Miles Quaritch (Stephen Lang). His attitude towards the natives is one of abhorrence and repugnance. He does not attempt to understand the Pandorans or their culture; instead he sees them as a threat that needs to be extinguished. The derogatory tone he adopts when talking about the natives reveals his deeply held racist views: 'Out there beyond that fence, every living thing that crawls, flies or squats in the mud wants to kill you and eat your eyes for ju-ju beads.'

Many reviewers and bloggers suggest that the character of Quaritch alludes to the former US President George W. Bush. They claim that the fictitious character's treatment of the Pandorans is similar to the stance adopted by the Bush administration when the US invaded Iraq. However, the film also inadvertently reminds the audience of historic practices of genocide, which typically occurred when Western forces attempted to take control of non-Western land. Quaritch flippantly discusses Na'vi fatalities, which could be read as a subtle allusion to the Holocaust: 'I'll do it with minimal casualties to the indigenous, I'll drop them out with gas first. It will be humane more or less.' Such instances clearly mark the film as anti-colonial (and more incisively anti-American). The film preaches caution against Western contempt for indigenous cultures. It highlights how destructive corporate imperial attitudes are. Yet in the same breath, the film can be read as a colonial fantasy.

The character of Jake is problematic because he offers a romanticized view of colonial relations. Initially opposed to the Pandorans as he looks to fulfil his military obligations, he soon becomes sympathetic to their plight. Jake and his scientist comrades are depicted as caring and wanting to learn from the Na'vi. Dr Grace Augustine (Sigourney Weaver) continues the age-old role of educator, setting up a school for her colonial subjects. Grace and her researchers are fascinated with the Na'vi culture and in particular their understanding of nature, Jack states:

> I am trying to understand this deep connection people have to the forest. She [Neytiri] talks about a network of energy that flows through all living things. She says all energy is only borrowed and one day you have to give it back.

The pro-environmental message is prevalent in colonial fantasies and typically seen in films about Native Americans. Jack offers an idealistic, yet archetypal, view of colonial interaction because he is willing to learn from the indigenous tribe. However, it is pertinent to ask whether his role is necessary in telling the story of the Na'vi?

Hollywood has historically explored foreign culture through the eyes of the white Western male. *Avatar* could easily have been narrated by Neytiri (Zoe Saldana). A female narrator would have been an interesting departure, warranting consideration in relation to Spivak's argument (although not strictly a subaltern, being the tribal leader's daughter, she could be classed as subaltern from the US perspective). James Cameron missed an opportunity here to break with the generic convention of depicting foreign races from the white Western viewpoint. Having a white protagonist highlights the voyeuristic exotic mystery of tribal life; they are seen as the alien 'Other' by the Western tourist.

Jared Gardner exposes the controversial subtext of *Avatar*. He likens the film to *The Jazz Singer*, stating that Al Jolson's adoption of blackface is no different from Jake Sully's 'blueface':

> As blackface did in 1927, blueface in 2009 allows Hollywood simultaneously to 'mourn' the loss of what is 'vanished' while also celebrate its rebirth and continuation through the indispensable mediation of the white male body [...] While the film on its surface appears to celebrate the culture being put on by the white man [...] in the end it is, as all Hollywood films inevitable [sic] are, about the white man and *his* culture – and the white man and *his* storytelling machinery. The tear shed or cheer raised for the Na'vi is no more authentic than the tear shed for the plantation black culture in *Jazz Singer* or the last of the Mohicans in James Fenimore Cooper's *The Last of the Mohicans*. It is all about white boys showing off how well they tell stories about the tragic loss of indigenous cultures, and how powerful that storytelling ability makes them. (2010)

Gardner's blackface metaphor highlights the Postcolonial legacy that is betrayed within this film. It is impossible to separate the fictitious tale from the history of Western domination over the East. Therefore *Avatar* can be read as either an anti-colonial tale of non-communication and aggression or a paternalistic colonial fantasy that is laden with the guilt of the white man.

The film *Avatar* does not necessarily demand a Transnational reading as the film is clearly an American blockbuster. However, closer inspection reveals a number of Transnational features. For instance, the lead character Jake Sully is performed by English-born Australian actor Sam Worthington. The cinematographer, Mauro Fiore, is Italian. Furthermore, the film was shot on two different locations: Los Angeles and Wellington, New Zealand. The cast was also sent to Hawaii in order to experience rainforest terrain.

Additionally, the language of the Na'vi was created by the linguist Professor Paul Frommer over a period of four years. He developed the language by mixing the grammatical and syntactic rules of existing languages such as Japanese, Spanish, Polynesian and languages of Eastern Europe. The language has gained a cult following, with numerous 'Learn Na'vi' websites encouraging fans to partake in this alien form of communication. This phenomenon, whereby aficionados learn a fictional language, occurred with J. R. R. Tolkien's Elvish language of Middle Earth (composed from Finnish and Welsh-language patterns). Another example can be seen in the *Star Trek* fans who converse in Klingon. These fictional languages can be learnt across the world regardless of nationality. They are a unifying tool, potentially providing a universal form of communication in a similar way to Esperanto, which was artificially created as an international language.

All of these attributes add to *Avatar's* Transnational credibility. Nevertheless, the cited examples are not necessarily indicative of a Transnational production but are instead representative of a big-budget commercial enterprise (the film was funded by four American companies and one UK-based firm). The film industry is a global network and accordingly crew and cast often move from country to country in order to gain employment. Therefore, most films will involve some

Transnational characteristics (cast, crew, location, funding, etc.). For that reason, it is important to consider the multifaceted nature of Transnationalism to fully identify texts that conform in ethos, aesthetics, economics and politics. In the case of *Avatar* maybe we should consider introducing the term transplanetary (Earth vs Pandora) rather than Transnational?

Reflect and respond

1   *Avatar* continues the generic tradition of viewing foreign cultures through the white man's lens. List other films that follow the same narrative blueprint.
2   Do you think *Avatar* is best understood as an anti-colonial text or as a romanticized colonial fantasy?
3   How would the narrative have differed if Neytiri had been the narrator and Jake Sully did not exist?
4   Drawing on your knowledge of Postcolonialism, discuss your reactions to the character of Colonel Miles Quaritch and Dr Grace Augustine.
5   Attempt a reading of *Avatar* as a modern political allegory.

Conclusion

Postcolonial Studies, in part, explores the aftermath of colonial rule and how indigenous people attempt to reinsert their voice into a culture that has to some extent been annihilated. It is suggested that initially, once the imperial powers have been removed, nations enter a state of 'Postcolonial amnesia'. This means that the historic trauma of oppression and exploitation is so great that native people are unable to even mention it. Consequently, many cultural artefacts fail to openly critique or discuss in any detail the Postcolonial condition. However, it is only once this silence is broken that wounds can begin to heal and it is poignant that a number of recent film texts look to address the historical shame, for example *Caché/Hidden* and *Manderlay* (Lars von Trier, 2005).

Transnationalism offers a way forward for Postcolonial debate. Rather than looking backwards to the tyrannical rule of Western forces, it attempts to interrogate and negotiate the relationship between the West and non-Western nations. It moves beyond the negative connotations of the colonized/colonizer and victim/perpetrator towards a more positive outlook. This is not to say that these old grievances are no longer relevant because they remain core to our understanding of national identity and foreign relations. However, in today's digital age, new technology and the internet have provided those who were once silenced a platform from which to be heard. Furthermore, sites such as YouTube enable filmmakers from remote corners of the globe to air their texts without having to conform to traditional aesthetic expectations of commercial (Hollywood) cinema.

Transnationalism signals a way forward. It is a way of moving beyond the isolationist stance of nationalism and it shatters the binary opposition of East against West. It is pertinent that Transnationalism has emerged at this point in history as filmmaking has gained a global interface.

Digital networks have enabled production teams to work in collaboration from different corners of the globe. As a result, the world has metaphorically reduced in size, whereas the opportunities for cross-cultural production have become infinite.

Bibliography

Bachchan, A. (2009) 'Official Blog of Amitabh Bachchan: Day 265'. Retrieved 14 July 2010. Available at http://bigb.bigadda.com/?p=1445.

Ezra, E. and Rowden, T. (eds) (2006). *Transnational Cinema: The Film Reader,* London: Routledge.

Fanon, F. (1967) *The Wretched of the Earth,* Harmondsworth: Penguin (first published 1961).

Fanon, F. (1986) *Black Skin, White Masks,* London: Pluto Press (first published 1952).

Gardner, J. (2010) 'Avatar: Blueface, White Noise', *Huffington Post.* Retrieved 19 July 2010. Available at http://www.huffingtonpost.com/jared-gardner/emavatarem-blueface-white_b_409522.html.

Higbee, W. and Lim, S. H. (2010) 'Concepts of Transnational Cinema: Towards a Critical Transnationalism in Film', *Transnational Cinemas* vol. 1 no. 1, pp.7–21.

Jhally, S. (1998) *Edward Said: On Orientalism,* Media Education Foundation.

Kotwal, K. N. (n.d.) 'Steven Spielberg's *Indiana Jones and the Temple of Doom* as Virtual Reality: The Orientalist and Colonial Legacies of *Gunga Din*', *Film Journal* no. 12. Retrieved 10 June 2010. Available at http://www.thefilmjournal.com/issue12/templeofdoom.html.

Said, E. (1978) *Introduction to Orientalism,* in G. Desai and S. Nair (eds) (2005) *Postcolonialisms: An Anthology of Cultural Theory and Criticism,* Oxford: Routledge, pp.71–93.

Shaheen, J. G. (2001) *Reel Bad Arabs: How Hollywood Vilifies a People,* New York: Olive Branch Press.

Shaheen, J. G. (2008) *Guilty: Hollywood's Verdict on Arabs after 9/11,* Northampton, MA: Olive Branch Press.

Shaw, D. (forthcoming) 'Deconstructing and Reconstructing "Transnational Cinema"', in S. Dennison (ed.) *Transnational Film Financing in the Hispanic World,* London: Tamesis.

'Slumdog Actor Given New Home' (2009) *Guardian.* Retrieved 14 July 2010. Available at http://www.guardian.co.uk/world/2009/jul/07/slumdog-millionaire-mumbai-danny-boyle.

Spivak, G. C. (1988) 'Can the Subaltern Speak?', in B. Ashcroft, G. Griffith and H. Tiffin (eds) (1995) *The Postcolonial Studies Reader,* London and New York: Routledge, pp.24–8.

Conclusion

In a book of this kind, there can be no conclusion. That is because we have offered a series of methods: ways of reading or interpreting films. None of these methods is definitive. Theory is not written in stone; it should not be thought of as a regimented, authoritarian way to approach texts. Rather, theory is a tool that can be used selectively. We want to argue that a three-way relationship can be set up between theory, text and reader (viewer).

What we have done is to set up a number of interpretative frameworks: Structuralism, Marxism, masculinity and so on. None of these on their own can account for the complexity of film culture; yet the insights they afford can stimulate us to think afresh about what films mean. In addition, we have surveyed a range of critical perspectives, such as audience reception, stardom, race and ethnicity. When used carefully, these can enrich our understanding and help us to see the mythologies (power relations, organization, etc.) that lie hidden beneath the film's surface. Films are not always predictable products of a capitalist system of production. Rather, they relate in a complex way to the world of dreams, ideas, subjective desires and sociopolitical power relations. And theoretical work will enable us to excavate underlying subtexts.

Up until now, film theory has developed primarily out of the discipline of philosophy and literary critical theory. It is possible to argue that other disciplines can profitably be raided – social history, cultural geography, art history, anthropology and so on. This would certainly be a way of broadening out the field, and providing new insights. But whatever explanatory model chosen, we have to make sure that we are flexible and inventive in its application, so that the readings produced are both thorough and appropriate.

This is not to say that specific theories are directly responsible for producing particular films, even though they may represent a sophisticated meditation on particular issues. In other words, do not fall into the trap of presuming a director/screenwriter made a conscious decision to create a narrative based upon a theory (Psychoanalysis, Star Studies, Postmodernism, etc.).

Furthermore, remember that you have recourse to more than one theory when exploring a film. In all our case studies, we have read texts through specific lenses: *Rabbit-Proof Fence* through the prism of Race and Ethnicity, the Dogme 95 movement via the prism of Realism. However, there are other ways of reading these films which can be equally revealing. A Marxist reading of the Dogme 95 movement would enable us to study its anti-capitalist manifesto and the way it looked to challenge commercial forms of filmmaking. Likewise, a Feminist reading of *Rabbit-Proof Fence* would throw up some fascinating conclusions, and invite us to think about the empowerment of the Aboriginal girls as they rebel against patriarchal order. Therefore, it is important to consider different theoretical approaches because these could produce alternative readings that go against the grain.

It is essential that you do not let theory restrict your imagination. Be aware of your own initial reading of a film. Do not ignore your intuition; often your textual analysis can bring a fresh perspective to established ideas. Occasionally you can become overwhelmed and blinkered by a theoretical position, which could result in the dismissal of vital information. Furthermore, your understanding of a text can be enhanced through a detailed examination of production history. This line of investigation may be more pertinent to your reading of a film than undertaking a traditional theoretical interpretation.

What we are suggesting, then, is that you use this book as a basis for further study, and that you should feel encouraged to use theory flexibly and without fear. It can be your friend rather than enemy and will help you to gain more understanding of the complexities of films and the way they relate to the societies that produced them and the audiences that respond to them.

Filmography

3 Hommes et un Couffin/Three Men and a Cradle (Coline Serreau, 1985)
42nd Street (Lloyd Bacon, 1933)
300 (Zack Snyder, 2006)
2001: A Space Odyssey (Stanley Kubrick, 1968)
À Bout de Souffle/Breathless (Jean-Luc Godard, 1960)
Abre los Ojos/Open Your Eyes (Alejandro Amenábar, 1997)
The Adventures of Priscilla, Queen of the Desert (Stephan Elliot, 1994)
The Adventures of Robin Hood (Michael Curtiz, 1938)
Aladdin (Ron Clements and John Musker, 1992)
Alexander (Oliver Stone, 2004)
Alien (Ridley Scott, 1979)
All about Eve (Joseph L. Mankiewicz, 1950)
Amar Akbar Anthony (Manmohan Desai, 1977)
American Graffiti (George Lucas, 1973)
American Psycho (Mary Harron, 2000)
Anastasia: The Mystery of Anna (Marvin J. Chomsky, 1986)
Annie (John Huston, 1982)
Annie Get your Gun (George Sidney, 1950)
Apocalypse Now (Francis Ford Coppola, 1979)
L'arrivée d'un Train à la Ciotat /Arrival of a Train at a Station (Auguste and Louis Lumière, 1897)
Avatar (James Cameron, 2009)
Back to the Future III (Robert Zemeckis, 1990)
The Basketball Diaries (Scott Kalvert, 1995)
Batman Begins (Christopher Nolan, 2005)
Battleship Potemkin (Sergei Eisenstein, 1925)
Beauty and the Beast (Gary Trousdale and Kirk Wise, 1991)
Being John Malkovich (Spike Jonze, 1999)
Bellissima/Beautiful (Luchino Visconti, 1951)
La Bête Humaine/The Human Beast/Judas Was a Woman (Jean Renoir, 1938)
Big Fish (Tim Burton, 2003)
Bill and Ted's Excellent Adventure (Stephen Herek, 1989)
The Birds (Alfred Hitchcock, 1963)
The Birth of a Nation (D. W. Griffith, 1915)
The Black Pirate (Albert Parker, 1926)
Black Swan (Darren Aronofsky, 2010)
Blackmail (Alfred Hitchcock, 1929)
Blade Runner (Ridley Scott, 1982)
Blade II (Guillermo del Toro, 2002)
Blazing Saddles (Mel Brooks, 1974)
Blue (Derek Jarman, 1993)
Blue Velvet (David Lynch, 1986)

The Blues Brothers (John Landis, 1980)
Bowling for Columbine (Michael Moore, 2002)
Boys Don't Cry (Kimberly Peirce, 1999)
Boyz 'n the Hood (John Singleton, 1991)
Breathless/À Bout de Souffle (Jean-Luc Godard, 1960)
Brick (Rian Johnson, 2005)
Bride & Prejudice (Gurinder Chadha, 2004)
Bridget Jones's Diary (Sharon Maguire, 2001)
Brokeback Mountain (Ang Lee, 2005)
Broken Arrow (Delmer Daves, 1950)
Buck and the Preacher (Sidney Poitier, 1972)
Bugsy Malone (Alan Parker, 1976)
Caché/Hidden (Michael Haneke, 2005)
La Cage aux Folles (Edouard Molinaro, 1978)
Calamity Jane (David Butler, 1953)
Camelot (Joshua Logan, 1967)
Captain Blood (Michael Curtiz, 1935)
Caravaggio (Derek Jarman, 1986)
Carrie (Brian De Palma, 1976)
Casablanca (Michael Curtiz, 1942)
Casino Royale (Martin Campbell, 2006)
Cathy Come Home (Ken Loach, 1966)
Chicago (Rob Marshall, 2002)
Un Chien Andalou/An Andalusian Dog (Luis Buñuel, 1928)
Child's Play 3 (Jack Bender, 1991)
Chitty Chitty Bang Bang (Ken Hughes, 1968)
Citizen Kane (Orson Welles, 1941)
A Clockwork Orange (Stanley Kubrick, 1971)
Cloverfield (Matt Reeves, 2008)
The Color Purple (Steven Spielberg, 1985)
Conan the Barbarian (John Milius, 1982)
A Connecticut Yankee in King Arthur's Court (Tay Garnett, 1949)
Coolie (Manmohan Desai and Prayag Raj, 1983)
Coorab in the Isle of Ghosts (Francis Birtles, 1928)
The Count of Monte Cristo (Kevin Reynolds, 2002)
Crash (David Cronenberg, 1996)
The Crimson Pirate (Robert Siodmak, 1952)
Cronos (Guillermo del Toro, 1993)
Crouching Tiger, Hidden Dragon (Ang Lee, 2000)
Cruel Intentions (Roger Kumble, 1999)
The Crying Game (Neil Jordan, 1992)
Curly Sue (John Hughes, 1991)
Dances with Wolves (Kevin Costner, 1990)
Dangerous Liaisons/Les Liaisons Dangereuses (Stephen Frears, 1988)
The Day after Tomorrow (Roland Emmerich, 2004)
Dead Man (Jim Jarmusch, 1995)
Desperately Seeking Susan (Susan Seidelman, 1985)
Do the Right Thing (Spike Lee, 1989)
Dogville (Lars von Trier, 2003)

Donnie Brasco (Mike Newell, 1997)
Don't Lose Your Head (Gerald Thomas, 1966)
Dorian Gray (Oliver Parker, 2009)
Duel in the Sun (King Vidor, 1946)
Earth (Deepa Mehta, 1998)
Easy Rider (Dennis Hopper, 1969)
Edward Scissorhands (Tim Burton, 1990)
Edward II (Derek Jarman, 1991)
Empire of the Sun (Steven Spielberg, 1987)
The Empire Strikes Back (Irvin Kershner, 1980)
Les Enfants du Paradis/Children of Paradise (Marcel Carné, 1945)
Enigma (Michael Apted, 2001)
El Espinazo del Diablo/The Devil's Backbone (Guillermo del Toro, 2001)
Evita (Alan Parker, 1996)
The Exorcist (William Friedkin, 1973)
Eyes Wide Shut (Stanley Kubrick, 1999)
Fame (Alan Parker, 1980)
Family Plot (Alfred Hitchcock, 1976)
Ferngully: The Last Rainforest (Bill Kroyer, 1992)
Festen (Thomas Vinterberg, 1998)
Fiddler on the Roof (Norman Jewison, 1971)
Fight Club (David Fincher, 1999)
The Fighter (David O. Russell, 2010)
Fire (Deepa Mehta, 1996)
Fireworks (Kenneth Anger, 1945)
A Fistful of Dollars (Sergio Leone, 1964)
The Flame and the Arrow (Jacques Tourneur, 1950)
The Fly (David Cronenberg, 1986)
For a Few Dollars More (Sergio Leone, 1965)
Fort Apache (John Ford, 1948)
Four in the Morning (Anthony Simmons, 1965)
Four Weddings and a Funeral (Mike Newell, 1994)
Frenzy (Alfred Hitchcock, 1972)
Gangs of New York (Martin Scorsese, 2002)
Germania Anno Zero/ Germany Year Zero (Roberto Rossellini, 1948)
The Girl Can't Help It (Frank Tashlin, 1957)
The Godfather Trilogy (Francis Ford Coppola, 1972–90)
Gold Diggers of 33 (Mervyn LeRoy, 1933)
GoldenEye (Martin Campbell, 1995)
Gone with the Wind (Victor Fleming, 1939)
The Good, the Bad and the Ugly (Sergio Leone, 1966)
Goodfellas (Martin Scorsese, 1990)
The Graduate (Mike Nichols, 1967)
La Grande Illusion/The Grand Illusion (Jean Renoir, 1937)
The Grapes of Wrath (John Ford, 1940)
Grease (Randal Kleiser, 1978)
The Great Train Robbery (Edwin S. Porter, 1903)
Grey Owl (Richard Attenborough, 1998)
Groundhog Day (Harold Ramis, 1993)

Gunga Din (George Stevens, 1939)

The Guru (Daisy von Scherler Mayer, 2002)

Guys and Dolls (Joseph L. Mankiewicz, 1955)

Hairspray (John Waters, 1988 and Adam Shankman, 2007)

A Handful of Dust (Charles Sturridge, 1988)

Harry Potter and the Philosopher's Stone (Chris Columbus, 2001)

He Who Rides the Tiger (Charles Crichton, 1965)

Heaven's Gate (Michael Cimino, 1980)

Hellboy (Guillermo del Toro, 2004)

Hellboy II: The Golden Army (Guillermo del Toro, 2008)

High Noon (Fred Zinnemann, 1952)

High Plains Drifter (Clint Eastwood, 1973)

High School Musical franchise (Kenny Ortega, 2006–8)

La Hora de los Hornos/The Hour of the Furnaces (Octavio Getino and Fernando Solanas, 1968)

The Human Stain (Robert Benton, 2003)

I Am Legend (Francis Lawrence, 2007)

The Idiots (Lars von Trier, 1998)

Imitation of Life (John M. Stahl, 1934 and Douglas Sirk, 1959)

Indiana Jones and the Temple of Doom (Steven Spielberg, 1984)

Invasion of the Body Snatchers (Don Siegel, 1956)

Iris (Richard Eyre, 2001)

Iron Man (Jon Favreau, 2008)

The Jazz Singer (Alan Crosland, 1927)

Johnny Guitar (Nicholas Ray, 1954)

Journey from Berlin (Yvonne Rainer, 1971)

Jubilee (Derek Jarman, 1978)

Kabhi Alvida Naa Kehna (Karan Johar, 2006)

Kabhi Khushi Kabhi Gham (Karan Johar, 2001)

Kes (Ken Loach, 1969)

Kill Bill: Vol. 1 (Quentin Tarantino, 2003)

Kill Bill: Vol. 2 (Quentin Tarantino, 2004)

A Kind of Loving (John Schlesinger, 1962)

Kindergarten Cop (Ivan Reitman, 1990)

The King of Kings (Cecil B. DeMille, 1927)

Koyaanisqatsi: Life out of Balance (Godfrey Reggio, 1982)

El Laberinto del Fauno/Pan's Labyrinth (Guillermo del Toro, 2006)

Ladies in Lavender (Charles Dance, 2004)

Ladri di Biciclette/Bicycle Thieves (Vittorio De Sica, 1948)

Lan Yu (Stanley Kwan, 2001)

Lara Croft: Tomb Raider (Simon West, 2001)

The Last King of Scotland (Kevin Macdonald, 2006)

The Last Waltz (Martin Scorsese, 1978)

The Legend of Zorro (Martin Campbell, 2005)

Léon (Luc Besson, 1994)

Little Big Man (Arthur Penn, 1970)

Little Caesar (Mervyn LeRoy, 1931)

The Little Shop of Horrors (Frank Oz, 1986)

The Lodger (Alfred Hitchcock, 1926)

Lola Rennt/Run Lola Run (Tom Tykwer, 1998)

The Loneliness of the Long Distance Runner (Tony Richardson, 1962)
Look Back in Anger (Tony Richardson, 1959)
The Lord of the Rings: The Fellowship of the Ring (Peter Jackson, 2001)
Lost in Translation (Sofia Coppola, 2003)
The Machinist (Brad Anderson, 2004)
The Magnificent Seven (John Sturges, 1960)
Magnolia (P. T. Anderson, 1999)
Mamma Mia! (Phyllida Lloyd, 2008)
The Man Who Fell to Earth (Nicolas Roeg, 1976)
Man with a Movie Camera (Dziga Vertov, 1929)
Manderlay (Lars von Trier, 2005)
Marathon Man (John Schlesinger, 1976)
Marnie (Alfred Hitchcock, 1964)
The Mask of Zorro (Martin Campbell, 1998)
The Matrix (Andy and Larry Wachowski, 1999)
Memento (Christopher Nolan, 2000)
Menace II Society (Albert and Allen Hughes, 1993)
Metropolis (Fritz Lang, 1927)
Mickey, Donald, Goofy: The Three Musketeers (Donovan Cook, 2004)
A Midsummer Night's Dream (Peter Hall, 1968)
Millions Like Us (Sidney Launder and Frank Gilliat, 1943)
Mimic (Guillermo del Toro, 1997)
Monty Python and the Holy Grail (Terry Gilliam and Terry Jones, 1975)
Moon (Duncan Jones, 2009)
The Moon Is the Sun's Dream (Chan-Wook Park, 1992)
Mother India (Mehboob Khan, 1957)
Moulin Rouge! (Baz Luhrmann, 2001)
Mrs Brown (John Madden, 1997)
Mrs Doubtfire (Chris Columbus, 1993)
Mrs Henderson Presents (Stephen Frears, 2005)
Mulholland Drive (David Lynch, 2001)
Muppet Treasure Island (Brian Henson, 1996)
My Big Fat Greek Wedding (Joel Zwick, 2002)
My Darling Clementine (John Ford, 1946)
My Own Private Idaho (Gus Van Sant, 1991)
New Jack City (Mario Van Peebles, 1991)
The News Boys (Kenny Ortega, 1992)
The Nightmare Before Christmas (Tim Burton, 1993)
No Country for Old Men (Ethan and Joel Coen, 2007)
North by Northwest (Alfred Hitchcock, 1959)
Notes on a Scandal (Richard Eyre, 2006)
Notorious (Alfred Hitchcock, 1946)
Oklahoma (Fred Zinnemann, 1954)
Oldboy (Chan-Wook Park, 2003)
Once Upon a Time in the West (Sergio Leone, 1968)
El Orfanato/The Orphanage (Juan Antonio Bayona, 2007)
Paint Your Wagon (Joshua Logan, 1969)
Paisà/Paisan (Roberto Rossellini, 1946)
Paris Is Burning (Jennie Livingston, 1990)

Partie de Campagne/A Day in the Country (Jean Renoir, 1936)
Pépé le Moko (Julien Duvivier, 1937)
Performance (Donald Cammell and Nicolas Roeg, 1970)
Peter Pan (Clyde Geronimi, Wilfred Jackson and Hamilton Luske, 1953)
The Phantom of the Opera (Joel Schumacher, 2004)
Phone Booth (Joel Schumacher, 2002)
Picnic at Hanging Rock (Peter Weir, 1975)
Pinky (Elia Kazan, 1956)
Pinocchio (n.a., 1940)
Pirates of the Caribbean (Gore Verbinski, 2003–7)
Pirates of Penzance (Wilford Leach, 1983)
Planet of the Apes (Franklin J. Shaffner, 1968 and Tim Burton, 2001)
The Player (Robert Altman, 1992)
Pocahontas (Mike Gabriel and Eric Goldberg, 1995)
Powaqqatsi: Life in Transformation (Godfrey Reggio, 1988)
Psycho (Alfred Hitchcock, 1960)
The Public Enemy (William A. Wellman, 1931)
Pulp Fiction (Quentin Tarantino, 1994)
Quantum of Solace (Marc Forster, 2008)
Les Quatre Cents Coups/400 Blows (François Truffaut, 1959)
Queen Christina (Rouben Mamoulian, 1933)
Rabbit-Proof Fence (Philip Noyce, 2002)
Raging Bull (Martin Scorsese, 1980)
Raiders of the Lost Ark (Steven Spielberg, 1981)
Rear Window (Alfred Hitchcock, 1954)
Rebecca (Alfred Hitchcock, 1940)
La Règle du Jeu/The Rules of the Game (Jean Renoir, 1939)
Requiem for a Dream (Darren Aronofsky, 2000)
Ride with the Devil (Ang Lee, 1999)
Riff-Raff (Ken Loach, 1991)
Rio Grande (John Ford, 1950)
Rocky (John G. Avildsen, 1976)
The Rocky Horror Picture Show (Jim Sharman, 1975)
Roma Città Aperta/Rome Open City (Roberto Rossellini, 1945)
Room at the Top (Jack Clayton, 1959)
A Room with a View (James Ivory, 1985)
Rope (Alfred Hitchcock, 1948)
Russian Ark (Aleksandr Sokurov, 2002)
Samson and Delilah (Warwick Thornton, 2009)
Sapphire (Basil Dearden, 1959)
Saturday Night and Sunday Morning (Karel Reisz, 1960)
Saturday Night Fever (John Badham, 1977)
Scarface (Howard Hawks, 1932)
Scary Movie (Keenen Ivory Wayans, 2000)
Schindler's List (Steven Spielberg, 1993)
The Sea Hawk (Michael Curtiz, 1940)
The Searchers (John Ford, 1956)
Sebastiane (Derek Jarman, 1976)
Serenity (Joss Whedon, 2005)

Seven Brides for Seven Brothers (Stanley Donen, 1954)
Seven Samurai (Akira Kurosawa, 1954)
The Seventh Seal (Ingmar Bergman, 1957)
Shakespeare in Love (John Madden, 1998)
Shane (George Stevens, 1953)
She Wore a Yellow Ribbon (John Ford, 1949)
The Shining (Stanley Kubrick, 1980)
The Shipping News (Lasse Hallström, 2001)
Sholay (Ramesh Sippy, 1975)
Showboat (James Whale, 1930 and George Sidney, 1946)
Shrek (Andrew Adamson and Vicky Jenson, 2001)
Shrek 2 (Andrew Adamson, Kelly Ashby and Conrad Vernon, 2004)
Singin' in the Rain (Stanley Donen and Gene Kelly, 1952)
The Sixth Sense (M. Night Shyamalan, 1999)
Sleepless in Seattle (Nora Ephron, 1993)
Sleepy Hollow (Tim Burton, 1999)
Sliding Doors (Peter Howitt, 1998)
Slumdog Millionaire (Danny Boyle, 2008)
Soldier Blue (Ralph Nelson, 1970)
Some Like It Hot (Billy Wilder, 1959)
Song of the South (Harve Foster and Wilfred Jackson, 1946)
La Sortie des Usines Lumière/Workers Leaving the Factory (Louis Lumière, 1895)
The Sound of Music (Robert Wise, 1965)
The Spaceman and King Arthur (Russ Mayberry, 1979)
Spellbound (Alfred Hitchcock, 1945)
Stagecoach (John Ford, 1939)
Star Wars (George Lucas, 1977)
The Stepford Wives (Bryan Forbes, 1975 and Frank Oz, 2004)
Stop! Or My Mom Will Shoot (Roger Spottiswoode, 1992)
Strangers on a Train (Alfred Hitchcock, 1951)
Straw Dogs (Sam Peckinpah, 1971)
A Streetcar Named Desire (Elia Kazan, 1951)
Sunset Boulevard (Billy Wilder, 1950)
Supersize Me (Morgan Spurlock, 2004)
Sweeney Todd: The Demon Barber of Fleet Street (Tim Burton, 2007)
Sympathy for Lady Vengeance (Chan-Wook Park, 2005)
Sympathy for Mr Vengeance (Chan-Wook Park, 2002)
Target for Tonight (Harry Watt, 1941)
A Taste of Honey (Tony Richardson, 1961)
Taxi Driver (Martin Scorsese, 1976)
The Ten Commandments (Cecil B. DeMille, 1956)
The Terminator I–III (James Cameron and Jonathan Mostow, 1984–91, 2003)
Terminator: Salvation (McG, 2009)
La Terra Trema/The Earth Trembles (Luchino Visconti, 1948)
They Live! (John Carpenter, 1988)
The Third Secret (Charles Crichton, 1964)
The Thirty-Nine Steps (Alfred Hitchcock, 1935)
This Sporting Life (Lindsay Anderson, 1963)
Three Men and a Baby (Leonard Nimoy, 1987)

The Three Musketeers (Roland V. Lee, 1935 George Sidney, 1948 and Richard Lester, 1973)

Timecode (Mike Figgis, 2000)

Titanic (James Cameron, 1997)

Todo Sobre Mi Madre/All about My Mother (Pedro Almodóvar, 1999)

Tongues Untied (Marlon Riggs, 1990)

Top Gun (Tony Scott, 1986)

Trainspotting (Danny Boyle, 1996)

Transamerica (Duncan Tucker, 2005)

Treasure Island (Fraser Clarke Heston, 1990)

The Truman Show (Peter Weir, 1998)

Twins (Ivan Reitman, 1988)

Umberto D (Vittorio De Sica, 1952)

Unforgiven (Clint Eastwood, 1992)

The Usual Suspects (Bryan Singer, 1995)

V for Vendetta (James McTeigue, 2005)

Vanilla Sky (Cameron Crowe, 2001)

Vertigo (Alfred Hitchcock, 1958)

Le Voyage dans la Lune/A Trip to the Moon (Georges Méliès, 1902)

Walkabout (Nicolas Roeg, 1971)

Walker (Alex Cox, 1987)

Water (Deepa Mehta, 2005)

Week End (Jean-Luc Godard, 1967)

Went the Day Well (Alberto Cavalcanti, 1942)

West Side Story (Jerome Robbins and Robert Wise, 1961)

When the Levees Broke: A Requiem in Four Acts (Spike Lee, 2006)

Why We Fight (Frank Capra, 1943–4)

The Wife of Monte Cristo (Edgar G. Ulmer, 1946)

The Wild Bunch (Sam Peckinpah, 1969)

Wild Wild West (Barry Sonnenfeld, 1999)

Willy Wonka & the Chocolate Factory (Mel Stuart, 1971)

The Wizard of Oz (Victor Fleming, 1939)

The Wrong Man (Alfred Hitchcock, 1957)

Young Guns II (Geoff Murphy, 1990)

Young Mr Lincoln (John Ford, 1939)

The Young Victoria (Jean-Marc Vallée, 2009)

Zanjeer (Prakash Mehra, 1973)

TV shows and documentaries

24 (Various, 2001–11)

The Apprentice (Various, 2005–)

Big Brother (1997–2010)

Edward Said: On Orientalism (Sut Jhally, 1998)

Ellen (Various, 1994–8)

A Fine Romance (Bob Larbey, 1981–4)

Firefly (Joss Whedon, 2002)

Imagine: Bollywood's Big B: Amitabh Bachchan (C. Lockhart, 2007)

Living with Michael Jackson (Julie Shaw/Martin Bashir, 2003)

The Oprah Winfrey Show (1986–)
Pride and Prejudice (Simon Langton, 1995)
Race, the Floating Signifier (Stuart Hall, 1997)
Who Wants to Be a Millionaire? (Various, 1991–)
The X Factor (Various, 2004–)

Index